Pounding along to Singapore

A story of the 2/20 Battalion AIF with the letters and diary of
Capt. EW (Bill) Gaden of 'D' Force, POW
1940-1945

by

Caroline Gaden

With best wishes Al
Caroline Gaden

CopyRight
Publishing
Brisbane

Pounding along to Singapore

DEDICATED

to

Bill Gaden's

Grandchildren and Great-grandchildren

The next generations who need to learn about our past heroes to give them the fighting spirit to carry on.

IN MEMORY

of all the

Men and Women

who went 'into harm's way'
to protect Singapore and Malaya
in the Second World War

First published 2012

Published by CopyRight Publishing Company Pty Ltd
GPO Box 2927
Brisbane Q 4001

http://www.copyright.net.au
info@copyright.net.au

The language of the letters reflects the attitudes of many Australians towards people of other races at that time.

Printed in China

ISBN 978 1876344849

Contents

Chapter 1 - War is declared

On 3 September 1939 the world was plunged into crisis when Britain announced she was at war with Germany.[1] That day twenty-one-year-old Bill Gaden, an officer in the Sydney-based volunteer 17 Battalion Militia unit, was walking home from work when he met his two teenage sisters Sue and Elizabeth and their school-friend Penny. He told them all sternly 'Go home at once! War has been declared'.[2]

Just a few days later the Gaden family was plunged into a major crisis of its own when their father Noel took his own life, the Coroner's report showing it was due to 'the effect of a bullet wound in his head wilfully inflicted by himself'.

Noel's Will, written on 28 March 1939, indicated his wish to leave half his estate to his wife and three children in equal parts and the other half of his estate, including all picture books, photographs, watches and other personal effects to Patricia Louise Todd (or more often known as Lawson) of Robert Street, Marrickville.[3]

So the Gadens lost all their family memorabilia. However what Noel did leave to his family was a number of debts, amounting to nearly one thousand six hundred pounds (£1,600) which Bill, aged not quite twenty-two, undertook to settle. Young Bill had to grow up very quickly and assume the role of breadwinner for the family.

It would have been very difficult on a shipping clerk's wages in 1940, but Bill managed to pay off all the accounts shortly after he signed up for active service. In one of his early letters home from army camp in 1941 Bill refers to the fact that both he and his mother Vera were finally debt free and should congratulate themselves.

They certainly should.

It was just a short nine months after his father's death that Edward William Gaden enlisted in the Australian Imperial Forces (AIF). He became NX12543. In the queue that day was his good friend David MacDougal NX12539 who joined him in the 2/20 Battalion, and John Albert Boss NX12540, Kenneth William Parry NX12541, Richard Clive Thompson NX12542 and Graham Stanley McLeod NX12544 who all became officers in the 2/30 and also sailed to face the enemy overseas.[4]

Nine hundred and ninety-three thousand Australians enlisted in the Second World War. Seven hundred and thirty thousand chose to join the Army.[5] All these men and women had families and friends at home; all were forged and shaped by their personal circumstances. All had to be weaned from the familiar world they knew to coalesce into a new 'family' group, the specific unit of men and women with whom they would live and train, struggle and fight, survive or die.

By the middle of 1940 the 'phony war' was well and truly over. The Germans occupied northern Europe and the war was not progressing well for the Allies. Paris had fallen. The Italians had joined the Germans as partners. The evacuation at Dunkirk had brought as many men as possible off French soil and back to England.

The Australian Government was worried that Japan would see her ideological allies winning in Europe and would in turn be tempted to strike in the Pacific. They knew the garrison at the British naval base in Singapore would not be strengthened. Australia would have to defend herself from any potential threats from the increasingly aggressive Japanese.[6]

Many young Australians decided it was now time to join the Army. They were looking to help the 'Mother Country' and fight the Germans. Those who had enlisted very early in the war had been often been labelled 'economic conscripts' as some had been seeking a regular income,[7] but many were looking for an overseas 'adventure'. However the fall of France proved to be the signal to act and thousands of young men made a considered decision to serve, many because of their British heritage. In 1936 the number of Australian residents coming from British stock was 97%.[8] Enlistment in the Australian Army jumped from 8,000 in May 1940 to 48,500 in June.[9]

No doubt many were inspired by the words of British Prime Minister Winston Churchill. On 4 June 1940 Churchill gave a stirring speech to the British Parliament.

> We shall not flag or fail. We shall go on to the end. We shall fight in France, we shall fight on the seas and oceans, we shall fight with growing confidence and growing strength in the air. We shall defend our island, whatever the cost may be. We shall fight on the beaches, we shall fight on the landing grounds, we shall fight in the streets, we shall fight in the hills. We shall never surrender: and even if, which I do not for one moment believe, this island or a large part of it were subjugated and starving, then our Empire beyond the seas, armed and guarded by the British Fleet, would carry on the struggle, until, in God's good time, the New World, with all its power and might, steps forth to the rescue and liberation of the old.[10]

Bill Gaden jumped the gun on Mr Churchill. He had volunteered for the Australian Imperial Forces three days earlier, on 1 June 1940.

Bill was posted to the 2/20 Battalion of the Australian Imperial Forces (AIF) which, along with the 2/18 and 2/19 Battalions, made up the 22nd Brigade (a Brigade is usually made up of three Battalions), part of the 8th Division (a Division is usually made up of three Brigades).[11]

The story that follows is the chronicle of Bill and his comrades in the 2/20 Battalion.

On 13 July 1940 fourteen officers completed their final medical examinations and received their pay books at Victoria Barracks.[12]

Bill Gaden is fifth from the right and David MacDougal is third from the right. The officers are carrying walking sticks, there was obviously a shortage of batons ... there was a shortage of rifles and other arms too.[13]

The Battalion's *War Diary* of Sunday 14 July 1940 reported from Wallgrove Camp that officers had been appointed to the Battalion and arrived for an intensive ten days of training. The officers listed were Lt Col WD Jeater, Maj. GE Ramsey, Maj. RO Merrett, Maj. AE Robertson, Capt. RDJ Richardson, Capt. ACM Ewart, Capt. RH Cohen, Lt EW Gaden, Lt J Hepburn, Lt KW Hutton, Lt AG Davies, Lt BD Richardson, Lt AI Yates, Lt DC MacDougal, Lt G Maxwell, Lt DF Thompson, Capt. JG Fairley.

To this disparate group of young men would fall the task of moulding themselves into a team of officers and then shaping a group of heterogeneous civilians from all walks of life into a homogeneous battalion of fighting soldiers. Bill already knew some of them, Rod and Bart Richardson from school, David MacDougal from sailing and Arch Ewart from the 17th Militia.

The individual battalions of the 22nd Brigade worked hard to shape their men into efficient fighting individuals who, in turn, were moulded into cohesive fighting units. Within each Battalion the four Companies competed to be best and within the Companies the individual Platoons also aimed for excellence. They had to work together as small groups which could easily mould into larger units as circumstances dictated. Men had to identify with their battalion and develop an *esprit de corps* which helped them adapt and co-operate, and ultimately survive under fire and during the appalling conditions of the POW camps. The development of battalion spirit was encouraged by the attitude of the officers but also very much from the individual soldiers ... they realised that the battalion was to become their 'family', especially once they were overseas and 'in harm's way'. It helped that Australians in general are a 'tribal lot' who align themselves with like-minded groups.[14] For soldiers the common shared goal was to defeat the enemy.

Military training was something many men endured as a means to an end. They were not parade ground soldiers but were volunteers in a short-term army whose only purpose was to fight; some had the attitude *Why be a soldier when all one needed was to be a fighter?*[15]

Sport became an important part of training. Inter-battalion rivalry was shown on the sports field. It allowed the young men to burn off their testosterone but it also taught them how to become good team players.[16] In addition, various concert parties also helped to develop the *esprit de corps* which is so important for any military unit. Whilst at Wallgrove camp on the western outskirts of Sydney, the men were allowed weekend leave from midday Saturday to midnight Sunday which was an additional boost to their morale.

Troops received their inoculations and were blood typed. Individual well-wishers and organisations such as the Lord Mayor's Patriotic Fund sent the Battalion 'comforts' such as socks and dilly bags.[17] Troops were warned of the danger of imparting information about troop movement in letters or verbally. They were reminded that a prophylactic clinic for venereal disease was available. They learned that vineyards were out of bounds when on manoeuvres.[18]

According to his friend Reg Newton, in October 1940 Bill was sent to the Senior Malayan Officers Administrative course which he passed before being posted back to the 2/20 as a Captain.[19] He became Second in Command (2I/C) to Capt. Charles Moses then later to former school friend Capt. Rod Richardson, the Company Commanders of 'D' or 'Don' Company.[20]

Routine orders were used to remind troops that admission to the Battalion Orderly Room was granted for transaction of official business only. On this day when Lt EW Gaden was Battalion Orderly Officer the drivers were given instruction for crossing the Harbour Bridge.

> SYDNEY HARBOUR BRIDGE
> Damage to Toll Shelters. Military truck drivers are instructed that when crossing Sydney Harbour Bridge they are to use the outside lines only, as damage has been caused to Collectors' Shelters by military vehicles attempting to use the inside lines.[21]

The men were also told not to try and make their boots shiny ... spit and polish was out!

Boots had:

> ... been subjected to various treatments i.e. washing in soda, water, petrol, etc, with a view to removing the fat dressing from the leather in order that they may be polished.
> The leather of the Army Boot is specially treated with this dressing in order to render the boots reasonably waterproof and serviceable under Active Service conditions and the dressing should on no account be removed.[22]

On 7 November 1940 the first trainload of personnel left Ingleburn, their base in south-western Sydney, for Bathurst. Here the men detrained at Kelso and marched in full kit the seven miles to their camp at Glanmire, north of Bathurst.[23] The time spent here was to be an important phase in consolidating the individual Sections into Platoons and those in turn into Companies, thus becoming an efficient and effective Battalion unit. Bart Richardson recalled they also became very used to the thousands of flies which accompanied the troops whenever they were outdoors.[24]

In late 1940 Bill wrote his first letter home to his mother Vera who was nicknamed Doukie. His sister Gwyneth Mary was always known as Sue and younger sister Elizabeth Balcombe was known as Ginge, a reflection of her hair colour.

Dear Doukie 10.11.40

At last dear we have arrived at our new home in the country. I am sure we shall like it.

Our troops moved from Ingleburn last Thursday by train and arrived here in the afternoon. We detrained at a siding called Kelso which is 2 miles from Bathurst and then commenced a 6 mile march out to camp - arrived 8.30 pm tired and cranky.

The camp is approx 6 miles from Bathurst but the roads are indirect and make the distance longer. All the Coys are quartered in groups of huts and each group ½ mile apart. Our own Bn area is so extensive that we have motor transport to take us to mess and back and also to visit other Coys. The country is undulating - wheat fields surround us and there are very few trees. On all sides we can see hazy blue mountains in the distance - these worry us a little because we all know that we shall soon be training on the high ground and have to walk.

We marched through Bathurst on Friday. The lads turned on a great show but I think they were treated rather coldly by the local inhabitants. We can see clearly now that the 7th Division did a tremendous amount of damage to the town and we are expected to do the same. Our chaps are moaning because the local girls stay at home and do not walk the streets at night. There are plenty of girls about but these followed us from Sydney and are not a very excellent type.

Leave into town is good. We are allowed every night off - provided we are not working or on any duties. The snag is getting into town. The bus service is rotten and there are no taxis. In actual fact I have very little interest in Bathurst and the only day I saw the town was when we marched through. The local golf club invited some of our officers to a dance. I did not attend and from all accounts I am truly thankful.

I have been transferred to 'D' Coy, and the CO has again mentioned 3 pips. They are now on the way, thank heaven. This move is a good one and I am now permanently a 2I/C. Capt. Moses is OC 'D' Coy and I think we shall make a good team.

Our sleeping huts are excellent. I have a room with decent cupboards, 2 tables and a bed built in to a wall. My predecessor was in the 2/13 Bn and must have been a carpenter. We have our own rooms and therefore have a lot more privacy than previously in other camps. Most of the huts are new and have not been occupied before. We feel very stylish and quite pleased.

Unfortunately a rule has come out from army that we shall not spend any night out of camp whilst at Bathurst. They make an exception of our Xmas 9 days of course but that is the limit. I shall definitely not be home before the 9 days leave.

We have received a lot of rain here. I have no idea of the quantity in inches but think at least 1½.

I have to close dear. Give my love to Sue and Ginge.

Much love dear

Bill

Bill's letter indicated 'Leave into town is good' and some troops took advantage of this. On 18 November a large bush and grass fire started in the unit's Training Area. It swept across the ground and all the troops were moved into positions encircling the fire and gradually gained control. The men bivouacked on their training areas overnight to keep the still-burning area under control. The Battalion's war diary reported *a great deal of organization was required on account of this happening and was excellent training and experience.*

On 20 November a Regimental Ball was held at the Trocadero in Bathurst, attended by a thousand troops from all units of the 22nd Brigade, but not Bill, he decided to stay in camp.

Commander of the 22nd Brigade, Brigadier HB Taylor MC, VD, and Mrs Taylor did attend the ball.[25] Harold Burfield Taylor had won the Military Cross in the First World War and later the Volunteer Decoration for twenty years of efficient service. He was to survive the war and was eventually discharged from the Australian Army on 8 January 1946.[26]

On 19 December the troops were allowed home on final leave, they were warned of the time, place and expiry of their Active Service Leave. Their Divisional Commander, Major General Gordon Bennett, also sent best wishes for the festive season writing:

> *The Div. Comd. Wishes to convey to all ranks his best wishes for a Happy Xmas and Prosperous and Victorious New Year.*
>
> *Though we are impatient to set out on the task for which we enlisted, we are fortunate that we are able to spend this Festive Season among relatives and friends in sunny Australia rather than among the discomforts of alien land.*[27]

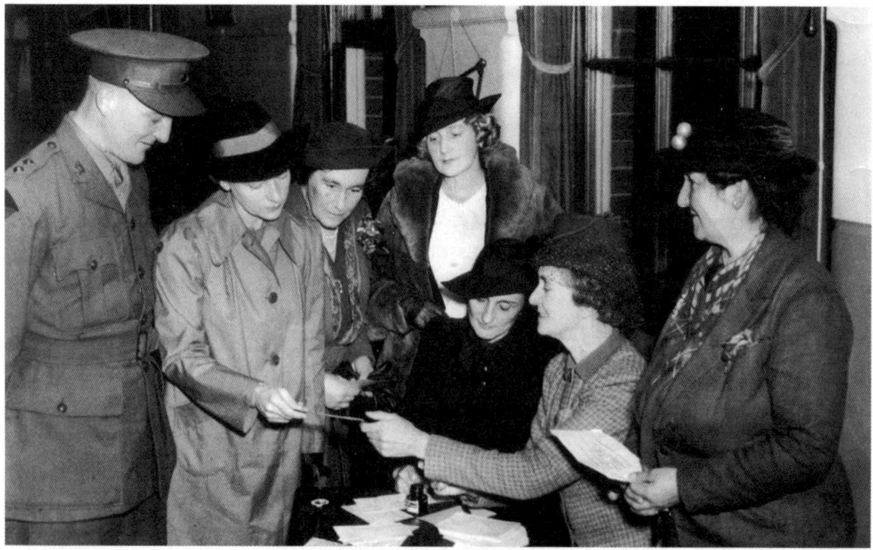

Bill, still with his Lieutenant 'pips', on his final Christmas leave, with some of the ladies of the 2/20 Comforts Fund. His mother Vera [Doukie] is seated and wearing the dark hat and coat.

Dear Doukie 2 Jan '41

I wish you a happy, lucky, prosperous and successful New Year. If I have left any out dear you wish them.

Our dance on New Years Eve was a great success. We were troubled early by rain and had to abandon our beer garden but that did not stop the party moving with a swing. The hall was 'excellently' decorated and the supper inclusive of haggis was also good. I feel sure that all present enjoyed themselves and got pretty drunk. The Fruit Cup was good and we used most of it. Unfortunately we did not have sufficient time to mix any complicated cocktails. The mixing we did consisted of one bottle gin, jar fruit juice, 4 gallons water. The stuff went like hell. In one lot the waiters put two bottles gin and I am sure that this bucked up the party considerably.

Owing to the rain the beer kegs had to be removed from the beer garden to the back of the stage. This was a very bad move because the drips from the beer came through the floor and fell on the freshly laid supper tables below. Incidents such as that one kept me busy practically all night.

Today one of the local creeks came down in flood whilst we were out digging. On our way home it was necessary for us to cross the creek and what a shimozzle [sic] the crossing was. The water was about 4 feet deep and we 'waded' across. It was good fun but very wet. Wish the girls all the best for me dear.
Love
Bill

...

Dear Doukie 3 Jan '41

Thank you very much indeed for your newsy letter. You may possibly receive two of mine in return because I posted one this morning which I am practically sure will catch the same mail as this one.

We have been walking about in the rain all day. Officially we have been inspecting the digging work done by other Bns. but in reality we spent the day endeavouring to pacify our troops who did not like walking in the heavy rain and muddy ground. The morning was reasonable but during lunch we received a huge deluge which lasted throughout the afternoon.

It is really bad luck about the house. [Sale of Marooan, the family home in Scone where Bill was born and spent his childhood.] However we can only live and hope.

You and I both started the New Year with a clean sheet. My only debt is to the 17 Bn Officers Mess which I am not going to pay until I receive some money from them. I think we can both pat each other on the back.

I am pleased that you are going down to see Barbara although I am very much out of favour in that direction at the moment - 'sans fait rien'.

Last night I listened to a German propaganda talk on Ken Hutton's wireless. It was good and very humorous. Much love to the girls.
Love
Bill

...

Dear Doukie 5 Jan '41

I have written to Stan Spain and congratulated him on his son's majority. Ian is somewhere north of New Guinea with part of an artillery unit.

The school at Duntroon I was going to is off as far as I am concerned. It appears that nominations from this Bde were in excess of the numbers that the school could handle and some had to be crossed off. Being junior I was taken off the list and promised the next available school.

At last the weather has cleared up. Since our return from leave rain has been falling here every day. Being Sunday we have visitors in camp today. I have made a resolution not to entertain any ladies this afternoon and accordingly I am in my room dressed in a pair of shorts only. Capt. Moses gave me a bonzer cigar which I am enjoying at the moment.

All around the camp mushrooms are plentiful and our cooks have been kept very busy. There are so many that a couple of chaps can easily fill a bucket in half an hour. We fed our Coy with mushrooms at breakfast this morning.

We are still digging on a big defensive system each day. We have had to take buckets with us each morning to bail out the trenches before the lads start working. I believe the owner of the property we are digging up has complained to army headquarters that we are ruining his land, however still we dig.

Church parade this morning was terrible. The C of E padre is an awful looking bird and our troops (2/20) insisted on singing the wrong hymns too loudly and generally wrecking the show. It was a Brigade parade of about 2000 men and the other units were just as bad as ours at the finish. One party of lads in the 2/18 Bn sang deeply, loudly and precisely each Amen. Generally I think the show was a flop. When nearing the end of his boring sermon the padre announced that he had received a 'brain wave'; the congregation roared with laughter. We never found out what the brain wave was because he finished hurriedly, gave us his blessing and cleared out.

I have spoken to the Pay Sgt. here about your allotment money. The extra money that I have allotted to you is being deducted from my pay here now but he says that you will not receive the extra money for a couple of weeks when a big cheque will arrive.

I am now going to have a decent sleep until mess time.

We have a new scheme in action every morning. Every officer must be dressed and shaved before 5.55 each morning and parade at Bn HQ at that time. Normally we arise about 5.30 but this new rule necessitates even earlier rising. I know I shall waste away.

Much love dear to yourself and the girls. I hope Sue has found a job.
Love

Bill

Stan Spain was a friend from sailing days on Sydney Harbour where Bill was a keen yachtsman. Stan was born 1873, and, despite his age, enlisted to serve his country in June 1940 and on discharge was a Lieutenant with Area Staff. His son Major Ian Alfred Hamilton Spain, NX107755, survived the war and was discharged from Headquarters 1 Australian Army on 17 July 1946.[28]

Dear Doukie 10 Jan '41

I am very pleased about the house. Even though it went for £300 the liability is partly off our hands. We are coming home on leave again next Friday morning early, for 5 days. We cannot complain that leave has been scarce. I seem to always be coming and going.

Yesterday rain fell in torrents and partly flooded the camp. However we only received a little compared with other parts of the district. Scone I believe has had another flood. Fortunately I have not been out in the bush digging. I have been working in camp but the troops have been out in the rain and mud. The lads have dug a couple of miles of trenches already and are still going flat out.

My job in camp has been to keep the troops in the field fed. This has been difficult because they are working two platoons of 30 men in shifts and we have to have their food ready for them as they come off duty. Some of the platoons come off duty at 6 o'clock in the morning which means we have to start cooking their breakfast in camp at 3 a.m.

I have to be up and constantly about because the cooks don't like it and are inclined to become slack. For the last two nights I have been sleeping in short spells and really today I feel very weary.

I hope Sue can come to terms with the Gidley King lass. I feel that Sue would be capable of running a small business herself although the books may give her a bunch of trouble.

I will finish now dear and supervise the cooks in action again. Love to all

Love

Bill

Bill did not realize it, but the lessons he learned here in the organisation and administration of food supplies for the troops were to prove invaluable, saving the lives of many men during the subsequent prisoner of war years.

The business that Sue took over was most likely the manicure shop within the Hotel Australia in Castlereagh Street, formerly run by Kathleen Gidley-King.[29] The hotel was the premier hotel in Sydney, describing itself as the 'Hotel of the Commonwealth'. It had been opened by famous actress and film star Sarah Bernhardt. Lavishly furbished with polished granite, imported Italian marble columns and staircase, there was another imposing staircase nine floors in height made of mahogany. There were reception rooms, the Moorish Lounge and a huge dining room called the Emerald Room complete with chandeliers, fountain and statues.[30] The clientele would have been those people with plenty of money.

At this time Doukie received a couple of letters from Agnes. She had been nanny and housekeeper to the family when they lived at Marooan in Scone. Agnes had arrived when Elizabeth (Ginge) was just three months old. She was engaged for five years but wouldn't leave until Elizabeth was eight years old and could look after herself. She eventually married John Court in 1929 in Muswellbrook.[31]

Dear Mrs. Gaden *Post Office, Forster 20/1st/'41*

I hope you are all well. We are very well here and having a nice holiday. Mrs. Mackay told me tonight Mrs. Throsby told her Bill was on his final [leave?]. *I wonder if it is right. I did want to come and see him before he went. How is Elizabeth and Susie? I hope they are well and enjoying life. Mrs. Gaden is Keith Gaden a relation of yours? Mrs. Mackay's sister's son, who is in the Air Force, said a Keith Gaden was his instructor and what a nice chap he was.*

Jim and Joe [Agnes' sons] *are having a lovely time down here. Mr. Mackay takes Jim out fishing with him and he catches quite a lot of fish. Mr. Mackay said he got a lot of*

fun watching Jim pulling them in, his eyes get bigger and bigger. I hope I hear from you soon Mrs. Gaden.

All my love and best wishes to you all.
I remain yours faithfully

Agnes Court

There were two instances of similar family names, the Gadens being one. When the Battalion was posted to Bathurst, Corporal David Thompson was told by his mother that he had relatives there. He never heard from them. One day the Adjutant called him over, much to David's consternation, wondering why the officer wanted to see him. He was told 'I think I owe you an apology ... I've been several times to visit a family who think I am their relative, but they have the wrong David Thompson. I think you'd better come with us to their tennis party next weekend'. So both Lt David Frederick Thompson (NX34958) and Cpl David Sidney Thompson (NX51413) went to the tennis party and finally caught up with David's mother's relatives.

In the second instance, according to the Nominal Roll for the Second World War, there were just two Gadens in the RAAF, both descended from William Hart Gaden, the first of the line to migrate from Newfoundland to Australia in 1840.[32] They were Robert Henry Gaden and Charles Burton Gaden. Both were Flight Lieutenants. Robert Henry was a great-grandson of William Hart and he survived the war. Charles Burton was the son of Dr Keith Burton Gaden, another great-grandson who was also cousin to Bill's father Noel. Flight Lieutenant Charles Burton Gaden died on 13 December 1940. His squadron of six Gladiators came across five S79 bombers escorted by eight Fiat CR.42s. Gaden, in Gloster Gladiator II N5765, was shot down by the rear gunner of a S79[33] and killed near Sollum, Egypt where he is buried. (Grave 22 B 1)[34] No record has been found to indicate Keith himself was an RAF or RAAF instructor.[35]

Dear Mrs. Gaden *Post Office, Forster*

I was so glad to hear your voice this morning. I made a mistake with the number of the house phone, it is (7) seven. I will be so excited to see Bill's photo. I am sure it will be nice. We are having a lovely time down here the Mackays are so nice and different to the Paynes they are more like you people.

Young Proudfoot from Scone died of wounds, his Father is the man in Asser's. Young Moxham is wounded.

I am glad Sue is starting on her own, I am sure she will do real well. Betty will be turning up to see her I suppose. We have had a lot of rain up at Scone since I came down here. Mrs. Savill is living down here, Mr. Savill is in the army. I must close hoping you are all real well.

Yours faithfully, Agnes

The Gaden family would know the Proudfoots from their many years of living in Scone. Young Proudfoot was Edward Wallace Proudfoot, the son of Hector Proudfoot. His Service Number was NX1419, he served in the 2/2 Infantry and died on 4 January 1941.[36] His father worked for the Asser family who ran a store in Scone, selling 'Drapery, Mercery, Boots'.[37] No specific Moxham could be identified from the Nominal Rolls.

Dear Doukie 28 Jan '41

Please excuse pencil. I have nothing better with which to write at the moment. I received your letter and also the garters. Thank you very much; they are A1. We are terribly busy dear. I have been sleeping whenever possible and working consistently. I hope the photos come soon. They should have them ready by now.

How is Sue getting on with her business? I hope she still has plenty of clients.

Please understand dear that all my letters in future will be censored and that only very limited information can be given.

Ralph sends his best wishes and hopes you are well. He is looking the very picture of health and is in very fine spirits

Yesterday I had a buster from a push bicycle. At Glenfield I was quite proud of having survived a fall from a horse but having come off a bike in the AIF I feel most humiliated. No wounds.

Connie Cay wrote me a long letter. As soon as I can locate a pen and ink and have a few minutes I shall return it.

I am enclosing one of my new colour patches and two old ones. The new ones are on our uniforms and look very smart. Please keep them because you will often see the new colours in Sydney worn by our reinforcements.

I have fired the little automatic and found it very accurate and easy to shoot with. Cheerio dear

Love

Bill

Much love to girls

PS the green and white diamond is the colour of the 20 Bn last AIF.

Ralph was Rolphe Waldo Uther Barker NX28141 38 who was in 2/20 with Bill. He was destined to die in Burma on Mission 204 on 5 December 1941.

Connie was the former matron at Broughton School where a young Bill had been a boarder. During the war she kept in touch with many of 'her boys'.

In the First World War, the 20 Bn AIF had these same colours. They were reintroduced for use by the 2/20 in the Second World War.

The motto of the 2/20 battalion was '*Nullesecuneus*' which means 'second to none'.[39]

Dear Doukie 29 Jan '41

I posted you a letter this morning but since then the good news has arrived a few minutes ago - a letter authorizing my third pip. I expect to be called up any moment to receive the works.

If you have time dear would you please endeavour to obtain a copy of the Government Gazette. Mr. Hart at the enquiry counter of the GPO will be able to advise you where to get them. I do not want it here but it would be great if you had a copy at home.

This morning we had a big brigade parade. 3000 of us marched past the Brigadier in slow time. This parade has no special significance it was only turned on for practice and to help wear out the lads boots. All the dark badly cut uniforms our lads have been wearing have all been returned and in their place we are receiving a very smart drill uniform similar to the light one officers wear. The lads look very smart and well dressed.

At the moment I am sitting at my table in the Coy orderly room and am practically smothered with paper. We are working under pressure now.

Much love dear to yourself and the girls.

Love

Bill

The old winter gear was returned and sea kit bags were issued.[40] The new uniforms were lightweight and the drill trousers could be buttoned up to become shorts or dropped to cover the legs and then tucked into short ankle puttees[41] which provided ankle support and took the place of a leather or cloth gaiter.[42]

Dear Doukie 30 Jan '41

I am now actually a Captain. The troops seem to [sic] just as pleased as I am and the other subalterns here are all trying not to look envious.

Today we went on a long trek over very rough country. We are all tired and for the most part happy.

I have received a lot of letters of congratulations etc. already. Bush wireless certainly works fast.

The back pay that has been credited in my pay book amounts to £14. I cannot draw it out yet but will be able to later.

Lately I have been working in camp and today out in the bush I received a good dose of sunburn. The old nose will commence peeling any minute.

The photographs have not turned up. If they do not come soon you will have to choose the best of them and distribute. Connie Cay wants one and so do Margaret [Taylor] and Elaine [Warren]. I shall send you sufficient cash when we receive our next pay.

I must close now dear but will write again at the earliest opportunity. Much love to all

Love

Bill

By the beginning of February 1941 the men knew embarkation for overseas was imminent. The camp was 'closed' and the unit was packed and ready to move. Senior officers went to Sydney ahead of the troops and the men rehearsed entraining and embarkation drill. The Battalion left Bathurst by train on the first Sunday and Monday of February, heading for Sydney and then 'destination unknown'.[43]

Dearest Doukie Sunday 2 Feb '41

I have received two of your letters and expect to receive the third on tomorrow morning.

It is rotten luck that the sale of Marooan fell through. I hope that some kind Samaritan shall come forth and buy soon. Scone must be looking very green and prosperous after the recent rain and some people may decide to live in 'pretty country'.

Ralph was very lucky being sent to Sydney. I missed out because, knowing the ropes they considered me of more use in camp where I am always on tap to give advice re packing, entraining etc.

All my letters in future are to be addressed:

NX 12543
Capt. EW Gaden
'D' COY
2/20Bn
Aust Imp Forces
Abroad

Please write often and give me all the tit bits of news.

I think the photographs are awful and at the first opportunity I shall have some more taken. I am enclosing a £1 note in case you want them.

Recently I have written letters to people everywhere and possibly will receive the replies 'somewhere'. Please do not endeavour to evade the censors etc. by giving people letters because it may get us all in trouble.

Today is windy and hot, washing day for everyone here.

I am in a bit of a spot because the gear I have here will not fit in the bags and trunks we are not permitted to take. I can clearly see that I will have to pack another case marked 'stationery'.

The garters are still in action but they have been regarded with too many covetous eyes to remain with me always. There is something I would like very much indeed; flare to dangle from the tops of my sox. The colours are green and white dear, this drawing will give you an idea how to make them. Since we changed our colour patches a remarkable change has taken place within the unit. The lads have reacted to the brighter colours and are very keen. They have a traditional significance having been worn by the 20th Bn last war.

Gordon and Mrs. G both wrote to me. I am replying by this mail. [Griersons were next door neighbours.]

Please give a photograph to Margaret. If you don't she will clamour for one.

Ralph has just been to see me and has his head covered in bandages. He has just had a piece of grit taken out of an eye but otherwise he is blooming and sends his regards.

No more news at the moment dear. Love to all. Stick to the paperwork dear, I am pleased you like it. Cheerio, good luck and happiness.

All my love
Bill

By hosting the troops during their training phase, the people of Bathurst contributed in no small way to the war effort. However the war was to create a huge burden on Australia, both economic and industrial. With a total population of just seven million people, over one million joined the armed services and a further half a million were employed to build roads, construct airfields or were engaged in munitions. Ration coupons were issued for petrol, food and clothing (there were none available for the purchase of sheets and towels); prices and rents were fixed.[44] Women became a huge labour force working on farms, in factories, building ships and assembling aircraft as well as working in the transport and communication industries. Even children were involved by growing vegetables; schoolboys made the wooden needles used by the women who made the camouflage nets.[45] Those who were not employed were often involved in the Comfort Funds, the mothers and wives, sisters and sweet-hearts, raising some pounds and shillings for a few luxuries for 'their lads'. Their emotional burden was immeasurable.

The war was a war to which every single member of the Australian population contributed in some way.

At Bathurst a Memorial Wall was eventually built and covered with plaques dedicated to the various battalions who trained there. The plaque for the 2/20 reads:[46]

MALAYA 1941
MERSING
ENDAU

NITHSDALE ESTATE
KRANJI
SINGAPORE 1942

Second to None

DEDICATED TO THE GALLANT MEMBERS OF
2/20 BATTALION
AUSTRALIAN IMPERIAL FORCE

22nd BRIGADE 8th AUSTRALIAN DIVISION
WHO TRAINED IN THIS CAMP DURING THE SECOND WORLD WAR
PRIOR TO EMBARKATION FOR ACTIVE SERVICE IN MALAYA

LEST WE FORGET

ERECTED 10 AUGUST 2002

1 *Chronology of Second World War*, < http://www.spartacus.schoolnet.co.uk/2WWchron.htm >
2 Penny Fussell, personal recollection.
3 Will of EN Gaden, in the possession of the author.
4 DVA Nominal Roll < http://www.ww2roll.gov.au/>
5 Australian Bureau of Statistics, *Year Book Australia*, 1946-47 <http://144.53.252.30/AUSSTATS/abs@nsf/featurearticlesbytitle/F19B5A51A60904F3CA2569DE00>
6 Molony, *The Penguin History of Australia*, p. 282.
7 McKernan, *Drought the red marauder*, p. 170.
8 Mackay, *Turning Point*, p. 37.
9 Elliott and Silver, *A history of 2/18 Battalion*, p. 15.
10 Pitkin Pictorials, *The Right Honourable Sir Winston Churchill*, a pictorial memorial, p. 15.
11 AWM note <http://www.awm.gov.au/atwar/structure/army_structure.htm >
12 *War Diary 2/20 Bn. A.I.F.*, 13 July 1940.
13 Wall, *Singapore and Beyond*, p. 1.
14 Mackay, *op. cit.*, p. 36.
15 Elliott and Silver, *op cit.*, p. 18.
16 Pease and Pease, *Why men don't listen*, p. 281.
17 *War Diary 2/20 Bn. A.I.F.* 2 October 1940.
18 *ibid.*, 6 October 1940.
19 Newton, Reg, personal communication.
20 Newton, Reg, Interview, AWM S01739.
21 Routine Orders 2/20 Bn AIF, 30 Oct 1940.
22 *ibid.*, 6 November 1940.
23 Elliott and Silver, *op. cit.*, pp. 23-4.
24 Richardson, Bart, Address at Dedication of 2/20 plaque, AWM, 30 Nov 2007.
25 *War Diary 2/20 Bn. A.I.F.*, 20 Nov 1940.
26 DVA Nominal Roll, AWM web site link to awards and decorations and Digger History web site < http://www.diggerhistory.info/pages-medals/00-medals-cat-index.htm >
27 Routine Orders 2/20 Bn. A.I.F., 19 December 1941.
28 DVA Nominal Roll.
29 Sonia Gidley-King and Diana Bradhurst, personal communication.
30 Hotel Australia < http://en.wikipedia.org/wiki/Australia_hotel >
31 NSW BDM index, 8455/1929. Marriage of Agnes O'Donohoe to John Court.
32 Gaden family history researched by the author and David Sidney Thompson, personal communication.
33 Commonwealth biplane fighter aces < http://www.surfcity.kund.dalnet.se/commonwealth_gaden.htm >
34 David Gray <http://www.3squadron.org.au/subpages/roll.htm >
35 DVA Nominal Roll and Gaden family history researched by the author.
36 DVA Nominal Roll.
37 Scone Historical Society records.
38 DVA Nominal Roll.
39 Bathurst Army Camp Memorial Wall < http://www.skp.com.au/memorials2/pages/20505.htm > and Army Battle Honours < http://www.army.gov.au/AHU/HISTORY/Battle%20Honours/Battle_Honours_WWII_Infantry_Unitsp1.htm >
40 Elliott and Silver, *op. cit.*, p. 24.
41 *Sydney Morning Herald*, 20 February 1941.
42 Puttee <http://en.wikipedia.org/wiki/Puttee >
43 *War Diary 2/20 Bn. A.I.F.* 1 and 2 February 1941.
44 Higgins, Australian Bureau of Statistics, 1301.0 *Year Book Australia 1946-1947.* Australians at War <http://www.abs.gov.au/ausstats > p. 5.
45 Personal communication from members of the < AUS-NSW-SYDNEY@rootsweb.com > mailing list.
46 Bathurst War Memorial < http://www.skp.com.au/memorials2/pages/20505.htm >

Chapter 2 - Pounding along to Singapore

Leaving their homeland and sailing away to war was an emotional time for the men of the 2/20 Battalion and the rest of the 22nd Brigade and 8th Division on board the troop ship *Queen Mary*. They had to farewell their family and friends; they didn't know if they would ever see them again. From now on the other members of their platoons and companies would have to become a surrogate family for each soldier.[47]

The officers of the 2/20 had become Bill Gaden's family and protected him when they could. There was an altercation at a restaurant at embarkation time. Bill Gaden was bailed up by someone with forthright views on the war. Bill eventually lost patience, took a swipe at the person and the police became involved. No one was allowed to serve overseas if there was any hint of a problem with the police, so when embarkation time came, the 2/20 officers rallied round and made sure Bill was quickly on board and hidden on the large vessel.[48]

The departure of the 22nd Brigade was supposed to be secret, but with a ship the size of the *Queen Mary* (over 81,000 tons)[49] in Sydney Harbour, and hundreds of uniformed men travelling to the quay and boarding, it would have been a very open secret that she was there to transport troops to an area of conflict. Bart Richardson remembered that people waved all the way along the railway line and the shores were lined with people.[50] One wife recalled: 'They had the biggest crowd waving them off from the docks you could ever imagine'.[51]

There was an inspection of troops by His Excellency the Governor General, with 2/20 troops forming up on the Sun Port Deck Side Forward, hardly a secret exercise! Even at this late stage two members of the unit disembarked, one being medically unfit and the other found to be in a reserved occupation.[52] The ship sailed from Sydney and into harm's way at 13.30 hours on 4 February 1941.

Bill Gaden could see his home 'Valhalla' at 8 Raymond Road, Neutral Bay from the decks of the great liner.

He wrote:

Darling Doukie

One hour has passed since I lost sight of 'Valhalla' and you waving. The lump around my tonsils seems to have departed.

The big vessel is wonderful at sea, hardly any movement has been apparent up to date. Our accommodation is quite good but not palatial. Most of our troops are in hammocks and are very cramped for space. We call the hammock area 'Calcutta', remembering a certain black hole. The messing for all ranks is excellent.

A plane from our man-o-war escort patrols our convoy and gives us excitement as well as protection. The plane at times flies so low that from the high decks we can look down on it as it zooms past.

I have a small cabin with David MacDougal. We are happy together and quite comfortable.

Today is Wednesday and all is well. The old crate is plunging about a little but I have not been sick.

Each day I shall write a little and at the first opportunity post it home to you.

Thursday - We are bounding over the ocean and soon I believe this note is to be posted.

Life has been pleasant. Gradually we are becoming adapted to the conditions on board and are fast becoming good sailors.

Yesterday I was 'Captain of the Day'. This is not an honour but a duty taken by each one of us in rotation, starting at the bottom. The period of duty lasts for 24 hours during which time you are responsible for the maintenance of good order and discipline on board. I am the first officer of this unit to have ever been 'Capt. of the Day'. We did not have such duties on land.

Our canteens are cheap and have reasonably good stuff. Beer and cigarettes are cheap, no excise. I purchased 50 'Sunripe' cigarettes, English brand, tonight for 1/6. Everything else seems to be cheap also.

I believe the mail closes tomorrow so dear I shall close this note now and write again if time permits. Good luck. All my love to yourself and the girls.
Love
Bill

PS Now showing 'Diamond Jim' in Officers lounge. The above show was mournful and not good entertainment.

The fighting-fit men, used to long route marches around Bathurst, obviously became bored with the confines of the ship and their journey to war. Lt-Col WD Jeater, their commanding officer, issued orders that they were not to play with the fan and light switches nor was gambling allowed, 'gambling devices' would be confiscated. Rubbish was not to be placed in the latrines, it caused blockages; cigarette butts and matches were to be placed in the appropriate receptacles, not strewn on the decks. The most ominous warning was:

'MAN OVERBOARD' The Regulations prevent this ship from stopping under any circumstances in the event of personnel falling overboard. Troops are to be advised of this and that it is useless in any way to affect a rescue.[53]

As the *Queen Mary* progressed through Bass Strait other vessels joined the convoy. The *Aquitania*, at 45,647 tons, was carrying troops embarked from Melbourne, *Mauretania* at 31,938 tons and the Dutch ship *Nieuw Amsterdam* at 36,667 tons carried troops from New Zealand.[54]

On 10 February the ships arrived at Fremantle. The *Queen Mary*, at 81,237 tons, was the largest vessel in the convoy and too large to enter the harbour, so no shore-leave was possible for the boys of the 22nd Brigade.[55]

Bill sent a telegram home to the family:

TELEGRAM
Office of origin S66 SANS ORIGINE 13 words Time Lodged 5P
Received by the Chief Telegraph Office, Sydney 11 Feb 41,
Neutral Bay stamp is timed 10.30am 12 Feb 41
GADEN, RAYMOND ROAD, NEUTRAL BAY, NSW
WELL HAPPY NOT SEASICK LOVE TO ALL BILL

When the convoy sailed from Fremantle on 12 February 1941, the sea was particularly calm and that evening the Ship's Officers hosted a dance.[56] The next day the men were officially told that the 22nd Brigade was bound for Singapore. Officers received daily briefing lectures about Malaya and were then expected to pass the information on to their men.[57]

During the voyages the troops had many different training exercises, the program allowed for the rotating of training decks for all personnel so everyone had a fair share of sun and fresh air. Daily swimming was also a pleasant feature. First pay on board was made available for troops on 14 February, the rates allowed were: - Field Rank and above £10, Officers below Field Rank £5, Warrant Officers and Sergeants £2, Corporals and Specialists £1.10.0 and Privates £1.

Darling Doukie 15 Feb 41

Once again we are at sea and charging steadily along.

The last port of call was rather a disappointment. We did not have leave and could only see the town from our anchorage about 3 miles out. However the view, especially at night, was beautiful and poignantly reminiscent of home.

During the last week we have been sweltering in oppressive heat. I always thought that life on a ship would be cool and pleasant even in summer.

I have received two of your letters dear, and also one from Vivian Fowler . [The Fowler family were friends from Goulburn where Vivian's husband was a local bank manager.]

I am sorry that old Bill Badgery is 'fading away', and I am in complete agreement with your decision to refuse their invitation.

The lads are happy and are enjoying the cruise. The heat enables them to wander about half nude.

Our officer's lounge is air conditioned and we hold dances and concerts with an occasional talking picture. Last night was a great and happy occasion. The AIF officers turned on a cocktail party and entertained all the nurses and ship's officers. The success of this venture was clearly shown by the Commodore who led a 'crocodile' from the lounge, through corridors to our mess hall.

This note leaves us at sea and is carried to you by airmail.
Cheerio dear. Love to the girls.
All my love

Bill

It was at these dances and concerts on board the ship that Bill and the other officers first met nurses such as Elaine Balfour-Ogilvy and Wilhemina (Ray) Raymont of the Australian Army Nursing Service. He would see them again when they were able to go on leave from their various stations in Singapore and

Malaya. These brave young women had volunteered to sail into danger to care for sick and wounded troops. Many nurses, including these two, were to die at the hands of the Japanese, never to return to their beloved Australia.

The battalion's war diary recorded that on 16 February the convoy split up, with some ships heading for the war in Europe and Africa, the *Queen Mary* heading for Singapore at a faster speed.

William J Noonan recalled the big day for the Malaya-bound boys of the 8th Division.

> *Somewhere in the Indian Ocean a convoy, consisting of two ships of war and four of the greatest liners in the world took part in a magnificent manoeuvre prior to separating for 'destinations unknown'. At 3 o'clock the* Queen Mary *swung round in a huge circle, passing very close to a gloriously lined Dutch vessel, crowded with Kiwis yelling their heads off. The gigantic Cunard liner continued her arc, and came up on the starboard side of another liner at the rear of the convoy. She was packed with thousands of cheering Victorians, and cheer after cheer went ringing across the water from both sides. The spirit of brotherhood in a single cause carried in every cheer - a very moving moment. Then it subsided until the* Mary *drew level with another veteran troop ship.*
>
> *The greatest ships in almost telepathic communication, laden with the world's finest fighting men, each heart going out to the other in a gesture of well wishing - a rare glimpse of mass emotion in a moment of admiration and bewilderment. It may never happen again. The blood surged through my veins and within myself I said 'I am proud to be a part of this'.*
>
> *The convoy divided, the* Queen Mary *speeding at an increased rate behind the destroyer H.M.S.* Durban. *The others faded until they were mere silhouettes on a tropical horizon, following an ocean greyhound. And we were alone; pounding along to Singapore.*[58]

Bart Richardson recalled they were in box formation with *Queen Mary* on the left front. The ship then did a complete circle round the other ships and he remembered the rigging and two masts of each ship could not be seen for khaki.[59] It would have been a magnificent sight.

HMS *Durban* was *Queens Mary's* escort. *Durban* was part of the British Malayan Force along with the cruiser HMS *Dragon* which also escorted troops to Singapore.[60]

The *Queen Mary* had a top speed of 40 knots.[61] But it is unlikely that she kept to her top speed for too long. In hostile waters ships 'become nervous' with less than 70% of their fuel on board and even today our modern frigates will double their usage going from 24 knots to 30 knots.[62] At 40 knots the *Queen Mary's* fuel consumption would have been huge. Apart from that HMS *Durban* would not have been able to keep up with her. *Durban's* top speed in her heyday was about 30 knots and she was well past her prime (she was commissioned in November 1921 and expended in June 1944).[63] It would be a needless risk to put super-heated steam under the pressure required for such a speed.

The troops bound for Singapore were now known as 'Elbow Force'. The men continued training but were entertained by band and concert parties and they enjoyed the shipboard activities of the swimming pool and sporting events. They even received a newspaper edited by one of their own, Oswald Ziegler of 2/18 Battalion.[64]

The *Queen Mary* berthed at the Naval Docks in Singapore Harbour at 1500 hours on 18 February 1941. The troops disembarked and travelled to their barracks by train. At 0830 the next morning they stopped at Gemas for breakfast, provided by one of the British Garrison regiments, The Loyals. The Australians then moved to Bagan Pinang where they marched in pouring rain and heat to their new barracks in Haig Lines, the original camp of the Volunteer Forces at Port Dickson.[65]

The Battalion's war diary reported that Capt. EW Gaden disembarked with the 10 AGH as patient. So Bill Gaden was taken straight from the ship with the 10 Australian General Hospital personnel in Singapore, not the best way to start a campaign overseas.

Meanwhile the people of New South Wales were being kept well informed of world events by radio and the newspapers of the day. The *Sydney Morning Herald* ran a daily column headlined THE WAR, DAY BY DAY. Its Military Correspondents discussed the happenings of the week in the various, sadly expanding, theatres of war. The Australians were heavily involved in the fighting, with thousands of troops facing the Germans and Italians in Europe and Africa. Many people had a very vested interest in the events overseas.

The newspaper also discussed events closer to home and the Australian population was well aware of the build up of Japanese aggression over the weeks and months. The *Sydney Morning Herald* of 5 February 1941 advised ALARM AT JAPAN'S MOVES and discussed the defence plans for the naval base and Australians at Singapore. Maps of the places mentioned in the article brought home to the readers just how close to Australia the aggressors really were.[66]

The *Sydney Morning Herald* of 20 February 1941 headlined JAPANESE SHIPS IN GULF OF SIAM. There was a short mention of Malaya's defences and another discussion of the 'Fate of the Dutch East Indies'. There was also a detailed description of the arrival of the Australian troops in Malaya, following weeks of secret preparations. It advised that they were a well equipped force. The news was welcomed in London but the Japanese were critical, saying the arrival of Australian troops in large numbers in Singapore '*could not be interpreted as a gesture contributing to peace in the Far East*'.[67]

A year later peace gestures were far from the minds of both the Australian and Japanese troops. Many of the young men and women who disembarked from *Queen Mary* had lost their lives, the rest became prisoners of the Japanese. The families did not learn of their fates for many painful months or even years.

[47] Elliott and Silver, *A history of 2/18 Battalion*, p. 25.

[48] Penny Fussell, Personal communication.

[49] Smith, *Singapore Burning*, p. 50.

[50] Bart Richardson, Address at Dedication of 2/20 plaque, AWM, 30 Nov 2007.

[51] Peters, 'The life experiences of partners of ex POWs of the Japanese', *AWM Journal* 28 April 1996, p. 1.

[52] *War Diary of 2/20 Bn. A.I.F.*, 4 Feb 1941.

[53] Routine Orders 2/20 Bn. A.I.F. 4 Feb 1941.

[54] Ocean liners < http://www.ocean-liners.com/ships/asp > and < http://en.wikipedia.org/wiki/RMS_ > and < www.gallagher.com/ww2/chapter11.html >

[55] Richardson, *op. cit.*

[56] *War Diary 2/20 Bn. A.I.F,* 12 February 1941.

[57] *ibid.*, 13 February 1941.

[58] Noonan, *The Surprising Battalion*, p. 1.

[59] Richardson, *op. cit.*

[60] <http://uboat.net/allies/warships/ship/1207.html >

[61] Smith, *op. cit.*, p. 50.

[62] Lt Cmdr Philip Gaden, RANR, Personal communication.

[63] <http://uboat.net/allies/warships/ship/1207.html >

[64] Elliott and Silver, *op. cit.*, p. 25.

[65] *War Diary 2/20 A.I.F.*, 19 February 1941.

[66] *Sydney Morning Herald*, 5 February 1941.

[67] *ibid.*, 20 February 1941.

Chapter 3 - From Ship to Hospital

The troops of the 22nd Brigade AIF disembarked in Singapore on 18 February 1941.[68] Bill Gaden was sent straight to the Middleton Hospital, the infectious diseases centre built in 1907 on the Moulmein Road, Singapore.[69] The rest of his battalion went to Port Dickson on the west coast of Malaya. The following weeks of training were missed by Bill, so his troops had a head start on him in adapting to work under local conditions. They went on route marches, mounted guard, organised swimming, sport and games and learned to overcome administrative problems, especially in relation to finding out their 'entitlements with regard to employment of native labour'.[70]

Darling Doukie 22 Feb 41

In my last screed home I mentioned that our cruise was nearly over. This letter is written from dry land! I have a rather sad story: - on the day of disembarkation I was admitted to the isolation ward of the ship's hospital, under observation for scarlet fever. Early in the afternoon, same day, another lad and myself were carried on stretchers to the wharf and were eventually taken to an excellent isolation hospital.

The hospital is really fine. We are all fed with every dish we care to order. A native servant is available 24 hours each day to each patient. An atmosphere of happiness prevails everywhere.

The basis upon which these merits have been built is sound British organization and efficiency. I have not developed scarlet fever; in fact I have developed no disease at all. However because I still run a temperature sometimes the powers that be have decided to keep me in luxury for a little longer.

Please let me know where John Barton is stationed.

This will be my only letter to Australia this mail. Please announce the news over 2WC. [Is it family jargon for 'the grape-vine'?]

Much love to all.
The only letters I have received were those acknowledged. Love to Sue and Ginge
Cheerio dear
Love
Bill

On 24 February the troops commenced training in earnest with compass marches through the jungle. At this stage they were allowed a two hour siesta until they were better able to cope with the heat and humidity of Malaya. Swimming and other recreational activities were organized after the siesta. Companies rotated through the various training programs to ensure all troops had access to equipment and activities.[71]

There were some soldiers who used brothels, many took no precautions, and venereal disease became an issue. General Bennett asked authorities for a special VD hospital to be set up in Malaya (this was refused).[72] A detailed description of treatment for VD was issued to troops on 25 February 1941.

Routine Orders by Lt Col WD Jeater Commanding 2/20 Bn AIF, 25 Feb '41 PORT DICKSON included:-

VENEREAL DISEASE PROPHYLACTIC TREATMENT At present the Preventative Ablution Centre is established at the 2/9 Fd. Amb. [Field Ambulance] Block in the down-stores ablution area and is indicated by a blue light. The Centre will be open from 2000hrs to 2300hrs and all personnel granted leave must report to this Centre before returning to their lines. Those that have not exposed themselves to the possibility of infection need not be treated, but all others must receive treatment and will receive a note to that effect. Personnel who contract V.D. and do not possess such a note will be charged with a self-inflicted wound.

Units will be responsible that all personnel arrested in an intoxicated condition receive treatment before being placed in the Guard House.

The following standard prophylactic treatment will be carried out at Preventative Ablution Centre for the time being. The patient will proceed as follows:-

1. Pass urine.
2. Wash hands thoroughly in soap and water and rinse in plain water.
3. Roll up shirt and drop trousers to knee.
4. Pull back foreskin and wash penis and surrounding areas thoroughly with soap and water.
5. Dry the parts with cotton wool.
6. Rub calomel ointment obtained from blue light outfit over the head of the penis, scrotum and groin. The whole of the contents of one tube to be used.
7. Hold penis vertically and separate lips of the mouth of the urethra.
8. The attendant will then drop from an eye dropper 10 drops of 1 in 8000 potassium permanganate freshly prepared daily.
9. The patient will not pass urine for four hours after this treatment.

All those who returned drunk to barracks had to be treated ... and then not pass urine for four hours!

Other health issues were of concern to the unit's command. Troops were warned to use only British tooth and shaving brushes as those of Japanese or Chinese manufacture could harbour anthrax. Two showers per day were ordered to help prevent skin 'affections' [sic] and smoking whilst under a mosquito net was forbidden.[73]

A week after arriving in Port Dickson the Battalion's administration were still having issues with their entitlement to native labour. This was in fact quite a problem. Work on defences could not be carried out using local labour because the army was not allowed to pay the 'coolie' workforce more than the rubber plantations paid them as it was said to be 'unfair competition'.[74] Thus many planned defensive structures were not built unless done so by the soldiers themselves. However the soldiers needed time to train to fight in the jungle, rather than dig trenches or build beach defences.

The men had to learn how to cope in these new conditions. The early training hours meant a new routine was called for with many more duties than before. Refrigeration of food, especially meat was a difficult problem. The Australian troops also were not used to the smaller and different British rations issued to them.

Lack of knowledge of the native language was a handicap which retarded progress and efficiency. Lectures on health issues were given to all ranks.[75]

Sporting fixtures were arranged between units and outside teams, a soccer match saw the 2/20 beaten three goals to one by the local police team.

Gradually more vehicles arrived for the unit and training began on the Bren carriers taken over from the 'Loyals'.

Invitations to visit local dignitaries began to arrive. The *War Diary* of 5 March reported that:

> C.O., 2I/C, Adjt. and 16 officers and 2 Nursing Sisters today attended afternoon tea at the residence of His Highness the Yang Di-pertuan Besar of Negri Sembilan. The drive to H.H. residence was most interesting, and the party was entertained on arrival in a right royal and interesting manner.

Meanwhile, as his troops were learning and adapting to local conditions, Captain Bill Gaden was still ensconced in the military hospital back in Singapore.

> Darling Doukie 5 Mar '41
>
> Since my last letter I have moved from Middleton Hospital, Singapore to Alexandra Military Hosp. which is situated about 5 miles from the heart of the city. My pneumonia has practically departed and I am now 'convalescing in the country' and feeling well.
>
> This hospital is tremendous, very modern and is controlled by the British Army. The Australian patients are happy and contented and find this splendid hospital a pleasant place to recover from their various illnesses.
>
> My room-mate is Capt. Reg Newton from the 2/19 Bn. He is recovering from a very stiff dose of pneumonia. We enjoy each others company and in fact have quite a good time in 'Australia Ward'.
>
> The rainfall here is prolific; rarely does a day pass without a heavy shower.
>
> The building we occupy is three stories [sic] high. Our ward is on the top floor and the view excellent. I can see, from my bed, the British Army barracks, several native thatched huts, banana trees, palms and in the background a mountain which appears to be cloaked with dense tropical vegetation.
>
> Today John Barton [school friend from Scone] came out here to see me. John has been a regular visitor and always brings good books and magazines. He has a big Studebaker car, but his mileage is limited owing to petrol rationing.
>
> Singapore still remains an unknown quantity to me. I was able to see a little from the ambulance when I was transferred from Middleton Hosp, but not sufficient to gain a lasting impression.
>
> Each day visitors arrive to see us. Fortunately some of our officers still remain in the city and have not moved to country stations.

'Australia Ward' is a very cheerful place tonight. Our diet has been supplemented by Malt and stout. This should help bring our weight back to normal again. It is very pleasant medicine.

I am reading 'Northwest Passage' and enjoying it thoroughly.

At Middleton I obtained quite a good book on colloquial Malay, as spoken by the natives. I have been spending an hour or so each day learning the language and can now ask for most of the things I require. Fortunately it is not necessary to speak Malay in hospital but both Capt. Newton and myself often corner an orderly who has been out here some time, and learn as much as we can from him.

We have received many visits from Officers of the British Army who are stationed out here permanently. We have learned a lot from them and I feel sure that we shall leave this hospital much wiser men.

Ralph Barker has returned to the unit. I thought he would still be in hospital here when I arrived but evidently his ailment has left him and he has been sent up country.

Give my love to Sue and Ginge dear. Cheerio
All my love
Bill

This friendship with Reg Newton and the developing language skills would prove invaluable to their survival in the coming years.

Alexandra Military Hospital was a sanctuary in peaceful, sprawling grounds. It was a stately building, three storeys high, with wide cooling verandahs. The officers' wards, open on both sides, were located on the top floor where the refreshing breezes were most available. At the time it was considered to be 'the most up to date and one of the largest military hospitals outside Great Britain'.[77] It had three hundred and fifty six beds for military personnel but this was considered inadequate if war was to break out; the hospital needed to double its capacity by 'increased beds in wards and using some verandah

The Alexandra Hospital in 1942

space'.[78] In 1942 the hospital was close to an Army storage facility whose large fuel tanks are clearly visible on the upper right hand side in the photograph. The original photograph was located in the Hospital's conference room in February 2007.

On 6 March 1941 Malayan Command began a large scale exercise. The 2/20 Battalion did not take a very big part in it but were subjected to a blackout that night. The next day they obviously were still not involved as several officers and men travelled to Sepang and were entertained to afternoon tea by Mr Brunton, the manager of a large rubber plantation, after which his 'coolies' gave practical demonstrations of the tapping of the trees. The party were then conducted by Mr Brunton over the rubber factory. (Mr FH Brunton was Manager of the Sepang Estate, Selangor from 1935.)[79] The Adjutant reported that:

> This gentleman has today shown a most wonderful interest in the welfare of the Private soldier and his hospitality and generous entertainment as well as his most interesting conducting of the party over the Estate has not only been most instructive to the troops, but has helped build up in this small portion of the unit a little more of the very necessary understanding between all ranks of a unit. The troops paid tribute to Mr. Brunton and his wife and returned in convoy to Camp very much wiser in many things and particularly happy (A great help).[80]

A second football match was arranged between players from the 2/20 and local police, this one 'created great interest and was very entertaining' and resulted in a win to the Australians.[81] This was one of many football matches of all codes arranged between different local teams as well as inter-Battalion matches. In Malaya, sport was popular and truly multi-racial.[82] It was excellent for fitness of the players; it kept men occupied and entertained and was an important part in maintaining unit morale.

With troops from both the 'Mother Country' and the 'Colonies', it was inevitable that already-established sporting rivalry would soon lead to matches on the local *padangs*.

The first cricket match played by the 2/20 was on 9 March, against the 2/9 Field Ambulance, the 2/20 winning by 8 runs. Sport was a temporary panacea against homesickness, boredom and frustration that they were not fighting the Germans but playing a waiting game against the Japanese who they thought would never come.

Back home, on March 8 the *Australian Women's Weekly* magazine had published an article about the 'Laughing Soldiers', the Malayans' name for the AIF in Singapore. Reporter Margot Heale told the readers that the troops were a real inspiration to her. She said they looked to be first rate soldiers and their hard training had built them up into 'superb specimens'. The light-hearted Malayans welcomed the 'happy-go-lucky' soldiers from a far off land. The mothers, wives and sweethearts were told that everything was being done for the comfort of their boys, with clubs and hostels being arranged by the ex-patriot Australians for their entertainment.[83]

Bill Gaden, despite his talent and love of sport was still confined to hospital. He wrote to his aunt. Nicknamed Dorky, she was Doris Miriam (Balcombe) Grant, wife of Hugh Grant. Her son was Hugh Balcombe Grant (known as Bob) who initially joined the Army, NX28293, but he later moved to the RAAF.

Dear Dorky 9 March '41

Today I received a very nice letter from Mrs. Hughes. She has extended me an invitation visit her at Kuala Lumpur. Unfortunately I am in hospital and shall not be able to go up country for a couple of weeks. I have had pneumonia, not very badly luckily.

I am in Alexandra Military Hospital, Singapore and being very well looked after.

This is the first time that I have been in a hospital and the experience has not been bad at all. The hospital is very modern and my room is on the third floor of a large cool building and has an excellent view. Visitors have been arriving daily, most of them officers from both the British and Australian services. The patients on this floor are very congenial and generally we have a fairly good time.

Singapore is still a mystery to me because I have only been in the city in an ambulance. I was taken to hospital as soon as our vessel arrived here. I am walking about now and should be able to pay the town a visit within the next few days.

I have been taught to play an excellent card game - Solo. We play for cents and delight in 'skinning' an RC padre who is a very good sort and who is also convalescing with us.

There are several Australians here and my room mate is Capt. Newton an Australian officer. We manage to have a lot of fun. Our room is called 'Australia Ward'.

Have you had any recent news from Bob? I had hoped to see him when I sailed for oversees but now we are on different sides of the world.

I am gradually learning to speak the Malay language and my vocabulary at the moment is about 60 words. The colloquial Malay is not very difficult.

Thank you very much indeed for writing to Mrs. Hughes. I shall see her as soon as possible.

I have received no Australian mail at all so far. The letters have all been delivered to the wrong hospital. Love to you all
Love
Bill

...

Darling Doukie 9 March '41

I am practically well again and should be back with my unit in a couple of days. At the first opportunity I shall cable you from Singapore.

Today I received a letter from a Mrs. Hughes; she is a friend of Dorky who has invited me to their home at Kuala Lumpur. At the first opportunity I intend to visit her.

We are a happy family here in hospital. Each day and often at night we play a card game called Solo and enjoy it immensely. For a few days I was not very good and lost frequently. The lads called me their 'meal ticket'. However I have improved and an RC padre is now the 'meal ticket'.

Letters have arrived from my unit and locally but still none from Australia. I know they are in Malaya because they have been sighted at our Australian hospital. I hope they arrive here soon.

Yesterday I received a long letter from Capt. Moses. He says the lads are happy and like Malaya. They are playing football, soccer and are waiting for my return to add some weight to the Bn team. I shall not be in condition to play for quite a long time. I have lost two stone in weight but am speedily regaining it on malt and stout.

I have not been numbering my letters but intend to do so the future. This is the fifth I have written from Malaya so I shall number it accordingly.

You have probably seen in the local newspaper an account of 'Joey' the 19 Bn. kangaroo that was smuggled into Malaya in a box marked 'Medical Supplies'. Joey is liking the climate and so far is doing very well. Capt. Newton who is with me here in hospital was largely responsible for Joey's voyage to the East. He gave instructions for the making and marking of Joey's box.

The currency out here is in dollars as you know. A dollar is worth about 2/11 Australian currency but it has a purchasing value of about 1/6. I mean that you have to pay one dollar in Singapore for goods that could be purchased in Sydney for 1/6. Some articles such as clothes and tobacco are very cheap but European foodstuffs and beer are very expensive. I may be incorrect in this observation but I don't think that I am far out.

I am writing this epistle in the Officer's lounge and a short distance away the Solo school is in action. They have discovered another 'meal ticket', a lad from the RAF.

We have here bath chairs with three wheels. These are most popular and have names. Australia Ward have lost theirs because we have arrived at the walking stage. We called it 'Alor Star'.

Darts are a popular sport. We have a board in the dining room. I have not seen any experts and all of us are about the same standard which is very low.

I have finished reading 'Northwest Passage' and am now wading through a detective yarn.

No more news dear. I shall write again soon. Love to Sue and Ginge.
Love
Bill

Meanwhile the 2/20 Battalion were involved with all other allied troops in a Far Eastern Defence Exercise. They moved from camp by motor transport.[84]

Darling Doukie 10 March '41

Whacko! Today I received my first mail from Australia and what a pile thirteen letters and I know that your parcel and some more mail is still 'somewhere in Malaya'. I have received two of yours - numbers 4 and 5 - one from Mrs. Wilkinson and one from each of her daughters, two from the office and the remainder from girls including Elaine but none from Margaret. I have taken your advice about 'poise and breeding' to heart and intend to act accordingly.

In yesterdays letter I gave you all the local news from here but since yesterday sufficient has accumulated to fill these pages.

Last night we played Pontoon. We were fortunate in having nine players and the game was good fun. I think I enjoyed it more than my colleagues because I won successfully.

'Australia Ward' has been winning well recently.

Today I ordered some clothes to be made from a tailor, an Indian who visited the hospital at our request. I am having one uniform, 2 pairs of shorts and two shirts made for $20, about £2.18.0., the Australian price about £7.10.0. These are rather expensive articles out here. Cheaper ones can be obtained but they are not so good.

Our Solo school has been broken up because the RC padre was discharged from hospital this morning. However we still have plenty of convalescent patients and a possible 'meal ticket' with us.

Today I had a long talk with an RAF lad. He came originally from South America prior to joining the air force in England. He is very interesting to yarn with. We have been telling each other about the beauty spots of our home countries.

I am pleased you enjoyed your day at Freshwater with Mrs. Caldwell and Ross. Sue tells me that Mrs. C has legs that are even thinner than her sons.

Capt. Newton is having a hair cut. The barber, a Malayan, really enjoying himself. The native word for a person or man is O'rang and hair is utang. We have just discovered that a hairy man is an orangutang. The language is delightful in its simplicity and I am not finding it difficult to learn.

We are developing the Eastern habit of sleeping in the afternoon. Our lads in camp have not had the opportunity. They play sport. We shall have difficulty adjusting ourselves to the new order on our return to the unit.

Today is Monday. Last night was a black out but we managed to find a spot with sufficient light for pontoon. 'Aust Ward' won again.

The local authorities have been practicing [sic] with the air raid siren. Yesterday morning we heard it for the first time and I could not understand why a fog signal was bellowing here, so far inland. The chaps soon enlightened me.

I hope you like the new neighbours. Write and give me all the news. Thank you very much for your pages of news in these last two letters,

Love to Ginge and Sue. I shall write to them soon.
All my love
Bill

On 11 March the Far Eastern Defence Exercise saw the 2/20 move approximately 160 miles, the unit arrived at its appointed rendezvous and went into a 'perimeter' camp until daylight. The transport was very effectively screened in the 'Harbour' appointed to them. This second phase of the exercise was well handled and quite efficiently carried out. At 1300 hrs a message was received for the unit to move to KLUANG there to entrain for camp.

Back home in Australia the *Sydney Morning Herald* of 11 March reported that in Malaya the AIF MAKES FRIENDS. Their special representative of the AAP advised that contrary to malicious stories circulating, the AIF men 'were on the friendliest terms with all sections of the population, especially the Asiatics'. The rumours suggested the troops had been offensive to the native women, there were consequent brawls and they had a boorish attitude towards the locals. However the AAP representative had investigated the stories and proved them to be wrong. It was thought the circulation of the story was due to fifth columnists and was deliberately designed to stir up trouble.[85] (A fifth column is a group of people who clandestinely undermine a larger group, such as a nation, from within, to the aid of an external enemy.)[86]

In the meantime Bill wrote to his two sisters.

Dear Sue, 11 March '41

Have you ever seen a sarong? I am sure you have not so herewith follows a description: - a couple of yards of highly coloured silk like material about four feet wide, then wrap this sheet around their middle and legs and use it as a substitute for pyjamas; not all men but many. I believe they are cool substitutes. I intend to try one out.

Chinese women generally appear to be wearing their pyjamas in the street. This costume is a two piece garment with a long top and the trousers have the bell bottom effect. These observations have been made from a distance. I am still in hospital.

Ladies shoes in Singapore are cheap. I am told that many of the Chinese shoemakers in the town can copy even the most expensive shoes and although the quality of the leather may be doubtful the shoes wear and keep their original shape reasonably well. The cost here is one-third approx. of the Aust price.

The speed of the Indian and other native tailors is amazing. A tailor at the hospital here made me a shirt yesterday morning. Our drill uniforms are cheap and the material excellent compared with Sydney materials.

The value of money in the East is a mystery to me. A naval officer told me yesterday that a certain type of wireless could be purchased in Shanghai for $400 and also cost $400 in Singapore. A dollar in Shanghai is equivalent to 5s and in Singapore 2/11 Australian currency.

I intend sending you all samples of Singapore millinery. However it may be a month before this promised parcel arrives because I have only been paid $3 since I arrived in Malaya and Malay cash is getting short. I have a large credit in my pay book but cannot draw the money until I return to the unit in the jungle.

I am pleased your business is progressing satisfactorily and that you are keeping your head above the surging seas.

Stick to it Sue, cheerio old bean. Good luck.
Love
Billy

...

Dear Ginge 12 March '41

I am sure that Mac or any other of the lads you know would like to hear from you. We are still Australians even though we live in a jungle and often think of home and friends. The old, old question is constantly being thought by all of us 'what is so and so doing now' and for answers the army depends on you. Write Ginge and 'give us the works'.

Your shining circles don't get a chance to float in the sky of the East. From what I am told of the morals of the East I think that the devil must be constantly in action collecting shining circles on the prongs of his pitch fork.

The swim at Freshwater must have been super. If you sunbake out here the moist atmosphere causes the body to perspire trickling streams. You would have no difficulty keeping your weight down in Singapore.

Europeans out here have to wear shoes or slippers always because little parasites called hook worms creep through the skin on the feet and play havoc somewhere inside the body. Natives I believe can walk with their feet bare - most of them have worms.

I have been informed that the type of mosquito that carries diseases such as malaria and dengue stands on its head when biting. Last night I saw a mossy on my arm. He certainly was standing on his head. The first swipe got him and the corpse (squashed) was retained for further inspection because of the black out. We use dull blue lights in a black out. Unfortunately this morning our treasure was dusted away by an orderly before we had a chance to examine the corpse. In the hospital area mossies are very rare and the odd ones that appear are not dangerous. We always use nets with a very fine mesh.

We often have a good laugh at our pyjamas. Some officers prefer to wear their own silk suits, usually white and sometimes with a Chinese inscription like a Mah-Jong cabbage in green on the pocket. Many of us wear the suits supplied by the hospital. These are striped but in different colours, mostly blue, pink and brown. It is unusual to see a patient in a suit of the one colour. My scheme today is pink top and blue pants.

For the next few days our ward is going to be very quiet. One of our number is to be operated on this afternoon. He is to lose his appendix.

I did not mention before that because of the increased number of Australian patients we have been moved to a four berth ward. The other lads are a naval officer from Melbourne and an RAAF officer from Adelaide. More lads are coming in so we shall have to establish two Australian wards.

Today my weight is 12 stone exactly. Even though I am two stone lighter than I was in Sydney I feel well and should put pounds back on when I can exercise again.

Cheerio Ginge. Keep working and write us often.
Yours much love
Bill

Meanwhile Bill's troops arrived back in camp at 0400 hrs on 12 March. The Far Eastern Defence Exercise was thought to have been of great value to all concerned and went to show with what mobility troops could be moved from one place to another. This was another valuable training exercise missed by the sick officers.

Darling Doukie 13 March '41

Today two letters arrived numbers 7 and 8. They were packed with news and have made me happy.

The girl with me when I met Mr. and Mrs. Brooks at Bathurst was Jean Thatcher. I have told you about her. She is very close to forty and certainly not pretty. I met her at our Bn Dance and she came out to visit us in camp twice. She gave me a tin of cigarettes when I left and I have written to her recently from here.

I am sorry that Barbara has to spend another three weeks in hospital. I do not wonder that Margaret has moved to the Raymond Club.

I have no idea how Elaine [Warren] received her letter before any one else because they all went together at Fremantle and they should all arrive together. I wrote letters to all my friends in Neutral Bay and I hope they won't put their heads together and find I dispatched a similar screed to each one. You should be receiving a letter every mail now.

I was surprised to read about Reservoir St advising you of my evacuation to hospital. I tried to send a cable to you from Middleton Hospital but experienced difficulty there because they did not understand EFM rates and neither did I at that stage. I gave up trying to cable because I had posted letters par avion and thought they would only be 5 days in transit. I have only missed two mails and those could not be avoided because I did not have paper to find the mail notices. My letters must be rolling in now.

We are still going happily along here in hospital. Excitement never happens but we walking patients find amusements in small things, time passes pleasantly.

A lad in our ward from Adelaide had his appendix removed yesterday. He is very chirpy this morning and pleased because he did not talk when coming back to consciousness last night.

Leave is surprisingly difficult to obtain from hospital. Two of our colleagues who have been here since our arrival have a couple of hours in town today. They are British Army officers and very lucky because they have their messes handy. Capt. Newton and I hope to see Singapore before long. We are planning to go together to town and visit the places we have heard so much about. This morning we had a very heavy dew and even now at 9 o'clock it is heavy on the ground and our view is like an ocean of cloud.

I have a very pleasant letter from Gran. She says that she is happy but I am sure that she is feeling B's army absence terribly. [Her grandson Hugh Balcombe (Bob) Grant NX28293.]

I am very pleased that Dorky's friend Mr. Hughes is with Bonstead & Coy. They are shipping agents and we should have much in common to talk about.

I shall send you the cash for the photographs. At the moment my funds are getting low but soon I shall be able to draw on the credit that has mounted up during my stay in hospital.

Toby Barton has been unable to obtain leave from his work and has not been to see me for several days. I am expecting him today.

We have a British Army officer here who has had a great deal of sailing experience. He has represented England in a 6 metre boat and has done a lot of ocean racing and cruising. We yarn for hours on end about boats. He is a very brilliant chap, a thorough Scotsman and a university graduate in philosophy. Sailing in Singapore is quite popular and there are several clubs. John Hordern [NX70270 HQ 22 Inf Bde][87] visited one club and he was not impressed with the boats at all. I have since found out that he went to one of the smaller clubs that was more concerned with social activities than with sailing. I am told that there are many fine sailing craft here and I hope that I shall be granted sufficient leave to see them. The method of washing clothes here is unique and I fear expensive. The clothes are wet and then banged about on concrete or stones. The method is undoubtedly efficient and clothes return from the 'do-bee' reasonably well laundered. In the humid moist heat of this country it is necessary to change clothes twice per day and so the life of the 'do-bee' must be busy. Yesterday afternoon I lost at Pontoon but last night managed to redeem my chips. The lads are not finding that their expenses in the country are very great. I intend to increase my allotment, 2/- per day, and if you do not require it your Savings Bank Acct is the best place I know of. Sue may need a little cash to expand her business and I feel that you all should have all that I can spare. Your paper work is certainly holding your interest and occupying your time. Keep it up dear. Love to the girls

All my love

Bill

[Which Barton did Bill mean? 'Toby' was the nickname of David Edmund Barton of 2/3 Machine Gun Battalion stationed in the Middle East. His brother John, former school friend of Bill, was a pilot in the RAAF stationed in Malaya and was destined to meet Bill while on leave at Fraser's Hill. The Barton brothers were the grandsons of Edmund 'Toby' Barton, the former Prime Minister. Their father, Oswald, also known as 'Toby', was the doctor in Scone, and a good friend of Bill's father.][88]

The EFM telegram came into use for troops at this time. This meant the sender was no longer permitted a free choice of words in the text but had to use one or other of the expressions shown on the list of standard texts. A flat rate of 2/6 per telegram was charged.

The battalions of the AIF had been in Malaya a month now, a month of acclimatisation and training missed by Bill Gaden and Reg Newton. On 14 March the *War Diary* reported that the 2/20 lodged the requisition for the first large pay in Malaya, for $27,000. All officers of the unit staged a football match, the teams being captained by the two junior subalterns, the match resulted in a win for the CO team.

At this stage all great-coats were recalled by Ordinance. One wonders why troops heading for hot and steamy Singapore were ever issued with great-coats in the first place!

Troops were kept occupied and morale was high. Some platoons of the 2/20 were busy performing for the Cinesound news-reel, showing off some jungle tactics. General leave was granted for all troops and the first lot of surface mail arrived from Australia. Football and cricket matches were in full swing and the entertainment committee had their first concert which proved to be a huge success.[89] After a month of sick leave, Bill Gaden was soon to return to his troops.

Darling Doukie 17 March '41

Good news - on Wednesday I return to the Bn in the jungle fit and well. Wednesday is the day after tomorrow.

My stay in the two hospitals was not unpleasant and was really a very good rest. I regard it as a reward for the work I put into this new army since the early days of Wallgrove and Ingleburn.

Tomorrow Reg Newton and I have applied for leave. We hope to walk along the dim lit streets of Singapore and purchase small things for you at home. We are both going to send cables.

Wed 19th March

Our leave was granted and Reg and I left hospital after lunch yesterday to see what Singapore was really like. We were fortunate in getting a lift into town in Ambulance and hope now to give you a full description of what we saw and did.

The Ambulance dumped us in a crowded street heaven knows where, we did not, and for the first time we saw Singapore's population in action. There were Chinese, Indians, Eurasians and other coloured people crowding the streets, stinking like hell and all talking in the Malayan jabber that is becoming familiar to us. We decided to clear out but found it not so easy. Shop keepers sprang from doorways inviting us to buy junk and fortune tellers hovered around persistently. We decided the middle of the road would be a safe place but there blokes in pants only, with filthy rickshaws, blocked our way and noisy little Ford taxis hooted at us.

Eventually we arrived at an open road but not before a Chinese boy had yelled, attracted our attention and blatantly invited us to his house of ill fame, one storey above a row of shops. We decided on a plan of action and set off to find the Post Office. Raffles Hotel loomed up and provided a very disappointing spectacle. The building looked old, worn and in need of paint. An Indian spat from the balcony as we sauntered past. Raffles is a pub famed in the East for high prices and a good stock of liquor. We walked on and found a harbour full of sampans and stinks.

(I commenced this screed in hospital on Monday. Wrote a bit more in the waiting room at Singapore railway station and I am now in the train bound for the jungle. The time is 10.25pm).

After leaving the harbour chased by stinks we continued our search for the Post Office and found Robinson's a large European store. Reg was anxious to purchase some imitation jewelry and was duly robbed. The prices in that shop were terrific. I wanted some cigars for Capt. Moses and was astounded at their prices. We were told by a clerk at Robinson's that 'Change Alley' was the place for us, so away we went.

'Change Alley' was a familiar name to me. I had heard of it in Sydney, on the Queen Mary and at the hospitals, but when I saw it I was 'rocked'. As wide and as long as Rowe Street, with fifty times as many shops, 'Change Alley' was a seething mass of humanity. The shops were owned by Malays, Chinese and Eurasians but the people bargaining for goods were from every country. We saw more Europeans there than in the whole of Singapore. Reg wanted pyjamas and a kimono and I cigars. We shoved our way in and Reg was robbed in no time although he did not find the spots and holes in his new pyjamas until we were back in the hospital (safe). I bought nothing. When I showed interest in a tobacco shop those hungry shrewd black eyed cows pounced and I fled.

We decided to give up our hunt for the Post Office and take a taxi to the Cable office. A taxi found us in no time and away we went. After traveling about 200 yards we both burst out laughing; we were passing the Post Office. Our taxi ride was a short one and the driver was a sucker. He only charged us 40 cents; if he only knew!

We sent our cables. Mine was worded 'Leaving hosp Wednesday Love all'. Six words to Australia cost us £1. The address is free. Again we faced the robbers but now we had confidence.

I don't like rickshaws and we decided taxis would be just as cheap if we shared expenses. We found a taxi to go back to Robinson's for advice. We did not know that Robinson's was only one block away. When we arrived the taxi driver's black face barked out 50 cents. I gave him 25 and a policeman hunted him off. At Robinson's we obtained the address of Yamada and Co.

We walked out of Robinson's and stood on the edge of the pavement debating as whether we would catch a taxi or not. Eventually we decided to do so and I called 'Taxi' like 'attention'. To our amazement there was a roar of engines and a line of 12 or so vehicles raced across the street and formed a traffic jam in front of us. I did not realize until a few minutes later that I was facing a taxi rank and that those black eyed devils were warming their engines while we were debating. Next time I visit Singapore I shall play that game at every taxi rank and go for a 20 cent ride.

Yamada and Co is an excellent shop. The attendants are gentlemen at least they do not try to influence your purchasing by producing junk. All the stock we could see was really good stuff and I was very sorry that you cannot be with me to help buy things for yourself and the girls. We saw kimonos, china, carved images and countless other things. I was fairly short of cash and did not buy anything. Reg spent £20 and came out with his arms laden.

We set our sails for the hospital and decided to visit a British unit on the way.

At 7.30pm we arrived back at the hospital full of beer and feeling very well. We were severely scolded by a cranky Sister at the hospital for arriving late for dinner, but, sans fait rien, we had seen Singapore.

I can now write a lot about the hospital and our doings there that I had to leave out of previous letters because our letters were censored by the CO of the hospital. However that can wait till my next letter and also today's visit to See-ha-pore as the natives call it.

Cheerio dear. My next letter should arrive with this one. Love to the girls.
All my love
Bill

The 2/20 troops continued training, practising attacking and defending out in the jungle, away from their base camp. They became used to maintaining blackouts, moving round in the dark, sleeping under the stars ... and mosquito nets. Many useful lessons were learned from these exercises, lessons which would be put to use in the months ahead.[90]

Back home in Australia, the families would be reassured to read that the Allies COULD PUT UP A 'GOOD SHOW' after the arrival in Malaya of further reinforcements of regular troops. The Commander-in-Chief, Far-Eastern-Command, Air Chief Marshall Sir Robert Brooke-Popham said he was certain that Malaya could put up a really good show in defending itself. A fine esprit de corps had developed between the troops and there was good fellowship among the 'various races inhabiting the Empire'.[91]

What a pity such optimism would prove to be so badly misplaced.

68 *War Diary 2/20 Bn. A.I.F.* 18 Feb 1941.

69 Thulaja, *Communicable Diseases Centre*, <http://www.infopedia.nlb.gov.sg/articles/SIP_336_2005-01-03.html>

70 *War Diary 2/20 Bn. A.I.F.* 20-22 Feb 1941.

71 *ibid.*, 24 February 1941.

72 Dodkin, *Goodnight Bobbie*, p. 32.

73 Routine Orders 2/20 Bn. A.I.F. 25 February 1941.

74 Taylor, *British Preparations*, <http://www.britain-at-war.org.uk/WW2/Malaya_and_Singapore/html/body_british_prepare.htm >

75 *War Dairy 2/20 Bn. A.I.F.* 27 February - 3 March 1941.

76 Framed print hanging in Alexandra Hospital, photograph by Bob Gaden, 14 February 2007.

77 Partridge, *Alexandra Hospital*, p. 20.

78 *ibid.*, pp. 25-6.

79 Photograph collection of British Association of Malaysia and Singapore, <http://www.janus.lib.cam.ac.uk/db/node.xsp?id=EAD%2FGBR%2F0155%2FBAM%202%2F46 >

80 *War Diary 2/20 Bn. A.I.F.*, 6 March 1941.

81 *ibid.*, 8 March 1941.

82 Smith, *Singapore Burning*, p. 18.

83 *Australian Women's Weekly*, 8 March 1941, p. 9.

84 *War Diary 2/20 Bn. A.I.F.*, 10 March 1941.

85 *Sydney Morning Herald*, 11 March 1941, p. 10.

86 Definition from < en.wikipedia.org/wiki/Fifth_columnist >

87 DVA Nominal Roll.

88 DVA Nominal Roll and information from Scone and Upper Hunter Historical Society.

89 *War Diary 2/20 Bn. A.I.F.* , 15-17 March 1941.

90 *ibid.*, 19 March 1941.

91 *Sydney Morning Herald*, 21 March 1941, p. 10.

Chapter 4 - Training at Port Dickson

Bill Gaden left Alexandra Hospital and was able to return to his unit on 19 March 1941. He had to catch up with the many new skills learned by his men and also learn to negotiate the inevitable army politics.

```
From CABLE OFFICE 327, SINGAPORE
RECEIVED TELEGRAM dated 24 March 1941 Neutral Bay, NSW
LEAVING HOSPITAL WEDNESDAY LOVE ALL
GADEN 10 23PBB
```

The Divisional Commander Gordon Bennett, never one to shirk criticism of his contemporaries, whatever their rank, was appalled at the 'laissez faire' attitude of the British High Command. The British believed the jungle to be impenetrable and concentrated their training on beach defence. Bennett realised that the troops who had arrived from Australia would be faced with fighting in the jungle but they were not trained in jungle warfare. This had to change, so, along with the Argyll and Sutherland Highlanders, the Australian Battalions devised a jungle training syllabus.[92]

The jungle through which the men were now training could not have been more different from the open grassland round Bathurst where they had been posted back in Australia. In Malaya

> *the jungle grew down to the water's edge with the water surfaces apparently as solid as the earth. Each giant tree was a pillar of climbing lantana, orchids and other parasitic plants with the tree tops forming an almost solid barrier to sunlight, a strong wind would allow some sunlight to filter through, throwing a cascade of colour downwards. Day changed to night suddenly. For the hour both sides of noon all seemed ghostly still and quiet as birds and animals took a siesta.*[93]

The jungle was like a huge green maze and even seasoned bush men lost their way without local native guides. Scattered in jungle clearings were native villages or kampongs. These villagers knew all the tracks through their own area. Some of them were fifth columnists, which meant they were on the Japanese side. They subsequently provided detailed maps of these local routes to the Japanese soldiers which allowed them to encircle the Allied troops and make deadly use of this world so naturally suited for silent movement and ambush.[94] The Australian soldiers were told:

> *you must learn stealth and silence - learn to be as cunning as the wild animals themselves; don't underestimate the enemy. Japan has crack troops, trained in jungle warfare for years. They own rubber estates and tin mines and have detailed plans and knowledge of the country and will probably sneak around our flanks and rear and catch us unawares. But remember, two can play at that game. We must learn to stalk the Japanese like animals.*[95]

So the Australian troops learned to use the jungle to their own advantage; not to fear the jungle or its animals, to move through it silently and to go for long periods without food, water and sleep. Within a few months they would need to remember every lesson learned; their lives would depend on it.

> Darling Doukie 21 March '41
>
> My last screed was a lengthy description of my first visit to Singapore on Tuesday 18 Mar. In this one I shall give you the news of my second visit and something of our 'country home'.
>
> Reg Newton and I departed from the hospital fairly late on Wednesday morning and after leaving our bags and valises at the railway station we visited Mrs. Bramwell for lunch. Mrs. Bramwell is the wife of a naval officer at the hospital and we met her there. Our 'tiffin' was very nice and we departed at 3.00pm with many addresses of shops to locate.
>
> Most of the time we walked from street to street. I bought some small ebony elephants with white ivory tusks and will post them tomorrow. We saw plenty of silks etc. but the experience of the previous day warned me against rash purchases. I only bought you elephants which were very much reduced after an argument and later on I shall send you kimono etc. We were pleased when our train took us away from the smells of Singapore.
>
> I arrived at our camp at 6.30am yesterday and found the lads happy and healthy.
>
> We are camped in a beautiful spot close to the sea and within walking distance of a swim. Our quarters are good; cool two storey buildings most of them, a few grass huts and our mess is a large house. We have tennis courts, football ovals and a golf course surrounds the camp. We have no time for relaxation at tennis or golf but the lads do manage football.
>
> Rubber plantations are numerous and occupy most of the cleared country. The jungle is only a short distance from camp and is not alive with snakes, tigers, elephants etc. Today I explored a little with Capt. Moses and the only life we saw had wings. Monkeys are common and the cooks have a pet one called 'Sally'. We bought home a lot of cane, mostly Balacca, the type that chairs are made of. I shall give you more details when I have seen more jungle.
>
> Yesterday I received three more of your super letters and a parcel containing the garters and flares. They are excellent. Thank you very much indeed dear.
>
> A letter and parcel from Connie was also waiting for me. She has made me an excellent hold-all and included in her parcel a tin of butterscotch and some malted milk tablets.
>
> Cheerio dear. I shall write again soon and give you more news. Love to the girls.
> All my love
> Bill

As an officer Bill was lucky to be on the invitation list of several British colonial families, but the other ranks were often met with open hostility. There was no civility and no gratitude that the troops were there to defend them, too many civilians felt the increased garrison numbers were unnecessary, the Japanese would not attack. Soldiers wrote letters of complaint back to family in Australia, and these evoked many protests back to various friends in Malaya. Then things improved.[96]

The wives and mothers of the troops read the *Australian Women's Weekly* report headlined 'General saw AIF fighting fit in tropics'. Major-General J

Bill with Mrs Bramwell at 'The Flat' 20 March 1941

Northcott, Deputy-Chief of the Australian General Staff told the women of Australia that their troops looked fine and were in excellent spirits and very good health. The unnamed reporter told how initially the local population was somewhat afraid of these big foreigners but now the atmosphere had really changed as the troops made friends with them and tried to learn the local language. The Aussies enjoyed the rickshaws and the native shops where many souvenirs were bought. In many of their northern locations the troops were housed in local schools or had palm huts for their mess and they coped well with the climate. Each had a mosquito net for their bed but malaria was initially not a problem; preventative steps would be taken once they moved into the jungle.[97] Morale had been boosted by the presence of a kangaroo mascot (which had been smuggled across with the assistance of Capt. Reg Newton).[98]

Darling Doukie 22 March '41

Today another letter. Thank you very indeed. I am pleased that the last one of mine only took five days and I hope you have received the others equally as quick.

I really like our camp and I know all the lads do also.

The elephants are packed up all ready for their voyage. You should receive them in about 4 weeks.

Sue tells you have been made an instructor. Good work dear. I hope the film turns out successfully and that you are well to the fore.

I laughed about your excursion to the *Orpheum* [Theatre] one week too soon. Did you eventually see the play?

Our Bn soccer team had an easy win against another Army team today [the Malay Volunteers at Si Rusa, score 3 to 0]. We have a good team and it should do very well.

Capt. Moses has been admitted to hospital locally. He damaged a knee yesterday playing soccer. He should be well again soon.

Connie's butterscotch has caused a mild panic. I hid the tin in a drawer among my underclothes and even then the ants found it. The little black blighters are all prancing among my clothes. Tomorrow I shall 'air' the drawer in the sun and burn them out.

Each day I travel into the rubber and jungle per truck and work with the troops as much as possible. I have been taking it fairly easily and not taking too much exercise. At the end of next week I should be back to normal again.

Today I visited a plantation manager, Mr. Hosking. He produced his collection of Eastern trinkets and they are excellent. I know now what to buy and send you. I am very pleased indeed that I did not purchase silks etc in Singapore because he produced some materials that are far superior to any I saw in my rounds.

Today we had a lot of fun with a hurd [sic] of Indian children, Tamils they were. We stopped our truck near a native village and the kids swarmed out jabbering. One of the lads produced a camera and they all lined up waiting to be taken.

Tamil children are usually thin and rather ugly but the Malayans are often handsome chaps. We often see natives in our travels and they are quite friendly. We bought some bread fruit from some boys yesterday. It tasted like a mixture of pineapples, bananas and Singapore.

The women rarely venture near the camp for obvious reasons although they are ugly creatures with no appeal. I think they would be quite safe on our Bn parade ground at night provided an old Indian buck was not prowling about.

Cheerio dear. No more news. Love to Sue and Ginge.
All my love
Bill

The troops continued to play inter-unit sports fixtures and another group were entertained by the Bruntons at Sepang, their invitations being much appreciated.

On 29 March 1941 the 2/20 moved out of the Port Dickson area and transferred to Seremban. The locals turned out in force to witness their final Retreat Parade, giving the troops a boost in morale.[99]

Darling Doukie 29 March '41

Today we packed up and moved to a new camp. We are now close to a reasonably large town and our troops and ourselves are in excellent quarters. I have purchased a camera and shall be sending you snaps when I have my first film developed.

A few days ago a party of officers from our unit visited the local Yam Tuan. This chap occupies a position something like a President and lives in a palace like a Sultan. We were introduced to His Highness and were given afternoon tea at the Palace.

I thoroughly enjoyed the afternoon but do not hope for another visit. The old boy possesses three wives and a hurd [sic] of daughters. We saw one wife but missed out on the daughters. I was surprised to find an Indian atmosphere prevailing at the Palace and it reminded me of that super book 'The Rains Came'. We examined collections of magnificent curios and antiques in large glass cases and really enjoyed our afternoon. I became very interested in everything I could see and very nearly departed without bowing and scraping to the Yam Tuan and his wife.

We have been working hard as usual but the climate here does not permit working all day. In the afternoon we have a 'siesta' from 2pm till 4pm and play our sport from

4pm to 5pm. I like the warm sultry days and, in spite of the essential perspiration, I am putting on weight.

I am enclosing £3 in Australian notes. These should help to pay for the photographs. I hope to be able to send you a snap of myself taken with the new camera. It will have to be an enlargement because the prints are very small; smaller than the top of a matchbox. The camera is a Kodak 35 with a 5.6 lens. The type is very similar to a 'Leica' and takes 36 snaps on each film. Cameras are fairly cheap out here and this type is cheap to run.

Charles Moses is still in hospital with a crook knee. He should return to the fold soon.

I have not been able to see Mrs. Hughes at Kuala Lumpur as yet, but leave in the future looks fairly bright, so 'here's hoping'.

In Singapore taxis are everywhere but here we only have rickshaws. They are not very pleasant things to travel in. I shall do most of my traveling on foot.

Today I had my first shower since leaving Bathurst. It was marvelous. In our last camp we bathed in tubs or went dirty which is a very stinking practice in Malaya. Our water supply was limited. Here we have excellent showers.

I have received another letter from Connie. She is a regular old pen pusher.
Cheerio dear, give my love to Sue and Ginge.
I shall be posting a parcel to you tomorrow.
All my love,
Bill

The local Yam Tuan's home was the Sri Menanti Palace, built between 1902 and 1905, with no nails or screws used during the construction. An earlier palace was burnt down during the civil war between Yam Tuan Antah and the British. The new palace is four storeys high and has 99 stilts which represent the 99 warriors of the various 'luaks' or clans. The architecture style is Minangkabau 'Rumah-rumah Adat'.[100]

In the 29 March issue of *Australian Women's Weekly*, reporter Adele Shelton Smith excitedly told her readers she had been given the most thrilling assignment of all her years in newspaper work. She and photographer Wilfred (Bill) Brindle had been sent to Singapore and Malaya as 'Special Correspondents'.

She wrote that she was going to see the AIF training and find out what the women back home wanted to know most … what the camps were like, the accommodation, the food, the recreation time and what the troops do on leave. She looked forward to seeing the familiar slouch hat and khaki against a background of native colour. In particular she wanted to send a first hand account to the women of what their husbands and sons were doing to 'preserve the common ideals of which that [pre-war] friendliness is the outward sign'.[101]

Throughout the *War Diary* troops were listed who 'marched out' to take training courses, to exchange with other units or to act as umpires for military exercises; also if they went on leave and when they returned. Usually the officers were named and their service number given, but sometimes only the number attending was listed. Soldiers who went to training courses or to detention barracks for some misdemeanour were named and again their service number was noted. It also listed what was considered to be adequate rations for these fit young men and their training regime. 'Restricted diet No. 2' consisted of:[102]

BREAKFAST (Daily)	DINNER (Daily)	SUPPER (Daily)
Bread 6 ozs.	Bread 6ozs.	Bread 6ozs.
Porridge 1 pint	Meat 4 ozs.	Porridge 1 pint
Marg/butter $^{1}/_{2}$ oz.	Potatoes 8 ozs.	Marg/butter $1^{1}/_{2}$ oz.
Water	Rice 2 ozs.	Water
	Water	

The administrators within the 2/20 found their new location of Seremban to be more inconvenient than Port Dickson as troops were spread out over a larger area, duties were greater in number. However it was recognized that the additional pressure was good training. Officers were taking it in turns to visit other units on exchange, to learn new skills, to referee 'war games' and to experience different ways of training and to liaise with British, Indian and local regiments. Bill's friend Arch Ewart went on exchange with the 2 East Surrey Regiment, Rod Richardson went to the 3/17 Dogra Regiment and Bill Carter went to the 2/16 Punjab Regiment.[103]

The troops themselves preferred being closer to town, their morale and behaviour was much improved. 'Great goodwill' existed between troops and the locals who took much interest in Retreat and Church parades. Consequently the troops made great effort to put on a 'good show'. When their pay arrived the lads went into town to enjoy themselves in a 'most orderly manner'.[104] Senior officers had dinner with the British Resident of Negri Sembilan, the Colonial administrator.[105]

Back in Australia the *Sydney Morning Herald* ran some photographs of the AIF troops training in Malayan rubber plantations, sighting a rifle, doing bayonet drill and moving through the plantation.[106]

Darling Doukie 4 Apr '41

I am enclosing a few snaps which I hope will convey a pleasant impression of our surroundings. They were taken with my new camera and some are quite good although many turned out much overexposed etc.

We are happy and really enjoying life. The town we are in is sufficiently large to provide a fair variation of entertainment for our troops. Picture shows and dances are popular. The lads do not receive the opportunity of leading a gay life although I believe the facilities are available.

On Sunday I am going to visit Mrs. Hughes. Dorky will be pleased. I shall write and tell her all the news next week.

This morning, being Friday, we saw a crowd of Malayan men and boys going to a Mosque. They were dressed in their most colourful clothes and really made a striking picture. Their garments are of soft coloured flimsy materials, mostly silk, but they all wear a very bright sarong around their middles and usually a dark fez on their heads. The sarongs we saw today were mostly blue, purple and green.

Hockey is becoming a popular game and I think that it may take the place of rugby football. Soccer is a popular game with the troops but the humid climate is not conducive to rugby.

I have my first decent heat rash. Small red pimples have sprung up on my shoulders and neck. They are not very unpleasant but rather frightening to look at; something like measles.

Tonight our Coy mounts the unit duties, guards, picquets [sic] etc. The duties are so numerous here that the only people in our Coy not engaged will be Capt. Moses and myself. We have quite a lot of work to catch up with and so we will be fairly busy. Having no troops for a day is quite a new experience.

Capt. Moses has returned from hospital and is working as hard as ever.
Cheerio dear. Give my love to the girls.
Yours ever. All my love.
Bill

PS I have written a couple of letters to Margaret but she has never answered them. I shall write no more.

PPS Enclosing Menu card HT 'QX'. [QX refers to the ship *Queen Mary*.]

Adele Shelton Smith's first *Women's Weekly* article from Malaya was headlined 'Gee it's good to see someone from home'. She had spent a weekend at a 'colourful coastal town' and had met troops swimming in a millionaire's pool, singing and dancing with the taxi-girls at a cabaret and sightseeing. They had been invited to the homes of several Chinese hosts. She also went sightseeing and saw the troops 'out in droves with their cameras' and holding rickshaw races, followed by admiring children calling 'Hello Jo' to all the Aussie troops.[107]

Darling Doukie 7 Apr '41

Yesterday, Sunday, I visited Mrs. Hughes. She is a very nice woman and with her husband provided pleasant entertainment for me throughout the afternoon.

Their house is a large mansion and is about two miles out of town. The address I was given did not indicate a dwelling of importance and I was very surprised when my taxi crunched up a pretty gravel drive and came to rest under the portals of a Tuan Besar [Besar means 'big' and Tuan means 'master' in Malay].[108] Mrs. Hughes had many questions to ask and we found ourselves on common ground when she told me that she had spent many holidays with the Parburys at Middlebrook, Scone. She is an Australian and has been living in Malaya for 23 years. [Following the Japanese invasion, the fate of the Hughes family is unknown.]

8/4/41 After driving about the countryside for an hour or so we visited a local club, had a drink and then the car, a large Hillman, was placed at my disposal with a Malayan driver. I did not use it very much because I know petrol rationing is severe but I spent a great afternoon and took many snaps. The club we visited was a sports club and one of the best in the country. A golf course equally as good as Royal Sydney, many tennis courts and a swimming pool were all available for energetic members. I was very interested in the tennis courts. They were surrounded by tall narrow hedges and not one sported the usual wire netting. I believe it is quite the normal routine for business people to leave home about 6.00a.m. in the morning, have a swim and breakfast at the club and then proceed to their offices. I personally would never leave the club.

Your 10 page letter dated 29 Mar has just arrived. The news about the garden and the fish pond is excellent. Please keep me advised with your progress. I am pleased those red flowers have been dug up.

Ginge should like her new job [with the Permanent Trustee]. Sue was happy in Macquarie Street and I feel sure that Ginge will also do well there.

I am pleased that you are not waiting patiently for a kimono to arrive. The lads have been buying the things and sending home parcels of cheap silks etc every mail. I have been looking for something that you would really like and I am sure that it shall not come out of a Chinese silk store.

No snaps this letter. I am waiting on these films that are being developed. The local film developers have been rushed with so much business that they take weeks to produce a print.

I can only write on one side of each sheet of paper. Local censorship does not permit writing on both sides. Thank you very much for posting the block because paper is scarce out here. Your last letter only took five days to arrive. The service is getting better each week.

Our lads are endeavouring to learn the local language. Every day we hear funny stories about their chats with the natives who have now obtained quite a lot of English and Australian phrases. One lad was trying to converse with a local boy and was making a pretty poor job so the youngster grinned and piped up 'Your Malay is incomprehensible; speak English'. The native children are taught English in the school. The kids have very soft pleasant voices and are really delightful to listen to. In this town they always greet us with 'Hello' but in another town a few miles away they say 'Hello Joe'.

Yesterday I went for a rickshaw ride down the town in search of my photographs. On my way back to camp I passed one of our Guards and the Officer of the Guard gave me a smart 'eyes right'. I wish that I could obtain a photograph of myself taking a salute from the guard whilst reclining in a rickshaw.

My letters will not be arriving as often as in the past. We are working much harder now and our time is pretty well filled up. However I shall write when every opportunity arrives and you should receive one each week.

I hope Gran manages to sell 'The Briars' [The Balcombe family home in 14 Woonona Street, Wahroonga, built in 1895].

It will be a loss to us all but really the house is far too big and expensive to keep.

Cheerio dear. Love to the girls.
All my love
Bill

Many of the locals who were developing the soldiers' photographs were later suspected of being fifth columnists who were collaborating with the Japanese, passing on vital information collected from photographs. In the following months some of their shops were classed as 'out of bounds' to troops.[109] However the local Chinese were usually friendly toward the troops who were sometimes entertained at large banquets by local Chinese merchants.[110]

Adele Shelton Smith's second posting from Malaya was published in the *Weekly* on 12 April, Easter Saturday. She had lunched with Major-General Gordon Bennett in the bungalow he shared with senior officers. He assured her that the troops were behaving very well, in fact better than when at home. Mail was arriving regularly but newspapers from home were needed. Ex-patriot white women were running a club for the troops, providing food, cool drinks and a place to chat about home. The troops were training hard and on their return to camp were able to have showers behind nipah palm shelters. They slept on their stretchers on the school verandahs with sheets changed weekly and mosquito nets to keep out the small lizards.

'Smithy' reported that the boys were becoming naturalists and told her about the beautiful orchids and huge snails and scorpions. There were monkeys, orang-utans, panthers, tigers to see … and avoid. The country was criss-crossed with drainage ditches.

The officers held a cocktail party, complete with the band, for European guests, to try to repay some of the hospitality they had received.

The same bulletin had a photograph of a soldier becoming acquainted with a 'Dutch wife', a long bolster used to absorb perspiration when sleeping. A third page of information told the womenfolk that the Australians were known as the *tid apa* boys, very appropriate as *tid apa* means 'why bother' or 'why worry'. The local rickshaw boys were making a fortune with the frequent rickshaw races, just as often with the owner getting a ride whilst he was pulled along by the troops. They also had an open invitation to the beachside home of a Chinese business man and were able to swim in his pool and have races along the beach. Smithy's message to the womenfolk back home was 'Don't worry. They are as happy as sand-boys!' and from the many accompanying photographs of them dancing and singing, swimming and climbing trees, rickshaw racing and bargaining for purchases, the troops were having a lot of fun.[111] There was little mention of hard work or training.

Bill at the athletics carnival

Sporting fixtures continued in this new location. A cricket match against a Seremban XI was organized, the troop's captain being Private Tom Scollen, born Armidale NSW. Like Bill he was an all-round athlete, good at running, cricket and football and was often listed in Battalion teams. The 2/19 beat the 2/20 easily in cricket. Every afternoon saw sporting events of some sort on the local *padangs*, cricket, hockey, soccer and even boomerang throwing which was popular with the Unit Pioneer section.[112]

As well as sporting fixtures, movies and concerts were provided for their entertainment. Some troops attending the Seremban picture theatres were in the habit of purchasing a 25 cents seat ticket and then occupying seats priced at 60 cents. They were warned that

> *If this practice continues the proprietors will have no alternative than to abolish the concession already granted troops. And men will be warned that offenders will render themselves liable to disciplinary action.*[113]

Major Dick Cohen ran the 'All in Fun Revue' which was a great success.[114] However military training took a large part of their days. A weekly syllabus was organized and the individual companies took turns at various 'stations' learning about new weapons, practising attacks on specific locations, navigation, negotiating the large drainage ditches, surviving in the 'bush'. Moving through jungle and rubber plantations was very different from the open paddocks around Bathurst, so these exercises were invaluable.

The countryside in Malaya was composed of many rubber plantations. It was decreed that a £5 fine would be imposed on any soldier who damaged a rubber tree, however slightly, even if it was in pursuit of his training. Russell Braddon commented that 'Nothing could have been more calculated to interfere with mobility and efficiency'.[115] Even when the fighting subsequently started, the men were not allowed to damage the rubber trees because reparations would have to be paid to the rubber companies.[116]

2/20 Bn. AIF Outline Syllabus of training
Week ending 19 Apr '41. All Coys.

Mon 14	Coy exercise with tpt.[transport] Area Circular Road, Seremban Test from issue of Coy order - zero Packing of kits and stores Organised loading of vehicles Movement to dispersal harbours tactically and occupation Reports to Bn. H.Q. when in position 1600-1700 Maintenance Parade, smartening up drill, P.T and organized sport under officer's control.
Tues 15	Bn. Exercise, Area Circular Road, Seremban To cover loading vehicles Moving into dispersal harbours Mid-day meal in harbours Move to embussing point Road discipline will be enforced and traffic control etc.
Wed 16	Bn Exercise Area 2½ miles S.E. Seremban

```
          Attack against enemy in semi jungle and rubber
          Object To test Bn H.Q. O. Op
          'I' sec functioning
          Communications
          Initiative of junior officers and leaders
          To develop speed
          Concealment from air
          1600-1700 As for Mon 14.
Thurs 17  Coy Trg [Training]
          Compass bearings and movements across country
          Object to test keeping distance
          To check speed in the hour for cross country moves
          1600-1700 Preparation for Div Exercise
Fri 18    Div Exercise
Sat 19    Maintenance parade and rifle and S.A. inspections,
          kit inspections. Medical inspections etc.
                         Signed J.M. Lowe, Capt. Adjt 2/20 Bn. AIF.
```

In her next *Woman's Weekly* article, published on 19 April, Adele Shelton Smith finally had some photographs of the troops in uniform and training hard, but no details were given for censorship and security reasons. In her article she reported on a sumptuous Singalese meal given by a wealthy Indian businessman in honour of the troops. Several different kinds of curry were served as well as chutney, pickles and fruit. The local Malay Police band was in attendance and the Aussies sang 'Advance Australia Fair' with great gusto. She also reported on the social life in Singapore itself, advising that no night club was permitted to stay open after midnight and the strict rules about evening dress had been relaxed to only one formal dress night in the week at Raffles. She advised that there were more men than women in each party so the girls were treated like 'pampered princesses surrounded by courtiers'.[117] Imagine how that was received by the womenfolk struggling alone back home!

Darling Doukie 22 Apr '41

I have been rather busy during the past week and have not written. However 'here is the news'. A few days ago I was out on an exercise with Capt. Moses and we saw a small crocodile, about 6 ft. Capt. Moses managed to fire one shot at it but I was so excited that I tried to take a photograph and shoot with my little automatic at the same time. The result was no photo and no shot. The croc escaped with ease.

I am enclosing a few snaps. I have written an explanation on the back of each. I hope they prove interesting. I have started a book of these snaps. It should be worth while later. We entertained the local European residents at the club last Saturday night. We turned on an excellent concert. The whole night was a very good one.

Social activities here are very expensive. We are not trying to cope with all the hospitality offered us. I have received two letters dear. You are a Briton. We are all happy because our mails have arrived. Last week only a few letters turned up. Something must have gone wrong with the system. We welcome the mail so much here that when letters were distributed this morning some of our chaps read their mail and did not worry about lunch. The mails usually arrive about mid day and we read them during afternoon siesta.

> The fish pond must be super. Gordon has been a stout fellow.
>
> Gran received a fair price for 'The Briars'. She should be satisfied.
>
> Ralph sends his regards. He is well and happy.
>
> I have spots all over my body like measles. This is prickly heat. I have a powder and dust myself after each shower. The complaint is very common, we all have it. The medical fraternity do not consider it serious.
>
> I am playing hockey. Officers are not permitted to play football. Hockey is the next best sport but I don't like it very much. However it should keep me in condition.
>
> Last night I saw a bottle of 'Mynor' juice in a shop window. These natives must obtain their stores from the world over. I have searched the town and can find nothing that you would really appreciate. Most of the decent things that are available are easily obtainable in Sydney. I hope to find a decent type of basket, fill it full of treasures and post it.
>
> No more news dear. I shall make up the weight with snaps.
> All my love
> Bill

The great depression of the 1930s had obviously hit the Balcombes hard as they were mortgaged to the Bank of Australasia from 1935. The ensuing war would not have helped their financial situation. In 1941 Jessie Balcombe sold 'The Briars' to Winifred Laura Phipps, wife of Joseph John Flower Phipps of Chatswood, a merchant.[118]

ANZAC Day 1941 saw the 2/20 joining other Australian troops in a large parade in Kuala Lumpur on the Salangor Club Padang (playing field). The ceremony was considered to have been 'simple and very satisfactory'. The General Officer Commanding (GOC) Malaya took the salute accompanied by the British Resident of Selangor. The Sultan of Selangor and the GOC AIF were present. After a meal at the Kuala Lumpur Racecourse the troops were given two hours leave and then returned to Camp by truck. The following day a cricket match was arranged between a Seremban XI and the 2/20. Bill Gaden was part of this team.

In her *Women's Weekly* article of 26 May, Adele Shelton Smith reported on the more hum-drum aspects of life in the tropics. The headline was 'Tip-Top Tucker in the Tropics' and she reported that the Army seemed to have the same formula as every woman - 'feed the brute'. The men didn't like the sweet flavour of the local bread, so they now had an Australian bakery. There had been Hot Cross Buns for Easter. Bacon was from Queensland, meat from Argentina, potatoes, carrots and turnips from England, butter and frozen meat from Australia and jams and tinned fruit from Canada and Australia. Fresh vegetables were hard to obtain locally and the Army cooks had to become familiar with them and learn the best method of cooking. Indian and Chinese *dhobis* were contracted to wash 30 pieces of laundry per week per man, the dirt literally being thrashed out of the clothes by bashing them onto stones.[119]

Darling Doukie 30 Apr '41

Yesterday two of your letters arrived dated 7th and 15th April. Thank you very much for the news.

I am sure you must feel very small sleeping in the large 4 poster [the bed was inherited from Gran Balcombe]. It must be very comfortable.

The rent will surely be raised if you continue the improvements. However as the 'rent collector' invariably comes to the back door she will be none the wiser. The fish pond sounds super. Connie gave me an extravagant description in her letter. I hope the carp live.

My insurance policies are both very good. I made inquiries and had them fixed up before leaving.

I intended increasing my allotment but because many others have done that and their people back home have not received the cash I decided against it. The only other means of sending you money is by cable through the pay office at Sydney. I shall endeavour to send a cable as soon as possible - amount £25.

Mother's Day must be very close. I shall be thinking of you when it comes dear. We cannot wear a white flower on our uniforms but we can still think of you.

I have represented the Bn at cricket and hockey. Tomorrow we have a sports meeting. I have been doing a little training on the quiet and hope to surprise some of the favourites. Most of the power I lost in Singapore has returned and I feel very fit. Very few of the officers are competing in the Bn Championship events. They have a handicap 100 yards for themselves. I am entering in some of the Bn championships in addition to the officer's race. Because I have been in hospital they have given me 15 yards start in the Officers handicap. Whacko!!

Our ANZAC day parade at Kuala Lumpur was evidently a great success. We are turning the same show here on Friday.

No snaps in this letter. The last lot of films have not been developed. I can get them enlarged here dear. If you particularly want any of the snaps I sent you enlarged I can have it done here or send you the negatives. Perhaps it would be better to post the negatives because of the cheaper postage.

Gran G wrote me a cheery letter. She is sending me 'Bulletins' regularly.

Whilst I was in hospital I wrote to Capt. Lowe our adjutant. The letter arrived here yesterday. It had been to Cairo. It has been recorded in our unit war diary.

Soon after my arrival in Malaya I wrote to Margaret [Taylor] at Neutral Bay. The letter came back last week with post marks all over the envelope and marked 'Not Known' etc. I am sending her the envelope.

I am pleased you had a yarn to Lady Wakehurst. One of these days you will be dropping in to Govt House for a 'cuppa.'

I have not heard from Brian Badgery as yet. Hope to soon.
Cheerio darling. Love to the girls and regards to Gordon and Co.
All my love
Bill

PS My Malay is improving. Today I managed to ask a native to cut Capt. Moses and myself some sugar cane. He understood and we went away chewing.

[Lady Margaret Wakehurst, was the wife of the Governor of NSW who served in Australia from 1937 to 1946. She was the President of the Women's Land

Army of NSW as well as the Women's Australian National Service (WANS) which she founded.][120]

On 30 April the Battalion held its first sports meeting with a large number of entries. According to the War Diary, all ranks were 'very keen'. The leaders of the Armed forces were also very appreciative of the locals who provided entertainment for the troops. It made it easier to maintain discipline and morale.

A Ceremonial Parade was held on 2 May 1941 followed by the finals of the Sports Meeting. Brigade Command and local dignitaries were invited, including HH The Yang Di-Pertuan Besar of Negri Sembilan and the British Resident.

Darling Doukie 2 May'41

Yesterday I sent you a cable worded 'Love best wishes Mother's Day' and also a present of £25. The documents relating to the cash were sent by airmail direct to the Pay Office, Reservoir Street, Sydney. You should receive notification from the pay office to collect the cash about 15th May '41. If you are not notified hop along and see them and they will pay you the money. I am sorry that I cannot send you the cash direct to yourself. They only allow us to send cash through our pay people. Anyway the money is worth a little bother.

Our sports were not completed yesterday owing to rain. We are to finish them this morning. I shall give you the results at the end of this letter.

Our address has been changed. The mystic word 'abroad' has been wiped and our letters are now to be addressed 'Malaya'. This is to stop our mail going to the Middle East.

News is scarce dear. I wrote it all a couple of days ago in my last letter.

I hope Sue and Ginge are getting along successfully. Where is Ginge working now?

In Malaya every pond has fish in it. I believe the fish are quite good to eat but they look dirty like catfish. I am looking forward to the day when I can spend a few leisure hours fishing in the pond at 'Valhalla'.

The sports are now over and I feel stiff. I managed to run 3rd in three sprint events. I need a lot more training before I shall beat some of the lads in this Bn. The times in the running event were very good.

The time is now 10pm. This afternoon we turned on a ceremonial parade and showed the people of this town that the AIF could really drill well if they tried. The parade was quite successful.

Tonight we entertained some of the local Chinese and Malayan residents. We gave them an excellent dinner. I think they enjoyed it. A few nursing sisters were present and the evening has passed happily.

I have bought you some baskets. They are good and well made. I shall post them tomorrow. Cheerio dear. Love to the girls.

All my love
Bill

PS When you go to Reservoir St to collect the money take your bank pass book with you for identification purposes.

```
From CABLE OFFICE 277, SEREMBAN
RECEIVED TELEGRAM dated 2 May 1941 Neutral Bay, NSW
LOVE BEST WISHES MOTHERS DAY
GADEN 10 30 AMLC
```

The final article written by Adele Shelton Smith was published in the *Australian Women's Weekly* on 3 May 1941. She wrote of the Australian nurses who told her the locals treated them like film stars, giving them orchids and fruit and plenty of invitations to social and sporting events. She said the girls all looked well in their crisp, grey uniforms and red capes. The quarters were plain but comfortable, some rooms with beautiful views. The girls had plenty of family photographs on display. All rooms contained the nurses' battledress with tin hats and respirators as compulsory equipment.[121]

In early May 1941 the 2/20 troops left Seremban and returned to their former 'home' at Port Dickson. They swapped places with the 2/18. An exercise had been arranged which was difficult for the HQ 2/20 men who had only just returned to the area. However the adjutant noted that 'fair results were obtained and a considerable number of points and ideas obtained'.[122]

The whole unit took part in the major exercise starting on 7 May.

War Diary of the 2/20 Battalion AIF PORT DICKSON 7 May. '41
Unit moved out of Lines to Assembly Area and carried out a Bn. Exercise covering Movement through the jungle, Attack, Organisation of Bn. H.Q., Movements of 'A' and 'B' echelon M.T. and the exercising generally of all Coys. Lunch in the field, the exercise finishing at 1800 hrs. This was probably the best conducted Bn Exercise yet held in one day and was umpired and organized by Bde. to produce situations and events in such a manner as to thoroughly exercise all personnel in their duties and co-ordinate all branches of the Unit, particularly Bn. H.Q. and H.Q. Coy. Personnel. A most interesting and instructive day.

As a result of lessons learned on this exercise, the troops themselves became far more interested in such tactical training.[123]

A Brigade sports meeting was arranged and, though the 2/20 did quite well, the lads of their great rivals, the 2/19 finished a long way ahead. The adjutant noted in the war diary that the troops 'need such distractions to keep them in good spirits'.[124]

Some of the soccer stars of the 2/20 were chosen to play for Negri Sembilan in the inter-state soccer match versus Selangor on Saturday 10 May '41. Ptes Sym, Storey and Serong were selected as players and Pte D Quinn selected to referee the match.[125]

Two of these talented young sportsmen were to die as prisoners of war, Gordon James Storey (NX33004) and Daniel Quinn (NX20485): the two survivors were Malcolm Thomas Sym (NX33003) and George Leonard Serong (NX33391).[126]

Darling Doukie 10 May '41

Once again our camp has moved. Our new location is quite a pretty spot but we have no town close to us. We have the sea close at hand and can swim in the warm tropical waters if the spirit moves us. The officer's quarters are excellent and the mess super excellent. I am living in a bungalow on the top of a hill. The garden is pretty, mostly flowering trees including frangipani. The surrounding vegetation is thick and our view is a green sea of tree tops. We cannot see the ocean. With me are my Coy officers, Lieuts Woods, Betterridge and Richardson.

The mess is 1/2 mile away but is a truly magnificent building on the side of a hill that runs down to the sea shore. The mess furniture is modern expensive and artistic. Tables with round glass tops, large easy chairs and sofas. Electric fans abound. The mess garden is delightful and extends practically to the sea and a little beach fringed by palm trees. We can sit on the lawn in front of the mess and see the ocean, bright blue, and the little white beaches appearing here and there along the coastline. The sea is as placid as the water of Sydney harbour. The ocean just lazily laps the beaches.

Whoopee - your letter has just arrived. I was expecting one but not until tonight.

I shall write to Dorky and catch the next air mail dear.

You did very well in selling the bed for £1.10.-.

I am pleased that you are going down to see the Sautelles, they are very nice people.

The comforts that the troops appreciate most of all here are; cakes, sweets, cigarettes, and tobacco, long socks, and razor blades. Local magazines such as Bulletin, Man (Junior and Senior), Home, Pix etc are lapped up by all of us. All the articles I have mentioned are difficult to obtain out here.

Our army food is mostly tinned and the menu never includes cake of any description. You should see the scramble around a fruit cake from home. Agnes sent me a beautiful one and Mrs. Wilkinson also. I like my fruit cake heavy and not iced.

Our CO is in hospital. He has been away for one month already and we are not expecting him to return for a couple of weeks. He has a skin disease caused by using too many cheap remedies for prickly heat. Capt. Moses is also in hospital with some sort of dysentery. He is not very ill and should be back with the Coy soon. His wife and family live in flats called 'The Rockies' on Kurraba Point. You may meet them someday.

Ralph sends his regards. He is a cheerful soul but I think he finds army life in Malaya very much different to the farm at Muswellbrook.

Our batmen live in the bungalow with us. They think they are the most important people in the land. We have a special taxi service (trucks) for them to travel to and from the troops mess. They are becoming expert gardeners and generally keep the bungalow in order. Tomorrow, Mother's Day, they will decorate the place with white flowers in jam tins. Our white flowers are frangipani, petunias and some small ones I have no name for.

My knowledge of the local language is increasing daily. I can now yarn a little with the niggers.

Cheerio darling - love to the girls.
All my love
Bill

Of the three lieutenants Bill names in his letter Alexander James Betterridge (NX70256) would be killed in the fight for Singapore on 9 February 1942.

William Jamieson Richardson (NX35011) was killed two days later. Harold Albert Woods (NX56116) would survive the war and incarceration.[127]

The Bulletin Magazine had been launched in 1880 with the masthead slogan 'Australia for the White Man'. It was known for its radicalism and its xenophobia and became known as *The Bushman's Bible*.[128] *The Home* magazine was launched by Sydney Ure Smith in February 1920 as a monthly publication for upper middle-class Australian housewives. Its articles had a focus on holiday destinations, home decorating, fashion, cosmetics, cultural events and other amusements of the independent and modern woman.[129] *Pix* was a slightly risqué girlie magazine. *Man* was started in 1936 by Kenneth Murray and it published excellent fiction and non-fiction articles. There were also cheeky cartoons, titillating photographs and artwork printed on heavy art paper with glossy card covers. Despite it being expensive at two shillings per issue, circulation was 60,000 at the start of the war. The pocket sized *Man Junior* was started in 1937. It had 96 pages with no advertising and sold for one shilling.[130]

Prickly heat remained a health issue for the troops, and a few days in camp away from strenuous activity helped keep it under some control. During May it was 'rather prevalent'.[131] For some men a day of leave was helpful. Leave was granted to 140 troops of all ranks to visit Malacca. Bill was one of them.

Darling Doukie 18 May '41

I have reams of news of an ancient and crusty nature. Yesterday I spent at Malacca.

The town is characteristic of the East, dirty, stinking, too many shops selling cheap junk and over populated. It was the history of the place that captured my interest and made me walk miles from one old building to another. I bought some photographs and am enclosing them with this letter. The snaps are each numbered and I shall explain a little about each one.

Nos. 1 & 2 The Old Gate of Malacca. The Portuguese when they first arrived out here built a stone wall around the town and the only entrance into the town was through this old building shown in the photographs. This 'Gate' was built in 1511 and even now after 400 years it still is a mighty solid structure.

No. 3 is an inside view of an ancient fort built by the Portuguese about the same time as the 'gate'. This fort is about 3 miles from the town and is situated on the summit of a hill and overlooks the whole district. This fort has been occupied by both Dutch and British throughout the ages. The fort appears to be in a state of general decay in the photograph but this is far from true. The old place is just as solid today as it was when the Pork and Cheese built it. Age has deposited moss on the walls but has done little damage. We jumped about from turret to turret and had a thoroughly good time.

Nos. 4 & 5 were both taken very near the old 'Gate'. You can see how placidly the open sea meets the land; no rolling surf, just a ripple. Malacca has no harbour. The large vessels anchor up to a mile off shore and the people come ashore in boats anywhere. Some vessels with shallow drafts are loaded from a dyke shown in No. 4.

No. 6 is a main street in Malacca. This snap might have been taken in any of the larger towns in Malaya.

No. 7 is an old church built around 1600. I believe it is magnificent inside. We stuck our heads in but found something R.C. progressing inside and hastily retired.

No. 8 is a scene that we see every day. The people are Malayan natives. They always parade like this when they see a camera coming. You will notice that Mrs. Malaya is absent. She always is when soldiers appear. In this case she is more than likely busy having another child. The numbers of children in a Malayan family varies from 8 to 18.

No. 9 The fisherman is a Chinese coolie. Fishing like this is rather uncommon because of the danger of crocodiles. The normal method of angling is to crouch on the bank with a short rod.

In addition to these snaps I took 37 snaps myself but do not hope to have them printed for weeks.

I concluded my day at Malacca by taking one of our nurses to dinner at a place called 'Palm Beach'. We joined forces with several other officers and nurses and had quite a lively party. Unfortunately we had to break things up and leave Malacca at 9pm for camp. This was the first time that I have shown any inclination towards friendliness with the nursing staff and I still think they are a hard faced, hard hearted bunch. We all enjoyed ourselves anyway.

Love to the girls dear.
Much love
Bill

PS I received parcel of socks and cigarettes from the office today.

By now the 2/20 Battalion had been in Malaya for close to three months. The troops had originally thought they were to be deployed in Europe or North Africa and were frustrated that they had to do what they thought of as 'garrison duty' and wait for the Japanese to come. In the meantime they had to learn about the jungle, something new and quite difficult to move through. It had vines that tripped, bamboo spikes that pierced and an all-pervading stink of leaf mould, bugs in the bark of giant trees, fungus and stagnant water.[132] The men were angry that they were so far from 'Action'; some became troublesome and tested unit rules. It was important, but more difficult, for officers to maintain morale and discipline.

May 21 saw a rest day arranged at Si Rusa beach, about 7 km south from Port Dickson near the Alor Gajah peninsula.[133] Boats were hired and the men enjoyed the change of activity.

A check of personnel admitted to hospital with V.D. complaints showed the very small figure of 2.55% of Unit active strength, since arrival of unit in Malaya.[134]

Darling Doukie 24 May '41

Your letter dated 12 May arrived today and with it the excellent photographs of Valhalla and the view from the verandah. Thank you dear very much indeed.

I am pleased those little black Bs - arrived at last. You shall not receive the baskets for many a long day to come. After I had posted them the other day I discovered that I had left one of them out of the parcel. I was able to retrieve the parcel and I have been holding it because I have been on leave a little recently and hoped to acquire something more to put in it. I shall post it soon.

I shall certainly buy you some beads 'as per diagram'. The shops in the small towns have only rubbish but in Singapore I saw crates of those things in every colour. Some were very pretty; jade with good chains, others red stones and silver chains. The cheap ones, bone and string, are even obtainable here. At the first available opportunity I shall locate them and send you some. I could have purchased stacks of jewelry etc before this, but to me it never appeared pretty; always too ornate or too bulky or too cheap. The prices here are practically the same as in Australia but there is a very much wider selection and I think a better article out here.

Today's mail brought along a letter from Mrs. W.G. Ayrton. Who is she, dear? I believe Dorothy Bell gave her my address. I am not sure who Dorothy is. Rene (Ayrton) has invited me to pay her a 'rest-cure' visit in a town quite a long way from here. I shall write and say 'thank you' today and hope to see her as soon as I can. Please let me know in your next letter what I am likely to strike.

Things are certainly changing about at home. Gran should be very happy with you but I can see that your hands will be 'very full' each mealtime with Gordon and Gran extra. However I know that you like them both and that they will be no trouble.

I am wondering if you have received the cash I sent you. It should be with you and possibly spent by now.

Recently I have been doing a spot of sailing. The water is very calm and the breezes are very light. Not many thrills but very pleasant.

I am well and fit dear.

How is Ginge agreeing with the Permanent Trustee? The job should be sound and steady for her. I think that she will be happier in that type of job.

I am pleased that the girls saw Gran G [Gaden] and family in town. I hope your flu passed over quickly dear and that you are well as ever again.

This letter is far too heavy for any airmail to carry at the normal rate. I shall just throw it in the post and trust to luck that it is not weighed.

I know many of the names that have appeared in casualty lists. In the cutting you sent me there were chaps mentioned who were in camp with me at Liverpool in 1937. They were with the 30th Bn NSW Scottish.

Love to the girls and regards to Gordon dear. I have received the 'Smiths' that Gordon posted to me. Love to Gran

All my love
Bill

'Gran G' was Bill's paternal grandmother Agnes Lilian Gaden. 'Gran' was his mother's mother, Jessie Balcombe. Gordon was Vera's brother. Gordon Tyrwhitt Balcombe was a solicitor who joined Abbott, Tout and Balcombe, in Sydney in 1910. In the mid 1920s he withdrew to practise alone in the suburbs. He did not marry until later in life.[135]

Smith's Weekly was a Sydney-based independent weekly newspaper-style magazine, patriotic in flavour and aimed at men. It covered sport, finance, short stories and focused on cartoons, satire, controversial views and 'sensationalism'.[136] In short, it was ideal reading material for a soldier of the time.

As well as imported material the troops had their own magazine to read. On 28 May the first issue of *Thumbs Up* was distributed, made possible through the tireless efforts of editor and manager Pte Francis (Joe) Wilfred Wilson. (He survived the war and was awarded the Distinguished Conduct Medal.)[137]

Bill Gaden is mentioned a couple of times in *Thumbs Up*. In the Company Report there is a 'Dither From D' which reported that *after a well timed illness Capt. Gaden also is with us again - a regular gloom chaser with his cheery smile and bright manner.* Noel Harrison recalled his nickname was 'Horse'.[138]

Bill was also listed in the Social Activities as President of the Surf Life Saving Club.

> *This Club has been handicapped by the protracted illness of its popular President and by continued uncertainty of the final whereabouts of the Unit, President attending baths sessions in the 'QX' watching for likely members. Secretary Bill Dalley, ex Queensland surf nobility, has contacted the Sydney Surf Association and is now considering plans for giving instructions in Resuscitation and Physiology branches. What-ho a sub-department of Fishing, Bill?*

Meanwhile troops continued to train with the Bren guns and watch demonstrations of anti-tank mines and Bangalore torpedoes. Such very military activity refocused the men and discipline problems ceased.[139]

The Officers invited the Nursing sisters of Malacca and Port Dickson to a dance in the Officers Mess. The evening 'proved most enjoyable'.[140]

> Darling Doukie 31 May '41
>
> I have received a letter from Brian [Badgery]. He is well, sweating, but he likes the country. At the first opportunity I shall visit him.
>
> Our first Bn Magazine has been published and I have posted you a copy. This magazine is our first attempt at a unit publication and I feel sure that you will consider it a creditable effort.
>
> Copies of the Woman's [sic] Weekly have been coming into our hands and we are both amused and annoyed by the glowing articles written by Adele Shelton Smith. The articles do not indicate a true picture of our activities in Malaya.
>
> The troops and officers are leading a very much more prosaic existence than in Australia. They rarely venture far from the camp areas and the large dinner parties described are just sheer bunk. Most of us have been entertained by the local Orientals sometime or other but never on a lavish scale. A severe pain and diorohea [sic] usually follows a Chinese dinner. The average troop finds plenty of amusement with his friends in camp, and only proceeds into the towns to take photographs and purchase a few small trinkets to send home.
>
> We officers are honorary members of clubs etc. but we never visit these places regularly. Most of the officers have only been to one, perhaps two parties since our arrival in Malaya. Normally at night we stay in camp, work, yarn and read our papers and mail from Australia. There is really nothing else to do. We have all developed a habit of retiring to bed early. Working in the open air and in the close humid atmosphere makes us very sleepy.
>
> Sunday 1 June 41 Capt. Moses has returned to the unit after a month in hospital and convalescent leave. He is looking very fit and is ready for work. I believe Mrs. A.E. Robertson, our Major's wife, is endeavouring to organize comforts for the

2/20 Bn. She is a very nice woman and I am sure she is not prepared to spend money right and left herself. I am sure you could give her a hand in an 'advisory capacity' but don't attempt it dear if your hands are full.

All my love
Bill

Around this time over three dozen troops were returned to Australia as being medically unfit. Those remaining spent time camouflaging all the motor transport which was then used to transport troops to regular swimming training. This noticeably improved troop morale: on these swimming parades there is always a very cheerful and bright atmosphere, which 'proves the great relaxation that they are'.[142]

On 6 June Pte W.G. Wilson (NX27699) died in his quarters from injuries sustained from a shot from his rifle. He died at 2.00 am and was buried that evening with full military honours. A Court of Inquiry was assembled on the same day. Battalion officers were in charge. Was it an accident or suicide? Had Pte Wilson received a 'Dear John' letter from a loved one? Had he received 'flack' from someone because he was in Malaya rather than facing the Germans or Italians in Europe or Africa? Or was he upset at not leaving camp the day before to return to Australia with some medically unfit friends?[143]

In a further attempt to improve morale for troops who were becoming frustrated at playing a waiting game with the Japanese, two Companies adopted a new leave scheme by bivouacking for the weekend alongside the beach. No Reveille, no parades of any kind. Control was maintained by Officers and NCOs without any difficulty and the troops voted this weekend an excellent idea.[144]

Darling Doukie 7 Jun '41

Another two letters arrived today and they are excellent. I feel that I know everything that happened at home after reading your letters. The censor usually pens the envelopes but so far he has not cut anything out.

Today Betty Bryant, star of 'Forty Thousand Horsemen', arrived at our camp in person. The lads were pleased and made a lot of noise. I am sure her popularity was due to the fact that she is a white girl with a good figure and was not due to her film success. White people are scarce enough here and girls are as rare as emus.

All our crocks have returned from hospital. Capt. Moses is fit and sparking and Lieut Bill Richardson has lost weight but is quite well. I shall be able to take a spot of leave now.

Arch Ewart and I have been discussing our leave together for weeks now. I think we should actually get away about next Saturday 14th Jun. Our programme at present includes a visit to Mrs. Ayrton at Ipoh and a day with Brian [Badgery]. I have not seen Brian up to date.

I am sorry Jacob Badgery is ill. I hope he recovers and will be available for Gran's inspection.

The weather must be very cold at home. I wish we could have just a little cold breeze here. We are sleeping in underpants only and our only bedclothes are mosquito nets. The temperature is pleasantly warm and we sleep soundly. The constant heat is causing our blood to become very thin. A little cut bleeds much more freely than in Australia. One officer recently spent a week high up in the mountains. The temperature up there was evidently cold. He used blankets. I have not slept with a blanket since our ship left Fremantle. When the officer came back to camp he went off duty immediately and has taken a couple of weeks to recover from the change of temperature.

I received a letter from Gwen Clarke, Stewart's daughter. I believe she rang you and had a yarn. [Stewart Clarke had worked with Bill at Birt and Co.]

I posted you the baskets during last week. They should turn up in a month or so.
I am enclosing a few little snaps. Give my love to Gran and the girls dear.
All my love

Bill

[Lieut Bill Richardson was William Jamieson Richardson NX35011 who was destined to die in the fight for Singapore on 11 Feb 1942.][145]

Darling Doukie 11 Jun '41

I am writing this letter in the jungle. A small stream is quietly flowing past me as I sit propped against a mass of tree roots. A big yellow butterfly has decided to be friendly and is sitting contentedly on my chest.

This morning I had no intention of writing from the jungle but a few minutes ago I managed to borrow some paper and a fountain pen, so here it is. The butterfly has flown.

Smithy is still very much with me. He is still exactly the same as in Australia. He washes for me, polishes for me and thieves for me. I sent you a photo of him with his monkey about 2 months ago. I shall take another one of him and send it along as soon as I can. Smithy has no parents dear, and is keeping his young sister at home. He has not been receiving any parcels and I know that very few letters have arrived for him. Do you think you could send him something? He does not smoke but eats like a rhino/sore/ arse. He follows me around like a puppy and is always doing something to make life in this place comfortable for me.

My only regret today is that I have no fishing line with me. The little stream is full of fish, mostly small ones but I suspect a large one will be lurking in the shadowy depths. The rest of the Coy are all out working our patrols. They should return any time now.

My leave has been postponed again. Possibly I shall get away next week. Capt. Moses is going away for the week end to attend a broadcasting conference.

The towns I have seen include Singapore, Kuala Lumpur, Malacca, Seremban. When my leave is over I hope to write more about many other places.

Yesterday I received a tremendous newspaper mail. Jean Thatcher from Bathurst posted me a dozen or so Heralds. Elaine [Warren] came to light with some Heralds and a Sunday paper. Gran sent along her usual Bulletin. The lads have now returned and they are all stirring up the fish. We will soon be moving back dear.

Cheerio dear. Love to the girls.
All my love
Bill

Bill's batman 'Smithy' was not who he made out to be, Robert Smith (NX 20508) was not his real name. He was really Oswald Charles Burne who resumed his true name by Statutory Declaration after the war.[146] No wonder he received few letters. One can only speculate why he had enlisted under an assumed name.

Darling Doukie 13 Jun '41

I am enclosing a poem. One of the lads wrote it and our P&O Cpl typed it for me. I think you will like it. Some of our lads are returning to Australia. They are the few who have been boarded out of the army as medically unfit. One of them, Cpl H B Flanagan was in my Coy. He is a decent lad, perhaps a little rough but still a good chap. He will be able to give you all the first hand news of Malaya and our doings. Heaven knows how you will get hold of him but anyway if you ever see him he will be able to tell you all about us.

I am being fairly swamped with newspapers. Evidently both Elaine and Jean Thatcher have been posting papers regularly and the postal people have been holding them up. I have received practically every Herald for April and May.

News is pretty scanty dear. Pictures and an occasional camp concert summarise our nightly entertainment. Last night I saw 'The Great Dictator'.

Cheerio dear. More news next letter. Love to the girls and Gran.
All my love

Bill

OUR PICNIC

The Sixth are getting battered; the Seventh copping hell.
The Ninth are on no picnic, they're getting theirs as well.
While in the distant jungle, many thousand miles away,
The Eighth are on a 'rest cure', all we do is play.

Because there are no shells here, no bullets flying thick,
We have the name of 'Glamour Boys' and that will always stick.
Every time we take a step the sweat falls from our brow,
And if they only knew it, we have B.O. - and HOW.

Ploughing through the jungle with mud up round our waist
With every step a mouthful, it has a putrid taste
Fighting 'mozzies' by the score and cobras by the ton
It's no use denying, we're having lots of FUN.

If you don't believe me when I say it's bloody hot,
I'll now state a Native custom to show just what is what.
Every man is buried with his overcoat as well
Just because he'll need it in case he goes to Hell.

Give the Japs malaria, it isn't worth a zac.
They won't keep it very long before they give it back.
Although we need the rubber and find uses for the tin
If we stay here any longer, we'll soon be mighty thin.

Take us to the Middle East, where it's cold at night
So we can join the others and help to win the fight.
If they grant us this favour Miss Adele Smith may say,
'Those Eighth Division 'Glamour Boys' are on no holiday'.

Free, gratis, and for nothing........i.e., Buckshee.

SECOND TWO NOUGHT

Weekly Bulletin of the 2/20th Bn. A.I.F., Malaya.

Authorised by Lt.—Col. W. D. JEATER, C.O.

Sponsored by 2/20th Bn. Social Activities Committee.

Passed by Censor Officer H.Q., A.I.F., Malaya, for transmission through the Post to Australia.

Editor & Manager:—PTE. F. ("JOE") WILSON.

No. 1. *Saturday, 14th June, 1941.* *Somewhere in the Jungle.*

AUSTRALIAN NEWS PARS

Our greatest hour

"This is the greatest hour of Australia's history, and we are the custodians of it," Prime Minister Menzies said recently. "There is only one fight to-day, and I call upon the whole of Australia to go through with it".

Lessons of defeat

In a broadcast this week, Mr. Menzies admitted mistakes and miscalculations in the Middle East had been made by Imperial leaders, but, he said, lessons of the defeat were being learned.

Tobruk may turn scale

Mr. Menzies expresses the opinion that the heroic defence of Tobruk might be the turning point of the whole of the Middle East Campaign.

Speeding up tank production

Minister for the Army announces establishment of an Advisory Committee of the Mechanisation Board to speed up mechanisation, particularly in the production of tanks.

A ship a month

Federal merchant shipbuilding programme provides for one ship a month during the next five years.

Forced Loan envisaged

Federal Cabinet will be asked to discuss a scheme of compulsory lending to war funds as part of budget proposals. Conference will discuss, before the end of the month, uniform State taxation.

Our exports decline

Australian exports for the last eleven months have fallen by ten million pounds as compared with 1939/40.

More smokes in sight

Best news of the week for Australians at home is that the tobacco shortage is likely to ease next month.

Think of it!

The Australian Alps are snow—covered. Melbourne experienced its coldest day of the year on Monday. Kiandra recorded a temperature of 6 deg. below zero on Tuesday. A tornado hit Orange, N. S. W., last Sunday night causing heavy damage.

Us, too?

Federal Cabinet is expected to reconsider sending women welfare units to the Middle East for the A.I.F.

A.I.F. in the Middle East can now send home special air mail letter cards for threepence each.

Next one in a pram?

Further claim in unofficial contest to find A.I.F.'s youngest soldier comes from Geelong. They assert that Pte. W.T. Harrason, posted wounded, enlisted a fortnight after his fifteenth birthday.

Malayan babes—one pace forward!

GIVING YOU THE PICTURE

THE C. O. CONGRATULATES US

Having seen the proofs, I consider this paper will be an excellent thing for us all. Whoever originated the idea is to be congratulated, for behind it all is the old hope of so welding our Unit that always we work hard—or at least, should work hard—and then recreate hard. In days gone by it was frequently stressed that once abroad it would be ever so much to the good to have our own facilities for amusing ourselves, thus putting all ranks in the right way of producing the happy, hard-working, hard-fighting Unit I so deeply desired.

Of soldiering in general I would say, from many years of experience, that it is the hardest profession of all. There is ever so much to know about ever so many things; there is the highest level of discipline to be reached: to be able to do those things we don't wish to do, cheerfully; there is the knack to be acquired of being in the right place and doing the right thing both at the right time. Not until these difficult obstacles have been cleared can we justifiably claim to be called soldiers.

To soldiering in Malaya I must, of course, refer specially. General McNaughton, the Canadian Force Commander, chiding his troops in England, the other day, on their impatience for action, reminded them that by far their biggest job was the defence of the homeland—Britain. Their training was well advanced, he said, but to cope with the invader would call for all the best in them. Similarly, I wish to remind you that we are defending our homeland—Australia, and although we might wish to be elsewhere, as soldiers we obey. And as I said above, we do it cheerfully. (Yes, I know!)

Well, all the best to the new paper. I hope you lads fill it with some of those ideas for which I have long looked and may soon now find. Good luck!

W. D. Jeater, Lt.-Col., Comd. 2/20 Bn. A.I.F.

Let's Iron Out This Bulletin Business

This production marks the birth of a small weekly news sheet as distinct from our Unit magazine. But why a weekly paper at all? And can it be maintained as an interesting and useful organ? In answering these questions we find opportunity to say some vital things.

Our answer to the first is based on the thesis that while a soldier should be skilled in fighting he must also be proficient in the art of living. Probably, he fights best who lives fullest: and there occur periods such as we are experiencing right now when the ability to live is even more necessary than the ability to fight. We read of the exploits of our contemporaries in Greece and Egypt—with envy. To emulate them would require Guts: to endure many of their discomforts unaccompanied by their thrill of risky adventure requires Guts, too, of an even rarer sort. It's finding some of us out—this "standing and waiting to serve". The staff we must lean upon is dissolution of our grouches in richer living.

A richer life implies something beyond more ricksha rides and increased supply of "Anchor" beer. Circumstances of Active Service do not, and could not, always place within our reach the fundamental comforts—wine, song, and feminine society: but if there is an Australian trait outstanding above all others it is the spirit of comradeship, which, exploited to its full limits, could could result in this, or any other, Unit becoming one big socially satisfied body. The day's training finished, we might all escape from a mood of depression, a touch of home-sickness, empty pockets even, to the Cricket field, or to Hockey, League, Union, Soccer, Tennis, Athletics, Swimming, Chess, Ping Pong, a Concert, or the Library—all according to group tastes. This satisfaction of the desire for social intercourse is the ideal; its practical realisation can only be achieved through hearty co-operation and organisation; effective organisation, we have found, is nigh impossible without a sound system of publicity; and this, our basic problem, finds its solution in "Second Two Nought", the major purpose of which is to keep you always "in the picture" socially.

The answer to the second question lies etirely with YOU.

—The Editor.

CONTEMPORARY 'ROOS AND KIWIS

(Composed from H.Q., A.I.F. bulletins and local newspapers over the past week.)

Anzacs can take it

Correspondents state that the blitz in Crete against the Anzacs was more savage than at Dunkirk. Amazing tributes are still being paid to the courage, resource, and determination of the Anzacs.

\+ \+ \+

Western Desert heat halts fighting

A press correspondent with the Middle East forces, writes that there has been practically no activity in the Western Desert, where the heat has been terrific in the last few [illegible] the thermometer registering [illegible] degrees. The Germans still hold Halfaya ("Hell Fire") Pass and several posts including Mussaid, along the Egyptian frontier. At Tobruk the only activity has been spasmodic bombing.

\+ \+ \+

Slessor Cables—from Syria

June 10– Australians formed the spearhead of the advance from Palestine into Syria. Many were fresh from the Home country, others had served in Greece and the Western Desert.

\+ \+ \+

June 10– One body of Australian troops in Syria is moving up the coastal road, supported by English cavalry who, owing to the nature of the country, are using horses for the first time in this war.

\+ \+ \+

June 11– Australian flank has penetrated more than 30 miles from the frontier. The men are facing shell-fire from Chenenne. The first Australian casualty was an officer shot by a French 25 mm. gun.

\+ \+ \+

June 12—The A.I.F. occupies Tyre, on the coast of Syria. The inhabitants welcomed them with a fervour that made them feel as though they were coming home. As the A. I. F. passed up the coast road, villagers garlanded their hats, rifles, and vehicles with roses. West Australians prepared the way for the occupation of Tyre by Victorians. There was no resistance in the town after the Vichyites had left. Residents cheered triumphant entry of A.I.F., whose police helped to keep order.

The Weekly Bulletin of the 2/20. Issue Number 1 dated 14th June 1941.[147]

Meanwhile routine in Malaya continued. Yet another soccer match took place between the local police force and the Battalion, and the rugby team played a team of lads from the Riverina. All ranks were advised that the Sunjei Ujong Club was out of bounds, a restriction which became more common leading up to the fighting with the fear that some 'locals' were spies for the Japanese.[148] It wasn't long before the properties Hythe and Salcombe opposite the Malay School and Telak Kemang at Si Rusa were also out of bounds to all troops.[149]

District Court Martials were held on 18 June with two 2/20 men on charge. Pte JH La-Hay (NX53385) and Pte WJ Kemp (NX51509) were charged with various offences:- resisting an escort, striking an officer, common assault, malicious damage to property and conduct to the prejudice of good order and military discipline. Pte La-Hay was sentenced to 80 days detention and Pte Kemp to 150 days detention.

Pte James Harold La-Hay died as a POW in Sumatra on 25 May 1944. Pte William Joseph Kemp was discharged from the Army on 20 August 1941. According to the DVA Nominal Roll, he did not become a POW so was repatriated to Australia well before the fighting began. Was his poor behaviour a deliberate ploy on his part to make sure he was sent home?[150]

Two days after the court martial five 2/20 officers marched out as umpires to the 11th Indian Division exercises. Bill Gaden was one of these officers. He returned on 28 June where he would meet newly arrived Salvation Army officer George Woodland who was to become highly regarded by the troops.

A thief was found to have been on the prowl in camp in late June, with a steel filing cabinet containing about $994 returned pay stolen from the Battalion Orderly Room. The cabinet was subsequently found on the beach with some small change and nearly all the papers that were in it, but not the cash. A week later almost half the lost money was discovered by Pte Gardiner in a disused Malay kitchen in 'E' Coy Barracks.[151]

Written in the top corner of Bill's next letter is Smithy's address:

NX20508 Pte R. Smith
D Coy
2/20Bn AIF
Malaya

Darling Doukie 29 Jun '41

Last week I was away on business - up in the north. On my return here three of your letters were waiting for me. Thank you dear. I look forward to each mail and your letters.

I have been to many places. Here they are:-

Penang - a beautiful little city, full of life and not affected by war or troops. Penang is an island one mile from the mainland. When our ferry was taking us across the little town was bathed in the golden glow of the setting sun and the harbour was packed with native fishing boats with flapping sails. I stayed at the Eastern and Oriental Hotel and there found perfect bliss - no not like that. The pub is magnificent and the accommodation leaves nothing to be desired. My room was large and beautifully

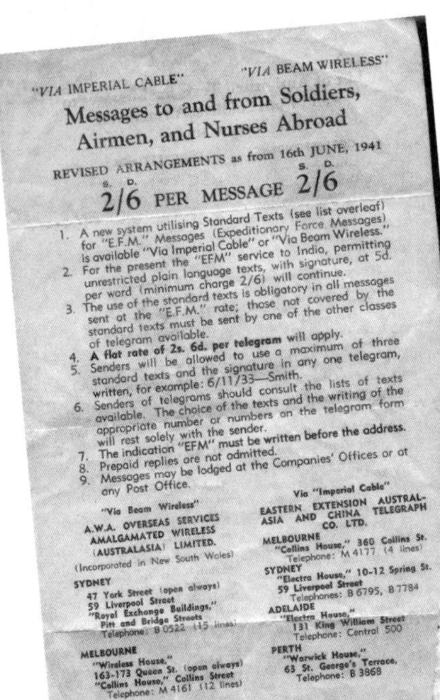

"VIA IMPERIAL CABLE" "VIA BEAM WIRELESS"

Messages to and from Soldiers, Airmen, and Nurses Abroad

REVISED ARRANGEMENTS as from 16th JUNE, 1941

S. D. 2/6 PER MESSAGE S. D. 2/6

1. A new system utilising Standard Texts (see list overleaf) for "E.F.M." Messages (Expeditionary Force Messages) is available "Via Imperial Cable" or "Via Beam Wireless."
2. For the present the "EFM" service to India, permitting unrestricted plain language texts, with signature, at 5d. per word (minimum charge 2/6) will continue.
3. The use of the standard texts is obligatory in all messages sent at the "E.F.M." rate; those not covered by the standard texts must be sent by one of the other classes of telegram available.
4. **A flat rate of 2s. 6d. per telegram** will apply.
5. Senders will be allowed to use a maximum of three standard texts and the signature in any one telegram, written, for example: 6/11/33—Smith.
6. Senders of telegrams should consult the lists of texts available. The choice of the texts and the writing of the appropriate number or numbers on the telegram form will rest solely with the sender.
7. The indication "EFM" **must be written before the address.**
8. Prepaid replies are not admitted.
9. Messages may be lodged at the Companies' Offices or at any Post Office.

"Via Beam Wireless"

A.W.A. OVERSEAS SERVICES AMALGAMATED WIRELESS (AUSTRALASIA) LIMITED.
(Incorporated in New South Wales)

SYDNEY
47 York Street (open always)
59 Liverpool Street
"Royal Exchange Buildings," Pitt and Bridge Streets
Telephone: B 0522 (15 lines)

MELBOURNE
"Wireless House," 163-173 Queen St. (open always)
"Collins House," Collins Street
Telephone: M 4161 (12 lines)

Via "Imperial Cable"

EASTERN EXTENSION AUSTRALASIA AND CHINA TELEGRAPH CO. LTD.

MELBOURNE
"Collins House," 360 Collins St.
Telephone: M 4177 (4 lines)

SYDNEY
"Electra House," 10-12 Spring St.
59 Liverpool Street
Telephones: B 6795, B 7784

ADELAIDE
"Electra House," 131 King William Street
Telephone: Central 500

PERTH
"Warwick House," 63 St. George's Terrace,
Telephone: B 3868

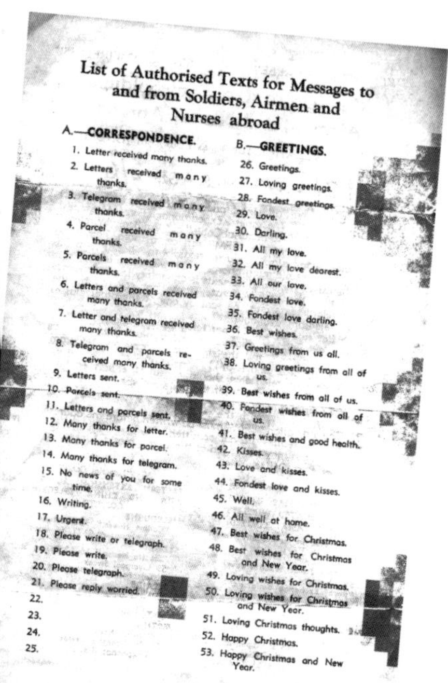

List of Authorised Texts for Messages to and from Soldiers, Airmen and Nurses abroad

A.—CORRESPONDENCE.

1. Letter received many thanks.
2. Letters received many thanks.
3. Telegram received many thanks.
4. Parcel received many thanks.
5. Parcels received many thanks.
6. Letters and parcels received many thanks.
7. Letter and telegram received many thanks.
8. Telegram and parcels received many thanks.
9. Letters sent.
10. Parcels sent.
11. Letters and parcels sent.
12. Many thanks for letter.
13. Many thanks for parcel.
14. Many thanks for telegram.
15. No news of you for some time.
16. Writing.
17. Urgent.
18. Please write or telegraph.
19. Please write.
20. Please telegraph.
21. Please reply worried.
22.
23.
24.
25.

B.—GREETINGS.

26. Greetings.
27. Loving greetings.
28. Fondest greetings.
29. Love.
30. Darling.
31. All my love.
32. All my love dearest.
33. All our love.
34. Fondest love.
35. Fondest love darling.
36. Best wishes.
37. Greetings from us all.
38. Loving greetings from all of us.
39. Best wishes from all of us.
40. Fondest wishes from all of us.
41. Best wishes and good health.
42. Kisses.
43. Love and kisses.
44. Fondest love and kisses.
45. Well.
46. All well at home.
47. Best wishes for Christmas.
48. Best wishes for Christmas and New Year.
49. Loving wishes for Christmas.
50. Loving wishes for Christmas and New Year.
51. Loving Christmas thoughts.
52. Happy Christmas.
53. Happy Christmas and New Year.

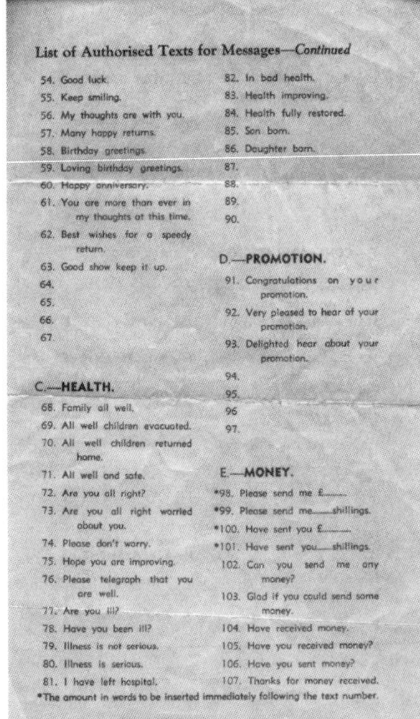

List of Authorised Texts for Messages—*Continued*

54. Good luck.
55. Keep smiling.
56. My thoughts are with you.
57. Many happy returns.
58. Birthday greetings.
59. Loving birthday greetings.
60. Happy anniversary.
61. You are more than ever in my thoughts at this time.
62. Best wishes for a speedy return.
63. Good show keep it up.
64.
65.
66.
67.

C.—HEALTH.

68. Family all well.
69. All well children evacuated.
70. All well children returned home.
71. All well and safe.
72. Are you all right?
73. Are you all right worried about you.
74. Please don't worry.
75. Hope you are improving.
76. Please telegraph that you are well.
77. Are you ill?
78. Have you been ill?
79. Illness is not serious.
80. Illness is serious.
81. I have left hospital.
82. In bad health.
83. Health improving.
84. Health fully restored.
85. Son born.
86. Daughter born.
87.
88.
89.
90.

D.—PROMOTION.

91. Congratulations on your promotion.
92. Very pleased to hear of your promotion.
93. Delighted hear about your promotion.
94.
95.
96.
97.

E.—MONEY.

*98. Please send me £——
*99. Please send me——shillings.
*100. Have sent you £——
*101. Have sent you——shillings.
102. Can you send me any money?
103. Glad if you could send some money.
104. Have received money.
105. Have you received money?
106. Have you sent money?
107. Thanks for money received.

*The amount in words to be inserted immediately following the text number.

The EFM telegram came into being at this time. This meant the sender was no longer permitted a free choice of words in the text but had to use one or other of the expressions shown on the list of standard texts. A flat rate of 2/6d per telegram was charged.

If I could lay
my hands on
the woman journalist who
said soldiering in Malaya was
a round
of dinners and
dances
I'd wring her !!*! neck
WOULDN'T IT?
by S. J. McALISTER

Cartoon taken from The Weekly Bulletin *of the 2/20. Issue Number 2 dated 21st June 1941.*[141]

furnished. I had my own bathroom and a little drawing room attached. E & O to me sounds like perfect comfort. Parts of Penang were so like Sydney that once or twice I felt a 'frog' in my throat and I am sure the others did too. Photographs later.

Alor Star - this is the town that Hinkler visited during his epic flight. The name fairly breathes romance etc. but the town is dreary and surrounded by rice paddy fields. We stayed there a couple of days but saw little to write about.

On one occasion I went to the Thailand border and only saw jungle.

Other towns in the north are very native. They are full of stinks and Chinks.

The little writing pad I am using came from Sydney. Gwen Clark sent it with a tin full of sweets and cigarettes.

Tomorrow I actually depart on leave. Archie and I are off at last. Kuala Lumpur first stop thence Ipoh. After that we will take Mrs. Ayrtons advice and go where she suggests.

I have bought you some junk, a sarong and a wood carving. Penang had plenty of necklaces but they were fabulously expensive. The wood carving etc. will be posted tomorrow.

Cheerio darling. My love to Sue and Ginge.
Yours ever, All my love
Bill

So on 1 July 1941 Bill Gaden and Arch Ewart went for a well deserved period of leave. They missed the Brigade Parade held on the Malay Regiment's Pandang to celebrate the first anniversary of the formation of the 22nd Australian Infantry Brigade. They missed the beach picnics following the parade, they missed the return of Pte Gould who had been Absent Without Leave for over two weeks, they missed his escape from hospital to go AWOL again![152]

Pte Walter Alan Gould was eventually discharged from the Army on 21 December 1941. He did not become a POW so must have been repatriated before the fall of Singapore.[153] Was this another soldier who had found a way of getting home to Australia?

Darling Doukie 5 Jul '41

I am actually on my holiday with Archie and here is all that we have done up to date.
Monday afternoon:- Left camp and caught the train to Kuala Lumpur. At KL we spent the night in the most expensive pub and had a hell of a good time. I drank a little too much for the first time out here but it did not matter because Archie was just as bad as I. We did nothing bad, only celebrated the fact that we were 'off the chair'.

Tuesday morning: - We hired a car and 'syce' at Kuala Lumpur and at 12 o'clock set sail for Fraser's Hill and lunch. Fraser's Hill is a cracker spot; cool clear. It is one of the few decent holiday places around. It is not a town, only twenty or so houses, a golf course, tennis courts and perfect views. We booked for the night at 'The Admiralty', a boarding house. Tuesday night was extra good. Several girls, nurses, were on the last night of their leave and we were given a 'welcome' party. Everybody happy and everybody 'white'.

Wednesday:- We departed for Ipoh at 12.30pm and arrived at Mrs. Ayrton's place at 5.30pm. Mrs. Ayrton is a great scout and her husband is Scotch (very dour) and is great fun. They killed the fatted calf for us and turned it on properly. Both Arch and myself admit that we have never been entertained so naturally and so well. You would like both of them very much. Ipoh is a decent town and we saw all of it. Mrs. Ayrton came in our car and explained everything. She even took us into a Chinese temple. I took photos of the Buddas.

Thursday:- departed Ipoh with a feeling of regret at 2pm and arrived back at Fraser's Hill at 7pm. On our previous visit we found Fraser's Hill a grand place and because boarding house accommodation was not available we took a house. Our return to Fraser's Hill and our bungalow was an epic. A decent lady Estate Agent had hired Chinese boys and cooks for us and all was excellently prepared for our arrival. Some of the locals knew of our return and arranged for whacko party in 'Aus House' that night. The party was a howling success. We are considered the best hosts in Malaya. All we did was:-

(a) Provided a few cheap whiskies all round

(b) Made everybody take off their shoes

(c) Played murders with the lights out.

Our party was a wild riot and our guests walked home arm in arm just before the dawn.

Friday: - Golf, tennis and more golf. At night we had a few visitors but we were all tired and our guests left us fairly early. The golf course is short, pretty and I am playing not badly. I have not lost a ball and I have won $2. We are living like fighting cocks in our own bungalow. Chinese boys waiting on us hand and foot.

Tonight we are all going to a 'whacko' party at the local club. Today we had a meeting with the nurses and because they are returning tomorrow we have all decided to make tonight a really bumper show. There are plenty of English people about but we don't like them. The men are soupy and women have no morals or sense. The climate gets them.

On Monday when we were coming up we struck John Barton going down. He had been here a couple of weeks and was returning because he was broke. I loaned him $10 and will get it when I arrive back at camp. Our leave has been extended a little and we shall occupy our bungalow until Monday. This is really a heavenly place, 4000 feet up on the very top of a mountain. The air is cool clear and crisp. We really sleep with blankets.

I have bought Ginge a birthday present and shall post it when I get back to camp.
Cheerio darling, more when I have recovered from tonight's show. Love to the girls.
All my love

Bill

In his next letter Bill enclosed some postcards of Fraser's Hill and wrote some explanation on the back of each card.

Darling Doukie 6 Jul '41

We are still on our holiday at Fraser's Hill. My last letter written yesterday has all the information up to yesterday afternoon. Here goes from there.

Saturday night was grand. The local club provided us with a small happy dance. We were a merry party and arrived home about 3am feeling pretty tired.

Sunday: In the morning I played golf with one of the nurses. We had a grand game. Sister Ogilvy from S.A. was my partner. She plays a pretty good stick. I could not go wrong today and the local caddy master cum pro was astounded when one of my iron shots went 309 yards; dead straight. This fellow has been taking an interest in

This photograph shows the Golf Course at Fraser's Hill. Our house is behind the hill in the distance. You can clearly see here that the course is right on the top of a mountain (4000ft).

The 'shopping centre', Fraser's Hill. There is only one small shop and it sells everything. The inscription over the doorway reads 'Maxwell Arms'. Everybody meets at 'The Arms' in the late afternoon for a drink and a yarn. There is no 6pm closing in Malaya.

This view shows the rugged nature of the countryside very well. The houses at Fraser's Hill are far apart and are linked by narrow but excellent roads. Fraser's Hill is very like many places in our own Blue Mountains.

Sister Elaine Balfour-Ogilvy, Australian Army Nursing Service, 2/4th Casualty Clearing Station, 8th Division, 2nd AIF. She was from Renmark, South Australia. She was attached to the 2/9 Field Ambulance at this time.[154]

my golf and now 'I don't slice'. He tells me that my handicap would be 12. My old 'hit hard and hope' style has disappeared and this morning I made the green three times with my first shot.

Sunday afternoon very quiet. The nurses departed at 4.30pm. Both Archie and I slept until one of our boys called us for dinner at 8.30pm. Tonight we are spending at the house by ourselves. Tomorrow we return to camp.

Our holiday has been a great success. I am feeling just as well now as when I left Australia. The birthday presents I have bought for Ginge are quite good, a genuine Malayan silver bracelet and necklace. I shall post them immediately on my return. I don't know which one Ginge would like best so she can choose one and the other one goes to the family. I am enclosing in this letter some snaps I bought taken at Fraser's Hill.

Cheerio darling. My next letter will come from camp. Love to the girls.
All my love
Bill

Darling Doukie 9 Jul '41

Back again in camp - we had a glorious holiday. I hope soon to have the photographs ready to post.

Mrs. Ayrton will be leaving Malaya on holidays about 30th August and will be calling in at Sydney and I have given her your address, phone etc. She and her husband are going to New Zealand to visit their small daughter aged about 9. She may ring you. She looks like that old acid drop Mrs. Tandy but really she is a grand scout.

Please don't post Smithy any more socks, he has dozens. I asked him what he would like today and he said a cake and a few 'all day suckers'. His number in NX20508, Pte Smith R (Bob). Today he is all smiles. The mail brought him a letter from a woman in Manly I wrote to, who runs some sort of comfort fund. Enclosed in the letter was a canteen order.

A tennis party in Malaya. The members are thought to include Bill Gaden on left, nurses 'Ray' Raymont in centre with Elaine Balfour-Ogilvy standing next to her and Arch Ewart tying his shoelace.

I have become great friends with one of our nurses from South Australia. Don't worry. She has a face like the back of a trolley bus and muscles in her arms that ripple. She was at Fraser's Hill with us. Elaine Ogilvy is her name. I like her because she plays golf, tennis and swims. The boys say she has hairs on her chest. Anyway she is easily the best of our bunch of lasses and the most popular with everybody including her own crowd. I beat her at golf and swimming and thereby gained her admiration - whacko. News is scarce here dear. Camp still goes along.

At a mess meeting tonight I was elected with two others to inquire into the terrific cost of food locally. What a job! We have one formal dinner each week and these have been costing us about £15 each night. The lads want to know why we can't have a decent feed cheaper. So I start my inquiries with Ah Bing our local provider tomorrow.

Cheerio dear, All my love
Bill

When I arrived back from Fraser's Hill a letter of yours was waiting. Thank you darling very much. Thank Sue for her letters. I shall write to her soon.

(Smithy's all day suckers were probably large round flattened lollypops - often four or five inches (10-12 cms) across and about half an inch (1 cm) thick, with a stick attached, which supposedly took all day to eat. Usually made up of two colours in a spiral pattern, they were a treat to be had only at the local agricultural show, and one in the stocking for Christmas.[155] However another more practical possibility was a large spherical boiled sweet made from similar ingredients which changed colour as a layer was sucked away.)[156]

No doubt Bill was pleased to miss the Route March of $14^1/2$ miles done by the 2/20 lads the day before he returned from leave! A number of blistered feet and a few chafings were the inevitable result.

Over the next weeks the troops went on five day treks, with the only contact with camp during this period allowed to be the ration and water trucks. The men bivouacked in the rubber plantations. For extra authenticity a mock skeleton enemy also bivouacked facing them.

The War Diary also reported:

Exercises were most successful. Movement and control as well as bivouacking in rubber, jungle and open country was experienced as well as considerable night work. Very many lessons brought out. Stamina of troops very good.[157]

...

Darling Doukie 16 Jul '41

Four of your marvelous letters arrived yesterday. They are great.

I have read a few paragraphs out of them, about our comfort fund, to the other officers with me. We have had many a laugh.

Life has been good for me over the past few weeks. First of all a visit to the north, then a holiday at Fraser's Hill and now I have the Coy all to myself, camped on a beach miles from Bn.

Our little camp is as happy as is possible. The lads are in native atab huts and I have a small bungalow 30 yards from the beach. We are working hard and playing even harder.

The local State Athletic Championships are coming off soon. I have the Bn team with me doing some training. I am training myself for the 440 yards.

Last night some of us returned to the Bn to attend a picture show - we saw 'Forty Thousand Horsemen'. The lads enjoyed the show but immediately afterwards made a mad rush for the trucks to take them back to their beach home. They were all frightened of being left behind because I told them earlier that the trucks would wait for nobody.

In one of the Atab huts we have a ping pong table, Bobs table and others games.

We have divided the Coy into two halves - the 'itchies' and the 'others'. The 'itchies' are those with heat rash. They are the ping pong champs but the 'others' have the upper hand at the other games.

At last I have discovered a good army cook. Our meals have been excellent and cooked from army rations only. We rue the day when we shall from here depart.

The nights are glorious here by the beach. Lately there has been no moon but our little camp has an electric light engine and we have plenty of light. The cool breeze floating in from the sea through the palm trees is deliciously refreshing.

It is now 3.30pm. I am sitting on my verandah wondering where to start on all the news that I have for you.

We have some Indian soldiers camped near us and some of our lads are boxing with them now. The Indians seem good chaps, rather bashful but very willing to enter into any sport.

I have learned to ride a motor cycle. We have one with us and at low tide race it on the beach. Yesterday I let it go 'flat out'. One of the lads said to me afterwards 'Christ Sir you must have hit a hundred'. I didn't, but I know the warm air stung my eyes and face and tried to pull my hair out.

My camera has decided not to work and the snaps I took at Fraser's Hill are all blurred. The lens is dirty I am told but that should not cause every picture to be rotten. If it refuses to function when it comes back from Singapore I shall trade it in for something else.

The fishing at our seaside resort is good. The lads are keen and have been catching plenty.

There are two small Malayan shops here both of them authorized to sell food to AIF. These shops cook our fish and provide chips with them. Every morning the two shop-keepers rush me with morning tea and biscuits, free. They think that by keeping on my side I shall permit the troops to buy their goods. They are not far wrong and the arrangement suits me admirably.

David McD's aunts are grand scouts. I have seen them, met them, but do not know them very well.

I don't mind dear if you do not like Mrs. Moses. The skipper is not a bad chap. I do know plenty better. He is on leave at present.

Congratulations on being selected Assistant Secretary [of the 2/20 Comforts Fund]. Your work will never end. I think you will find the job right into your bag.

My Malay is improving. I can even tell the sanitary man to empty the 'rose bowls' and sweep the drains.

One of the boys just produced some oysters. I tried one but I still don't like them.
Cheerio dear - love to the girls.
All my love
Bill

PS Your parcel of writing paper, garters etc arrived 11pm tonight. Thank you dear.

[Bobs is a traditional snooker-like game where each player has six balls which are hit with a wooden cue. The balls are aimed to pass under one of a row of eight wooden arches; each arch has a 'value' from one to eight. The winner is the person with the highest score.][158]

Darling Doukie 22 Jul '41

Your big fat letter full of information turned up yesterday. Thank you dear very much.

News is pretty scarce. Nothing has been happening recently. I am back again in camp and being rolled along by routine.

Each night I train for the State Athletic Championships. The one race I am entering is for the 440 yards. Our big day is Saturday next. [Bill had every right to be optimistic about his chances in the athletics. At Broughton School he had proved to be an excellent sportsman, he loved football and athletics and was a good swimmer. In 1930 he was a member of the school's 2nd XV rugby team and the 2nd Athletics team and was promoted to the first rugby and the first cricket XI in 1931. He would have been around 14 years old. He subsequently moved to Maitland High School where he first met fellow officer Bart Richardson. He broke all the school athletics records. In 1933 he was awarded a medal, still owned by the family, for being Junior Champion in the 100 yards, 220 yards, Hurdles and High Jump.]

Your cable arrived. Thank you very much. Another parcel should reach you soon. With this letter I am enclosing a small Malayan Kris in real Malayan silver. The Kris is a small weapon carried by Malayan warriors and bridegrooms. This dagger has played a large and important part in the history of this country. When I return I shall bring with me a real one. The Kris is the Malayan national emblem.

Capt. Moses fell down our stairs tonight. He says that the smell from my pipe caused him to screw up his nose and close his eyes - hence the accident.

I intend to post you regularly a copy of our Bn newspapers. The verses and other bits you will find amusing.

My Coy made a profit of $46 on the bar during our week at the beach. This represents £7.12.0 in real money.

I have had quite a deal of explaining to do. The powers that be are thinking that we did nothing but booze. Actually we worked hard during the days but saved our thirsts for the tropical nights.

Tomorrow I hope to have a decent solo ride on a motor cycle. I shall be very careful because the sports are so close.

I am very sorry that old Mr. Brooks passed away. However I know it was for the better because he could never recover from his injury.

Agnes has written me a long letter. She gave me a description of the brooch you gave her. Good old Aggie.

David MacDougal is very pleased that his people have met you. He is a good chap and I am sure his aunts are well worth knowing.

Smithy will be thrilled with 'Quiz'. He is a cheerful little blighter but I know he feels his situation at times. He asked me a few days ago how much it would cost to educate a girl. It appears that he wants to send his young sister to school and wants to pay her fees with military allotment.

No more news dear. I am looking forward to your next letters. Love to the girls.
All my love
Bill

[Mr Brooks was most likely Canute Brooks a family friend from Scone. He was born in 1874, the son of James Norton Brooks and his wife Harriet Elizabeth.][159]

[*Quiz* magazine was aimed at the male market by Gardner Publications. It contained cartoons, yarns and short stories.][160]

Comforts for the troops continued to arrive from home, the Australian Comforts Fund sending:

> *Cigarettes 2676 packets, chewing gum 1683, matches 1506 packets, razor blades 892 packets, tooth paste 892 tubes, tobacco 446 1oz pkts, cigarette papers 223 packets, cake 445 lbs.*[161]

It was also reported at this time that Bill was one of the members of a Court of Enquiry to examine the loss of a specific rifle. These Courts were held to determine causes of death or injury, loss of equipment and other such disciplinary action as may be needed.

Darling Doukie 27 Jul '41

I left your little Kris out of your last letter. Here it is!

Cheers! I won the Negri Seremban State 440 yards Championship yesterday. Sending the cup and a medal soon. Our Bn scooped the pool. We won a silver Challenge Shield and fourteen trophies. I am pleased because I was given the job of training the lads.

After the prize giving ceremony a funny incident occurred. We were proudly exhibiting our shield and cups to a large crowd of AIF, Malays, Chinks, Tamils and mixtures. The show looked like a tremendous football scrum. Everybody was pushing and shoving. The sports committee feared that the precious shield would be pulled to pieces. Eventually they descended on us in a body and pinched back the works. We haven't seen it since.

Yesterday before the sports I was too excited to eat a decent lunch. After the sport I managed two whopper steaks and eight eggs.

Mrs. Badgery sent me a parcel of six magazines. They are great. Please thank her when you see her.

Charles Moses and I had a great laugh when your paper arrived with the photograph of that hypocrite Wells in it. Capt. Moses sacked him from the ABC sometime ago. He borrowed cash from the employees and failed to return some.

Elaine Ogilvy had departed to a station many miles away. I have a suspicion she regretted her departure more than I did. 'Sans fait rien' - we came here to fight. Although I did not see much of her in camp I think she is one of the finest lasses I have ever met. Gran would call her 'nice'.

Soon you will receive a cheque from Birts [Birt and Co., Bill's Sydney employer]. My bonus £13.9.0. The office posted me a great parcel a week or so ago. It contained biscuits, tins of barley sugars and café au lait. I was very pleased with it. They wanted to know what they should do with my money. I told them to send the cheque to you. The postage people are knocking back overweight letters. I shall have to be careful.

How goes the comforts fund business? Your name has been published over here in our weekly paper. What about sending me a few lines about the work done so that we can print it for the lads? I am sending you copies of the paper each week.

Love to the girls dear. Cheerio.
All my love
Bill

Could the 'hypocrite Wells' that Bill mentions have been one David Wells whose photograph appeared in the *Sydney Morning Herald* of 12 June 1941 in a series of photographs under the headline 'Hospital and Comforts Funds Workers'?[62]

Enclosed with this letter was a column from the *Malay Mail*, Monday July 28, 1941 which reported Capt. Gaden won the 440 yards, Othman was 2nd and E Jones 3rd - time 56²/5 seconds and the Inter Club relay was won by Capt. Gaden's AIF team in 1 min 40 secs. The Champion Unit was AIF Port Dickson (2/20 Bn) with 24 points.[163]

The weekly bulletin of the 2/20, *Second Two Nought*, (No. 8, 2 Aug 1941) reported the results of the athletics. The relay team was Gaden, Scollen, Want and Bell; Capt. Gaden won the individual 440 yds and Cpl Bell the individual 220 yds.[164]

Sadly two of these fine young athletes were to die at the hands of the Japanese. Thomas Patrick Scollen, NX 57377, died Sandakan, Borneo on March 7 May 1945; Irwin James Want, NX 45422, was killed in action in Malaya on 10 Feb 1942. William James Bell, NX51489, survived being a POW with Bill in 'D' Force, 'U' Bn.[165]

The same newspaper reported that Capt. Gaden and Padre CG Sexton (NX35108) were the two officers on the committee to organize 'a Unit Party sometime in the coming week'.

Tom Scollen

Darling Doukie
3 Aug '41

News for letters has been rather scarce lately. This letter covers our recent doings.

Last night we held a dance in our mess. The show was very cheerful and we all enjoyed it. Our partners were nurses from their various stations and a couple of local lasses. I was pleased when my friend Ogilvy turned up - invited but not expected. The mess was beautifully decorated and the garden lit with coloured lights. Our big silver athletic shield and many cups were placed on a table by themselves and provided us with the opportunity to skite. The guests, I think, were favourably impressed.

I am now training our Bn football team. The lads are very keen and are all working well. Our ambition is to clean up the other units over here and gain as many places as possible in the State representative team.

Tomorrow I leave for the bush for a week or so. We are doing a really decent hike through jungle and rubber country. I hope to see some of the much talked about game - panthers etc. Mails may be difficult in the bush and letters hard to write. I shall try to overcome these difficulties.

I shall soon be able to post you my snap album with the photographs stuck in. My camera has just returned from Singapore where it received repairs.

How does Ginge like her job? The bottle of whisky she bought you must have been grand. We can buy large bottles here for about 7/6. We cannot post it away. Most of our drinks in the mess are cheap - duty free - but outside the prices are higher than at home.

Capt. Moses has departed once again on duty. I have the Coy. Every time we do anything the skipper is away. This arrangement suits me admirably.

Love to the lasses, dear. Please tell Gordon that I enjoy the 'Smiths'.
All my love dear.
Bill

On 7 August 1941 the Commanding Officer of the 2/20, Lt-Col WD Jeater left the unit and was posted to command the General Base Depot. It was a move welcomed by Bill as Jeater was known to criticize a junior officer in front of the men, treating them like Corporals. His conduct towards the men when they had complaints about the food created an unpleasant atmosphere in the mess. Jeater was replaced by Lt-Col CFA Assheton, formerly 2IC of the 2/18 Bn.[166]

Darling Doukie 11 Aug '41

The past five days have been fun and hard work. I have had the Coy out in the bush on a long hike. We ate and slept in the jungle and rubber. Each day we walked through rubber trees, crashed into the jungle and waded through stinking swamps. The nights were pleasant but the mosquitoes terrific. We had to be very careful with our mosquito nets because of the danger of dengue and malaria. You should have seen our little camps by night. The mossie nets were propped up on sticks and beneath them the lads slept on waterproof sheets. The white nets at midnight looked like a hundred ghosts. We all really enjoyed the stunt and hope to go again soon. Although we traveled through country that is reputed to contain wild animals we never saw them. I am certain now that nothing frightens tigers more than army boots.

We have a new CO, Lieut. Col. Assheton. He was previously 2IC of another unit over here. I like him very much. He works hard and I feel sure he will very soon gain the confidence of his new command. Old Bill Jeater has been given a job locally. I am not at all clear on what his job really is. We have not seen very much of him for months. He has been in hospital with a skin disease.

We are developing into a cracking good unit. The lads have been doing well at all sports. Our esprit de corps is rising to unexpected heights. Our football teams are all having a run of blazing success. Their colours are green jerseys, blue pants and socks with green and white rings. They look whacko! We have only one unit left to beat in this area.

Mails are slowing up again. I have not received a letter from you for over 2 weeks. Perhaps tomorrow will produce one. Cheerio dear, love to Sue and Ginge.
All my love
Bill

Meanwhile training continued for the troops of Bill's 'D' Company with plenty of exercises to occupy them:

War Diary 2/20 Bn. AIF
Outline Syllabus of training
Week ending 9 Aug '41
'D' Coy on a 5 day exercise in the Sua Betong-Tanah Meerah Camp

Week ending 16 Aug '41
'D' Coy.
Monday 11th Individual training
Tuesday 12th Dannert Wire Obs.

```
                              Recce boats
                              Molotov cocktails
Wednesday 13th Route March, fully loaded
Thursday 14th                 Coy as fighting patrol
                              (a) passage of defiles
                              (b) withdrawal into perimeter camp
Friday 15th                   Village fighting
Saturday 16th                 Administration
```

Dear Ginge 15 Aug '41

Many happy returns. This note will more than likely arrive too early but by posting it now it is 'sure to catch the worm'.

Last night spent out in the bush with the troops. The night was a nightmare. At 2 am rain commenced and it did not stop. We only have a couple of small groundsheets to keep the rain off on these stints. Very soon we were all soaking. At daylight a cloud must have burst. We were completely swamped. We picked our mosquito nets out of the drains and dumped them in the trucks. You should have seen us, wet, dirty but happy. On the way back to camp this morning we barged through four miles of jungle. What a night and morning.

David MacDougal (NX 12539) who left the 2/20 Bn to join Mission 204, the Commandos in China

David MacDougal has left us. He has been chosen for a job with a unit far away from here. I miss him. Dave is a great chap.

Capt. Moses has also departed. He has talked his way on to Divisional HQ. Mother will be pleased with this news.

Mrs. Fussell has been posting me books and magazines. I am handing them on to the lads. They are very much appreciated. Please give me Mrs. F's address. I want to thank her.

The mails have been rotten lately. It is ages since I received a letter from home. How goes the job?

Has Anthony Rutherford Walter (Tony with the wish) been located? Give me all the latest news? [Tony Walter, NX12271, was with the 2/1 Bn. He was a POW of the Germans and survived the war].[167]

Brian Badgery is stationed a long way from here. I have only seen him once. I hope to meet the old chap again soon.

I have lost quite a lot of weight over here - it must have melted off me. I now weigh 13 stone exactly [82.7 kg]. When I left Australia I was over 14 st. [89 kg]. However although my weight has departed I am in glorious condition and at present can play football or any game without feeling the slightest bit stiff.

Hope you like the silver neck businesses I posted you. They are fashionable.
Cheerio dear. Good luck and love to yourself and Mother and Sue.
Bill

Bill's fitness was evident with him being named in the Battalion's Routine Orders to play in the rugby union team against bitter rivals the 2/19 on 16 August.

Darling Doukie 18 Aug '41

A bale of letters arrived tonight. They have been held up recently and then suddenly let loose. Now that I have read them all the news is fairly swimming around my head.

The Comforts Fund is certainly progressing. I agree with Major General R [Robertson] that the thing we need most is cash. Sporting material and other things can be purchased here at present. However the time will surely come when we won't be able to purchase our needs and then we shall rely on you for razor blades, tooth paste, cakes, sweets, reading matter etc. Clothes and socks will I think never will be required by the lads. They have all got as much as they can possibly carry at present.

Sue is going great guns with Warwick. Surely she has had sufficient experience now to know what she is doing. Don't worry dear. She will be OK.

George Brookes has written to me. He wants me to arrange a meeting soon. My programme is a busy one and our meeting may not be for a week or so. One of my lads here knows him pretty well.

I am pleased that Gordon is playing tennis. He should play a good game. The tennis court idea sounds good to me. Old Mrs. Harrison should give it to you. She rolls in cash.

How are Ginge's carrots? The dammed catchment area must be in the wrong place. It has not had a decent supply of water in it for years.

I have been playing a little football - not seriously, just enough to keep in condition. Our teams are good and have been having plenty of success.

I know Mr. Moore. He comes from Muswellbrook. His son Joe is a great pal of Ralph's. Ralph by the way has left us temporarily. He went with David MacDougal.

Cheerio dear - news at the moment is pretty scarce.

Our new CO is a great chap. He is going flat out to build our unit into a great show. He will do it. Cheerio dear.

All my love
Bill

PS Love to the girls.

David MacDougal (NX12539), Rolphe [Ralph] Barker (NX28141) and Joseph Moore (NX20081) were all men of the 2/20 who were chosen for Mission 204, the secret Commando Unit in China. The medical standards for this select group were extremely high and all had to be single men with no dependants. They went on the ship *Karoa* to Rangoon in Burma. After training, on 25th January 1942, the Australians of Mission 204 followed the Burma Road into China. Their exploits were recorded in William Noonan's book *The Surprising Battalion*.[168] David and Joe survived but sadly Ralph became ill and died on 5 December 1941.

Darling Doukie 22 Aug '41

A couple of days ago I wrote and in that letter gave you all the news. Since then I have re-read your letters and now have a little more news.

Brian Badgery is a long way from here. I have only managed to contact him on one occasion. The distance between us does not stop me visiting him. The hindering factor is the necessary leave which is difficult to obtain. [Brian was with 8th Division Head Quarters.]

This is the first letter I have written to you in the morning. Usually I write at night. When we are awake over here the heat is always ready to greet you and we rarely start a day with that clean fresh feeling that we knew at home.

After we have been up for an hour or so things are different. The lazy oppressive feeling departs and we start work usually feeling full of beans.

Our camp is at present on a beach. I can see a native fishing fleet returning homewards. The junks are a pretty sight with their large sails glittering in the morning sun. Soon there will not be a ship in sight, just placid sea.

Must finish dear. The time for parade is very close.
Cheerio - love to both the lasses.
All my love
Bill

Darling Doukie 26 Aug '41

I believe a mail has arrived but as yet nobody has brought me any letters. I shall commence this note and if there is a letter for me I shall tell you about it later.

Recently I have developed a new hobby - drawing. I had a go with a few borrowed pencils the other day and found that I could make a reasonable job. Since then I have bought myself a packet of coloured pencils and have been going great guns. The pictures are fairly crude but I am improving. When I have a decent bunch completed I shall post them to you to keep. They will be good fun to laugh over later.

One of the lads produced a small newspaper cutting from a Muswellbrook daily about myself confronting a croc in the jungle. The few printed words are interesting but not quite true to detail. However they make good reading.

1 Sep 41: I commenced this letter a few days ago. In the meantime I have posted one to Ginge. Your letter arrived dear thank you very much indeed.

This camp is close to the sea. From our hill slope we can see below us patches of blue water through the palm trees. The camp itself is rather dusty. Rain I hope will come to clean it up for us.

We have been using a native grass hut for a mess but the bugs and rats became too vicious. We eat in the open now. Heaven knows what we will do when it rains. Eat in our tents I suppose.

Today I saw some fish that actually could walk on dry ground. They were in a muddy creek. I am told that they are common in these parts.

Some excitement was caused this afternoon when a native, shooting with a shot gun close to us, fired several shots into our officer's mess. He could not see the huts through the trees but it made us run for cover.

There is no more news dear.
Today I received Sue's letter about David B-P [Bjelke-Petersen]. I am writing to her by this mail.
Cheerio dear. Love to the lasses.
All my love
Bill

The walking fish were lungfish, *Neoceratodus forsteri*, which can move from the water onto land; they need to remain moist so are found close to the waters' edge on mudflats.[169] They can be over 1.5 metres long with scaly hides. They have 32 razor-sharp teeth.[170]

At the end of August the 2/20 lads moved camp from the west coast of Malaya to the east, to Mersing. They travelled by train but equipment had to be taken by truck. One carrier overturned and Pte LJ Hearn was killed. This was not a good omen for their new camp.[171]

92 Elliott and Silver, *A history of 2/18 Battalion*, p. 27.
93 *Sydney Morning Herald*, 31 January 1942, p. 11.
94 *ibid.*
95 Birch, *The 2nd AIF in Malaya*, <http://www.htansw.asn.au/teach/war/JBirch%20Malaya%20 Article.pdf>
96 Braddon, *The Naked Island*, pp. 40-1.
97 *The Australian Women's Weekly*, 22 March 1941, p. 7.
98 Reg Newton, Personal communication and *The Australian Women's Weekly, ibid.*
99 *War Diary 2/20 Bn. A.I.F.*, 29 March 1941.
100 Sri Menanti Palace, < http://www.malaysia.sawadee.com/negeri_sembilan/places.htm > and <http://www.malaysiahotels.cc/nsembilan.html >
101 Smith, Adele Shelton, *The Australian Women's Weekly*, 29 March 1941.
102 *War Diary 2/20 Bn. A.I.F.*, 30 March 1941.
103 *ibid.*
104 *ibid.*, 3-4 April 1941.
105 *ibid.*, 5-9 April 1941.
106 *Sydney Morning Herald*, 3 April 1941, p. 8.
107 Smith, Adele Shelton, *op. cit.*, 5 April 1941.
108 *Malayan Dictionary* < http://kamus.lamanmini.com/index.php >
109 *War Diary 2/20 Bn. A.I.F.*
110 *ibid.*, 10 April 1941.
111 Smith, Adele Shelton, *op. cit.*, 12 April 1941, pp. 7-11.
112 *War Diary 2/20 Bn. A.I.F.*, 13-14 April 1941.
113 Routine Orders 2/20 Bn. A.I.F, 25 April 1941.
114 *War Diary 2/20 Bn. A.I.F.*, 19 April 1941.
115 Braddon, *op. cit.*, p. 44.
116 Savage, *A Guest of the Emperor*, p. 11.
117 Smith, Adele Shelton, *op. cit.*, 19 April 1941, pp. 7-8, 10.
118 Information from John and Libby Fuller, current owners of The Briars.
119 Smith, Adele Shelton, *op. cit.*, 26 April 1941, p. 7, and http://dictionary.reference.com/browse/Padang
120 *Australian Dictionary of Biography* < http://adbonline.anu.edu.au/biogs/A160735b.htm >
121 Smith, Adele Shelton, *op. cit.*, 3 May 1941, p. 7.
122 War Diary 2/20 Bn. A.I.F., 5 May 41.
123 *ibid.*, 9 May 1941.
124 *ibid.*, 14 May 1941.
125 *ibid.*, 8 May 1941.
126 DVA Nominal Roll.
127 *ibid.*
128 < http://news.ninemsn.com.au/article.aspx?id=108987 >
129 Powerhouse Museum, Sydney < http://www.powerhousemuseum.com/collection/database/search_tags.php >
130 *Man* magazine, the Australian publishing icon <http://collectingbooksandmagazines.com/man.html >
131 *War Diary 2/20 Bn. A.I.F.*, 16 May 1941.
132 Braddon, *op. cit.*, p. 197.
133 Google Maps, < http://www.google.com.au/help/maps/tour/ >
134 *War Diary 2/20 Bn. A.I.F.*, 19 May 1941.
135 Gaden family history researched by the author.

136 *Smith's Weekly* < http://www.paperworld.com.au/magazineinfo.php?Mag=Smiths%20Weekly >
137 DVA Nominal Roll and *Second Two Nought* issues 1-11, in possession of the author.
138 Noel Newton Harrison (NX45896), personal communication, 25 April 2008.
139 *War Diary 2/20 Bn. A.I.F.* 29-30 May 1941.
140 *ibid.*, 31 May 1941.
141 *Second Two Nought*, Number 2, 21st June 1941, in the possession of the author.
142 *War Diary 2/20 Bn. A.I.F.* 4-5 June 1941.
143 *ibid.*, 6 June 1941 and DVA Nominal Roll.
144 *War Diary 2/20 Bn. A.I.F.*, 7 June 1941.
145 DVA Nominal Roll.
146 Wendy Taylor, DVA Nominal Roll team, Personal communication, 18 July 2007.
147 *Second Two Nought*, 14 June 1941, in the possession of the author.
148 Routine Orders 2/20 Bn. A.I.F. 16 June 1941.
149 *ibid.* 23 June 1941.
150 DVA Nominal Roll and Wall, *Singapore and Beyond*, p. 376.
151 *War Diary 2/20 Bn. A.I.F.*, 25 June and 3 July 1941.
152 *ibid.*, 2-5 July 1941.
153 DVA Nominal Roll.
154 National Archives of Australia, record of service of Elaine Lenore Balfour-Ogilvy.
155 Marie Donaldson <aus-nsw-sydney@rootsweb.com > Personal communication, 27 October 2007. and< http://www.lollyshopwangi.com.au/aussie-favourites/lollypops-lollipops/ > <http://www.goodygoodygumdrops.com.au/shop/cart.php?target=product&product_id=945&category_id=65 >
156 Bob Gaden personal communication.
157 *War Diary 2/20 Bn. A.I.F.*, 14-28 July 1941.
158 Bobs game, < http://www.qualitycaretraining.com.au/active%20games.htm#Table%20 Bobs >
159 NSW BDM register entries, 21336/1874 and 16952/1941.
160 *Quiz* magazine < http://www.tnet.com.au/~wirrigalozpulp.html >
161 Routine orders 2/20 Bn. A.I.F., 24 July 1941.
162 *Sydney Morning Herald* 12 June 1941, p. 16.
163 *Malay Mail*, Monday July 28, 1941.
164 *Second Two Nought*, No. 8, 2 Aug 1941, in the possession of the author.
165 DVA Nominal Roll.
166 Wall, *Singapore and Beyond*, pp. 3, 14 and 21.
167 DVA Nominal Roll and family letters in the possession of the author.
168 Noonan, *The Surprising Battalion*, pp. 29, 77.
169 Lungfish <http://www.nativefish.asn.au/lungfish.html >
170 Lungfish<http://www.goworldtravel.com/ex/aspx/articleGuid.cc5f87d4-34cb-489e-b70b-9919e3b131da/xe/article.htm >
171 *War Diary 2/20 Bn. A.I.F.*, 28-29 August 1941.

Chapter 5 - Digging-in at Mersing

By now the 22nd Brigade had been in Malaya for close to six months and the troops were familiar with the climate and surroundings. August 1941 saw the arrival of the 27th Brigade AIF in Malaya, transported by Dutch ships. The number of troops Gordon Bennett had under his command now reached 15,000.[172]

The battalions of the 22nd Brigade, the 2/18, 2/19 and 2/20, moved across to the east coast and set up camp at Mersing. Here they were to build beach fortifications to prevent any Japanese landings on the coastline closest to Japan. The 27th Brigade took their place on the west coast of Johore.

An ex-patriot who had lived in Mersing in the mid 1930s described the town as just one street with a few shops and no government buildings. There was no electricity so lights were powered by oil and the fridges ran on kerosene. The climate was hot and humid but there was plenty of shade under the coconut palms and Casuarina trees.[173]

The town was isolated; there was a twisting road through the jungle to Singapore 100 miles (160 km) away. Cold storage supplies came from Singapore by train to Kluang, then had to be hauled 60 miles (96 km) by road in the mail-car. Travellers often saw wildlife which included elephants, panthers and tigers, monkeys and musangs. (Musangs were nocturnal omnivores, also known as palm civets. They were expert climbers and spent most of their lives in trees. They ate small vertebrates, insects, ripe fruits and seeds and were very fond of palm sap.)[174]

The few Europeans in the town were involved with the rubber industry. The several thousand local Malayans were mainly fishermen, with lorries taking the whole catch to the Singapore market each day, so it was very hard for the locals to obtain good fish!

There was also a large guest house for visitors from Singapore who came for weekends and holidays.

Mersing was a coastal town with beautiful views for miles across to the many little islands in those parts. Ships could be seen in the distance going regularly between Singapore and Bangkok. The small town had the sea on one side and the river on the other. Originally there was no bridge across the river, travel was by punt. In the mid 1930s the road north to Endau was finished, before that the only way to reach the northern village was by boat. Japanese boats were often seen off the coast at this time, on what business no one knew.[175]

Routine was quickly established, with Bill one of the members of a Court of Inquiry into the death of twenty-three year old Lionel James Hearn (NX55850), a lad from Crookwell in the Southern Tablelands of NSW.[176]

The men were also told to be far more aware of malaria over there on the east coast, they had to wear long sleeves and long trousers after 1700 hours.

It was a pity they had not taken as much care when on the west coast as it was only a couple of weeks later that the adjutant commented on the unit strength being low due to the large incidence of malaria contracted at Port Dickson.[177]

Water was in short supply in this camp, it had to be carted in by truck. Drinking water was kept separate from water used for washing and ablutions. The storage tanks were close to the area the troops named 'Castlereagh Street'.[178]

Bill wrote to his sister Elizabeth about their new camp.

Dear Ginge 30 Aug '41

Today is your birthday - do you feel any older?

Congratulations on being elected President of the 'Younger Set' [of the Comforts Fund]. You will have a stack of hard work coming to you now - arranging parties, dances etc.

Our Pay Sgt. tells me his sister is on your committee. His name is Hutchinson. [Sgt John Noel Hutchinson, NX16527, was to die on 4 Feb 1945 in Sandakan, Borneo.][179]

The lads here are very keen on the Comforts Fund and Younger Set schemes. We will give you all the support we can. What can we do? If you intend sending the boys 'comforts' for heavens sake don't send short sox. They all have plenty. Long socks are OK. I think that the best presents are those that we can eat and read - especially cakes and bawdy magazines. Cigarettes, tobacco and papers are always wanted by all of us. We are in a new camp, living in tents with the rats and bugs. Not as bad as that but a hell of a change from the rather palatial barracks and bungalows we so recently vacated. Old Black Jack [Lt-Col F. Galleghan] would have a touch of the horrors if he saw this camp. He always liked straight lines of tents. We have not one straight line in the camp. Our tents are dotted about on the rocky slopes of a hill. We have tracks running everywhere. These have been given familiar names such as Macquarie St, Castlereagh St, etc. My lads are painting a 'Wait here for trams'.

The lads have changed in appearance since we left home. They look tough and sun tanned. Some of them could pass for natives anywhere. We take our shirts off as often as possible to avoid the itch etc.

I hope you like the necklace and bracelet. They are genuine Malayan silver although the bracelet was not carved it was made by natives at Kelantan. I have half a dozen spoons to send to Mother in my next parcel.

We are working flat out in this camp. Siestas are a luxury we enjoyed in the past. We work all day here.

David MacD has left us. You know that I think. He wrote to me and wished to be remembered to you.

Mother tells me that you have a new job in the office. That's the stuff, dear - keep it up.
Cheerio dear - give my love to Mother and Sue.
Many happy returns.
Love
Billy

Another soldier died at this time, twenty-one year old Sydney lad Kevin William Dallas Veness who died of illness whilst on guard duty on Magazine Guard. Bill was again a member of the Court of Inquiry into this death.[180]

Meanwhile the rest of the troops were engaged in a thorough and complete recce of their areas checking depositions, wiring, and routes. They were advised that when returning .303 cartridge cases to the QM Store, they had to separate those fired from automatic weapons and pack them in boxes distinctly marked in block letters 'F.A'. They were also advised that the latrines situated near the NAAFI Canteen were for the use of natives only, and were out of bounds to all ranks. Urine tubs for the troops were provided in the vicinity of the Canteen between the hours of 1900 hrs and Reveille.

September 3 was the second anniversary of the outbreak of war. His Majesty the King requested that the following Sunday, September 7, should be observed as a National Day of Prayer throughout the Empire. In accordance with His Majesty's request, church parades were held, with a combined parade for 2/20 Bn, 15 A/Tk Bty, 2/10 Fd Coy, Bde HQ at 0900 hrs in Pandang opposite the 2/20 Bn Lines, with the Catholic services held that evening.[181]

Darling Doukie 8 Sep'41

Tonight it is raining. I have just finished scratching the drains around the tent and have now settled down to write and answer your letters.

A mail today brought along a letter of yours with the Jack Davey cutting about the soldiers increase in pay.

Ginge must have been pleased with her birthday presents. She wrote me a long letter recently. I answered it a couple of days ago.

How did you get on with Mr. and Mrs. Ayrton? They wrote to me before leaving Malaya and I only saw them once and liked them.

Thank you dear for making the cake for my birthday. What a party I shall have in my tent when it arrives.

I have just re-read your letter and discovered that I missed out the page about your party with the A[yrton]'s at the Winter Garden when I read it the first time. I can easily picture you having a bright party. They are quite good fun when they warm up, particularly 'the old Scot'.

The dust has been rotten here since we arrived. The rain that is pouring down now should wash most of it away.

There are a few sharks about. One of the lads shot one a couple of days ago with his army rifle. He was reprimanded for wasting ammunition.

The bush we are working in is quite decent. My area has no jungle or swamps, only countless rubber trees.

Mr. Brookes has no chance in the world of seeing me here. Perhaps I may meet him on leave if I can get away. We are working flat out and leave is something that is not being considered at the moment.

Harry Woods [Lieut. Harold Albert Woods, NX56116][182] is sharing the tent with me. He is a good chap and tidy. Really I am not untidy in a tent myself these days so we get on well. His only complaint is that I always eat his coffee and milk out of the tin. I can usually pacify him by producing some tins of asparagus that Birt's sent me. Harry is now across the table writing feverishly.

My old Rolls razor broke down about a month ago. I bought another one, I have repaired the old one so possess two and 3 blades. Each blade should last 6 years so

I need not worry about buying any more for 18 years. The razors are fairly expensive but they are worth their weight in gold in wartime.

[The Rolls Razor was manufactured by Rolls Razor Limited, Cricklewood, London, England, it was a safety razor that used a permanent blade, rather than a disposable blade. It was packaged in a beautiful solid and compact metal case containing a self-sharpening device for the nickel-plated razor blade. The compact case had two removable lids - one on each side. Only one lid was removed at a time, and both lids contained a sharpening surface on the inside. One was a gray honing surface, only used occasionally, when the blade became blunt. The other sharpening surface was a strop, used to sharpen and maintain the blade between every shave. When not attached to the shaving handle for use, the blade remained inside the case, fitted into a fixed sharpening mechanism, protecting it from being damaged. The edge of the blade had a guide to prevent the blade from cutting too deep into the skin, making it safer than a cut-throat razor. The blade was stropped between each use and honed when necessary.][183]

I caught a rat this afternoon. He hopped into my tin trunk when the lid was open. I saw him go in and promptly closed the lid. We are still debating how to grab him when we open the lid. He is safe where he is and can only eat old socks.

I received a letter today from Dowling, the lad who went up to Gran G on his return to Australia. He tells me that he has been trying to contact you but can't because you are always out when he rings. He was a bit of a squirt but a hard worker over here. He mended the Coy boots.

Cheerio dear. No more news. Love to the girls.
All my love
Bill

PS I am enclosing a snap taken at Fraser's Hill during my leave - from the left Sister Raymont, Elaine Balfour-Ogilvy, Arch Ewart.

...

Darling Gran 11 Sep '41

I have some news for you about our new camp which we moved into recently.

We are living in tents. They are comfortable and safe when you remember where the ropes and gutters are. The camp is situated not very far from the sea and the surrounding county is pretty, palm trees etc.

A small town, very native, is close handy but it is of no use to us. The shops have a very limited stock and only sell goods suitable for the local natives. The town smells of fish and black people, not very pleasant. Before we arrived the locals made their money fishing, now they make it doing our washing.

There are only 9 or 10 white people permanently resident in this district. They would like to depart. They manage rubber estates. One white man I believe is employed by the Government to run the Customs business. The place has absolutely no amusement facilities but still we are happy.

Our tents are pitched here and there on the slopes of a hill overlooking a small beach and the sea. We have given the paths, roads and some of the tents familiar names. My troops occupy one side of Castlereagh St. I live in Wynyard Square. There is also Martin Place and many others.

We have no showers and washing is a funny business. We take a bucket behind a native grass screen and tip water over ourselves. I believe we are to have showers soon, until then we shall manage to keep clean somehow.

Dowling wrote to me. He said he had seen you and was trying to contact Mother. He is really quite a good lad but I think that soldiering was a little too much for him. He was always conscientious and worked hard. He was our boot-maker and was quite a good one.

Many of our lads have seen crocodiles and some have really seen tigers. However they have not managed to shoot any as yet. There are quite a lot of wild animals about. We find their tracks etc. often but rarely see the real thing. Personally I have not seen anything worth writing about in this camp.

After the war we will have many strange tales to relate. I have religiously kept a diary of our doings. Already it is worth reading and laughing over.

How is Nancy, Gran? I have not heard about Jim and Lorner [sic] for ages. Their son, young Ted, must be growing up fast now. Please give my regards to them dear.

Remember me to Moya.
Yours, Love
Bill

'Jim and Lorna' were Bill's uncle and aunt. James David Gaden was his father Noel's younger brother. His wife was Lorna R Jeanneret and they had married in 1932.[184] Son Edward James (Ted) was born in May 1940. Jim Gaden ran a farm near Jindabyne, NSW, on the Thredbo River. He was a keen fisherman, a member of the Monaro Acclimatisation Society, and the farm later became the Gaden Trout Hatchery, officially opening in 1953.[185]

Darling Doukie 14 Sep'41

I wrote to you a couple of days ago. The next few days may be busy ones so here goes for this letter.

I am sending you some money, £10. The system will be the same as last time. You wait until the pay office at Mary St. advises you that the money has arrived. Possibly they may send you a cheque. This cash is for yours and Sue's birthday. There is simply nothing in this town worth posting. The place is dead and dirty.

A few small things that I bought some time ago will be on their way to you very soon. They would not possibly fill a cake tin. Later I shall return the tins full of 'treasures'.

There is very little news. I wrote to Sue and gave her all the happenings.

Tonight is Sunday. The Salvation Army Hut is busting forth in song. The lads gather around an old piano and fairly yell. The Sallies hut is a structure made of grass and sticks and labeled GPO. The hut is waterproof and serves an excellent purpose. One Officer has to sing a solo song each Sunday night. My turn may come, but not if I know it. [The 2/20 had their own song book with the words to over 125 patriotic and popular songs of the time.]

Our tents are standing up well to the weather. Rain caused us a little trouble at first but now we are experts with tents. My troops had quite a lot of trouble with the first two decent showers of rain. Their tents were badly pitched. I made them take each one down and put them up properly, with new pegs and ropes. They moaned with the work but now they are very pleased.

I have lost my rising sun hat badge. Next time you are in town dear could you please buy me a couple. They can be bought in most of the big shops. The ones I require are the big chaps that we wear on the turned up side of our hats. By the way the unit has lost dozens of these badges. The Comforts Fund would be more popular than ever if a few could be sent to us. They are not really a necessity but they do mark us definitely as Australians. The local native Regiment wears turned up hats like ours and also some of the Indians. The Australian is the only soldier in the world who could still look really at home under our hats.

Some of Black Jack's officers have been along to see us. Capt. Bob Morrison, he got his commission with me, was in this party. Gee! I was pleased to see them. [Robert Harold Ker Morrison, NX121519, was in 2/30 Bn. He survived the war.][186]

Charles Moses [NX12404] is a Major. He talked his way into a job on Div Staff. Really he was given the boot from this unit because he talked too much and worked too little. The old dog certainly struck things pretty rich at HQ. He is now a staff officer, something I hope I shall never be and anyway I don't expect to have the opportunity. Charles has completely thrown us off his speaking list. He has been down in this area recently but he never really took the trouble to come and see us. He wrote a typed and very formal letter to us a few days ago wanting to know where some money was that we were supposed to owe him. As a crowd the unit says C---- Moses.

Cheerio dear. I hope to write again soon but because the next few days will be busy I may not have the opportunity.

Give Sue £2 and keep the rest dear. I know you shall both have very happy birthdays.

All my love

Bill

PS I have just discovered that I can send you a set of silver spoons cheaply by air mail in six separate envelopes. They should arrive all together.

A step up in fighting-readiness occurred when all ranks were advised that they had to carry respirators whenever they were absent from the Unit on duty for more than 24 hours. On such occasions respirators were not to be worn while in public places but held in readiness in such quarters as may be occupied during these periods.[187]

The Battalion's Routine Orders and War Diary for this time show the scope of the work put in by the troops. They trained hard and made extensive preparations. The men laboured for weeks to dig defensive works and they lived in dug-outs that they also constructed. The defensive works had trenches and weapon pits which all had to be timbered. They dug tank traps the full length of the beach; they rolled out barbed wire; they fortified the sites of the Vickers guns; they laid anti-tank mines; they constructed dummy roads for camouflage. The fire power was enormous and the defences at Mersing were very well prepared.[188]

Darling Doukie 19 Sep'41

The old postman was very good today. Two excellent letters. You must be making full use of the tennis court. I think that the game is great and excellent for the girls.

Fancy old Hordern loaning you the chairs. He should give them to you.

The Comforts Fund must be developing into a good show. If Mrs. Assheton is like her husband the organization will go ahead under her leadership.

I knew Mason, the lad who has been in touch with you. He is not a bad chap but he never really worked with us. I would have cheerfully left him at home because we knew at Bathurst that he would not 'take' the hard stuff overseas. Most of the men that have been returned are practically 'dead beats' where the army is concerned. Some of them are genuine chaps but most of them were just 'passengers' to us.

If you can, get in touch with Mansfield. He lost an arm in a motor accident. He is a really decent lad. He was in 'D' Coy for a while. He should be home soon.

The Battalion's *War Diary* shows there was a motor vehicle accident on 6 July 1941 and lists Private Robert James Auld (NX31973) as being the soldier involved who lost his arm. However Auld was not repatriated to Australia, an unlikely scenario with such a serious injury. He became a POW in 'E' Force in Borneo and died 5 June 1945.[189] There seems to be a case of mistaken identity in the *War Diary*. The actual soldier injured was Private Neville William Mansfield (NX32782). The Battalion's *War Diary* shows no record of any accident involving Neville Mansfield. However the Court of Inquiry papers show that Mansfield was the injured man, not Auld.

COURT Of INQUIRY held at Port Dickson and Malacca 15, 16 and 17 Jul. 1941. D.O.32/4556

INJURY (Accidental). FINDING:

1. NX32782 Pte. Mansfield, N.W. 2/20 Bn. and NX45720 Pte. Thompson, R.E. 2/20 Bn. were traveling in a 3 ton Chev. lorry L9037 on the night of 6 Jul. 41 when at about 2300hrs. this vehicle came into collision with Chev. 30 cwt. lorry L10894 on the Malacca-Port Dickson Rd. about 150 yds. south of the P.D. 3 mile pig.

2. The injuries sustained by the personnel mentioned were:-

(a) Pte. Mansfield - Traumatic amputation through the right upper arm - Fracture of right mandible (lower jaw bone), severe surgical shock.

(b) Pte. Thompson - Depressed fracture of right malar bone (cheek bone) and communited fracture (broken or crushed into many pieces) of the right maxillar (upper jaw bone).[190]

3. In the opinion of the Court Pte. Mansfield sustained the injury to his right arm in the following manner. He was sitting with his back to the offside of the lorry on his pack containing articles of clothing, sheets and mosquito net and it is considered had at least his right elbow resting on the top of the side of the truck. There is no direct evidence that any part of his body projected beyond the truck, but the inference is inescapable that his arm was at least resting as above described, and that either willfully or involuntarily, or as a result of the first impact of the two vehicles when the channel irons collided his arm became extended outside the truck and was shorn off as the centre canopy supports of the vehicles passed each other. With regard to the fracture of the right mandible the court has no direct evidence as to the exact detailed cause but considers that when Mansfield's arm was caught between the canopy supports of the two vehicles

his head and body would be swung around to his right and in all probability his right jaw collided with the canopy iron.

4. In the opinion of the Court Pte. Thompson sustained the injury to the right upper bones by being struck by the back of Cpl. Dalley's head. It will be seen from the evidence that Dalley was seated on the right of Thompson and the jolt of impact may well have caused both injuries as above suggested. Dalley states that he received a blow on the back of the head but made no complaint at the time. This was not serious and is not the subject of this inquiry.

5. The Court finds that Pte. Mansfield is permanently incapacitated for active service and accordingly reports that at the date of the accident his rank was Private and his rate of pay was: Deferred 2/-, Active 5/6, Allotment 3/-.

6. Pte. Thompson, on the medical evidence, will probably be able to resume duty on the 17 Aug. 41. He has a permanent minor deformity on the right side of the face with a slight asymmetry. He also has a disturbance of vision which is thought by the medical authorities to be only transitory.

7. Both Pte. Mansfield and Pte. Thompson were returning from leave in a military convoy and were under the orders of an officer. It is considered that they were on duty within the meaning of AMR&O 698 (5).

8. With regard to Pte. Thompson there is not evidence to suggest that he was guilty of a misconduct or negligence contributing to his injuries.

9. In the case of Pte. Mansfield as mentioned in Para 3. of this report, the court considers that at least his arm was resting on the side. It should be added that he was drowsing and says he does not remember having his arm either resting on or over the side of the vehicle, and it is a possibility in either case that the placing of his arm in either position was an involuntary act for which Mansfield was not responsible. Having regard to the possibilities the Court finds that he was not guilty of any mis-conduct or negligence contributing to the accident.

10. There is no evidence that either Mansfield or Thompson was in any way affected by intoxicating liquor.

Both William Bede Dalley (NX45236) and Pte Robert Edward Thompson survived the war.[191]

After the accident Neville Mansfield was transferred from the Port Dickson CRS to the 10th Army General Hospital on 12 July 1941, then to 2 Convalescence Depot Malacca on 2 September 1941 and ultimately disembarked from the hospital ship *Wanganella* on 2 October 1941 and discharged from service on 11 March 1942.[192] He joined the NSW Department of Agriculture and in the 1970s was to spend several years working with Bill's son Bob ... but not once did he mention to Bob that he had been in the 2/20 with his father.

Bill's letter of 19 September 1941 continued:

> I am not in reality OC 'D' Coy, although I have commanded the show practically all the time in Malaya. Charles Moses was my OC for a long time. He was always sick, in hospital, on leave or broadcasting. When work was about Charles was always absent. Capt. Rod Richardson is at present my OC on paper. I never see him. The CO has given him a special job so I run the Coy. In fact I have run the Coy ever since Bathurst. Rod Richardson was at Broughton School with me. We get on well together. He has been with the Coy for 3 days during the past 6 weeks. This suits me. All the lads, and most of all myself, consider 'D' Coy the best in the unit. Evidently many others do also because we are constantly receiving applications from other chaps to transfer in. We have our black sheep, but very few.
>
> Arch Ewart is with us again and is sparking. He is pleased that Jean [his wife] has made friends with Ginge and has been to our house. Jean is a nice lass. I do not know her well but I have met her.
>
> Arch saw a crocodile a few days ago. I suppose you have already heard the story. I believe he nearly trod on the reptile. I wish I had seen it because I could have gone into action with my portable artillery. I always carry my little weapon and a big army job. Anything alive on four legs or more runs a risk when it crosses my path these days. I also carry a native parang (long knife) and a handy type of pig stabber. These weapons are necessary for jungle work.
>
> The Salvation Army are really doing a great job for us in this camp. I was rather scathing about their preachings in previous camps but they have certainly come good now that we are more or less exiled from civilization. The Sally chap is a decent type of man. His name is Woodland. He turns on community singing, concerts and various other entertainments for the troops. Our church and the RCs are doing practically nothing. Woodlands [sic] is very popular with the troops. I can hear the click of ping-pong balls playing on one of his tables as I write.
>
> I hope the spoons arrived home safely. The cash should be with you soon. Cheerio dear. Love to the girls and Gran. I can't imagine Nancy G in a flat. I bet she turns on wild parties.
>
> All my love dear
>
> Bill

Nancy G was Bill's aunt Gwendoline Gaden, known as Nancy. She was the youngest of Noel's sisters and suffered from epilepsy. She did not get on well with her mother and, following her father's death, she moved into a flat away from her mother. Nancy was a sheltered child, she was never known to do any work, she didn't even know how to make a pot of tea. There was no way she would have known how to 'turn on a wild party'.[193]

The Woodland to whom Bill refers was George Woodland, one of the Salvation Army personnel allocated to the troops in Malaya. Salvation Army (SA) Major William Blaskett was with the 8th Division DHQ, SA Major Walter Birt was allocated to the Divisional troops and SA Adjutant James Kinder and SA Captain George Woodland worked at the Brigade level.

According to the Salvation Army magazine *War Cry* of August 1941, they arranged for messages to be sent home from troops passing through by train. They wrote out four hundred cables in seventy-five minutes for the grateful soldiers.

The troops really appreciated the work of the 'Salvos'. They provided writing paper and envelopes (300,000 sheets of paper and 26,000 envelopes reported in the Salvation Army newspaper *War Cry* of June 14, 1941). One soldier wrote *but for the Salvation Army I would not have been able to write this. Before we had been here 24 hours the Salvos had come along with equipment and writing materials.*

George Woodland organized Sunday night sing-songs at 'Red Shield House' within the camps where the motto was to 'bring your cobber and your mug'.

'An inspiring building' in Singapore was donated to the Salvos and opened as a Red Shield Centre in October and the local Chinese President of Rotary lent a piano for their use. *War Cry* also reported that a digger could walk in have a cup of coffee or tea and a huge buttered bun, toast or biscuits, have a read, play games or write a letter and it costs nothing.

The same newspaper told how hot meals were provided on Sunday with 175 men fed in groups of fifty. The menu consisted of stuffed roast duck and a variety of vegetables. Australian potatoes were sourced from a market sixty miles away and beans and cabbage also brought a long distance. By then the Red Shield had seven centres operating in Malaya. They reported 'Under trying circumstances we are doing our best for the boys who appreciate our efforts so much'.

The 'Salvos' organized mobile canteens to do the 'all night coffee patrol' when, keeping a weather eye out for Japanese planes, and sometimes carrying messages to troops, they would set up on a lonely road and provide a hot coffee and biscuit for passing troops, be they dispatch riders or troop trucks on patrol. They provided a cheer up for some mother's son. Their efforts were very much valued by the troops ... one night a patrol was stopped by the Salvos and offered coffee. The troops responded by offering the Salvo man a piece of Christmas pudding from their food tins from home, making sure that he was the one who found the three-penny piece they had surreptitiously slipped in.[194]

Darling Doukie 24 Sep'41

A parcel mail has arrived. I only received one parcel of books from Mrs. Fussell. The others must still be coming. Plenty of papers arrived. I have been reading your two *Smiths Weekly* tonight.

I mentioned in previous letters that this camp is practically exile. We just can't go anywhere because of three very good reasons, no leave, no transport and no place to go to. Still we are really happy here and I think we are all enjoying our isolated camp better than any we have previously been in.

The lads' sense of humour has improved to a marked degree. They turn on their own concerts etc. and have lots of fun. Something has developed in every one of us that has previously been dormant. Today a lad was told he had to stay in his tent all day because of his itch. This chap had a great day. He waited until some passer-by strolled past his tent and he would then yell out 'Get off my bowling green you ... ' or something equally silly. When a truck passed he would yell out 'One way traffic' etc.

> Last night our mess barman was seen squatting beside a dry drain with a long walking stick in his hand. He would proudly exhibit the 'fish' he was catching by pointing to a heap of empty beer bottles. His bait was a bottle opener. Most of us whistle up our dog every now and again. I heard a long whistle a few moments ago. There is not a dog within coo-ee but we all have them - and so forth.

The troops organised 'greyhound meetings' and had a lot of fun but some took the imaginary dog idea a bit too far. One soldier, 'Murty', wanted to be classed as mentally unfit and therefore be sent home. He took an imaginary dog everywhere he went, tied its lead to the chair and so on. However another soldier pinched the idea and did manage to convince the authorities he was mentally unstable. Once he arrived back in Australia he sent a card to 'Murty' 'You invented the dog but I rode it home'.[195] Bill's letter continued:

> Arch Ewart has a toy snake that has a very realistic appearance. He has used it to advantage everywhere. A couple of months ago we would have burnt the thing but now it helps to provide heaps of fun.
>
> I am sure that the local people think we are crazy but I defy anybody without an imagination and sense of humour to exist here.
>
> One of 'C' Coy troops yesterday ran madly in and out between tent ropes waving a stick. When he arrived at 'Martin Place' he stopped, jumped up and down and said to a Sgt. 'Hold my bloody horse'. Such is life.
>
> We have learned to anticipate some sort of nonsense around every corner.
>
> Until the last few days our officers have been working very hard. Lately however we have relaxed a little, mainly because our jobs are progressing smoothly, and pontoon schools have been in action. I have not been playing but many of the lads have knocked a lot of fun out of it. We also possess Monopoly sets and Chinese checkers.
>
> I listen to our newly acquired wireless and read some home newspapers. The wireless is quite a good set, battery, and the programmes are super. We were without a wireless for a couple of weeks and when the new one arrived it brought music that still sounds like nectar from the Gods.
>
> I read John Richards poems in the 'Advocate'. They are good. I hope this war will knock sense into JPR and knock out the filthy rot his mind used to be filled with.

This is one of John Richards poems printed in the *Scone Advocate* edition of 25 July 1941. John Pendemmis Richards, NX 47619, Gunner 2/4 Field Regiment: he was discharged 29 December 1942. He was born in February 1917 so was a few months older than Bill and no doubt one of the lads who he spent time with when growing up in Scone.[196]

> *The following verses were written by a young Scone gunner, under fire in an advanced observation post, in the recent Syrian push. 'Sonny Jim' is his mascot - a small black cat, which has already seen three campaigns:*

THE SMILE UPON THE FACE OF 'SONNY JIM'

When the shrapnel starts to fly,
From the shells that burst nearby,
And hardy gunners shake in every limb;
When I have one moment free,
I can drop my eyes, and see
The smile upon the face of 'Sonny Jim'.

And the confidence I gain
Is a thing I can't explain.
It seems to come from out those twinkling eyes,
A flame that's never gone;
Seems to signal, 'Carry on!'
And, like the Torch of Life, it never dies.

When I dive into a hole,
Flat out, digging like a mole,
I seem to hear him whisper in my ear:
'You can't scare me with a war,
I've been three times before;
So, cut out all the panic, d'yer hear!!'

So I take myself in hand,
Thinking, don't be stupid, and
Though snatches of this war are pretty grim,
You can bear up quite a while
If you emulate the smile
Of contentment on the face of 'Sonny Jim'.

There are some days when I find
I can read his small black mind;
He's thinking of the days of long ago:
'This forty-forty-one's,
A mere skirmish with the Huns,
But nineteen fourteen-eighteen was a show'.

But as for me, I say,
When these clouds have blown away,
In years to come he guides another chap
I know a small black cat
Will be purring 'I was at
The last World War--that WAS a scrap'.

Yes, he's just a little bloke,
And some treat him as a joke
As he swings there on his little silver chain,
But he radiates a charm
That keeps me safe from harm,
And I wouldn't lose him now, the world to gain.

When the shrapnel starts to fly
From exploding shells nearby,
And hardy gunners shake in every limb,
When I have one moment free,
I just drop my eyes to see
The smile upon the face of 'Sonny Jim'.

Bill's letter continued:

I have been out of writing paper and so has the canteen and normally I write twenty odd letters each week and the paper fairly flies away. Most of my letters are to various people I know in Australia and to fond mothers who are curious about their sons etc. You would laugh at some I receive. Also I write quite a stack of letters to people locally in Malaya who have been decent to the lads. And I sometimes write to my blokes when they are in hospital. What I really need is a nice blond shorthand typist. Please post me one 'on appro'.

One of my officers tells me that my old flame Cecily is about to 'spring a nipper'. Phil Murray told me. [Phillip Charles Murray NX34248, died 10 Feb 1942.][197]

I believe he knew Cec before he joined up. Last night I wrote to her but wasted my time because I have forgotten her address.

I have developed a patch of itch between the cheeks of my tail. 'It must be going to rain'- perhaps monsoons. Itch is really tinea. People called it Surfers Foot in Australia. I have a Surfers ω.

Cheerio dear. Love to the girls.
All my love
Bill

...

Darling Doukie 29 Sep '41

Today a decent mail arrived. Two of your letters and a couple of others from Margaret and the Wilkinson family were for me. Also a cheery note from Mrs. Waite. Things are looking up.

You are having fun with the Comforts Fund. You have no idea how pleased the lads are. They feel they are no longer 'the forgotten legion.' I agree with your endeavours to send us canteen orders instead of tobacco. The tobacco is great to receive because we have difficulty obtaining it over here but the canteen orders were super great. A number of my lads are in hospital. I posted them the orders and dished out the rest to 'deserving cases'. The lads really appreciated them. Capt. Richardson should have thanked you before this. A few minutes ago I gave him a 'dig in the ribs' about it. He will write today. Some new chaps have turned up to fill in the places of those who went back home. I noticed a lad from Scone and had a yarn to him. Heaven knows what his name is. I will soon find out.

Now have a good laugh. My new batman is Lennie Leadbeatter (-dinkum! He is a big tall self conscious lad about 22, a great chap). [Leonard James Leadbeatter NX25962, survived the war.][198]

Lennie has been with us ever since the show started. He always worked well but has not got the necessary oomph to push himself up in the Army. He came along the other day and pleaded with me to let him have a try at being a batman. I was only too willing and now Lennie has the job. He is doing well and really is much better than Smithy. Lennie never says a word. He just plods along and does things in a quiet sensible manner. Smithy is in hospital having a 'lump' taken out of his neck. The lads were pleased he went because ever since he left me he has been growling and grumbling. The boys say the tropics have 'got him'. Perhaps they have.

It is now nearly 4 o'clock in the afternoon. All morning I was in the bush working but this afternoon I am giving my itch a rest. The old itch is clearing up but is still irritating after a good sweat.

Yesterday was Sunday. Some of our officers hired a launch and went on a pleasure trip to some local islands. The day was hot and I stayed at home. Scared of sunburn. This boat was a small open crate and provided no protection at all. Last night when the lads returned they were a sorry sight - red and scorched like cooked prawns. This week we are having a cover made for the boat so I may venture out next Sunday.

We have been over here now for about 8 months. During that time I have spoken to only 37 different white women. This is really true. Occasionally we held parties at our old camp and brought along a few nurses. I knew only a couple of them at each party and we never had more than 20 at any of our shows. Apart from nurses I have spoken to Mrs. Ayrton (a thrill), Mrs. Hughes and daughter and a couple of virtuous matrons at our canteen.

Harry Woods has just been calculating hard. His total is 25. He did not have a spell in hospital at Singapore. I have another advantage over Harry because it took me 5 minutes to say 'No' to a Eurasian tart in Seremeban one night. He can't recall having had a similar opportunity of talking to a native woman. Most of us are in the same position. At home we used to see about 1000 each day and perhaps talk to 40 or 50. Now we see a few chinks and Malays each day and talk to ourselves. I am not complaining on behalf of the AIF but we would like to see more of the romance in 'this 'ere East'.

One of your letters dear, was written on the 23rd and I received it at lunch time on 29th. Really 5½ days to get here. Good work. I hope the post will break this record next mail.

I have kept my diary up to date and now it is really good to read. I wish I had recorded the dates on which I actually yarned with somebody who was not in the Army.

The canteen, the town and I have all run out of writing paper. I hope the office supply lasts. I can't stand that Salvation Army stuff.

Cheerio dear, love to Gran and the girls. This letter sounds cranky but really I am perfectly happy and enjoying a little peace and quiet this afternoon, 'calculating and figuring'.

All my love
Bill

...

Darling Doukie 3 Oct '41

A mail departed this morning. I missed it worst luck but this letter will follow on fairly soon.

A couple of days ago one of our drivers told me that he had taken several movie pictures of our lads working and playing in their various camps. He wanted to know if the Comforts Fund would like to see it. I gave him your address and he said he would write. The film is only very small size - 8 mm and will require a projector. I am sure that Kodak's would lend you one. The duration of the film will be about ½ an hour. More information will be forthcoming when you receive his letter.

Tomorrow I am going to Singapore with a couple of officers and shall have my birthday down there. I shall be able to buy Xmas presents, etc.

Your cable was a great surprise. I was very bucked by it. The spoons have evidently arrived, I was worried about them. They are excellent examples of Malayan silver.

News is difficult to find here. Nothing ever happens and we spend our days working.

I have been doing a good old bludge on the Army for the past few days trying to get rid of my itch. Sweating causes the itch to sting a little so I have been resting and reading.

Ginge, Doukie and Sue holding the cat

This is really the first time that I have ever taken 'time off' when in camp. Fortunately I have borrowed a couple of good mystery yarns to keep me busy. Today however I was back at it again and find that my ailment has improved 'out of sight' or nearly.

The tropics as you know make you feel sluggish and weary if you let the weather get you. We have coined a word, 'tid-apathy'. The Malay word tid-apa has a most expressive meaning, something like 'never mind' or 'don't worry', 'I don't give a damn' sort of thing. The new word is typical of the Australian soldier's happy-go-lucky acceptance of tropical conditions generally.

Arch Ewart is next on our list for a Majority. Fancy Jean thinking old Arch a 'sugar daddy'. I have never met a man more unlike one. My name is still very far down on the list. Anyway blokes of my age should not be thinking of such dizzy heights. Things are not going badly with me as they stand.

Connie has written and sent a photograph of yourself, Sue and Ginge. The snap is excellent of you but the girls are not too good. My old pal Jean Thatcher from Bathurst wrote and said that she had recently been photographed in Sydney and now she is determined to stay at home for the rest of her life. She reckons she knows what she really looks like now.

Up to date I have received a few letters with birthday greetings but no parcel. They will come along later I hope. I forgot to tell you. A letter of yours arrived about an hour ago just after I started this epistle. Thank you dear for all the news.

John Gaden is with BJ. [John Burton Gaden, NX26103, was in the 2/30 with 'Black Jack' Galleghan]. That is great news. I am all the more keen now to visit the lads. Up to date they have been far beyond my reach.

Our band will be full of style when they get their music. They are quite good but their operations have been hindered by the lack of music. We cannot buy band music in this country. They have gradually been making their own which is slow and not very satisfactory. You and your happy band are a God send to this unit.

Heaven knows what is wrong with Brian. His life should be paradise compared with ours. He is still back at base, of course, but that is where the comfort is. I can understand that he would grumble at leaving his old home at KL [Kuala Lumpur] but damn it, his present location is nearly as good. I don't think that old Brian is really moaning, and I do think that Mrs. Badgery is worrying far too much. I am very sincerely sorry that 'Mick and Marge' have both been ill recently.

Nancy must appreciate your visits dear. She appears to be just commencing to take an interest in life. Cheerio dear. My love to Gran and the girls.

Yours love
Bill

The film Bill referred to was made by Don Wall and Wallace Chauvel Lewis. It was 24 minutes long and an extensive coverage of life for the troops in Malaya. It showed the men on route marches, in the accommodation areas, with their weapons, digging deep trenches, laying wire and training as well as some shots of Singapore and the villages.[199]

During the time the AIF was in training and building fortifications, the Japanese were themselves busy. Colonel Masanobu Tsuji and ten staff officers of the Taiwan Army Research Centre were given twelve months for the task of collating all conceivable data connected with tropical warfare. This included weapon choice for humid conditions, amphibious landings, transport of troops on land, how to deal with malaria; in essence they developed a very practical 'soldier's hand book' full of helpful hints and useful information.[200]

As early as the beginning of 1941, Tsuji's deadline had been brought forward by six months. By October 1941 the Japanese rulers agreed they would set an internal and secret deadline to go to war with the Anglo-Americans. The Japanese planned to launch almost simultaneous attacks over a seven hour period on Malaya, Pearl Harbour, the Philippines, Hong Kong and the Pacific Islands of Wake and Guam. Operations in Burma were to start a week later.[201]

Meanwhile within the ranks of Allied Command some divisions were appearing. 'Operation Matador' was planned; this was to be a pre-emptive strike into Thailand to prevent Japanese troops from landing. It was a bold 'forward defence' plan but needed to be initiated twenty-four hours before the Japanese actually landed on the Kra Isthmus. South-East-Asian Commander-in-Chief Brooke-Popham wanted to make the final decision on its deployment himself but London refused this permission.[202] Britain wanted to avoid war with Japan at all costs and didn't want to be tricked into responding to a Japanese feint. This would give Thailand the opportunity to then appeal to the Japanese for protection. Britain's representative in Bangkok, Sir Josiah Crosby, wanted the Thai government to ask the British for protection against the Japanese. He considered it to be a matter of timing. He was also against the local military men being allowed to make the decision.[203]

Britain failed to inform new Army Commander Arthur Percival that they had set up a Special Operations Executive (SOE) force in both Thailand and Malaya. They were to be sabotage groups working undercover throughout the Malayan peninsula in the event of the Japanese overrunning the Allied defence. Crosby, worried about offending the Thai leadership, had foiled their work in Thailand, ensuring the operatives were deported from that country.[204]

When Percival learned of the activities of the SOE group who had been training recruits in Singapore, he was angry. He was also worried about morale, both civilian and military, should their work come to light. He argued that, as Europeans, they would be unable to merge in with the civilian population as their counterparts had done so successfully in Nazi occupied Europe. There was to be no army co-operation and SOE were asked to withdraw. However Churchill favoured their deployment so it was agreed they should work in Malaya but only close to the Thai border region.[205]

Percival was short of troops and equipment. He knew he did not have enough troops to assist SOE, he did not have enough troops to mount 'Operation Matador', he did not have enough troops to defend the whole of the Malayan peninsula and he did not have enough troops to defend Singapore Island following any fierce fighting that may have taken place on the mainland. Nor did he have any tanks and not enough of the promised aircraft.

Percival needed forty-eight infantry battalions and two regiments of light tanks capable of crossing the weaker wooden road bridges found in Malaya. He had just thirty-three infantry battalions and no tanks at all. The promised tanks, four hundred and forty-six of them, had been filtered away by Winston Churchill to support the Russians who had been invaded by the Germans, a futile gesture by the British Prime Minister as they were not as good as the Red Army's own tanks.

The Russians were given six hundred and seventy-six aircraft which should also have gone to the Far East. Percival desperately needed three hundred and thirty-six front-line planes which had been promised by London earlier in the year. By December 1941 he had just one hundred and forty five, of which none had the dog-fighting capabilities of the Spitfire. There were no long range bombers, no transports, absolutely nothing capable of matching the Japanese planes in the air.[206] Allied Command and their troops in Malaya were badly let down by Churchill and their other superiors who were overseeing the country's defence from afar.

Darling Doukie 6 Oct '41

I am enclosing a little piece of Siamese silver for your birthday. The lady engraved thereon is the 'Thai Goddess of War' so the jeweler told me. The natives use these clips to keep their flowing robes in the correct place when they go places. I hope you will be able to find a spot to stick it on when you go places. Genuine Thai silver ornaments are difficult to obtain in most countries. You can boast a little about this chap.

I spent a rather quiet birthday in Singapore. I told nobody of the 'happy day' and enjoyed it just by myself. There were three other young officers with me but none of us 'went on the spree'. We obtained leave for the weekend only to purchase Xmas presents. On the Sunday I shouted myself a special treat and accepted Ogilvy's invitation to afternoon tea at her new station a few miles out. The afternoon was really great and made me feel really cheerful. I had not seen the lass for a couple of months prior to Sunday.

We returned to camp early that night in the back of an old army truck. Heavens what a trip. Miles and miles of bumps and exhaust fumes. Saturday night in Singapore was quite a bright night although I went to bed early and felt super virtuous. After dinner we strolled through the crowded streets and inspected a few shops. This was not very exciting so the four of us took a taxi to the famous 'avenue of sin', Lavender Street.

We inspected a couple of dirty cabarets and saw the scum of Singapore. All slickered and revolting. These places were for the most part exactly similar to the Eastern dens that occasionally appear in Wallace Berry's pictures. We all received invitations from women of various nationalities but the very sight of them nearly made me sick in the gutters. The lowest price offered was $2 or 5/10 in real money.

I got fed up after about an hour and went back to the pub. The others stayed for a while but soon returned determined never to venture off the main street again. Later on they went to a dance of some sort but I was tired and went to bed early. The novelty of this country has completely worn off me. Some places are interesting but generally I feel that I have seen all that I want to see; for the time being anyway. I am hoping for leave soon and hope to do another week at Fraser's Hill.

I stayed at the Rex Hotel in Singapore and met a couple of decent chaps from Qantas Empire Airways. One of them knew me by sight. He used to catch the Neutral Bay boat. These chaps produced papers for us that were only 3 days old. They came straight from the plane. Raffles Hotel was booked out when we arrived and perhaps that was just as well. They charge 24/- for bed and breakfast so to speak.

Everything we want to buy over here is terribly expensive now. The shops know we are after presents for our people and they fairly rock on the prices. This has our chaps worried because on 5/- per day they just can't buy anything decent. I can remember the first afternoon I spent in town just after coming out of hospital. I thought that things were expensive then but now many things are 3 times as expensive without exaggeration. Even the taxis that used to be reasonable are tough. Fortunately I have plenty of money saved to see me through but I do feel sorry for my troops.

Your letters are all arriving dear. They are grand. I always look forward to them and the news. One arrived today, all about Gran having her lobster supper and the girl's tennis parties. I am pleased Ginge is playing well, she must be the belle of Neutral Bay these days. Sue has evidently recovered from her latest 'affair' - good old Susie.

Cheerio dear. My love to Gran and the lasses. All my love
Bill
PS Many, many happy returns

Security was stepped up with troops reminded that photography near military positions was not allowed and the identity of all persons using cameras near defensive works had to be clearly established by taking the offender to the nearest police post and confiscating the film. This week the strength of the Battalion increased with men returning from the sick list.

Among the many names listed was 'NX31973 Pte Auld R.J. 'B' Coy.' which confirms this soldier was definitely not the one who lost his arm in the motor vehicle accident on 6 July.

Darling Doukie 12 Oct '41

Your cake and the other parcel of treasures arrived last night. I got up in the middle of the night to collect them when they arrived. Thank you dear very much indeed. I am keeping the cake for a special occasion but the Fullers Earth has already been in action. [Fullers Earth was a talc-like powder which was used to absorb moisture. It would have been used to try and keep dry any skin subject to the unpleasant 'itch'.][207]
Agnes sent me a cake and a tin of strawberry jam. She also put a few sweets in the parcel. Margaret's parcel had a big pottery beer mug in it packed in oceans of paper

and packing. Jean Thatcher contributed a pair of sox, she did not know it was my birthday. Old Jean T is a sticker. Really I hardly ever saw her at Bathurst. I think she must regard me as her 'lonely soldier' or something like that.

Generally I did pretty well last night with everything except sleep.

This morning Harry Woods and I had a beaut morning tea of tinned fruit salad, cream and a heap of crushed ice. Ice is a luxury here. I fortunately saw the truck arrive with it.

Today, Sunday, is wet but our tents are dry. I am loafing about in underpants only.

Yesterday we had two super football matches on our own ground here. We have a beaut competition going and the standard of football is very high. Many of the lads over here have played for various states and even Australia. The games are fast, open and wonderful to watch. I have given football up. The sport is serious and requires too much time for training etc.

At last my itch seems to be really getting better. I won't know myself when it eventually clears up.

I am enclosing a couple of snaps dear. They were taken some time ago. You saw some of them before. I remember you mentioning it in your letters. The snap of our shield is particularly good. My cup, the 440 one, is on the right of the shield. Unfortunately I can't send home that cup. I have another small one here in the tent waiting for a parcel. I shall post it home in your cake tin when I have eaten the cake.

Today our church parade was taken by a C of E Padre. We normally have our Salvation chap. The service was dull and not a patch on the Sallies. We are all for the Sally Army, they do things.

How goes the Comforts Fund? According to our Major, Mrs. R [Robertson] seems to be doing all the work!! That is catty but is just between ourselves.

That verandah where I tried to sleep is a cow of a place when it rains. I wish old Mr. P would fix it up for you. He should, the old dog.

How is old Gordon Grierson [next door neighbour] looking? He has his share of worries in this world. I suppose Betty [Grierson] has decided to just 'sit and hope'. If she intends to cash in on her pretty face she had better start pretty soon.

Cheerio dear, love to Gran and the lasses.
Yours, all my love
Bill

Routine Orders by Lt. Col. C.F. Assheton Commanding 2/20 Bn. AIF 15 Oct '41 MALAYA included:-

SNAKE BITES Coys are to see that all working and recce parties carry with them at all times the necessary snake bite outfits.

SANITATION All ranks must be continually warned of the urgent necessity of keeping all latrine lids closed.

MALAYAN In order that personnel may learn progressively short Malayan phrases which may be of assistance later, a daily phrase will be published under NOTICES in B.R.O.'s and Pl Comds will check at weekends and ascertain proportion of men absorbing the language.

Berapa harga	=	How much (price)
Berapa jau	=	How far
Banyak Mahal	=	Too dear

Other phrases in later orders included:

Pukul berapa	=	What is the time
Nan Pergi	=	Where are you
Sila dudot	=	Please be seated
Nana awa datang	=	Where do you come from

The troops had been in Malaya since March ... why did it take so long for them to be taught some Malayan words and phrases?

By 15 October the adjutant was reporting morale was high and the defence plans had reached an advanced stage. One of the 2/20 Pioneers, Sgt Raven, had devised a trip wire for a Molotov cocktail which was successfully demonstrated to Brigade staff. More locations were placed out of bounds, these were Kokio Shokai, Japanese merchant, Jalan Awang, and S. Chooma, Photographer, Jalan Sultan, both in Segamat. Troops were considered to be in 'exceptional health', the best health since leaving Australia, with very few worried by skin complaints.[208]

Troops were also issued with another security warning:

> not to write, post, transmit, deliver or communicate to any person other than in the execution of his duty, any message of a secret or confidential nature, or is likely to be useful to the enemy, or relating to the numbers, description or destination of troops, transports or warships or likely to prejudice public safety, the defence of the Commonwealth, the efficient prosecution of the war, or the maintenance of supplies or essential services.[209]

Darling Doukie 27 Oct '41

News - plenty of it. I have been on the loose again ... Really scooting about. I spent last week end in luxury at the 'Sea View Hotel', Singapore. It was simply glorious after the old tent and dirt.

On Saturday morning I was doing a job a long way from here and suddenly found that I was half way to the big city when the job was finished. Fortunately I had brought my bag, packed, with me in case luck turned my way, and it did 'with a bang'. At 5pm I had booked in at the pub and had made arrangements for a party with another officer and a couple of nurses. Elaine came with her ears back and at 7.30pm we were all met and yarning at the 'Sea View'. This pub is easily the best in Singapore, including Raffles and the rest.

We had a super dinner, dancing between courses and eating far too much. Later we took the girls on a Cooks tour of Singapore's bright spots and they are numerous. We danced at the 'Great World' and inspected other places worth seeing. At 12.30pm our party broke up. The other half had to return to their respective work houses. Elaine and I carried on at the Singapore Swimming Club until 2am. She stayed with some 'approved' friends and I slept in luxury at the 'Sea View'.

The following morning we kicked off at 10.30 and walked Chinatown in search of Xmas presents and after lunch had a wonderful swim at the Club. Such doings would have seemed ordinary to me a couple of years ago but here it has a vast difference. I have only been really off the chain twice, at Fraser's Hill and now Singapore. I took my charge home at 5pm. She was to go out with a couple of Colonels or something to an official party at the Sultan's palace. I came straight back to camp without even having dinner. My tummy is not accustomed to the curried tiffins etc that I pushed into it. Today I am feeling extra sprightly and ready to work like a CPR locomotive. [CPR refers to the Canadian Pacific Railway, a long haul train over the Rocky Mountains.]

It is really worthwhile living in the 'ulu' for months just to really enjoy the simple things that are so normally taken for granted.

The tortoise was a slow old fellow. Your letter arrived at lunch time today. I had a good laugh.

Maj. Merrett has a very attractive beer garden rigged up. He is fortunate because he has his company away in a little camp of his own. We are stuck with the rest of the unit in a spot that is not nearly as attractive.

Cheerio dear - Black out tonight. Love to Gran and the girls.
All my love
Bill

Officers and men continued to transfer between different regiments for observation and training purposes. In late October the Battalion's *War Diary* reported that Capt. JM Lowe detached to and Lieut Wan Rahim B Ngah attached from the Johore Military Forces for one month. Lieut Stanistreet, Lieut Brooks and 12 OR's detached to the 1st Manchester Bn for one month and 2 officers (Lieuts Gardner and Gaisman) and 12 OR's from 1st Manchester Bn attached to the 2/20 Bn for 1 month. One soldier went to assist the Salvation Army Welfare Officer whose work was 'much appreciated'.

Darling Doukie 3 Nov '41

A couple of your letters are with me waiting to be answered. I have been going like blazes lately and just haven't had time to write before this.

I am terribly sorry Nell Giblin passed away. I never knew her but I know she was a very dear friend of yours. [Nell Giblin was Eleanor Giblin, the daughter of Donald and Ann.][210]

Xmas is nearly with us. Everybody is posting parcels full of rubbish. I shall send you all something in my air mail envelopes later and post only one parcel.

Tomorrow the Melbourne Cup is to be run. Sweeps are going everywhere. The lads are terribly keen about it. I have drawn a couple of fair horses. Worst luck; the mail closes tomorrow morning so I shall have to let you know the result in my next letter.

Mrs. Waite wrote me a long letter. She is very anxious to write to a 'lonely soldier'. I told her that there are thousands of lonely soldiers over here, but, so far as I know, they are all receiving letters fairly regularly.

What are the girls generally doing at home? A whole bunch of my chaps have been 'jilted' or something similar. The lads don't take it badly but at the same time many of them would like to have a crack at the men at home who talk about 'V' for victory etc.

We have our own cards printed for posting home at Xmas. They are not a brilliant effort but sufficiently good enough.

Major Maud, Major Robertson have had their holiday. They went to Fraser's Hill and stayed at Staff House, the place that Arch and I hired. The house has become a boarding house now. They had a great time and are full of stories. Last weekend they both went down to Singapore on shopping leave. Neither of them had seen the big city before and both were much impressed. I am going down there with Arch in the near future. We hope to stay at a small pub and do things quietly. I have had enough of gay life in Singapore to last me for many a long day and Arch complains that he is broke so we should get on fairly well together.

We have a young Malay officer staying with us. He is only on loan from a native military show. We have to be darned careful with our references to natives and also with our opinions generally. He speaks English better than most of us which is a little disconcerting at times. Capt. Jim Lowe has gone to the natives (there were some units of local soldiers) on loan. He knows more about the language than the rest of us. I can talk about most things with the 'boongs' but have not had the practice to talk fluently.

Cheerio dear. More news next letter. Love to Gran and the girls.

Yours All my love

Bill

Capt. Jim Lowe (NX35117) had been born in Gorahkpur, India in 1909.[211] He may have been fluent in some of the languages of the other Allied troops.

Enclosed in this letter was the Battalion Christmas card.

Darling Doukie 8 Nov '41

I have just returned from a night out in the scrub, a little tired, dirty but quite happy. We were on an exercise.

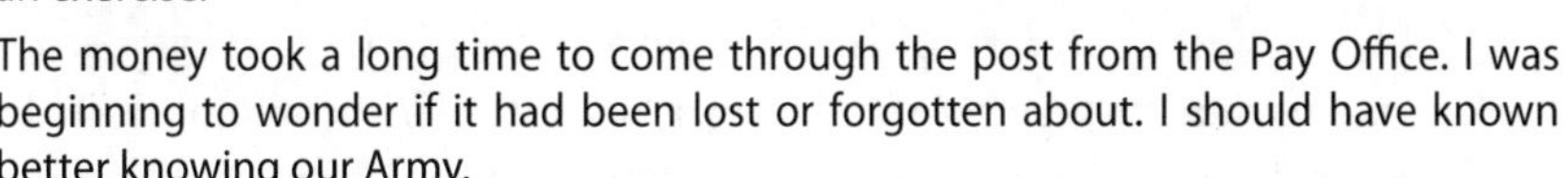

The money took a long time to come through the post from the Pay Office. I was beginning to wonder if it had been lost or forgotten about. I should have known better knowing our Army.

The things you send us from the Comforts Fund are being properly looked after and distributed. We have one on the job doing practically nothing else. At present Porter is in sole charge. We are getting quite a heap of stuff from home both from yourself and the ACF [Australian Comforts Fund]. Until recently we were not getting anything at all from ACF.

The latest acquisition to our show is a Salvation Army mobile canteen. These are really a blessing and do a grand job. Woodland, the Sally bloke, drives it round the camp and into every area where the lads are working both night and day. He gives them hot coffee and biscuits free.

A party is going full swing in the bar led by Major Merrett. I drew out quietly to write this letter. We have a young officer from an English unit with us and he is being royally entertained to his own bewilderment.

Your last few letters have mentioned several of the lads' mothers. Keep it up dear. The chaps are always pleased to hear about their people even through me.

I doubt that I have ever felt better physically than I do now. I have lost heaven knows how much weight but it must have been fat because I don't want it back. I sweat nearly twice as much as anyone else round here. The reason is simple, I run round more I suppose.

Arch Ewart has left us for hospital again. He has another slight dose of malaria the Doc tells me. Most of the chaps are back with us again from hospital who developed the disease some time ago. They are all pretty well and so far as I know they are not having periodic bouts. This camp is evidently pretty clear; we are only getting an occasional case.

The Monsoon rains are certainly heavy but hardly as bad as they are painted. It rains really hard for about an hour or so each day with an extra shower thrown in sometimes. The rest of the days are clear and bright. I think the weather is more pleasant during the Monsoon than at other times. I did not care for the long days of hot moist heat. They seemed to sweat out your energy and leave you with a perpetual thirst for booze. Cheerio dear. Love to Gran and the lasses

Yours love

Bill

PS I hope Ginge enjoyed her weekend at Bowral. By the way I believe that Gran G's income has been reduced to £250 per year now that Nancy has decided to live away from her. That will rock the old lady a bit.

This was a clause in her husband, Edward Ainsworth Gaden's will; her income was to be reduced from £400 to £250 should daughter Nancy move out.

The *War Diary* of 9 November showed that NX72769, Pte PE Lane was repatriated to Australia as he was under age. The DVA Nominal Roll shows NX72769 as being John Farrell. He was in 2/19 Battalion and died in the battle for Singapore. A search for PE Lane delivers two, Patrick Ernest Lane, N444985, date of birth 2 December 1924 (so aged 17 years) and Peter Ellis Lane, NX205668, date of birth 9 October 1926, so just 15 years old. Both survived the war and were discharged from the army at war's end.

The Routine Orders of 10 November mentioned the work of the Comforts Fund, advising that the Younger Set of the 2/20 Bn Comforts Fund were raising funds to provide for a Christmas tea and party for the troops' children. The men were advised to let their relatives back home know about the party and to contact the secretary Elizabeth Gaden, Bill's sister Ginge. Also acknowledged was the arrival of 900 packets razor blades, 900 packets tobacco, 180 tins of soup and 180 bars of soap.

This same Routine Order listed Bill as captain of the rugby team to play the rest of the 22nd Brigade.

Darling Doukie 10 Nov '41

A few letters ago I mentioned a film that one of our lads Pte Wall had taken over here and was sending across to Australia. Wall tells me that the film will be posted on Monday to his mother in Victoria next Monday by air mail and should arrive there about 20th Nov.

He is loaning the film to many people and organizations in Australia and I thought you would like it to be shown at one of your meetings or Comforts Fund parties. To that end I told Wall that I would ask you to write to his mother and arrange a date for the showing of the film. Mrs. Wall I believe will be in Sydney during the first week in December and could hand it to you then. I have not seen it but from an account it is a good show and is full of the lad's camps, parades etc in Malaya. Please write dear it will be worth while. The address is:

Mrs. CW Wall, c/o Mrs. L L Beauchamp, 4 Dudley Street, Brighton, Victoria.

The film is eventually to be passed on to a Newcastle CF and also a group of supporters at Parramatta.

Bob Stanistreet is an officer in our show. He was with me in the old 17th. At present Bob is far away in the ulu on a detached job but liking it. We call him 'Shicker Street' or just 'Shicker'. [Robert Woolcoot Stanistreet NX59135 survived the war.][212]

At last I am going brown. I can now exhibit my back with pride. The freckles are still there in millions but the pinky white background has gone. Whacko.

Yesterday I posted cards to everyone I can remember as a friend in old Australia. Dozens of them. Today your letter arrived, the one with the cutting about our dogs. Our 'sport' spread quickly to old New York didn't it.

The flats that the Blaxlands have taken are super. I wanted one of them but always thought they were more expensive.

I am really sorry that Mrs. Fowler has developed mumps. She should have 'grown out of them' years ago.

For heavens sake don't hire any Malay 'boongs' as houseboys. They are lazy and I think most irresponsible. The people here have mostly Chinese 'boys'. They are not bad but in any case they are always trying to cause trouble somewhere behind a passive, expressionless face. I never want to see a 'boong' when I sail again from this country.

Howard Porter is a decent young lad full of the joy of spring and what have you. I am glad you know his mother. Love to all dear
All my love
Bill

Howard Wilton Porter NX12556 was in charge of distributing the 2/20 Comforts. He was subsequently killed in the fighting on Singapore Island on 9 February 1942.[213]

At this time a Divisional exercise took place followed by a rest camp on Babi Kechil South Island which was located off the coast of Mersing, slightly north-east, taking about half an hour for the trip. The 2/20 boys went twice a week, on Mondays and Fridays. They were transported from Mersing Wharf. On the island duties were reduced to a minimum. It would have been a welcome and relaxing respite for the men, with beautiful beaches and good surf for sport and swimming.[214]

Darling Doukie 20 Nov '41

I am enclosing a little Xmas present for you. I hope you like it. The stones are moonstones, not very valuable but rather pretty. [Moonstones, a type of feldspar, are mined in Burma. They have a silvery blue-white colour which changes in relation to the light reflected from the cleavage planes on their surface.][215]

Last Saturday I played football in Singapore for the AIF. The game was a bit of a failure but the weekend was good. We played the Singapore Cricket Club and they fielded a strong team incorporating the British Army and Navy. The score was 24 to 6, we got stouched. Possibly you have read about it.

Whilst in Singapore I met some of the officers from my old North Sydney Unit and we kicked the tin a little. A couple of days ago we spent a sleepless night out in the rubber on an exercise. I didn't enjoy it much because rain was pouring a large part of the time and we were soaked.

Finding time to write letters these days is a bit of a trial. There always seems to be some work waiting to be done and demanding attention. David B-P has written to me but his letters did not mention his many troubles. The army should give him a soft job somewhere.

David B-P is thought to be Captain David George Bjelke-Petersen, NX12211, of Neutral Bay. His father Harald Frederick had married Isabel Davis in 1910. Harald was one of the Bjelke-Petersen siblings who ran a School of Physical Culture founded by brother Hans Christian in 1892. They ran courses of tailored exercise for men and women and had gymnasiums in Sydney, Melbourne and Hobart. They were responsible for a system of Physical Education in schools in the First World War and Harald was a recognised expert writer on matters relating to health and physical culture. He died in 1936. Classes were held in businesses such as Anthony Hordern, David Jones, Nestlés, and W.D. and H.O. Wills. The company is still in existence today, with students performing at events such as the opening and closing ceremony of the Sydney Olympic Games.[216]

Mail is not coming in to us satisfactorily these days. It is a long time since I received a packet and I feel sure there are packets on the way. It is a long time since I received one of your letters and longer still from most other people in Australia.

I am sending the girls a little Siamese silver brooch each. Their letters should catch the same mail as this one.

Birts have sent me another colossal parcel of tinned food and chewing gum. They are stickers. I am most amused at the impersonal short notes they put in the parcel. I always called the girls Miss So-and-So and they never include a personal note although I know they would like to scribble 'love from Joan' or something like that. I know!

I am gaining weight and looking more healthy then ever. Many of us are doing likewise. I can't help noticing how well the chaps look that came to this damned country with the first batch. Cheerio darling. More news next time.
All my love
Bill

...

Darling Doukie 23 Nov '41

Such a feast of letters from you today; five of them. The post people have been hanging on to our mail in the approved style and now they have flooded us with mail.

I shall get my news down on paper before I forget it and later shall answer your questions.

Last Saturday I played football for Johore against the RAF. The game was good but the ground wet and sloppy.

After the game I went to Singapore and thoroughly enjoyed a quiet peaceful weekend with a couple of chaps from here. We had to stay at a pub but this was OK because all we wanted to do was sleep and wallow in a hot bath.

I am enclosing a small necklace. The thing is very ugly and common but its origin is most interesting. I found it in a Chinese jewelers shop in the filthiest back street I have ever seen in Singapore. I paid approx 1/- for it after beating the chow down from $5 (15/-).

Singapore is becoming worse than ever as a leave centre for us. Our main recreation down there was drinking amid the colourful surroundings provided by its pubs and clubs. Now drink restrictions have come into force and we look at each other saying 'what the hell will we do'. There just is nothing to do unless you take a nurse to the respectable places and have your pockets fleeced. The picture-shows stink of sweating 'boongs' and the officers are not allowed to dance in Cabarets with taxi girls; not that we want to, but it would help to pass the time pleasantly and cheaply. Our nurses are stationed in outlandish places and even if we do manage to get one as far as the big city they have to leave early to get home at a reasonable hour. Sometimes they manage to stay in Singapore with friends but these occasions are rare and luxurious. I have not seen or heard from Elaine for a long time but that is not giving me much concern.

I have not seen John Barton for a long time. He is well and sparking because I have seen some of his friends.

We have an officer attached to us who has spent a long time in Australia and lived in Neutral Bay. His present job is rubber planting when the Army doesn't want him. His name is Capt. MacDonald. He started a lending library in Military Road called Bookery Nook some years ago.

In the various Cup Sweeps around camp I drew 5 horses. They were all duds but I have most of my money back.

I discovered that the broaches [sic] I posted to Sue and Ginge are really gentleman's tie pins. However they are suitable for ladies in my opinion.

Mrs. Badgery has posted me a bundle of magazines and a packet of butterscotch for Xmas. I have not seen old Brian for a long time.

Has Tony Walter been located? The last I heard he was 'missing' somewhere. [He was a POW of the Germans.]

Howard Porter has been on leave. I think he shall continue on his job, distributing Comforts, when he returns.

Your parcel of Xmas goodies has arrived. Thank you very much dear for everything. Somehow you seem to know exactly what I want. I still suck the coffee and milk straight from the tin. The golf tees will come in handy. A standing joke here is to say to some lucky lad opening a parcel 'Don't forget to send back the tin'. I won't.
Bye dear.
All my love
Bill

British Command became well aware of Japanese troop movements occurring at this time. On 27 November a signal was received from a Special Operations Executive (SOE) group at Tanjong Balai, a busy port on Karimun, one of the Riau Islands off the east coast of Sumatra. It warned of a build up of Japanese troops. The signal advised there was abnormal transport activity and 10,000 Japanese troops had been withdrawn from China that week and issued tropical kit. Plenty of merchant ships were available to move them.[217]

By 29 November Air Headquarters at Singapore were warned to be ready to launch 'Operation Matador' at 12 hours notice.[218] Australian troops were issued with ball ammunition, sentries were doubled, and steps were taken to combat fifth columnists in the Mersing area.[219]

On 30 November, at Samah Harbour in Hainan, Southern China, the Japanese Commander Lieutenant-General Tomoyuki Yamashita received a message. '*X day December 8. Proceed with plan*'. Tokyo had set the date of the invasion.[220]

The battleship HMS *Prince of Wales* and battle cruiser HMS *Repulse* docked in Singapore harbour on 2 December.[221] HMAS *Vampire* was part of the escort.[222] The light cruiser HMS *Durban*, which had escorted the troops on *Queen Mary* to Singapore back in February had been there for four weeks. They were joined by destroyers *Jupiter, Electra, Express* and *Encounter* all of which looked a 'bit battered'. These ships were all that could be spared from the war effort in Europe to help protect the distant British colonies. The aircraft carrier HMS *Indomitable* was meant to be with them but it was undergoing repair so had not arrived. Thus there was no air protection for the fleet. However the sight of the ships was a great boost to the morale of all.[223]

Lieutenant-General Percival allowed two Divisions of the 3rd Indian Corps to be sent north to unleash 'Matador' should the need arise. One division was to be allowed to go into Thailand. They were raw, only partially trained soldiers and he needed plenty of time to train them, time he no longer had. Nor did he have the junior officers, the Lieutenants and Captains who could speak Urdu and Gerkahal, to do the training; those officers had been sent to fighting battalions in Europe to keep up their strength against the Germans and Italians.[224] Why did he not send the more highly trained and seasoned Australian troops to meet the threat?

The increase in tension was obvious from Bill's next letter when he refers a couple of times to a 'crisis' but the bulk of his letter remains light-hearted.

Darling Doukie 3 Dec '41

Today a longer letter arrived with a note from Sue enclosed and also a scratch from the Singapore bloke.

I don't think I shall go to the Cameroon Highlands. Principally because he says in his letter that the place is all on its own in a nice quiet spot. Heavens I have been out in the 'ulu' for so long now that my holiday when it comes will be bright and noisy for preference.

We are in the middle of a crisis and a monsoon, so we have decided that a 'crisoon' has now arrived. Everybody seems to be in a bit of a flap except us, we are taking things peacefully.

There is even less news than usual dear for this mail. The letter may be a short one.

Ron Eaton came to see me a couple of nights ago. He arrived at 8 o'clock. I was out at a football meeting. The lads had pumped plenty of grog into him and he was pretty lively when I saw him. He is well and apparently happy with old Black Jack. [Ron Eaton NX70758 worked with Bill at Birt & Co. He was with 2/30 Bn.]

I have been whacking into some of the tinned stuff that the office has been sending me. Nestles cream and strawberry jam cakes, a delightful mixture but is really a bit too rich. I saw some of my troops earlier tonight enjoying a three course dinner out of tins from home. A couple of nights ago a party of officers led by Major Robertson each produced a couple of tins of something. We heated the lot over a primus and a tragedy occurred. The labels were boiled off the tins. The answer to this problem was obvious. As each tin was opened the contents was distributed evenly over all our plates and the final mixture was excellent to look at, awful to smell and surprising to taste. From memory our feast included tins of hamburger steak, sausages (super greasy), tomato soup, tomatoes whole, brussel sprouts, baked beans, spaghetti, and more beans. The party was a particularly merry one and was improved by Major M who seriously announced, at one stage of the show, that 'the fruit salad was hexalent'. He was eating baked beans out of a tin with a fork. The brussel sprouts gave off an awful odour. They nearly broke up the party, until we discovered it was the brussel sprouts.

I have been warned about going for another trip north to the Indians. The warning means; pack up and be ready to leave at a moment's notice. Owing to the crisis this visit is off for the time being. I hope it will soon be on again. I thoroughly enjoyed my last visit some months ago. Cheerio darling. My love to Gran and the lasses.
All my love
Bill

The day after Bill wrote that letter, on 4 December 1941, seventy Japanese battleships and transport ships full of troops and equipment, left Samah (on the Chinese island of Hainan which had been under Japanese occupation for two years) and headed south.[225] The equipment included 50,000 copies of a map of Malaya with Japanese characters and also many copies of a Japanese-Malay pocket dictionary. The presence of these supplies had been reported to the army hierarchy in Britain by their acting Consul-General in Saigon.[226] The British Government must have realised an invasion of Malaya was so very imminent.

On 5 December 1941 Air Chief Vice-Marshall Sir Robert Brooke-Popham, the Commander-in-Chief of all land and air forces in Borneo, Burma, Hong Kong and Malaya (which had been placed below the Middle East and Russia on the priority list) was finally given permission by London to launch 'Operation Matador' provided he 'had good information that a Japanese expedition is advancing ... to Kra Isthmus.'[227] The British Government were very concerned that they could be tricked into entering Thailand (to repel the Japanese) and then have the Thai government 'invite the Japanese' to assist against the British invaders. British Ambassador to Bangkok, Sir Josiah Crosby and the Thai Foreign Minister had appealed to Brooke-Popham: *For God's sake do not allow British Forces to occupy one inch of Thai Territory unless and until Japan had struck the first blow.*[228]

Unfortunately Brooke-Popham had already been advised that on 23 December he was to be replaced as Commander-in-Chief by General Sir Henry Pownall. He was serving out his notice. This was a huge blow to his confidence. He was wracked by indecision; what if he got it wrong?[229] A man whose authority had been so undermined by Churchill's dismissal notice was not going to make such a momentous decision.[230] No wonder that when the time came he did not order the launch of Operation Matador.

In his next note home Bill was more uneasy than in earlier letters. It was not a cheerful, chatty letter, but a more sober response to the situation. He said he was posting home his Savings Bank Pass Book by surface mail. This would ensure his mother had some money available should fighting break out and Bill be injured ... or worse.

Darling Doukie 5 Dec '41

This will be a short scratchy note but it is a letter and that's the most important thing.

Letter arrived from you and Gran this morning. Thank you very much. The sketch is grand. If you have any more please send them over. I know they take up a lot of time so I won't hope for many. I shall post you some of mine next mail.

The canteen order you posted was 'drunk' and enjoyed long ago. I should have let you know before this. The orders that Gran kindly sent me will be put to similar use no doubt.

I have made an allotment of £1.1.0 per week to my Savings Bank acct. I am posting you my pass book by surface mail. If you are stuck for cash at any time the money will be available for you to draw. Please send me across a few withdrawal slips and I shall sign them for you. You can fill in the amounts as you require them. With my deferred pay I am now saving £2.12.6 each week in addition to a credit balance of £30 or so in my paybook. By the way I increased your allotment 1/- per day 'Mrs. Spenders rise'.

Many of the chaps here are having mild financial trouble. They are spending their money on local junk and whacking up big mess accounts. I am quite happy but am keeping expenses low without being miserish.

Gran's holiday at Wollongong must have been a great break for her. She is surely going to the dogs.

Cheerio dear. I must catch the mail. I shall write a better letter soon.

All my love

Bill

On 6 December two days of typhoon storm passed, the weather cleared, and two Australian reconnaissance planes were able to spot about 70 Japanese warships and transports. They informed their bases but lost sight of the ships when they had to return home low on fuel. No one knew where the ships were heading. At 1800 hours the warning order 'RAFFLES', the pre-designated emergency code-word, was given to all units.[231] Troops moved by road transport to their prepared defensive positions. The *War Diary* of the day reported that troops were keen and morale was high.

More bad weather was to then cost the Allied planes another 30 hours of vital information.

Just after midnight, local time, a signal was flashed to Singapore H.Q. from the 8th Brigade at Kota Baharu that three Japanese warships were anchored off the coast of Malaya and their troops were wading ashore. Other signals also reported Japanese landings in Thailand at Patani and Singora. These were the exact ports where invasion was anticipated. They could have been covered if 'Operation Matador' had only been implemented twenty-four hours earlier.[232]

On 8 December 1941 at 0830 hours a Catalina flying boat from RAF 205 squadron in Singapore located the Japanese fleet but was shot down without radioing its position. The crew became the first casualties of the war between Japan and the Anglo-Americans. Japanese bombers attacked the Keppel Docks Naval Base at Singapore.[233] It would be another 10 hours before the attack on Pearl Harbour.[234] Why were the American authorities not prepared?

At 1545 hours on 8 December the Japanese fleet was finally located well north of Kota Baharu and its destination was obvious, heading towards landing places with many soldiers visible on the transports decks.[235]

All Allied troops were put on alert, quinine was issued as a malaria suppressive measure.[236]

Percival was surprised that 'Operation Matador' had not been launched by Brooke-Popham but realised how important it was not to precipitate a war with Japan. He even wondered if perhaps the Japanese troops were 'only a demonstration against Thailand'.[237]

At 1735 hours the British war ships which were berthed in Singapore's harbour, sailed north to find the Japanese fleet. They had no air support. It was to prove a fatal mistake.

By 1848 hours on 8 December 1941 Allied aircraft confirmed some Japanese vessels had landed at Singora and Patani and deployed their troops via landing craft. The chance to implement 'Operation Matador' had long gone, it required a 24 hour start over the enemy. By his indecision, Brooke-Popham had lost his opportunity to make an early strike against the Japanese. It was now too late.[238] The Allied forces had been dithering at the starting gates whilst their competitors took advantage of their indecision.[239]

Would 'Operation Matador' have stopped the Japanese? According to Ong it would certainly have held them up for a while, allowing time for Allied reinforcements to arrive; for how long is only in the realms of speculation. The myth persists that the British were surprised by the landward attack and their guns at Singapore pointed uselessly out to sea. This is incorrect. The steady progression of defence plans from Singapore Island Naval Base to then include the Malaya peninsula and then forward defence on the Kra Isthmus and 'Operation Matador' showed the British were expecting the attack to occur in precisely the way it did.[240]

[172] Smith, *Singapore Burning*, p. 57.

[173] Dimmock, Edna, House in Johore, The Road that leads to Singapore, *Sydney Morning Herald*, 24 January 1942, p. 11.

[174] *Rainforest animals: Common Palm Civet* < http://www.animalport.com/rainforest-animals/list/Common-Palm-Civet.html >

[175] Dimmock, Edna, *op. cit.*, p. 11.

[176] DVA Nominal Roll - NX55850.

[177] *War Diary 2/20 Bn. A.I.F.,* 12 Sep 1941.

[178] Routine Orders 2/20 Bn. A.I.F 29 Aug 1941.

[179] DVA Nominal Roll and Wall, *Singapore and Beyond*, p. 366.

[180] *War Diary* and Routine Orders 2/20 Bn. A.I.F. 3 Sep 1941.

[181] *ibid.*, 3 and 6 Sep 1941.

[182] DVA Nominal Roll.

[183] High-tech shaving < http://www.geocities.com/RodeoDrive/3696/Intros02.html?200825 >

[184] NSW BDM index, 13823/1932.

[185] Gaden trout hatchery < http://www.ausemade.com.au/nsw/destination/j/jindabyne/gth/gaden-trout-hatchery.htm >

[186] DVA Nominal Roll.

[187] Routine Orders 2/20 Bn. A.I.F., 12 Sep 1941.

188 *War Diary* and Routine Orders 2/20 Bn. A.I.F. Sep 1941 and Willcocks, *2/18 - Without glamour, the social history of the 2/18 Bn.*, p. 154.
189 DVA Nominal Roll and Wall, *Singapore and Beyond*, p. 371.
190 Dental terms < http://www.thefreedictionary.com/malar+bone > and < http://www.medterms.com/script/ > and <http://www.answers.com/topic/maxilla?cat=health >
191 DVA Nominal Roll.
192 Court of Inquiry documents sent to author by Graham Mansfield, son of Neville William Mansfield.
193 Bob Gaden, personal communication.
194 Hull, *Salvos with the Forces*, pp. 155-176.
195 Willcocks, *op. cit.*, pp. 197-198.
196 DVA Nominal Roll.
197 *ibid.*
198 *ibid.*
199 Wall and Lewis, *Malayan Moments*, AWM F03436.
200 Smith, *Singapore Burning*, p. 66.
201 *ibid.*, p. 107.
202 *ibid.*, p. 77.
203 *ibid.*, pp. 77-8.
204 *ibid.*, p. 81.
205 *ibid.*, p. 82.
206 *ibid.*, pp. 76, 97-99.
207 Fuller's Earth < www.netdoctor.co.uk/ate/childrenshealth/1203209.html >
208 Routine Orders and *War Diary 2/20 Bn. A.I.F.*, 15-24 October 1941.
209 *ibid.*
210 NSW BDM 22206/1941.
211 DVA Nominal Roll.
212 *ibid.*
213 *ibid.*
214 Google maps < http://www.google.com.au/help/maps/tour/ >
215 Moonstone, < http://www.exoticindiaart.com/jewelry/moonstone/ >
216 DVA Nominal Roll, NSW BDM record of marriage 57/1910 and record of death 14815/1936 and < http://www.australiadancing.org/subjects/4021.html >
217 Taylor, British Preparations,<http://www.britain-at-war.org.uk/WW2/Malaya_and_Singapore/html/body_british_prepare.htm >
218 Malaya-Singapore; tragic incompetence < http//www.diggerhistory.info/pages-battles/ww2/Malaya.htm>
219 Ziegler, *Men May Smoke*, p. 16.
220 <http://www.britain-at-war.org.uk/WW2/Malaya_and_Singapore/html/body_chronology_of_malaya.htm>
221 Falk, *Seventy Days to Singapore*, p. 63.
222 Malaya-Singapore; tragic incompetence < http//www.diggerhistory.info/pages-battles/ww2/Malaya.htm >
223 Smith, *op. cit.*, p. 96.
224 *ibid.*, p. 83.
225 *ibid.*, p. 116.
226 *ibid.*, p. 111.
227 Ong, *Operation Matador*, pp. 204-5, 249.
228 *ibid.*, p. 232.
229 Smith, *op. cit.*, p. 117.
230 Ong, *op. cit.*, p. 232.
231 <http://www.britain-at-war.org.uk/WW2/Malaya_and_Singapore/html/body_chronology_of_malaya.htm>
232 Parkinson, *Blood, Toil, Tears and Sweat*, p. 326.
233 Malaya-Singapore; tragic incompetence < http//www.diggerhistory.info/pages-battles/ww2/Malaya.htm>
234 Ong, *op. cit.*, p. 232.
235 Smith, *op. cit.*, p. 120.
236 *War Diary 2/20 Bn. A.I.F.*, 8 Dec 1941.
237 Smith, *op. cit.*, p. 120.
238 Ong, *op. cit.*, p. 233.
239 Smith, *op. cit.*, p. 121.
240 Ong, *op. cit.*, p. 250.

Chapter 6 - The Fighting Begins

Although Brooke-Popham had decided not to initiate 'Matador', he ordered that General Sir Lewis Heath's III Indian Corps should remain ready to commence the operation if necessary. However Heath had just one Division, the 11th, and two-thirds of a second, the 9th, to attempt to hold the northern airfields, to have troops available for 'Matador' and to also protect the very long border with Thailand over difficult terrain.[241]

Both the 9th and 11th Indian Divisions were under strength. The 11th Division was made up of just the 6th and 15th Brigades and their task was to hold Kedah as well as cover the Alor Star airfield. The 9th Division's 8th Brigade and a Battalion from the Indian 22nd Brigade was to hold Kota Baharu and the rest of the 22nd were to defend Kuantan.[242]

Four of these five brigades were forced to try and hold exposed positions. They could be easily cut off and there was no back up. Heath had no tanks to assist and there were simply not enough troops. It was these under-strength brigades that met the initial enemy thrust, with first contact on the night of 7-8 December 1941.

Lewis Heath, victor over the Italians in Abyssinia, was asked to do an impossible task in Malaya.[243]

The Japanese 5th Division troops landed unopposed at Singora and Patani in Thailand and had to cross Thai territory to reach Malaya. The third landing was at Kota Baharu on the north-eastern coast of Malaya. Here they met stiff opposition from the Indian troops and suffered many losses. They also inflicted many casualties.

As the Japanese moved south from Thailand towards Malaya they were met by the Indians who tried to block them. Less than 24 hours later one brigade of the 11th Indian Division had been reduced to one quarter of its strength and the other had suffered heavily.[244]

On the night of 8 December Singapore was bombed. The city was brightly lit, no blackout was in force. Luckily the main target of the Japanese attack was the Keppel Harbour docks and the airfields of Tengah and Seletar.[245] Some bombs did drop in Raffles Square and about 60 civilians were killed.[246] Finally the local population realised that war was more than just a vague possibility.

The Japanese advance continued down the Malayan Peninsula. They wiped out all but one of the Blenheim bombers based at Butterworth, near Penang.[247] This was the start of a week of intensive Japanese air raids on the RAF base.[248]

On 10 December the British warships HMS *Prince of Wales* (the ship on which Churchill had signed the Atlantic Charter with President Roosevelt just 4 months before),[250] and HMS *Repulse*, both bravely fighting without air

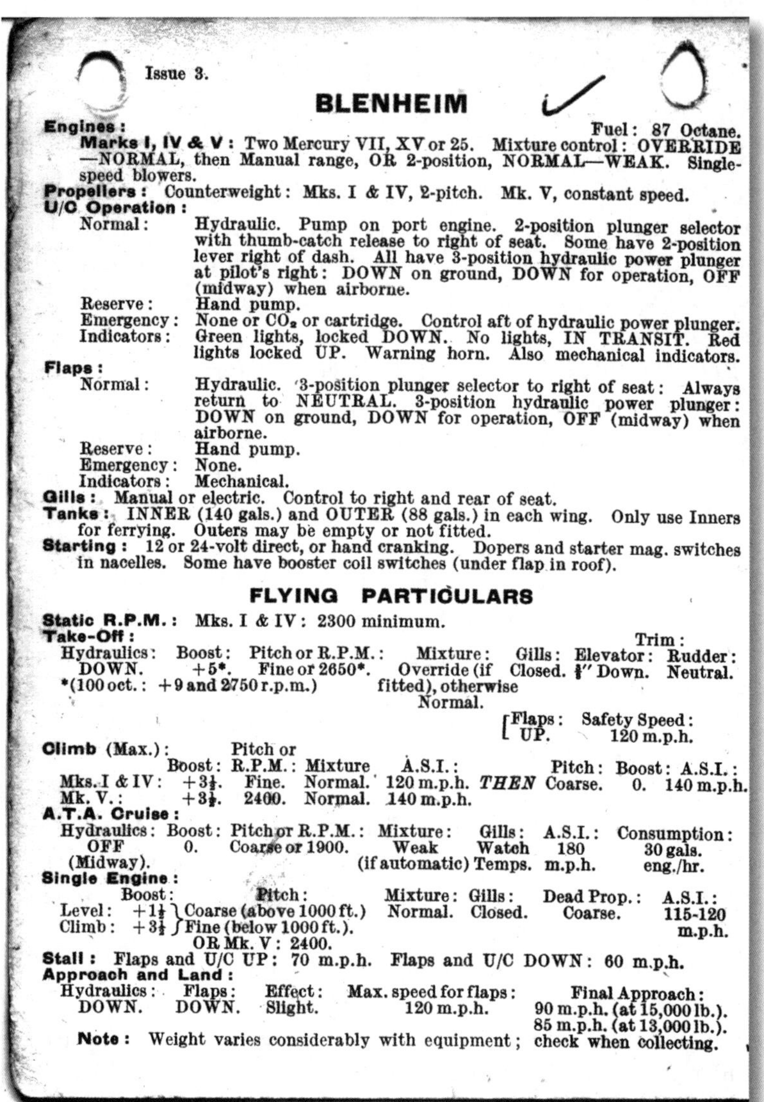

Issue 3.

BLENHEIM

Engines: Fuel: 87 Octane.
Marks I, IV & V: Two Mercury VII, XV or 25. Mixture control: OVERRIDE—NORMAL, then Manual range, OR 2-position, NORMAL—WEAK. Single-speed blowers.
Propellers: Counterweight: Mks. I & IV, 2-pitch. Mk. V, constant speed.
U/C Operation:
Normal: Hydraulic. Pump on port engine. 2-position plunger selector with thumb-catch release to right of seat. Some have 2-position lever right of dash. All have 3-position hydraulic power plunger at pilot's right: DOWN on ground, DOWN for operation, OFF (midway) when airborne.
Reserve: Hand pump.
Emergency: None or CO_2 or cartridge. Control aft of hydraulic power plunger.
Indicators: Green lights, locked DOWN. No lights, IN TRANSIT. Red lights locked UP. Warning horn. Also mechanical indicators.
Flaps:
Normal: Hydraulic. 3-position plunger selector to right of seat: Always return to NEUTRAL. 3-position hydraulic power plunger: DOWN on ground, DOWN for operation, OFF (midway) when airborne.
Reserve: Hand pump.
Emergency: None.
Indicators: Mechanical.
Gills: Manual or electric. Control to right and rear of seat.
Tanks: INNER (140 gals.) and OUTER (88 gals.) in each wing. Only use Inners for ferrying. Outers may be empty or not fitted.
Starting: 12 or 24-volt direct, or hand cranking. Dopers and starter mag. switches in nacelles. Some have booster coil switches (under flap in roof).

FLYING PARTICULARS

Static R.P.M.: Mks. I & IV: 2300 minimum.
Take-Off:

Hydraulics:	Boost:	Pitch or R.P.M.:	Mixture:	Gills:	Trim: Elevator:	Trim: Rudder:
DOWN.	+5*.	Fine or 2650*.	Override (if fitted), otherwise Normal.	Closed.	⅜" Down.	Neutral.

*(100 oct.: +9 and 2750 r.p.m.)

[Flaps: UP. Safety Speed: 120 m.p.h.

Climb (Max.):

	Boost:	Pitch or R.P.M.:	Mixture	A.S.I.:		Pitch:	Boost:	A.S.I.:
Mks. I & IV:	+3½.	Fine.	Normal.	120 m.p.h.	*THEN*	Coarse.	0.	140 m.p.h.
Mk. V.:	+3½.	2400.	Normal.	140 m.p.h.				

A.T.A. Cruise:

Hydraulics:	Boost:	Pitch or R.P.M.:	Mixture:	Gills:	A.S.I.:	Consumption:
OFF (Midway).	0.	Coarse or 1900.	Weak (if automatic)	Watch Temps.	180 m.p.h.	30 gals. eng./hr.

Single Engine:

	Boost:	Pitch:	Mixture:	Gills:	Dead Prop.:	A.S.I.:
Level:	+1½	Coarse (above 1000 ft.)	Normal.	Closed.	Coarse.	115-120 m.p.h.
Climb:	+3½	Fine (below 1000 ft.). OR Mk. V: 2400.				

Stall: Flaps and U/C UP: 70 m.p.h. Flaps and U/C DOWN: 60 m.p.h.
Approach and Land:

Hydraulics:	Flaps:	Effect:	Max. speed for flaps:	Final Approach:
DOWN.	DOWN.	Slight.	120 m.p.h.	90 m.p.h. (at 15,000 lb.). 85 m.p.h. (at 13,000 lb.).

Note: Weight varies considerably with equipment; check when collecting.

The Blenheim pilots never had the chance to use their notes to get the aircraft off the ground.[249]

protection of their own, were bombed and sunk in what was then considered to be Britain's greatest ever naval disaster.[251]

On 12 December, Lieutenant-General Arthur Percival gave permission for the defeated Indian force at Kota Baharu to withdraw and there was to be a general withdrawal south to start in three days, on 15 December, initially to the railhead at Kuala Krai.[252] It was to be the first of many withdrawals over the next few weeks.

By 13 December 1941 the Japanese who landed at Singora had reached Alor Star on the west coast of Malaya. The fleeing RAF personnel left in such haste that the Japanese found hot porridge still on the table. There was no time to destroy the thousand drums of high octane fuel and neatly stacked bombs stored at the airfield.[253] The Japanese were then able to use these 'Churchill Supplies' as they flew from the northern airfields on many bombing and strafing raids on the defenders.

Japanese disguised as local Malays began to infiltrate south.[254] The many local fifth columnists had given them detailed maps of jungle tracks and the location of stockpiles of timber available to repair any bridges destroyed by retreating Allied forces.

Darling Doukie 13 Dec '41

The world must have suddenly gone crazy; nations seem to be declaring war on one another right and left. However nothing really serious has happened lately and so far I am well clear of the guns.

We are living in the bush now and things are not bad at all. Fortunately I spent plenty of sweat building a decent dugout and now can live in comparative comfort. I have the place furnished with chairs and a table from our Bn Sgts mess and a couple of petrol lamps give plenty of light at night. A stream runs past quite close and is handy for washing and a gritty bath. The chaps are happy and are ready to pounce if the opportunity should occur.

I heard a wonderful story about Arch Ewart. He purchased a few typewriters a couple of days ago and was doing a great boast about giving one to each Coy to show us how generous he really is. I believe when he tried one of the typewriters, they all wrote backwards in Chinese!!

The tins of food that we have received from home are now invaluable. It is really amazing what variety we have. Our stocks include olives, sausage and vegetables and fruits of every type. Our small HQ group has pooled our tins and now find that we have everything necessary for several Xmas dinners.

I hope to find a bottle of ink soon and write my future letters with a pen. At present we are still in settling down stage.
Bye darling, I shall write when I can. Things are busy but I hope to catch every mail.
Love to Gran and the girls.
All my love
Bill

By 14 December 1941 the Japanese who landed at Patani in Thailand had reached Betong, close to the Thailand-Malaya border.

Back in London the overall mastermind of the Allied campaign, Winston Churchill, was under pressure at this time from many of the different theatres of war. Hong Kong was under heavy attack; Penang in Malaya was to be evacuated; an offensive against Rommel was launched in Africa and urgent calls for assistance came from Russia, Burma, Libya and Malaya. Churchill issued his first warning about Singapore:

Beware lest troops required for the ultimate defence of Singapore Island and fortress are used up or cut off in Malay Peninsula.[255]

Back home in Australia the Gaden family decided it was time that their few pieces of jewellery and their important War Savings certificates should be placed in a bank vault for safe keeping.

The Commercial Banking Company of Sydney Limited.
SAFE DEPOSIT VAULTS
Rent agreement 2354 Safe Number 1349, Received from Miss Elizabeth Gaden The Renter of the above specified Safe the sum of One pound five shillings being Rent in advance thereof up to and including the 14th Day of December 1942 subject to the terms and conditions of the Rent Agreement signed by the renter. Dated this 15th day of December 1941.

Found with the Rent Agreement was a hand written list of items placed inside:

War savings certificates (4)
1. £5 No G540850
2. £5 No G540851
3. £1 No 146122
4. £1 No 146123
Diamond Ring... Mothers
Broach [sic] ... *Sue's*
Diamond and ruby broach [sic]
Diamond pendant from Aunt Meddie
Pearl bar tie pin
Pendant - pearls and 2 blue
Bill's commission
6 Silver spoons (Malaya)

By 16 December the Japanese had advanced from Betong to Grik. Their other troops had advanced from Alor Star to Butterworth and the nearby Penang Island and harbour on the west coast. This was the oldest British colonial possession in South East Asia, where Raffles had started his overseas career with the East India Company. Penang was evacuated and abandoned by the troops and European civilians.[256] Unfortunately in their haste to escape from the advancing Japanese, they left the boats in the harbour intact rather than scuttling them. These boats became available to the enemy, leading to disastrous consequences for the Australian troops who later fought at Muar and Parit Sulong.

Dear Sue 16 Dec '41

Thank you for the cloth pips. They will come in very handy and save a lot of picking and unpicking the steel ones.

All my Xmas presents have been sent and now I have nothing else to say but good wishes.

The yellow B----s have not met the AIF face to face as yet. I am out in the bush with my troops and finding life quite pleasant. We are working hard preparing a tasty welcome for the Japs if they come our way.

I have plenty of tinned food and Xmas pudding stored away for the festive period. It looks like a party in the bush for us this year. I wonder what you will be doing.

Existing in this bush has taught me one thing … how to make coffee. I know exactly how much 'café au lait' to pour into a cup before the hot water. We have an enormous tin of ground coffee but experiments with it have not proved the best, mainly owing to the lack of sugar and the simple fact that it is ground native fashion into a fine dust.
Cheerio Sue. My love and very best wishes to Mother, Ginge and Gran.
Love
Bill

The next letter was addressed to 'Gran and Moya'. Gran was Bill's grandmother, Mrs EA Gaden of 'Vermont', Shepherd Street in Bowral in the NSW Southern Highlands. Moya Goff was a friend of the family from Bowral, she could probably best be described as a 'companion' to Bill's grandmother. Moya lived around the corner in Holly Street, Bowral. By this time her sister Biddy (Barbara Ierne) Moriarty had been widowed when her husband Boyd was killed in action in Crete. She was involved with the Australian Comforts Fund in Palestine and with the Red Cross in the 2/2 General Hospital in Kantara Egypt.[257] Her other sister, Helen Lyndon Goff had moved to England where, in 1934, she had had literary success with the first of the *Mary Poppins* series of books under the pen name Pamela Lyndon Travers.[258]

Dear Gran and Moya 16 Dec '41

Yesterday your parcel arrived. Thank you both very much indeed. The little draught board has already been put to good use and the butterscotch will find it difficult to survive another day.

At present I am living quite comfortably in a dugout somewhere in Malaya's 'ulu'. A little stream flows past, quite close, and provides water for a swim every day. Daily we add something to the 'bungalow' in the way of furniture, books, even a small stove.

Generally we are happy and cheerful. I always thought that life would be rotten in a situation such as this but really it is not bad at all.

Up to date the Jap [has not] met our chaps at all. Heaven knows what the blighters will do next. Anyway we are ready for him and prepared to fix him properly.

Our mail is coming in well and I have been receiving regular letters from the family and friends at home. Cottees sent me a plum pudding to be eaten over Xmas. I have resisted the temptation so far of opening it and I was quite pleased when I read Mother's letter today asking what the pudding was like. I can truthfully reply 'wait till after Xmas'. I have now acquired a case full of tinned food of all types for Xmas. Xmas will have to last a week.

One of my friends was seen a couple of days ago with several typewriters in his truck. He was guarding them because he knew we all wanted typewriters. Much to our delight all the typewriters wrote backwards in Chinese, and were, in due course returned to their rightful owners. Cheerio Gran and Moya.

Love
Bill

No military information was relayed in the letters home, but there is a feeling of confidence in Bill's comments to his grandmother and he tries to keep the letters light and humourous. No doubt the troops were missing the prospect of a Christmas at home with family but they knew the Japanese were finally on their doorstep. Some of their allies were already in battle 'up north'. Anticipation was high.

Darling Doukie 17 Dec '41

Most of the local news available I have already put in a note to Sue. This scribble will be short. The little flannel flowers arrived a little squashed but safely. What significance have they? Any? [Doukie probably sent the flowers to remind Bill of home. Flannel Flowers or Federation Stars are from the genus Actinotis. They have white, daisy-

> like flowers from September to December and grow as low herbs with silver-grey-green foliage. The name comes from the 'flannelly' feel of the petals. They are common in the Sydney area and were pictured on the official invitation to the original Federation celebrations held in 1901 in Sydney's Centennial Park.][259]

The letter continues:

> Yesterday we caught a tremendous butterfly. He measured 10 1/2 inches from wing tip to ditto. His markings are unusually brilliant and very pretty in a flashing manner. We have the old fellow stretched out over a plate and hope to have him identified as a rare specimen.
>
> I have not opened your Xmas pudding except of course to take the lid off and have a pick. I shall keep it until Xmas day and eat it then.
>
> The lads occasionally shoot wild pigs. All we have to cook with is a primus and a small one at that. However we are endeavouring to have pork of some kind for Xmas dinner.
>
> A panther lives in the jungle close by us and by night we often hear him making a noise that is like an angry cat with a deep voice. The lads have constructed a decent barbed wire fence and are quite willing to stay on our side after dark!! The snakes and various animals have not attacked any of us so we have ceased to regard them as a menace. I think they are more frightened of us and they have every reason to be.
>
> I hope Gran is comfortable in her new boarding house.
>
> Mrs. Assheton should make a very efficient President. She sounds as if she is very like her husband. No more news at present darling.
>
> Brian wrote to me a couple of days ago and mentioned some Bulletin's you had sent him. You are certainly acting as Fairy God Mother to the Army. Good for you dear. Please thank Mrs. Badgery for the many bundles of magazines she has forwarded me.
> Cheerio. Good luck. Happy Xmas.
> All my love
> Bill

On 17 December 1941, just one week after the sinking of the *Prince of Wales* and *Repulse* and one day after the evacuation of Penang, the most senior soldier in British uniform, Chief of Imperial General Staff, Field-Marshall Sir Alan Brooke wrote:

> *Personally I do not feel there is much hope of saving Singapore but feel that we ought to try and make certain of Burma.*[260]

The British General Officer Commanding Malaya, Lieutenant-General Arthur Percival, thought the situation serious but not hopeless. He hadn't committed the Australian troops yet; they were in Johore, just across the Straits from Singapore island. He was reluctant to remove Bennett's men north from Johore in case the Japanese tried to land on Singapore itself. He knew he must slow the enemy's advance as much as possible until help arrived in a month's time. The 'help' sailing to Singapore was two new divisions of troops, the 17th Indian Division and 18th British Division. These 40,000 men had been earmarked for this deployment in the Far East.[261]

The Straits Settlements Governor, Sir Shenton Thomas, and his administration had been attacked in the local media for their failure to prepare adequate civil defences. Sir Alfred Duff Cooper (Churchill's Special Emissary in the Far East) had written to Churchill:

There are no air raid shelters, no trenches even, no tin hats or gas masks for the civilian population. No preparations have been made for a system of food rationing, no registration of the inhabitants nor identity cards. The only sign that the authorities are aware of any danger is the large number of huts that have been set up for the reception of those who may be bombed out of their houses, but these are situated so close together and built of such flimsy material that a couple of incendiary bombs would sweep them all away in one magnificent bonfire.[262]

Sir Alfred Duff Cooper also wrote of Percival who he described as:

a nice, good man. He is a good soldier, calm, clear headed and even clever. But he is not a leader. He cannot take a large view; it is all a field day at Aldershot to him. He knows the rules so well and follows them so closely and is always waiting for the umpires whistle to signal cease fire and hopes that when the moment comes his military dispositions will be such as to receive approval. [263]

By 18 December the Japanese who had landed at Kota Baharu had advanced to Kuala Trengganu on the east coast. Percival flew to Ipoh for a conference with Heath. Both realised their front lines had been badly mauled and many men had been lost. Any protracted defence to the north of Ipoh was impossible.[264]

On 19 December Churchill wrote:

After naval disasters to British and American sea power in Pacific and Indian Ocean we have no means of preventing continuous landings by Japanese. The C-in-C (Far East) should now be told to confine himself to the defence of Johore and Singapore and that nothing should compete with maximum defence of Singapore.[265]

The Japanese had reached Selama on the west coast of Malaya by 20 December 1941. They took to rafts on the Perak River and infiltrated south to attack the British at Lenggong. This town was defended by the Argyll and Sutherland Highlanders who managed to inflict heavy casualties on the invaders before being instructed to withdraw south.[266]

Darling Doukie 20 Dec '41

Another letter in pencil dear, but it can't be helped. Ink is still a rare luxury. We are conserving our supplies for addressing envelopes.

So far I have seen no Japs. The war is going on without the AIF. We are happy, well and dirty.

Today two letters arrived and I know now that you have heard the news. I believe Sydney newspapers published a splash account of the AIF in action in Malaya. It was a lot of rot. We have not even seen an enemy.

The wives and mothers of our lads will surely be having a grand party. [This was the Christmas Party arranged by the Comforts Fund for the wives and children of the troops.]

I hope you did not do more than your share of the work, but, darling I know you did and I love you for it.

Rumours have already reached us to the effect that our Comforts Fund is far and away better than similar organizations. The lads are very pleased about it and are always talking about your doings.

We are knocking a lot of fun out of life these days. 'Roughing it' is grand sport. I don't think any man can really say that he has been places and done things until he has been placed with other men in a similar situation to ourselves at present.

Our meal times are extraordinary. We have breakfast at daylight, lunch about 11.30am and dinner at 4pm. These times suit our conditions admirably. We work all day digging, wiring and generally sweating. We wear shorts and boots only during the day but at night long pants and long sleeves to stop the mosquitoes biting. Washing is fun. A shallow jungle stream trickles past close to us and in that we try to scrape off the mud and dirt. I find that Lux toilet soap (super-creamed) makes an excellent paste with mud and water which comes off easily on a towel. The stream has little sharp stones on its bottom so we cannot sit down. I always think of old Norman H when I am trying to splash up enough water to 'supercream' my filthy person. Gran G provided the soap in her Xmas parcel. [Norman Hayes was the husband of Bill's aunt Essie Gaden; he was a 'rather correct' Englishman.][267]

You would delight in seeing one of the boys giving me a haircut with a safety razor. We have an old blunt pair of clippers but in any case the razor does a cleaner job. I still have plenty of hair on top but the sides of my head and the back have been shaved for ventilation. A lot of the boys are shaving their heads bald. I don't think that's necessary and I don't like the fashion. The short hair bristles under a tin hat and the mosquitoes have a wonderful feast at night.

After dark we 'black out' our dugout and use petrol lamps and lanterns inside. Really things are comfortable.

We are anxiously awaiting a big parcel mail. I have most of mine but many of the lads are still waiting for Xmas parcels. Your Comforts Fund parcels have been received by the three Majors and the works will be distributed on Xmas Eve.

Cheerio darling. This will not arrive until after Xmas. I hope the festive period was a happy one for you all. Yours truly,
All my love
Bill

By 22 December the Japanese from the two northernmost landings in Thailand had now joined forces and had reached Kuala Kangsar. They used rafts under cover of darkness to get behind Allied lines, aiming for the key road and rail bridges to the south. The British managed to get to Iskandar Bridge and withdraw over the Perak River before blowing a gap to impede the Japanese on the following day.[268] Only one section of the bridge was destroyed and it was quickly repaired by Japanese engineers.[269]

By now the 2/20 Battalion had lost a couple more troops to munitions accidents. Sgt WG Robinson had been killed by a mine on 16 December and just two days before Christmas they lost Pte CD Horne to a high explosive grenade. They had not seen action, the nervousness and anticipation must have been intense.

Capt. Hinder became acting Regimental Medical Officer at this time. This was Captain David Clive Hinder of the Australian Army Medical Corps, originally attached to the 2/19 Bn. He was subsequently the much loved medical officer for 'U' Battalion of prisoners and saved hundreds of POW lives. He survived the war and was revered by the 'U Beauties', the POW reunion group organized by Reg Newton.[270]

On Christmas Day 1941, Hong Kong surrendered to the Japanese.[271] It was also an unpleasant Christmas for the British and their allies in Malaya as the important tin mining centre of Ipoh faced imminent capture by the Japanese who continued their advance south.

What happened to Walter Ayrton and his wife Rene who had entertained Bill in Ipoh when he was on leave? We know they visited their daughter at school in New Zealand in 1941 but did they then return to Malaya? Did they become civilian prisoners of war? All we know is that they did survive those years as they visited Bill in the 1950s and donated a set of golf clubs with steel shafts to the Gaden household. The golf clubs, a set of Slazenger Air Flow Championship Stainless, are still in the family.

Darling Doukie 25 Dec'41

Xmas Day; and tonight is Xmas night. I have been thinking of you all - all day - and wondering where you are and how you managed to celebrate etc.

Our 'dinner' today was a happy occasion that I shall not forget for many years to come. We started with roast pork and roast duck and later crammed our tummies full of plum pudding, fruit salad and cream. The final course was supplied by our CF - sweets and smokes. These things would have looked well on a white table cloth, but to us they looked marvelous amongst the rubber leaves in our part of the bush.

The pig was caught and killed by a couple of the lads from the North Coast and beautifully cooked by a couple of shearers' cooks. The ducks were a present from Lieut Tony White. The party was improved for everybody by a present from Bn - one bottle of beer per man. I think the miracle of the day was the extent that your little Xmas pudding went. It fed the whole 16 in our group. I did not mention the money in it and the lucky members fairly yelled with delight when they struck it rich. I kept a large piece for myself and was rewarded with a 3d.

We swamped the pudding with brandy and tried to light it. There must have been too much wind, the brandy refused to blaze. We had to sleep all the afternoon. I still feel a little sick - too much pork.

The lads have all enjoyed this Xmas. They received parcels from the Salvation Army, the Australian Comforts Fund and our own Comforts Fund. I got a small packet of tobacco with a card with your writing on it. Some of your parcels met a tragic fate, doubtless Major R will tell you all about it however all the lads got something and they are truly grateful.

Yesterday I received a letter dear. Thank you. The PMG are lousy, only permitting you one page in each letter. It must be the censor.

The Japs have not come into our sector as yet and we have not seen any fighting at all. Things seem to have quietened down for the time being.

I have solved the mystery surrounding our native coffee and can now make it quite decently; 11pm is the time for coffee and toast.

Living out here in the bush is causing some of the lads to become more 'native' than ever. I believe some of them were quite disappointed when I arrived with a truck load of lavatory seats the other day. I suspect that they like squatting. Some chaps have not worn their shirts during the day for weeks. They are just as black as any 'boong'.

Letter cards are available for us but they are only one page and not nearly large enough for my purpose.

I have heard a rumour that poor old Ralph died in Burma. I hope that this is all wrong but I am afraid it is true. [NX28141 Rolfe Waldo Uther Barker died 5th December 1941.][272]

A decent pair of barber's clippers have been found and we no longer have to cut our hair with safety razors. Cheerio darling. Love to Gran and the girls.
All my love
Bill

By 28 December 1941 the Japanese had advanced to Ipoh. Japanese vessels were seen lying off Singora. It was thought this signalled a major reinforcement of the battlefront to move and infiltrate behind Allied lines. The British and Indian troops set up defence at Kampar in an attempt to hold Central Malaya. Over a four day battle the British forces, in particular the Argylls and Punjabis, inflicted severe casualties in hand to hand fighting and suffered many losses themselves but managed to hold their position.[273] Kampar was the strongest British defence position in the campaign and Percival staked much on its ability of hold the town and deny central Malaya to the Japanese.[274]

By 31 December 1941 the eastern advance of the Japanese had reached Kuantan and some headed inland via Maran and Temerloh to meet up with their compatriots at Kuala Lumpur two weeks later.

The Japanese were flying over Mersing on reconnaissance runs, but no bombs were dropped. During the month some evacuation of civilians from the district had taken place though there were still 'Natives' in the area. Engineers completed the necessary demolition of the township and no one was allowed into Mersing without an official pass from Bn HQ.

Meanwhile the British troops who had fought so hard and so bravely to successfully hold their position at Kampar were ordered to withdraw on 2 January 1942, just as the Japanese commanders themselves considered a retreat.[275] The Allied decision was just a few hours too early; what a difference to morale and confidence if they had had a victory at this stage.

The remainder of the Japanese eastern force headed south towards Endau and Mersing. This was where the 22nd Brigade AIF was waiting.

The Australian troops would soon be in the firing line.

241 Falk, *Seventy Days to Singapore*, p. 70.
242 Falk, *ibid.*, pp. 71-2.
243 Forbes, *Hellfire*, pp. 93-4.
244 Parkinson, *Blood, Toil, Tears and Sweat*, p. 334.
245 Falk, *op. cit.*, p. 72.
246 Smith, *Singapore Burning*, p. 126.
247 <http://www.britain-at-war.org.uk/WW2/Malaya_and_Singapore/html/body_chronology_of_malaya.htm>
248 *The Fall of Malaya, Master Media Guide to Pacific Battles* 1941-45.
249 ATA Ferry Pilot's Notes used by F/O Ron Ford, in the possession of the author.
250 Pitkin Pictorials, *The Right Honorable Sir Winston Churchill*, a pictorial memorial, p. 12.
251 <http://www.britain-at-war.org.uk/WW2/Malaya_and_Singapore/html/body_chronology_of_malaya.htm>
252 Parkinson, *op. cit.*, p. 334.
253 *The Fall of Malaya, Master Media Guide to Pacific Battles 1941-45.*
254 <http://www.britain-at-war.org.uk/WW2/Malaya_and_Singapore/html/body_chronology_of_malaya.htm>
255 Parkinson, *op. cit.*, p. 335.
256 Smith, *op. cit.*, p. 260.
257 Moriarty, Biddy, http://www.adb.online.anu.edu.au/biogs/A150477b.htm
258 Pamela Lyndon Travers, <http://www.sl.nsw.gov.au/mssguide/ptravers.pdf >
259 Flannel Flowers, <http://www.burkesbackyard.com.au/2001/archives/2001_archives/in_the_garden/flowering_plants>
260 Smith, *op. cit.*, p. 265.
261 *ibid.*, p. 265.
262 *ibid.*, p. 285.
263 *ibid.*, p. 286.
264 <http://www.britain-at-war.org.uk/WW2/Malaya_and_Singapore/html/body_chronology_of_malaya.htm >
265 Parkinson, *op. cit.*, p. 340.
266 <http://www.britain-at-war.org.uk/WW2/Malaya_and_Singapore/html/body_chronology_of_malaya.htm>
267 Gaden family history researched by the author.
268 <http://www.britain-at-war.org.uk/WW2/Malaya_and_Singapore/html/body_chronology_of_malaya.htm>
269 *The Fall of Malaya, Master Media Guide to Pacific Battles 1941-45.*
270 Newton, Reg, personal communication.
271 Smith, *op. cit.*, p. 284.
272 DVA Nominal Roll.
273 Smith, *op. cit.*, pp. 312-314.
274 *The Fall of Malaya, Master Media Guide to Pacific Battles 1941-45.*
275 <http://www.britain-at-war.org.uk/WW2/Malaya_and_Singapore/html/body_chronology_of_malaya.htm>

Chapter 7 - Australians in the Battle for Malaya

On the first day of January 1942, a Thursday, some of the Japanese Western Force troops were transported by ship to arrive in Telok Anson where they met up with more troops travelling overland. The combined force then moved south towards Slim River.

The *Sydney Morning Herald* this New Year's Day reported that the Japanese had a three pronged drive through Malaya towards Singapore. The newspaper suggested the most serious threat came from the west coast on the Perak front. The troops on the east coast were principally confined to patrol activity: the Japanese were gradually moving towards Kuantan in the east, but had not gained any strength in this direction. They were heading towards Kuala Lipis in the centre and were said to be making little progress due to poor communications. However the semi-official Japanese News Agency Domei was quoted as saying *the Japanese troops have surrounded and are wiping out a formation of Australian troops south of Ipoh.*[276]

This was not true, the Australians on the western side of Malaya, the 27th Brigade, did not see action for another two weeks when they sprung an ambush at Gemencheh Bridge near Gemas.[277]

However Gordon Gaffney (NX71862) of 8th Division HQ recalled travelling north, close to the Thai border with two Intelligence Officers. The troops had been told the Japanese:

> *aeroplanes were tied up with rope, and they couldn't see because they were short-sighted ... and their bullets were half rubber ... we ran into road block. I said 'turn around quick' to the fellow ... who was driving. As we turned, we heard this click ... and the bullet went straight through ... the little windshield at the back of the back seat, and it hit him all I heard was this fellow grunt in the back seat ... and they'd shot* [the English Intelligence Officer] *just above the temple ... They weren't made of rubber I can tell you.*[278]

Bennett's remaining troops, the 22nd Brigade AIF were still in the Endau and Mersing area on the east coast of the peninsula and, so far, also had not seen action. However some would meet the enemy this month.

The men of the 2/20 continued with their defensive work, fortifying the wiring, strengthening the field works, thickening the anti-tank and anti-personnel minefields. Unfortunately all carriers were grounded due to a steering weakness, a bit of a problem to discover at this late stage of proceedings. Officers and men, close to a thousand in total, were sent to Endau, north of Mersing.[279]

> Darling Doukie 1 Jan '42
>
> Yesterday I received your letter about Goulburn. I am pleased that you managed to make the trip. The change of air and 'atmosphere' must surely put your foo-foo valve in good working order.
>
> There is not a great deal of news from this part of the world. Every 'today' is like yesterday and we have not even seen a Jap.

Xmas dinner was good fun. We managed to 'find' a pig and some poultry and a couple of our shearer cooks made an excellent job of them. We have another pig, at present being cooked, for today's dinner.

Digging has been hard work but we are now reaping a harvest of satisfaction from our work. Our first few dugouts were called bungalows but the more recent ones have Sydney suburban names i.e. Central, Town Hall, Wynyard, and I occupy North Sydney. Most of us have our own house and each is furnished according to the owner's taste. The Jap seems to be giving us plenty of time to play about and the lads are applying their wits to many trades. Some have proved quite good carpenters and others are getting plenty of practice as barbers etc. We were fortunate in locating quite a store of oak 3-ply boards close handy and most of our dugouts are now lined with oak paneling. I am very proud of mine and find it clean, dry and comfortable. Some of our 'houses' are small, you can sit in the middle and touch everything you own without stretching but others are quite large. I can walk about without bumping my head on the rafters supporting the roof and I have black out screens of 3 ply that enable a light at night but when removed during the day let in plenty of sunshine.

The monsoons have been a farce, so far. It certainly rains quite often but never with the persistent force that we were led to expect. Perhaps the rains may commence pouring with a vengeance tomorrow but I doubt it.

My clothes have not seen an iron for over a month. They are none the worse for it. Every night I sleep on my trousers and put a passable crease in them, even after they have been washed by Lennie in the creek. I have also discovered that by folding a shirt properly, as soon as it has dried after washing, it does not look too bad at all.

Our cables, wishing us Merry Xmas, are just beginning to arrive. I have all mine but some of the lads have received their airmail letters first.

Heavens dear! I am putting on weight and fat these days. Weeks of shoveling and manual labour generally have raised a bit of muscle here and there but still my weight increases. A couple of days ago I won the over chest expansion comp with $7\frac{1}{8}$ inches.

Bob 'Shickstreet' (Stanistreet) is back with us again but I have not spoken to him. I can easily understand him not sending his mother much native jewelry etc. The stuff is fairly expensive and Bob has been 'on loan' to an English unit where mess bills are terrifically high.

I have just eaten my Lord Mayor's Patriotic Xmas Plum Pudding for morning tea. It went very well indeed. Our parcels from that source were excellent. They contained boot polish, fruit salad, paste, cream and tobacco as well as my morning tea.

If we stay out here I shall be nearly as wealthy as a king. I am spending practically 0, the only cash that has left my wallet has gone into stamps, there being no shops and nothing to buy.

Cheerio dear.

I am enclosing a little piece of latex, rubber straight out of the tree when it is collected in little cups on the tree; it looks like milk but after a few days it sets hard and gradually turns black. The rubber factories treat it chemically in its milky form, roll it out into flat sheets as it sets and then smoke it like fish. The rubber leaves the plantation factories in small brown sheets about 2 feet by 1 foot and $\frac{1}{8}$ of an inch thick. It is rough on the surface like a crepe sole. We have the floors of our dug outs covered with these slabs of rubber.

I found a beautiful leather-bound copy of Kipling's 'Kim' amongst some books given us by a planter. The yarn is really great and when I have read it I shall try to send the

book home but not if there is any risk of losing it because the copy is valuable.
Bye dear. Regards to Mrs. Fowler. Love to the girls and Gran.
All my love
Bill
Poor old Rolfe died in Burma from typhus. David MacD wrote and told me. David has some sort of fever himself. [They were with Mission 204, the Commando Force which went into China.]

Another sad story: Ogilvy has recently been trying to work with a broken leg in plaster. The lass cracked up and went down with some sort of fever. She is miles away. I have not seen her but have received a letter. The Jap has not improved the situation. He laid a few eggs on the town she happens to be in and since I have not even had a letter. Cheerio dear
All my love
Bill

Elaine was stationed in Bahu Pahat. On 22 November 1941 she was accidentally injured when walking on uneven ground whilst on duty. She stepped over a water pipe and fell causing a fracture to the left fibula. The official record states she was not to blame for the injury.[280]

On Friday 2 January 1942 the *Sydney Morning Herald* ran a detailed story about the battle in Malaya and the fighting at Kuala Lumpur. The correspondent advised that fifth columnists were very active and, through them, the invaders had intimate knowledge of local geography. The Allied troops were weary after two weeks of fighting and making constant withdrawals but remained confident in their ability to defeat the Japanese as soon as the tactical circumstances of the campaign permitted their making a stand.[281]

By Saturday 3 January 1942 Lieutenant-General Percival had made the decision to abandon Central Malaya where he felt that the extensive road systems of Selangor, Negri Sembilan and Malacca would make it too easy for the Allies to be outflanked by the Japanese. He decided they would withdraw in one bound of 140 miles, and would blow up the bridges rather than fight to retain them, and try to make a clean break from the Japanese.[282]

TELEGRAM TO MRS VERA GADEN, VALHALLA, 8 RAYMOND ROAD, NEUTRAL BAY
VIA CABLE FROM MALAYA 3 JAN 42
ALL WELL AND SAFE PLEASE DON'T WORRY
BEST WISHES FOR XMAS AND NEW YEAR
BILL GADEN 12 18B

This day's *Sydney Morning Herald* reported that *HEAVY PRESSURE ON MALAYA EXPECTED.* The correspondent advised that the increased tempo by the Japanese had been foreseen by the Imperial Commanders at Singapore who were waiting for the arrival of the promised substantial reinforcements. The enemy lost between three hundred and four hundred men in Friday's fighting. Air attacks were made on Singapore and there had been some enemy infiltration at Kuantan on the east coast.

The troops were involved in a desperate race against time between the Japanese in their thrust to Singapore and the Allies in getting their reinforcement troops to the Island so they could launch a counter-offensive. Sadly the immediate lack of Allied air support was obvious to all and was very bad for the morale of both troops and civilians. The *Herald's* correspondent from Kuala Lumpur was particularly scathing of this paucity of British aircraft.[283]

By 4 January the 2/20 troops on the east of the Malay peninsula were reassigned to strengthen positions facing the north and north-west; a land invasion was now considered more likely and more threatening than one from the sea.[284]

On 5 January the Battle of Slim River began. The British troops were defending a defile when the Japanese appeared with tanks and opened fire at close range. The tanks then moved on some allied artillery batteries. The Japanese infantry were backed by aircraft, engineers, tanks and artillery against the Hyderabads, Punjabis, Gurkhas and Argylls who had no tanks and no aircraft in support.[285] It was a total rout of the Allies and hundreds lost their lives in battle or fled into the jungle to try and make their way back to Allied lines. They were hunted down, few making it back to safety as the Japanese juggernaut rolled on.

At the end of the day the Indian 12th Brigade could muster just over four hundred officers and men (only two hundred were still armed). The 28th Brigade of Gurkhas could muster seven hundred and fifty troops. A Brigade normally has three battalions with a total of three to five thousand troops; the low number of survivors was an indication of the magnitude of the Allied losses. The few survivors were all utterly exhausted.[286]

Meanwhile over on the east coast the 2/20 troops were practising their jungle fighting.[287] They were yet to meet the enemy. It would not be too long. However these Company exercises showed that the troops had spent so much time digging and wiring the fortifications that they had lost some of their physical ability for sustained marching.[288]

The *Sydney Morning Herald* of Tuesday 6 January reported on more withdrawals in Malaya, with the Allies retreating to positions south of Ipoh. The withdrawal had been carried out on the previous Saturday night. The troops were closely followed by enemy armoured fighting vehicles which were successfully engaged, with high enemy losses. The Japanese were reported to have used landing craft seized further north to move troops southwards and infiltrate river areas ahead of the Allies.

There was also a report that an AIF Commando Unit had been behind enemy lines and captured and killed a whole party of Japanese, including a Brigadier. The enemy were travelling by car and the AIF used grenades and Tommy guns to attack. They then broke formation and withdrew back to the jungle and their rendezvous.[289] It is possible these were some Australians who had been on a raiding party behind enemy lines led by the Argyll's Major Rose.[290]

One Corporal and six ORs had 'marched out' from 2/20 on 23 December to become part of 'Rose Force'.

Despite knowledge of the fierce fighting that he would have gleaned as an officer and the documented advances of the enemy, Bill retained a light tone in his letter home.

> Darling Doukie 7 Jan 1942
>
> Nothing has been happening dear. These few lines are just to let you know I am well and sparking properly.
>
> This half civilized life is agreeing with all of us. The lads have changed slightly in appearance since the show began. The open air has made them appear tougher than before. Many are growing super special moustaches. The crowd of big, shy lads that departed from Sydney a year ago are fast developing into a tough, wild-eyed and be-whiskered lot of heathens. At least they must look a bit that way to a stranger.
>
> The Jap has not given us any attention up to date. Sometimes we hear one of his planes but more often we hear nothing.
>
> A little rain has been falling lately and our washing creek is nearly deep enough to swim in. We are going to build a decent dam across it tomorrow and try to make our daily wash a decent bath.
>
> Razor blades are becoming difficult to find. I am pleased as punch about my Rolls that does not require blades.
>
> You should see our poultry farm. We have 7 ducks and 12 fowls all waiting for our tummies. The boys 'find' these birds when they are out on reconnaissance. We even have a fair supply of birdseed to feed the birds on.
>
> Some of the lads are quite tired of poultry and even enjoy army tucker for a change.
>
> We have a monkey at Coy HQ. 'Minnie' has been in captivity now for 7 months. She has become very friendly and enjoys her fair share of popularity. She is owned by one of the boys and to him she shows more affection than the rest of us. We are not jealous!
>
> Cheerio dear. I have not received a letter from you for a week or so but they should turn up soon. Love to Gran and the girls.
> All my love, Yours truly
> Bill
> PS Ogilvy has recovered from both the fever and broken leg.

The *Sydney Morning Herald* of 7 January warned the Australian people of the increasing dangers in Malaya. The headlines screamed:

> *SITUATION IN MALAYA MORE SERIOUS, TWO NEW WITHDRAWALS, AIR ATTACKS ON SINGAPORE.*

The Japanese had now taken over the airfield at Kuantan on the east coast and fighting was still occurring to the west at Perak and Kuala Selangor.

An Official Correspondent advised:

> *Although the inaction of the Australians is proving galling to the AIF, the troops are accepting it without grumbling. It has become obvious to all others that their responsibilities will be doubled, but they above all others have been trained and specialised for the job that they will be called upon to perform.*

The reporter also remarked that:

In the meantime some of the Press cuttings from home are hardly good reading for men waiting hourly to put their long months of preparation to the test. All that is left for them to do is hold on and attempt to deal a temporary knock-out to the enemy who, so far, has had everything his own way.[291]

This was not encouraging reading for the worried families back home.

Endau force was formed from 'C' Company of the 2/20 Bn, led by Capt. WA Carter, and 'D' Company of the 2/19 led by Major T Vincent, with Major AE Robertson overall commander.[292] They were tasked with holding Endau and denying the mouth of the river and warning of enemy landings.

By 7 January 1942 there was a new Supreme Commander of all Allied Forces in the Far East.[293] General Sir Archibald Wavell arrived in Singapore to replace Duff Cooper. Wavell's new Chief of Staff was named as Lieutenant-General Sir Henry Pownall, who had replaced Brooke-Popham. It would be difficult for the newcomers to get a handle on the overall situation at this critical time in the fighting. Malayan Commander Lieutenant-General Arthur Percival was certainly concerned about continuity and thought the changes at this late stage were bad for morale.[294]

Percival's troops in Malaya were to be reinforced with the arrival of the British 18th Division who had left Liverpool, England on 29 October 1941 and had been at sea ever since. After so many weeks on board ship, they were not going to be fit for fighting, they were not going to have time to train on land nor would they be familiar with the weapons they would be using. The convoy was also bringing the 17th Indian Division which was a new formation mainly untrained.[295] They were due to land in around one week. Included in the cargo were fifty crated Hurricane aircraft which were also bound for Singapore to be reassembled in the Ford Factory on arrival.[296] The convoy ships were not bringing much needed tanks.

Percival knew he would need to hold Johore long enough for the deployment of these newly-arrived 17th and 18th Divisions and then, with Hurricane air defence, he hoped to launch a counterattack. But how much further would the Japanese have advanced before these reinforcements could be deployed?

Could the Allies hold Johore long enough?

There was a major communication problem emerging for troops on the ground. Percival's commanders had been ordered to do their best if outflanked by the enemy, but to keep their formations intact at all costs and withdraw rather than risk having to fight their way out. This proved disastrous as many withdrawals were prematurely triggered by a small number of Japanese setting off noisy firecrackers, giving the appearance of large numbers, a classic bluff.

If a handful of Japanese were reported to our rear the whole British army must perforce retire, infantry guns and armoured cars, often without firing a shot.[297]

It was a feeling which permeated the entire army irrespective of rank. There was no prize for being 'the only man left alive on the beach'. Thus many withdrawals happened sooner rather than later. Bennett, critical of Heath[298] and not believing in retreats, reported that:

I have seen a total absence of offensive spirit.[299]

Over on the east coast, the lads of the 2/20 were patrolling the river, and repairing damage done by the high tides to their defensive works. They also experimented with beacons made from tins of petrol ignited by permanganate and glycerine.[300]

Included in the *War Diary* of the 2/20 Battalion were seven carefully typed pages for their WAR PLAN FOR DEFENCE OF LEFT SECTOR MERSING. It covered troop dispositions, degrees of readiness, road blocks, beacons, mortar, artillery, beach lighting and other information, with details of vital localities, patrols and tasks. In reality they would hardly be given any time to make use of all their defensive efforts, all their preparations and all their training.

By Friday 9 January the Japanese had reached Kuala Kubu. The Allies withdrew from the city of Kuala Lumpur just hours before the Japanese arrived on 11 January. The day before, on Saturday, the British residents of the town had left in a 'shameful display of panic'.[301] The local population were left to their fate with the Japanese.

Saturday 10 January saw the *Sydney Morning Herald* headline BIG BATTLE RAGES IN MALAYA, THREAT TO KUALA LUMPUR, HEAVY CASUALTIES ON BOTH SIDES. The report told of the battle round the Slim River area in Selangor the previous Thursday. The enemy used tanks followed by infantry in lorries. The British troops were out-numbered by scores to one. The fighting was severe and casualties on both sides heavy. The main battle in Malaya was now said to be astride the railway running from Ipoh to Kuala Lumpur and there were many bombing raids by Japanese aircraft. But the most salient tactic they were using was infiltration along the rubber estate roads and forest paths which they appeared to know completely. Knowledge supplied by the locals was obviously most helpful. The fighting had, of course, severely curtailed the production of tin and rubber for export to Britain.[302]

Two days later, on 12 January, the *Sydney Morning Herald* was reporting the SLIM RIVER BATTLE GOES TO THE JAPANESE.

Surprise tactics won North Malaya for the enemy. Rubber stocks were destroyed by the Allies and also huge quantities of liquor to prevent them from falling into enemy hands, hoping thus to save the natives from the bestial orgies seen in the conquered cities of China.[303]

Sadly the Japanese soldiers didn't need the effect of huge quantities of liquor, they could do their rape and slaughter without its influence.[304]

On the western side of the peninsula the Japanese continued south, some moved to Gemas and yet more marched onto Malacca and took the coastal route to Muar. Other enemy troops took the road to Seremban then Port Dickson where the 2/20 had originally been stationed when they had first arrived in Malaya nearly a year before. Some Japanese troops, dressed as Malays, even attempted to land in south-east Johore from a fishing sampan but they were discovered and captured.[305]

Less than ten days had passed since Percival made the decision to abandon the Central Malayan cities of Kuala Lumpur, Port Swettenham and Malacca. These cities were the jewels in the crown of Malaya. The civilians would have been horrified at being left to be over-run by the advancing enemy.

Percival wanted to set up a new line of defence in northern Johore, a line of defence from coast to coast with the Australians remaining on the east coast. Bennett however was not impressed with this new tactic especially as the Australians had seen no action on the east coast; they were trained, ready and fresh. Heath's already tired divisions on the west coast were bearing the brunt of the attack.[306]

Bennett was anxious to not place the Australians under the command of Heath. He urged that Heath's troops should be placed under his own command. Percival hoped that Bennett's aggressive spirit may be just what was needed after the losses at Slim River[307] so Bennett was made commander of what was to be known as Westforce.

Bennett's elevation to Corps Commander came even though he had yet to fight his first battle. His Chief of Staff, regular soldier Colonel James Thyer, was not impressed with his immediate superior, knowing:

> *Between the wars he was a civilian and did not study military tactics and rested on his World War I laurels. He was moved by hunches and believed in the stars. He was tremendously ambitious and had his head in the clouds which is the last place a good battle commander's head should be.*[308]

The Allies Westforce consisted of the 9th Indian Division, the 45th Indian Brigade and the 27th Brigade of the 8th Australian Division. (The 22nd Brigade AIF would remain in Mersing.) The exhausted 11th Indian Division would be rested and the 12th Brigade returned to Singapore to re-form and re-equip.

Very heavy rain fell in the Mersing area at this time, damage was done to field works, all positions were sodden and water oozed from the ground.[309] It seemed as if the weather had joined forces with the Japanese. The troops laid anti-tank and anti-personnel mines and continued to patrol the north Mersing River area.[310]

War Diary of the 2/20 Battalion AIF MERSING 13 Jan '42

```
A/Tk and A/P Minefields-laying complete. An issue of special type
bombs constructed by 2/10 Fd Coy were made today.
Types  1. 'The Fish Fizzler' designed as a depth charge,
       2. 'The Putrid Pansy' a gelignite bomb issued to
       'D' Coy for coastal defence.
Heavy rain fell - interfered with Fd Works. S. [S= Sungai = River]
ENDAU rose 8 ft above normal level owing to torrential rain, the
barge boom carried away.
```

On 13 January 1942 the long awaited Allied reinforcements and the crated Hurricanes landed at Singapore Naval Docks. At this time the Japanese attempted even heavier air raids on the city.[311] The aircraft were rushed to the newly constructed Ford factory for reassembly.

The *Sydney Morning Herald* of 15 January reported that the communiqué issued in Singapore the day before had made no reference to the land fighting in Malaya.[312] But by now the Australian troops were under fire. The Australian 8th Division's entry into the Malayan campaign was signalled by the 27th Brigade's ambush of the Japanese at Gemenchlen River Bridge, Gemas from 13-15 January 1942.

AIF Commander Gordon Bennett issued this message in an order of the day to the AIF.

> *To a great extent the result of the present campaign will depend on your individual skills, courage and determination. After months of waiting the AIF in Malaya is face to face with the enemy. Each succeeding report of the fighting to date has convinced us that our training is on the right lines. It now rests with all of you officers, non-commissioned officers and men to prove your superiority to the Japanese. We have come into the fight at a critical hour. In your hands rests not only the fate of Singapore which we have come to defend, but the security of Australia itself; also the reputation of the AIF.*[313]

The 27th Brigade included the 2/29 and 2/30 battalions of the AIF. For some unknown reason, there had been a major breakdown in communication between the retreating allies and their backup - the AIF were not issued with the best anti-tank shells. The armour-piercing rounds seemed to go straight through the tanks so troops had to change to high explosive ammunition.[314] However if the Japanese expected another 'Slim River' victory they were mistaken. The Australians were a much tougher opponent and fought with a bravery the Japanese had not previously seen.[315] The 2/30 lost 17 men killed, 55 were wounded and 9 classed as missing in this battle.

The Australians sprang an ambush on Japanese cyclists, infantry and tanks who they had allowed to pass into a trap before opening fire. In a few minutes heavy casualties had been inflicted and six tanks destroyed. Later an enemy brigade with extra tanks made contact with the main force of the AIF whose artillery pounded the Japanese for several hours. The artillery also supported the Indian troops to the west. An Australian captain directed fire from his observation post and only withdrew when he was almost surrounded by the enemy.

Bennett reported back home to Army Minister Forde:

> *A severe defeat inflicted on the enemy on January 14.*[316]

The AIF had delayed the Japanese advance on Singapore by a vital 24 hours.[317]

Whilst desperate fighting was occurring on the west coast, life for the troops of 2/20 on the east coast remained peaceful, just manning patrols and carrying out repairs. This calm would not last long. At Rompin, on the coast to the north, Endau Force had made contact with 30 Japanese soldiers crossing the river. They wore steel helmets, black coats and khaki shorts.[318]

Darling Doukie 14 Jan '42

Letters from home are scarce these days. They are dribbling through slowly but not with the regularity that we knew some months ago. Mail days are past. Our mail arrives every day now in small packets. I usually manage one from you each week but there must be a hoard of your letters 'coming'.

Xmas in Goulburn must have been good fun. I am pleased you went down there. Reading my letters must have been a trial, there must be a hundred of them, or very nearly.

In my last letter I mentioned the monsoon was not unpleasant and not very wet. I spoke too soon. For the past two days rain has been pouring down. The weather is rotten and boisterous. Wind comes in vicious puffs, tearing through the rubber trees and trying to lift the iron off our dugouts. The rain comes in waves of intensity; sometimes it fairly crashes down for nearly half an hour and then eases off and just pours for a while. It never seems to stop.

Yesterday we were flooded. Water was lying everywhere and drains were gushing. Today we are marooned. Water covers the flat ground like a big brown sheet and the drains are out of sight.

Fortunately my dugouts are on the slope of a hill and beyond any sort of flood. They are reasonably dry and a 'blessing' in times such as these.

Drains in the rubber are deep and wide, something like Fig Tree Gully of Scone. In reasonable weather they have a trickle of water running in them that teems with little fish. These tremendous drains are everywhere and are usually crossed by 'boong bridges'; a couple of logs thrown across. We were not troubled by the flood when we could use these bridges but now these logs are out of sight and you can't tell, through the murky water, where the drains begin and end. There seems only one thing to do; smile, yell whoopee and reckon that we are all marooned.

This position is not all serious because as soon as the rain ceases the water will disappear like magic. It always does because the drains, although overloaded at present, are well and scientifically constructed to cope with this amount of annual emergency. Malaya is a poor sort of country but its drains are carefully surveyed masterpieces.

The Japs have not come our way. It seems that we are particularly good at keeping just out of the fight.

The letter is left unfinished for a few days but events were moving on swiftly in the war.

It was on 16 January 1942 the *Sydney Morning Herald* was able to report back to Australia that many of their troops had faced the enemy. The heart stopping headline read *AIF IN ACTION IN MALAYA*. They wrote that the AIF had defeated a small Japanese column comprising infantry and tanks, the action taking place in the eastern part of Negri Sembilan. The Japanese on the coastal routes in Malaya and in the centre aimed at a converging attack; the Allied strategy was to prevent the Japanese columns uniting. The Australians were always referred to as '*the AIF*' with no mention of the individual battalions, so every single family would have been very worried not knowing whether or not their loved one was directly involved.

Bill's letter continued:

> 19 Jan '42
>
> The past few days have been eventful. The Jap has met some AIF and received a hiding. I have been out of the fighting and have seen nothing more exciting than an occasional Jap plane.
>
> The local newspapers are making a big 'splash' of our participation in the show. Don't be alarmed dear; we are safe and sound and far away.
>
> Our floods have departed and things back to normal again. We had to use Sam-pans to collect our food etc in for a couple of days. I remember a photograph we used to gape at when we were kids of a rowing boat floating over West Maitland railway station. This place must have been flooded just as badly.
>
> The office [Birt and Co.] have again sent a tremendous parcel of tins and chocolate.
>
> Cheerio darling. Love to Sue and Ginge.
>
> All my love
>
> Bill

By Monday 19 January the Australian people were learning more of the ambush sprung by the AIF at Gemas, with the *Sydney Morning Herald* correspondent advising that the AIF had landed a real blow to the Japanese advance, one indication was the length of time, thirty-six hours, since any contact with the enemy. From eight hundred to one thousand enemy troops had been killed in both the ambush and when the bridge had been blown up. Australian casualties had been slight with not many men listed as 'missing'.[319] What a worry to the families who didn't know which battalions were involved in the fighting.

But worse was to come.

The Japanese Imperial Guards landed at the mouth of the Muar River and threatened the Australians left flank where part of 2/29 was deployed. Bennett held back a company and platoon of 160 men who moved to Bakri. They were reinforced by the 2/19 of the 22nd Brigade (the 2/18 and 2/20 remained in Mersing, guarding the East coast).

There was fierce fighting and the 2/29 were in trouble. The 2/19 were successful in holding the enemy but were then ordered to pull out towards Yong Peng to save the Indian's 45th Brigade which was also under heavy fire. The 2/19 ran into trouble themselves. Again the troops did not know which shells to use against the Japanese tanks. Armour-piercing rounds could go in one side and out the other but the tank continued on.[320]

The *Sydney Morning Herald* report said the enemy maintained pressure on the River Muar and Segamat fronts and had infiltrated troops southwards in the coastal belt.[321] They came down by boat using the craft which had been left intact when towns such as Penang were evacuated. The Japanese launched a vigorous attack with tanks and aircraft; the main thrusts were at the Muar River and further south at Batu Pahat.

The Battle for Muar was to be one of the most savage of the campaign. Even the Japanese Commander General Yamashita recorded that:

> *survivors of the enemy can feel proud, because in a week long bloody battle, without tank or air support, they held up the whole of my army. There is no doubt that the Imperial Guards in the Battle of Muar and the fact that the Commander and bulk of Officers and men of Japan's most famous Regiment, the Ogaki, had been*

lost, had a curious effect upon these elite troops for the remainder of the campaign, acting with unusual hesitancy.[322]

Whilst many of the AIF battalions were heavily involved on the west coast, things were now hotting up for the 2/18 and 2/20 on the east coast.

Endau Force was bombed and machine gunned and withdrew to Bukit Langkap and Jemaluang. Mersing was bombed. The troops were patrolling Mersing Tenglu, Bukit Sawah, and Mayong Estate areas.[323] Surplus stores and ammunition were moved to selected dump sites in Koti Tinggi Rd and Johore Bahru at night.

On 20 January the enemy continued to bomb the troops in the Mersing area. Four men of 'D' Coy 2/19 Bn, troops of Endau Force, who had been missing since being in contact with the enemy on 16 January approached and were brought through 'A' Coy area. These troops reported that Japs were in strength in Endau village occupying many houses and Japs had been encountered 5 miles south of the Endau-Mersing Road. This information was then passed onto Brigades. How different the speed of communication was at that time from what we now expect as the norm!

By 21 January the *War Diary* reported that troops engaged the enemy in Mersing, with 7 Platoon, led by Lieut Frank Ramsbotham, ambushing an enemy party at Padi Test Street. The main Japanese force then deployed to flanks and advanced through an anti-personnel minefield adjacent to the main road. Unfortunately the mines generally failed to explode (due to prolonged immersion in water caused by heavy rains) but the enemy were destroyed by medium machine gun, mortar and artillery fire. 7 Platoon opened fire from Lalang Hill and held enemy.

Major-General Bennett reported to the press that fighting had begun on the east coast area held by the AIF to which the enemy had infiltrated from the north. He advised that on Wednesday (21 January) the AIF had ambushed a Japanese party causing heavy casualties. The AIF patrol then rejoined the main force of troops.[324]

Back in the west some of the 2/19 troops who had survived the battle for Muar had to move to avoid being overrun by the Japanese. Under the command of Capt. Reg Newton, they made their way by compass bearings to try to return to Allied lines. They learned from some British troops that the bridge at Parit Sulong had fallen into enemy hands. Newton's force moved through the swamps then onto cultivated land. Eventually they split into ten groups of about six men who set off independently. Many were never heard of again. Newton stayed with the wounded men and they were betrayed by some locals. As prisoners they were taken to Malacca for interrogation, then to Pudu Jail in Kuala Lumpur.[325]

By 22 January other 2/19 troops under the command of Lieutenant-Colonel Charles Anderson tried to cross the bridge at Parit Sulong, not realising it had fallen into enemy hands. Eventually the Australians had to retreat and were surrounded. The Japanese refused to allow safe passage of the wounded, so Anderson had no choice but to allow the fit men to slip away in the night, 'every man for himself', and leave their wounded behind.

During the night these seriously wounded men kept firing towards the Japanese to disguise the retreat of their mates. The next day the Japanese realised they had been tricked. They herded the desperately sick and wounded men, over one hundred and fifty of them, into a small building the size of a tiny garage. They denied them food and water until the following morning when they kicked and beat the men before killing them with bayonets. Only three men managed to survive the massacre.[326]

The fighting at Parit Sulong, and the horrific aftermath has been recorded by several authors including Russell Braddon *The Naked Island*, Reg Newton *The Grim Glory of the 2/19 Battalion AIF*, Lynette Silver *The Bridge at Parit Sulong* and Colin Smith *Singapore Burning*. They make for exceptionally harrowing reading. Russell Braddon, NX8190, a gunner with the 2/15 Field Regiment, gives a first hand account of the troops' withdrawal through the jungle. Reg Newton also includes several personal stories of this action and escape in his history of the battalion.

The battle by the Australians against the numerically superior Imperial Guards between Muar and Parit Sulong was one of the epic encounters of the Malayan campaign and Percival considered the delay they imposed on the Japanese had saved a large part of his army from being cut off and annihilated at Yong Peng. The loss of the battle at Muar marked the end of any serious attempts by the Allies to hold onto part of Johore.[327]

The *Sydney Morning Herald* of 21 January 1942 reported that the Japanese were just seventy-five miles from Singapore[328] and the following day the distance was reported to have dropped to seventy miles. *The War Correspondent* reported that Allied troops were being severely tested and no details of the operation were known, the area was too remote. The Japanese were good at infiltrating and, though they had been hit hard in frontal attacks against the Australians, it was not long before '*his feelers are trying to get round*'.[329]

The *War Diary* of the 2/20 Battalion AIF MERSING for 22/24 Jan '42 included:

Enemy engaged in MERSING area, came under fire from Mortars, V.M.G.s, L.M.Gs. [Vickers and Light machine guns]

Enemy were completely routed. Intense bombing and machine gunning of MERSING area, particularly on any troop movements. Enemy sniping along banks and across S. MERSING.

Bde HQ and 2/18 Bn HQ moved to NITTSDALE ESTATE; B Echelon Bde Gp to concentrate Rubber area Jemaluang S.D Camp. Casualties estimated enemy killed 200, Own troops 1 KIA, 1 Missing believed killed, 2 missing, 4 wounded.

24th Jan: MERSING BRIDGE demolished, gap of 150 ft blown. Patrols reported Japanese concentration K. JAMARI destroyed by artillery fire.

Australians learned of this battle on the east coast on 23 January. It was reported that there had been -

contact with the enemy north of Mersing with enemy forces pushing south from the Endau River. Our troops successfully ambushed portion of the enemy forces inflicting a number of casualties with slight loss to themselves.[330]

Thus the families back home learned that now their lads stationed on the east coast, as well as those on the west, had been in the battle. Finally every Australian family would know their loved one in Malaya was directly in contact with the Japanese. Their stress and worry must have been intense.

On 24 January the *Sydney Morning Herald* reported that the allied Imperial Forces were making a general withdrawal from the various places where fighting was taking place. Acting Prime Minister Forde declared that the situation was more serious than it was just a few days ago.[331]

The defences prepared at Endau by the 22nd Brigade troops were abandoned to fall back to the Mersing-Kluang-Ayer Hitam-Batu Pahat line south of Muar on the west and Endau on the east. But soon they were ordered to withdraw south again.

Troops ordered to withdraw from Mersing had been preparing defences for months. They were not impressed at being ordered to leave.

Six months, fortifications, and all of a sudden we realised the Japs were all going down the west coast ... we were so disappointed that we pulled out of there without even trying.[332]

The *Sydney Morning Herald* of 26 January 1942 told Australians the grim news that many troops had been killed in the battle at Muar in previous weeks. Imagine the horror for the families on being confronted with the dreadful headline:

AIF's COURAGE IN MALAYA - ENDURANCE IN EPIC BATTLE 'SACRIFICE NOT IN VAIN'

MALAYAN FRONT January 25 Today it is possible to tell the epic story of self-sacrifice of two Australian Units - one from New South Wales, one from Victoria - in order to hold up the enemy for four vital days while the Imperial line was withdrawn.

Cut off after having been rushed to Muar to prevent the Japanese from getting behind British lines, the units refused to admit defeat at the hands of an overwhelmingly superior enemy force.

They fought day and night for a week until their ammunition and food ran out and then fought their way back 15 miles, only to find their retreat cut off.

Splitting up into small parties, they set out to steal through the enemy's lines by way of jungle and swamp.

Yesterday's Singapore communiqué revealed that considerable numbers of them and of the Indians they were sent to relieve have now reached the British lines after bitter fighting.

The Australian G.O.C. Major-General Gordon Bennett said on Friday that their sacrifice had not been in vain.

The Muar Road battle will mean sorrow in many Australian homes but Britons throughout the world will be proud of what has been done by men of Anzac fighting stock well led and expertly trained.

UNITS REFUSED TO ADMIT DEFEAT

This is the story of the men who refused to admit defeat and fought day and night for a week; whose ammunition and food ran out yet who are now gradually escaping for the jungle swamps and returning to their headquarters.

Two Australian units were involved in the battle which will take its place in history with the Charge of the Light Brigade.

The Australians have suffered heavily in the past week, but they have held up a whole division of the Japanese Imperial Guards, stopped enemy tanks, kept their wounded with them and fought through enemy lines for a distance of 15 miles to a position which they believed to be in our hands only to find when they reached there, exhausted, without food, and down to their last few rounds, that our previous position had been relinquished and the enemy was blocking the bridge of escape.

Major-General Gordon Bennett's last message to these surrounded troops will be quoted for years to come. Sent at 11.5 am on Thursday last by radio it read 'I regret that there is little prospect of any success of an attack between the 70 and 80 mile posts to help you. Lloyd's party [a commando unit that had already distinguished itself] *if successful should have appeared before this. Twenty of your men and many Indians have already returned to the road, which at present is in our possession at the 78 mile post.*

You may at your discretion leave the wounded with volunteers, destroy your heavy equipment and escape. Sorry I am unable to help after your heroic effort. Good luck.'

The consolation of this message was unfortunately not received by the lost battalions because it has been learned from survivors that the radio truck was destroyed just before.

The story of those brave men begins more than a week ago. Two weeks ago Indian troops were in the area south of Malacca where they were being hard pressed by a heavy Japanese infiltration farther south which was threatening their rear. Newly arrived Indians were sent to the Muar area in order to relieve the troops who were moving back from the north.

On January 18 the West Force Command decided to send in two Australian units which were rushed to Muar that day and accounted for 10 enemy tanks.

Then followed a dramatic account of the fighting which included hand-to-hand bayonets, sniping and machine guns. Some survivors who had made it back to their own lines told the story.

More harrowing was what happened to the wounded. Under the headline *JAPANESE MACHINE GUN WOUNDED* was the news of how the Japanese refused to allow Red Cross trucks and ambulances across the Parit Sulong Bridge and through to safety. The fit and walking-wounded had no option but to leave the seriously wounded and attempt to reach their own lines. The Japanese refused food, water and medication and massacred the AIF men.

There were two whole columns in the newspaper devoted to the story with an additional column under the headline *AIF LEADERS BRILLIANT* which discussed the battle and the fine work by the NCOs and finished with:

The people of Australia have every reason to be proud of them, their fighting spirit and their devotion to duty regardless of danger.

Even the editorial of the day was headlined *THE EPIC OF MUAR ROAD* which encouraged that:

Every Australian must respond to a thrill of pride at the tales of individual gallantry and self denial, at the disregard shown by our men for mere numbers of the enemy and not least at the splendid leadership of small parties maintained though leader after leader fell.[333]

Such words, such platitudes, would be of absolutely no comfort whatsoever to the families back home; they would want to know whether or not their own boy was still alive. Mothers don't want their sons to be injured or to die, even as heroes, they want them safely back home. Mothers hate war.[334]

What the Australians did not know was that members of the local population had also died at the end of a Japanese bayonet. Poh Woodland, then a small child, recalled -

My mother's sister and family were living in Muar ... I can still remember when we got the telephone message to say that the whole family was gone, all bayoneted, and only one child escaped by running into the jungle.[335]

The progression of the fighting was reported back in Australia.

NEW LANDING IN MALAYA - ENEMY THRUST IN EAST

Despite determined air attacks the enemy convoy sighted off Endau on the east coast of Malaya on Monday has landed a force and some transport ... Our bombers hit an enemy cruiser and scored twelve hits on troop transports and on stores dumped on the beach ...

Landing troops were machine gunned. At least 12 enemy fighters were destroyed. Our forces in this area are in contact with the enemy north of Jemaluang which is south of Mersing. This implies a withdrawal of the Imperial troops in the Mersing area.[336]

A further report added:

The troops who have been holding the Mersing area on the east coast, north of which the new landing has been made, have been preparing the defences for a year and there is no doubt these defences are formidable.[337]

The *Sydney Morning Herald* reported that an enemy convoy including warships and two merchant ships was sighted off Endau.[338] Thus the Japanese landed more troops by ship in the area. Despite the Air Force's valiant efforts in unwieldy and outdated aircraft, there was little to stop them. The Japanese then by-passed Mersing which was so recently vacated by the 22nd Brigade who by then had been ordered to withdraw to Singapore Island.

However the Australians did manage to get into the fray. Some companies moved ahead of the Japanese, the others moved behind, and there was fierce hand to hand fighting.

War Diary of the 2/20 Battalion AIF JEMALUANG 27 Jan '42

0330 hrs Firing heard in direction of 2/18 Bn Ambush area, 2/18 engaged with enemy LUO TYE ESTATE

0900 2/18 commenced withdrawing through our lines, 2/20 to cover 2/18 down to ULU SIDILLI then, after 1930hrs, 2/20 to withdraw to 29½ Mile Harbour and come into Bde. Reserve. At 2100 hrs 'B' and 'D' Coys by foot to 67 Mile Harbour embussed and ferried to ULU SIDILLE, Bn. HQ, 'A' and 'C' Coys by foot to 67 Mile Harbour and embussed to 29½ Mile Harbour.

A clean break was made with the enemy.

Troops of the 2/20 were to withdraw through the 2/18 lines and it was proposed to mount offensive action against the approaching Japanese. A trap was set in the area of the Nithsdale and Joo Lye Estates, between Mersing and Jemaluang, with the 2/18 setting up ambush positions. Grim fighting occurred in pitch darkness, with the troops showing desperate courage in the face of greatly superior numbers.[339] The Japanese lost 2,000 troops, with mainly one company of the 2/18 being responsible, but at a huge cost, with 'D' Company almost annihilated in the action.[340]

The article from *Sydney Morning Herald*, 5 February 1942*, p. 6, kept by Vera, was found amongst Bill's letters.

According to a Communiqué:

The enemy was caught between forward elements and artillery fire, enemy casualties are estimated at about 250 and ours at about 30. Our troops in this area made contact with the enemy around Ulu Sedili.[341]

The action went unfinished as the Brigade sent a withdrawal order. During the night of 27-28 January the troops moved to Sungei Ulu Sedili and carried out rear guard defensive action as East Force continued to withdraw.[342]

But the troop's artillery support was withdrawn prematurely and the troops were ordered to make their way to Singapore Island where the Causeway Bridge was to be blown up before 1 February.

The ambush of the Japanese by the 2/18, with backup by the 2/20 at the Nithsdale and Joo/Luo Tye Estates, with as many as 2,000 Japanese being killed for the loss of 83 Australian troops, was one of the most inglorious and costly fights of the whole campaign for the Japanese.[343]

This was the Muar Battle of the East Coast.[344]

Was this the same battle recorded by Shinozaki? He wrote that at some stage the Japanese fought a terrific battle with the Australians at Jemaluang near Mersing. He reported that it was fought between two hundred members of an Australian demolition party and a strong element of a Japanese brigade. The Australians were returning to Singapore after destroying Mersing Bridge and other bridges. Soon after dawn the Australians entered Jemaluang and

A.I.F.'s AMBUSH AT MERSING

Japanese Battalion Wiped Out

OFFICIAL CORRESPONDENT.

SINGAPORE, Feb. 4.—A Japanese battalion was ambushed and wiped out by two New South Wales battalions, which had remained at Mersing in the eastern sector of Johore, away from the main A.I.F. actions.

The two battalions hit the Japanese so hard before they fell back that all Imperial troops on the east coast were able to withdraw to Singapore without further contact with the enemy for four days.

It was at Mersing and Jemaluang that the main Australian forces had been concentrated in recent months and they had built defences that were regarded as virtually impregnable. The Japanese never attempted a landing there in what has long been regarded as "the gateway to Singapore."

When the desperate position in the west necessitated the main body of the A.I.F. going there, the two battalions left at Mersing were confident they could hold the Japanese. They had, however, to withdraw when the enemy looked like cutting them off from the west.

It was on January 26 that it was realised that these battalions would have to fall back, but their commanders estimated that the Japanese had only two regiments in contact with the A.I.F. on the Mersing River, although big forces had been landed about 30 miles farther north.

It was decided to try to trap the Japanese on the road south of Jemaluang. One battalion fell back through the other to the south of the Jemaluang-Kluang crossroads. Companies were then dispersed so that one covered the road, while others were placed on the flanks as far as 1,000 yards into the jungle. Artillery and mortars were hidden ready for action and by dusk all was ready with a seemingly unprotected road open to the Japanese.

Late in the afternoon a forward platoon encountered small parties of Japanese beating through the rubber trees and firing tommy guns and shouting. They did not, however, draw our fire, and the platoon silently withdrew.

FIERCE BATTLE

At 1.15 a.m. on January 27, Japanese troops opened fire from the road on our company covering it, but again no fire was drawn. Although it was their first time under fire, the A.I.F. men maintained perfect discipline and soon the reassured Japanese started to file past them.

At 2.20 a.m., the enemy made contact with the company holding the flank east of the road, and our troops went into action. Fighting was severe, but the Japanese were pushed into more compact groups to make better targets for the waiting gunners. At 3.30, a field regiment opened fire, backed by mortars. They got the range from the first shot, and their opening barrage lasted seven minutes. Then they laid down a creeping barrage, jumping 100 yards every two minutes, to enable our infantry to keep contact with the Japanese. This went on from 3.30 a.m. to 8 a.m., with the terrified Japanese meeting slaughter from every point.

Our infantry advanced 1,000 yards through rubber trees and jungle, of which they knew every inch. The enemy had got six mortars and numerous heavy and light automatic weapons into action, but these were silenced by our gunners, and by 8 a.m. a complete Japanese battalion had been destroyed. The last troops to leave the area reported that even Japanese reinforcements were retreating to Mersing. The past few months' hard toil of the A.I.F. in that area had been justified, as Mersing must be regarded as one of the most successful actions of the Malayan campaign.

**Sydney Morning Herald* 5 February 1942

came into contact with soldiers from Colonel Kiba's invasion force. It was a fight to the death in which the Saeki Tank Regiment from Kluang also took part. All two hundred Australians were wiped out. The Japanese were reported to have lost a thousand men killed or wounded.

The bravery of the Australians impressed the Japanese commanders Colonel Kiba and Colonel Saeki who, as a mark of respect, ordered a huge wooden cross be set up over the mass grave of the AIF men on the side of a hill facing the north-east just outside Jemaluang as the road curves to Mersing. On the cross was painted the words *To our Gallant Enemies, the Australians.*[345]

It is obvious that Malay Command planned to withdraw to Singapore Island during in the next few days. Despite the proposed ambush of the Japanese, Capt. Frank Gaven recalled that all the 2IC's, including himself, Capt. Maxwell, Lieut Mudie and Capt. Bill Gaden, were taken across the Causeway by Brigadier Dawkins and shown what was to be their allocated Battalion position, even their company positions, in the Kranji area on Singapore Island. These areas the troops were to hold if the Japanese invaded the Island. The officers were horrified. They had spent months working like beavers to make good fortification in the Mersing area, constructing fences on the beaches, digging trenches, laying mines, cutting tracks, but here, despite all the promises and money, there was nothing.

There were no fortifications, no sign of support, no sign of relief, not a glimmer of hope. Frank walked to the edge of an impenetrable mangrove swamp. He recalls feeling it was a desperate situation. An experienced soldier, he was full of gloom; they were going to be asked an impossible task and Frank thought that: *even Richard the Lionhearted would have felt desperate.*

He was also concerned that, however much the officers tried to remain positive, these feelings of desolation must have been visible and it would then be almost impossible to inspire the troops. Army HQ didn't seem to appreciate the urgency of the situation ... the orders coming through were to do with things like arrangements for recreation leave for the troops and laundering of troops clothing. As Frank said:

> *They were in Cuckoo-cloud land. It had no relevance to priority or urgency.*[346]

> ***War Diary* of the 2/20 Battalion AIF KOTI TINNGI 29$^1/_2$ MILE HARBOUR Jan 28 '42**
>
> Eng. Demolition party demolished wooden bridge and cratered road to delay enemy. Warning order received from BDE that 2/20 Bn. would move early on 29 Jan '42 to JOHORE BAHRU as centre Bn of an outer Br. Head Force which would cover the withdrawal of all forces on the Mainland to Singapore Island. Bn washed clothes and bodies, also rested. This was welcome having been in contact with the enemy for some days.

Bill found time to write a letter home. He tried to remain positive and keep things light but he alerted his mother to the money available from his bank account should he not return home. He also tried to give some 'brotherly' advice to his two sisters about their future.

Darling Doukie 29 Jan '42

I have not written for over a week. No paper, pens, time or post office.

We have been in action. Today our unit has been pulled well back to a quiet spot and we are resting, washing and looking at our feet. We have not seen the latter in days.

I am perfectly well dear and in the best of spirits. In fact not at any stage of the proceedings have I felt otherwise. My troops, I have not lost a man, are cheerful and confident. You should see them now. Nearly all of them are writing letters and most are stark naked with their clothes drying on nearby bushes. We found a creek to wash in.

Last night when we arrived back here there were 14 letters waiting for me. What a feast, 4 were yours and the rest from various people including the office who told me they had posted you a cheque for £25. Cripes I am really wealthy already, we can't spend any cash when times are like they are at present. My pay book must have £60 in it and my bank account in Sydney is now receiving a £1 per week allotment.

Goulburn must have been good fun and relaxation for you. You must slip away as often as you can dear.

Sue should find a decent job somewhere. She will find it hard to work for somebody other than herself but that is an obstacle her cheerful disposition will quickly overcome.

I think Ginge may be wise to stick with her present job. However if they won't pay her she is quite entitled to leave and find another, or rather find another before leaving. A permanent job on a steady salary is preferable to an unstable position even if the money is attractive.

Cheerio darling. I shall write as often as possible. Always remember that 'no news is good news'. My love to Sue, Ginge and Gran.

All my love
Bill

The day Bill wrote home the *Sydney Morning Herald* reported:

Fighting doggedly against superior numbers and delaying the progress of the enemy every inch of the way across Johore State, the Imperial Forces in Malaya are now defending a line roughly along the east-west road through Johore, 50 or 60 miles north of Singapore.

The Japanese are now attempting to move on Singapore along four main roads; from Senggarang on the west coast; from Ayer Hitam and Kluang in the centre and from Jemaluang on the east coast.

The worsening situation for everyone was evident when Major Blaskett of the Salvation Army wrote:

In the present emergency we are allotted a definite centre from which to work, touching all units en route as far as possible. The future is veiled in uncertainty. We are having experiences of which we cannot write. For three nights I have had practically no sleep. We made a hurried pack-up at 2 a.m. in the dark yesterday morning. I fear some of our equipment is lost. Some of our marquees were hurriedly pulled down and our stuff left.[347]

Back home in Australia the population was being warned by Deputy Prime Minister Francis Forde that an attempted invasion of Australia was a 'logical possibility'. Plans for a large scale evacuation of civilians would not be put into effect unless deemed necessary by the military authorities.[348]

The last day of January was a sad day for the Allies. At 0500 am they received orders to withdraw to Singapore Island and by 0630am the 2/20 Bn had commenced to cross the Causeway.[349]

At 0815 am, the last Allied troops of the Australian 22nd Brigade and the 2nd Gordons crossed the Causeway onto Singapore Island. Two surviving pipers from the Argyll and Sutherland Highlanders played them across the Straits, so the troops withdrew to the poignant and haunting strains of bagpipes playing 'A Hundred Pipers', 'Hielan Laddie' and possibly also a Gordon's piper playing 'Jenny's Black E'en' and 'Blue Bonnets O'er the Border'.[350]

The causeway (with its vital water supply pipe) was then blown up by Indian Sappers, creating a 70 foot wide gap.[351]

The last stand was imminent.

276 *Sydney Morning Herald*, 1 January 1942, p. 5.
277 Smith, *Singapore Burning*, p. 353.
278 Gaffney G, interview with Caroline Gaden now an AWM CD S01738.
279 *War Diary 2/20 Bn. A.I.F.*, 1 January 1942.
280 National Archives of Australia, record of service of Elaine Lenore Balfour-Ogilvy.
281 *Sydney Morning Herald*, 2 January 1942, p. 5.
282 Smith, *op. cit.*, p. 347.
283 *Sydney Morning Herald*, 3 January 1942, p. 5.
284 *War Diary 2/20 A.I.F.*, 4 January 1942.
285 Falk, *Seventy Days to Singapore*, pp. 148-153.
286 Smith, *op. cit.*, p. 347.
287 *War Diary 2/20 Bn. A.I.F.*, 5-6 January 1942.
288 Ziegler, *Men May Smoke*, p. 23.
289 *Sydney Morning Herald*, 6 January 1942, p. 7.
290 Smith, *op. cit.*, p. 353, and *War Diary 2/20 Bn. A.I.F.*, 23 December 1941.
291 *Sydney Morning Herald*, 7 January 1942, p. 11.
292 *War Diary 2/20 Bn. A.I.F.*, 7 January 1942 and War Plan for Defence of Left Sector Mersing.
293 Parkinson, *Blood, Toil, Tears and Sweat*, p. 352.
294 Smith, *op. cit.*, pp. 288, 291.
295 *ibid.*, pp. 265-6.
296 *ibid.*, p. 291.
297 *ibid.*, p. 368.
298 Falk, *op. cit.*, p. 161.
299 Smith, *op. cit.*, p. 302.
300 *War Diary 2/20 Bn. A.I.F.*, 8-11 January 1942.
301 Smith, *op. cit.*, p. 350.
302 *Sydney Morning Herald*, 10 January 1942, p.13.
303 *ibid.*, 12 January 1942, p.7.
304 Onn, Chin Lee, *Silent Army*, p. 54-6.
305 *Sydney Morning Herald*, 13 January 1942, p. 7.
306 Smith, *op. cit.*, p. 347.
307 Falk, *op. cit.*, p. 161.
308 Smith, *op. cit.*, p. 352.
309 Ziegler, *op. cit.*, p. 23.
310 *War Diary 2/20 Bn. A.I.F.*, 12 January 1942.
311 *Sydney Morning Herald*, 14 January 1942, p. 9.

[312] *ibid.*, 15 January 1942, p. 7.
[313] *ibid.*, 17 January 1942, p. 13.
[314] Smith, *Singapore Burning*, p. 356.
[315] *ibid.*, p. 359.
[316] *Sydney Morning Herald*, 19 January 1942, p. 15.
[317] *ibid.*, 17 January 1942, p. 13.
[318] *War Diary 2/20 Bn. A.I.F.*, 14 January 1942.
[319] *Sydney Morning Herald*, 19 January 1942, p. 5.
[320] Smith, *op. cit.*, pp. 360-365.
[321] *Sydney Morning Herald*, 20 January 1942, p. 5.
[322] Birch, *The 2nd AIF in Malaya 1941-1942*, < http://www.htansw.asn.au/teach/war/JBirch%20Malaya%20Article.pdf >
[323] *War Diary 2/20 Bn. A.I.F.*, 15-19 January 1942.
[324] *Sydney Morning Herald*, 24 January 1942, p. 13.
[325] AWM Summary details from Photograph of Capt. Newton P0385.001.
[326] Smith, *op. cit.*, p. 374.
[327] Smith, *op. cit.*, p. 397.
[328] *Sydney Morning Herald*, 21 January 1942, p. 9.
[329] *ibid.*, 22 January 1942, p. 5.
[330] *ibid.*, 23 January 1942, p. 5.
[331] *ibid.*, 24 January 1942, p. 13.
[332] Elliott and Silver, *A history of the 2/18 Battalion AIF*, p. 45.
[333] *Sydney Morning Herald*, 26 January 1942, pp. 4-5.
[334] Winn, *Scrapbook of Victory*, p. 119.
[335] Barrett, *Hidden Heritage*, p. 8.
[336] *Sydney Morning Herald*, 28 January 1942, p. 9.
[337] *ibid.*, 28 January 1942, p. 9.
[338] *ibid.*, 27 January 1942, p. 7.
[339] Ziegler, *op. cit.*, p. 23.
[340] Elliott and Silver, *op. cit.*, pp. 47-51.
[341] *Sydney Morning Herald*, 30 January 1942 p. 7.
[342] Ziegler, *op. cit.*, p. 23.
[343] Elliott and Silver, *op. cit.*, p. 47.
[344] *ibid.*, p. 99.
[345] Shinozake, Syonan, p. 77.
[346] Frank Gaven interview with Don Wall, AWM S04104.
[347] Hull, 'Salvos with the Forces, Red Shield Services during World War 2 reporting' *War Cry* Jan 31st 1942.
[348] *Sydney Morning Herald*, 30 January 1942, p. 7.
[349] *War Diary 2/20 Bn. A.I.F.*, 31 January 1942.
[350] Smith, *op. cit.*, p. 410.
[351] <http://www.britain-at-war.org.uk/WW2/Malaya_and_Singapore/html/body_chronology_of_malaya.html>

Chapter 8 - Battle for Singapore

Back in Australia the population did not know that withdrawal to Singapore Island had already occurred. The *Sydney Morning Herald* was busy reporting that the defenders were moving back and withdrawal was forecast. It also carried a story *ESCAPE THROUGH THE STEAMING JUNGLE,* telling thrilling stories of jungle marches through strong Japanese forces and helped by friendly Chinese. They reported that the Japanese were using motor bikes as well as bicycles to aid their journey south, advising the Allies had captured 250 motor bikes and 150 cycles in one attack on a Japanese position. There was also a tale of abuse by the Japanese on an elderly Civil servant who was saved by the bravery of Tamil and Chinese locals who untied his bindings and helped him to escape.[352]

By 2 February the newspaper's editorial advised:

> *The withdrawal of the Empire forces across the Johore Strait into the island of Singapore brings to an end a campaign which despite the heroism of the forces engaged will always be a depressing chapter in British military history because of inadequate preparation and in some respect performance.*

Readers were reminded that the invaders were now just 650 miles from Darwin.[353]

Once over the Causeway and back on Singapore Island, the troops were taken to their allotted defensive areas. The Australian troops were posted to the north-west corner of the island, with the 27th Brigade to the east of the Kranji River and the 22nd Brigade to its west. The 2/20 were the most northerly battalion, closest the Kranji River, the 2/18 were in the centre with the 2/19 the most southerly battalion.[354] Defensive work started immediately. Bill's Company, 'D' Company was in the centre of the 2/20 area, facing north on the Johore Strait.[355]

Stan Arneil revealed that the troops themselves were happy that they could withdraw no more, they were on the final perimeter and they could now stand and fight. They were exhausted from the continual fighting and withdrawing, fighting and withdrawing until they could scarcely walk from weariness. They felt that now they were reunited with friends and had plenty of food. They thought the probing attacks of Japanese patrols would not be problem, they just were eager to stand and fight.[356]

It was a time to re-group, rest and reflect, a time for a final letter to be written to loved ones back home. For both Allies and enemy it was to be a few days of respite before the final bloody battle, the battle for Singapore itself, began.

Brigadier Taylor's 22nd Brigade, the 2/18, 2/19 and 2/20 Battalions took on almost fifteen kilometres of coastline in the centre, where the Johore Strait was narrowest and where a Japanese attack was almost certain to come. The Japanese troops could be seen concentrating across the Straits.

The 22nd Brigade was only at about half strength (2,500 troops) due to losses in the fighting on the peninsula. The 2/18 and 2/20 were both given many kilometres of coast to defend, each given about twenty-five square kilometres of the area of operations. The 2/20 Battalion was to the west of the Kranji River, on the eastern side of the Lim Chu Kang Road.[357] They had to defend around seven kilometres of coastline.[358] The 2/18 men were to their west, in the Serembun River area and the 2/19 placed further down the coast towards the Berih River.[359]

On 1 February 1942 the 2/20 Battalion had just thirty-two officers and seven hundred and fifty-seven men.[360] Around eighty experienced men had been evacuated to hospital and some were sent to reinforce the depleted 2/19. Numbers were boosted by the addition of eighty reinforcements, but these men only arrived in Singapore on 5 February. They were unfit after the sea voyage, had insufficient training and no fighting experience.

By 8 February these men had to defend around seven kilometres of coastline, a coastline where no fortification or defensive structures had been built ... an impossible task.[361] In the next few days four hundred 2/20 troops would become casualties in the fighting, including ten officers.[362]

The Australians found that they occupied a deeply indented coastline with no defensive works whatsoever.[363] It was a dense wasteland of mangrove swamp and mud flats rather than open beaches, which made rapid enforcement during battle virtually impossible. Battalion posts were sometimes hundreds of metres apart and this was ideal for the infiltration tactics favoured by the Japanese.[364]

A gloomy assessment of the Australian's area was made by Lieutenant-Colonel Roland Oakes (NX12525) of 2/19:

> *A scraggy waste of stunted rubber and tangled undergrowth, apparently miles from anywhere, our vision limited to the next rise in the undulating ground and our means of movement confined to a few native foot-tracks winding through the wilderness ... Maps showed that we were a mile and a half from the west coast with ... the 2/18 away to the north in a similar desolation of waste and confusion ... A mile of single file track led through the belukar* [secondary jungle] *eight feet high, where visibility was no more than a stone's throw, to ... where 'D' Company looked out on the beauties of a mangrove swamp which was under water at high tide. It was not so much a thin khaki line of Australians but isolated clumps.*[365]

Even Bennett himself was concerned. On 2 February he had visited the northern area sector where the 2/20 were encamped. He looked at the entrance to the Kulai River across the Strait, a likely place from which an attack could be launched. Bennett reported that the men were cheerful but the posts were lonely. He commented: 'The gaps between posts are wide. The position is extremely weak'.[366] Two days later he visited the 2/18 and 2/19 Battalions. In his diary he noted:

> *This part of the island is thickly covered with timber, mostly rubber, with thick mangrove swamps growing right down to the water's edge. The posts, which are*

many hundred of yards apart, have a field of fire of only 200 yards. The gaps are patrolled regularly. I am beginning to worry about the extreme weakness.[367]

Darling Doukie 2 Feb '42

Last night I received three letters, all written from Goulburn. The holiday must have been great dear.

At present we are on Singapore Island. We have been here for a couple of days and during that time things have been very peaceful and sunny on the ground. The war is still going on above the clouds. Jap planes are continually coming over and our ack-acks are having great fun and bringing them down.

The planes keep up so high that they are only little black dots in the sky. The ack-ack shells bursting make a ring around the plane with little white puffs. The war is pretty; looking up at it from here.

The town we were in when I wrote about dugouts etc was Mersing on the East Coast. We held up Jap there for a week and only withdrew because our help was needed elsewhere. The AIF were never driven out of any position on the peninsula and the number of Japs we accounted for was terrific. At Mersing we got a couple of hundred of them and lost 3 chaps ourselves. Our artillery did most of the damage.

I believe that Sydney is to be evacuated. Heavens! Dear, where are you going? 'Marooan' may be useful but somehow I don't think you will go there. When I have the opportunity I shall send some more cash because you will surely need it.

The office were decent sending you £25 for Xmas. They are a great crowd.

This paper is crumpled badly. It came through the 'battle of Malaya' in my pocket.

All the clothes I own are on my back at the moment. The rest are somewhere about, not far away. We are all in the same boat, only carrying necessities and leaving the rest in dumps to be picked up by trucks. Unfortunately the Jap has been the first to arrive at some of these dumps. However we have not lost much and we have been taught the wisdom of traveling light.

Arch Ewart has been across to see us. He is well and sparking as ever.

The part of the Island we occupy is very pretty and clean. Rubber trees and native houses are everywhere but some small groups of palm trees on the coast make the place look just like a Metro Goldwyn Meyer tropic isle. There are a few magnificent houses with beautiful lawns but these we keep away from because the Jap likes to use them as targets for his eggs.

A phrase has come into our talk which will live forever; 'bomb happy'. A bloke is said to be thus affected when, at the faintest drone of a plane, will dive face downwards into the nearest hole and stay there. Most of us go for cover if a plane is directly overhead but otherwise we hop out to watch the ack-ack and dog fights. A few months ago it was difficult to make the lads dig, now there are some that rarely stop, but these in number are very few. Noise is far the worst part of bombing. The first few that came I thought were terrible but, after a hundred or so round about us at Mersing, I know that aerial bombing is a morale weapon and will never cause casualties in large numbers.

Cheerio darling. I shall write again soon. My love to the Girls and Gran.

Yours love

Bill

There were no more letters home before the fall of Singapore.

It was not until Monday 2 February 1942 that Sydney newspapers reported the withdrawal of the Allied troops from the mainland:

Imperial troops in Malaya have withdrawn to the island fortress of Singapore and are preparing to withstand a siege.

The Japanese invaders have reached Johore Bahru on the other side of the Straits of Johore and their way has been barred by the destruction of the Johore Causeway which formerly connected the island to the mainland ... the first 30 hours following the withdrawal were remarkable for the absence of battle. There were some air alerts and some bombing, three enemy aircraft were shot down, but no large scale attack.'

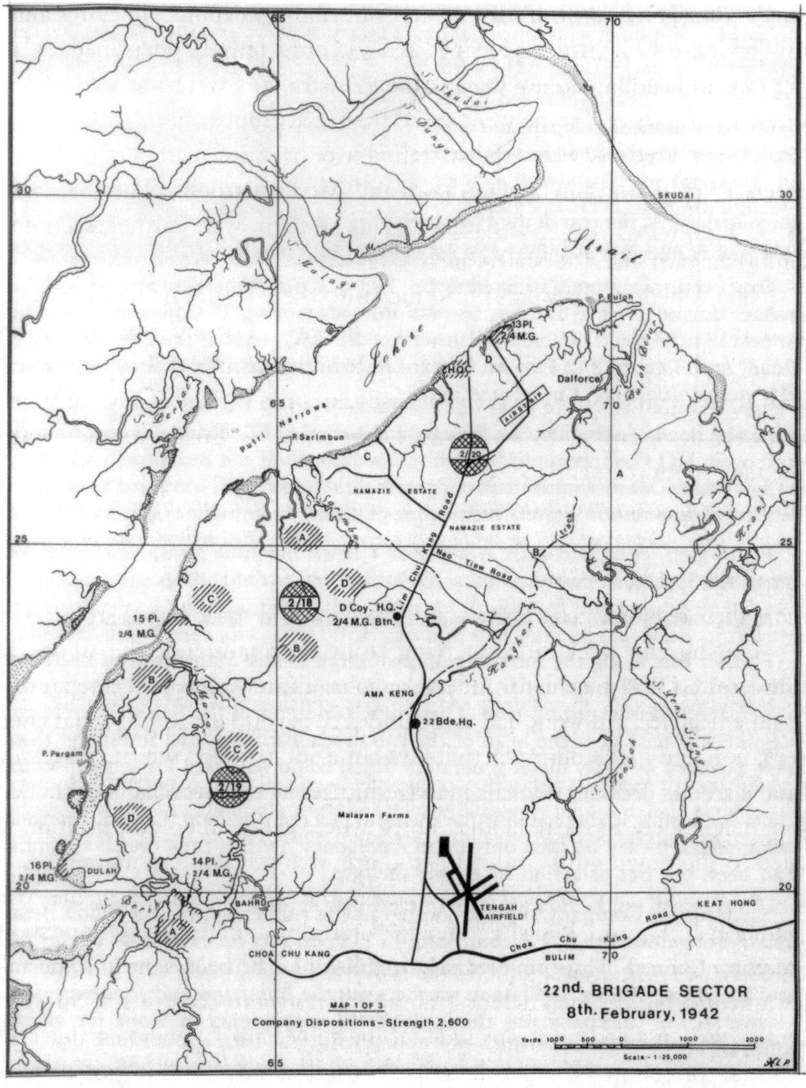

Map from Singapore and Beyond *by Don Wall - reproduced with permission*

An additional article gave the reasons for the move as the superiority of Japanese numbers, the convenient roads which they were able to use to outflank the British and their tank strength.[368]

The 2/20 were close to the Kranji River. 'A' Company were on the eastern sector near the Buloh and Kranji Rivers. 'B' Coy was in reserve near Namazie Estate, but soon were involved in the fighting, 'C' Company was also on the coast south of 'D', all overlooking thc Straits of Johore.

Bill's company, 'D' Company was deployed on the coast with the airstrip behind. To their east were Dalforce troops who were allocated an area close to the Buloh Besar River.[369] These local Dalforce troops were a Chinese Guerilla Force (named after Lieutenant-Colonel Dally the Commander of these local volunteers). They had no uniforms and not many weapons. They resembled many Japanese seen in the Mersing area so could only be identified as 'ally' by the white headband they wore. Many Australians were not told of these Chinese irregulars and some were killed by Allied troops.[370]

Interspersed between the battalion troops were members of Signals, Pioneers, Machine gunners, Transport and Medical troops. The Companies were each deployed into their platoons who, in turn, were in their sections to defend their particular allocated areas.

The Allied troops were spread too thin; there would be no interlocking fire so infiltration by the enemy would be easy. Despite this, the *Sydney Morning Herald* suggested there was room for optimism and they believed the British forces could hold off the Japanese until the arrival of reinforcements which were being rushed to Singapore. Prime Minister Curtin was demanding immediate reinforcements:

> *Assistance in great quantities must come at once otherwise it might be too late and even Hitler's defeat would be relatively unimportant in the face of an immediate catastrophe in the Pacific.*[371]

Some of these reinforcements arrived on 5 February.[372] It was to be too little, too late.

During the week since arriving from the mainland, the troops had fed and rested and began to undertake some limited defensive preparations along the beaches. All work had to be under cover of darkness to avoid enemy observation and fifth column activity was in evidence everywhere.[373] However Japanese troops dressed as locals managed to get across the Straits in the week before major shelling started. They noted where every allied gun position was located so their own guns could aim and fire with pinpoint accuracy.[374]

Six weeks prior to the fall of Malaya, the Chief Engineer of the Army, Brigadier Ivan Simson, had suggested to Percival that defence positions should be constructed in Singapore, precisely the task he had been sent to undertake. He wanted to build beach defences along the northern coastline of Singapore Island as well as fixed positions likely to be subject to Japanese assault across the Straits of Johore.[375] Percival refused to allow any building of defences, maintaining it was 'bad for morale both for troops and civilians'.[376]

Frank Baker recalled the coils of wire needed for the beach defences were all still in storage, so as not to upset the locals: as he remarked, 'Malay Command had a lot to answer for'.[377]

Even at this late stage life was proceeding as normal within the city itself with the picture theatre still running and the Anzac Club still serving meals.[378]

For Singapore, as with Hong Kong, the water supply was regarded as the greatest danger to the besieged, but feeding the substantial garrison and civilian population had also become a more serious problem.[379] There was plenty of food in storage, it just happened to be within range of the Japanese artillery as was the fuel and ammunition, a serious error of planning by those in charge ... basically Singapore Island was undefendable at close range.[380] The Japanese had seized control of the island's main water supply, the Gumong Pulai Waterworks north of the Causeway on 27 January. The supply was not disrupted until the Causeway was blown up by the Allied sappers a few days later. Subsequent bombing of Singapore also caused havoc on the water pipes, with huge amounts of water lost when pipes were torn apart in bombed buildings.[381]

On Thursday February 5 the *Sydney Morning Herald* reported the ominous order from Sir Archibald Wavell, the Supreme Commander of the Allied forces in the South West Pacific, to the defenders in Singapore. There was to be no retreat. He said:

> *I look to you to fight this battle without further thought of retreat and make the defence of Singapore as memorable and successful at the defence of Tobruk which British, Australian and Indian troops held so gallantly.*
>
> *Our part is to gain time for the great reinforcements which we and our American allies are sending to the eastern theatre. You must yield no strip of ground without fighting hard and leave nothing behind undestroyed that could be of the least service to the enemy.*[382]

Major Charles Moses, former OIC of the 2/20's 'D' Company, recited Wavell's order that there was to be no sparing of troops or civilians and no weakness was to be shown, 'Commanders and Senior Officers must lead their troops and if necessary, die with them'. The order did not reach many of the men, their officers tore it up and did not convey it. Just over two weeks later Moses had escaped from the Island and was heading for Australia with Bennett.[383]

The Japanese consolidated their troops at Johore Bahru before attempting a full scale attack against the Island. The Allied troops were reported to be busily preparing their defences on the miles of oozing mangrove swamps and network of greenish black tidal streams they were asked to defend. At one point a reporter was told 'Get down you silly blighter. No one must be seen here. Anyhow a sniper could get you.'[384]

According to David MacDougal, Capt. Bill Gaden told him he saw Japanese gathering in mass formation and many officers could be seen in the garden and on the verandahs of the Sultan's Palace on the mainland in Johore Bahru a mile away across the Straits.

David recalled:

Bill called for harassing fire from our artillery which would have caused huge Jap losses. The Brigade Artillery Commander refused because 'It might risk damaging the Sultan's Palace' and he wanted to conserve ammunition for the main attack on Singapore. This single mistake probably cost us Singapore.[385]

It seems that the British were horrified at the thought of damaging the building as reparations would have to be paid to the Sultan after the war.[386]

For the families back home the news of 6 February was becoming more ominous. The Japanese claimed to have begun a general offensive with heavy artillery. The Singapore communiqué reported it was with heavy mortars and light artillery. Whichever was correct, it meant all Australian troops were very much in the firing line.[387]

Saturday 7 February saw more dramatic newspaper headlines: *HEAVY GUN DUEL OVER JOHORE STRAIT* grabbed the eye on the front page. Inside, on the pages dedicated to reporting the war, families gleaned more detail.

ARTILLERY DUEL OVER JOHORE STRAIT SINGAPORE AWAITS ATTACK Large convoys of enemy transport vehicles were seen moving southward in Johore but being shelled by Allied artillery. The Imperial troops were said to be well settled in their defensive positions and ready for any move made by the Japanese. Air raids and bombing had occurred on the island.[388]

The stage was set for the final battle. The Japanese troops themselves had needed to take a few days to rest, regroup and prepare for the final assault across the Strait.

On this day Bennett reported the 2/10 Australian General Hospital at Manor House was shelled, the nurses remaining cool and courageous throughout the shelling, neglecting their own safety to care for the patients. He wrote:

These nurses are the nearest things to angels I can imagine. They never quarrel among themselves. They devote themselves wholeheartedly to deal with the rush of casualties. They never complain and always have a smile and kindly word for our wounded and sick men.[389]

This day also saw the *Sydney Morning Herald* publish a massive list of AIF casualties in Malaya, the first list for the 8th Division. There were over 400 names listed. The number from NSW 'killed in action' was 67 with another 71 'wounded'. A further 177 were posted as 'missing', another 68 were 'missing believed wounded' while 12 were 'missing believed killed'. The Victorian list was close to 70 lost.[390] What anxious eyes would have devoured those lists of troops. What gasps of sadness would have erupted as names were recognised. Sorrow and heartache would abound in the families of NSW and Victoria.

Prior to Christmas 1941 letters from home were regularly received by the troops. Once the serious fighting began the deliveries became far more erratic. A letter from Connie Cay, written on 8 February 1942 and a Christmas parcel she had posted to Bill on 29 December were both returned to her. Despite reading the list of casualties and knowing that fierce fighting was happening on Singapore, Connie's letter had tried to keep things light and newsy and looking to the future, just what a soldier at the battle front would appreciate. She tells of helping Bill's mother and sisters move into the house next door, from number 8 to number 10.

Connie had been House Mother at Broughton School, Newcastle, when Bill was a boarder there. She had moved to Neutral Bay, by chance met Bill one day on the ferry, and from then on kept in close touch with the Gaden family. She was a prolific letter writer to 'her boys' serving overseas, and keen to hear all their news. She kept the letters and parcel to give to Bill at the end of the war. What optimism!

Connie, registered as Annie Constance, had been born in 1893 in Randwick, the daughter of Sholto M and Florence L Cay.[391] She had two brothers, John and Max who she refers to in her letter. John Sloper Cay enlisted in the Light Horse (Service number 2018) to go to the First World War, leaving Sydney in RMS *Osterley* on 15 January 1916.[392] He survived the war and married Jessie Flora McLean in 1922[393] but had died by 1942.

Maxwell Robert Cay, was born 26 Nov 1899 and attended Shore School in Sydney, leaving in 1917. Connie remarked that Max was disappointed he had been unable to enlist when he left school. He was obviously inspired by his older brother and enlisted in Brisbane in the Army on 31st January 1942. His service number was QX34309 and next of kin was wife Violet. He survived the war, being discharged on 19 January 1945.[394]

44 Harriette Street, Neutral Bay *February 8th 1942*
My dear Bill

What fun you're in for on your return, adjusting yourself to your new surroundings and getting to know your way about your new home. You're going to love it and be jolly happy there. Not that you don't know it already. How we longed to have you with us yesterday, it was a regular working bee and all went at top speed. I fear your Mum and the girls were somewhat tired but they all promised me a 'sleep in' was to be strictly adhered to this a.m.

I loved your drawing room at Valhalla but the present one is a king pin having that glorious window. I looked round and found various bits of autumn tinted hydrangea which we put in the big green bowl and sat it on the window sill. Also got lots of phlox and zinnia from your own garden and had a great display. After getting my weekend bits and pieces I filled the thermos, buttered a griddle scone I'd got, grabbed an old dress and betook myself for action. Fairy Barton, dear soul, had dropped in on her way to the Top, and left some hot scones with your Mum. [Connie refers to Fairy Barton in several subsequent letters ... was she a neighbour of the Gadens, in the flat above, or a friend of them all?]

It was interesting meeting Joan Johnstone as I knew both her parents and heard lots of Armidale chat. She seems a nice lass and was a great help to your Mum. Gordon G was a true digger and was invaluable. As you'll hear we topped up the day with beer good oh too. Your Mum finally went next door to feed your name sake so Sue and I got busy and got your Mum's room ship-shape. How thrilled your dear brave Mum was to find it all looking gorgeous. All she wants now is firstly letters from you and then you home. Ginge is all agog getting your 'ship' licked into shape, you'll love your dug-out and will probably have to dong Ginge one to secure it. Sue has made her room look most attractive already.

You'd hardly recognise our city since the brown-outs have been put in force. It all looks most weird. I'm hoping I'll be in the city this week when we have our daylight trial. Bet there'll be a bit of confusion but it's most necessary to put the public through their paces.

ONE ON THE NOSE

On the principle that a cat, however scrubby, may not only look at a king, but scratch him, the American garbage-carrier Tahoe has rammed and probably sunk a Japanese submarine off the coast of the United States. That a nation so sensitive in its pride as Japan should have a ship destroyed in these ignominious circumstances demonstrates that war has its humiliations as well as its glories. Tokyo will doubtless stigmatise the episode as one of insult superfluously added to injury, but the Allies may be excused for seeing it rather as an act of poetic justice. An enemy who callously deals in treachery and unprovoked aggression is in no position, after all, to carp if his sailors are sent to the bottom with a mess of garbage. Like the satirist who plays hero to his own epigram, the Japanese warrior dotes on seeing himself as the idol of his own pugnacity. It should come as a salutary lesson to him, therefore, that the crew of a humble refuse boat considered themselves sufficiently exalted in dignity and status to engage him in combat. Though by the very nature of the encounter the personnel of the submarine may have been spared the chagrin of knowing what had struck them, we can take it for granted that the Japanese Admiralty felt the blow keenly. Remembering the normal usages of warfare, it may even agree that this is a case in which "comparisons are odorous."

Am sure the enclosed cutting from SMH[395] *(One on the nose) will amuse you and any you show it to. Old Granny has a bigger sense of humour than she's sometimes credited with.*

Yesterday's Herald had a delightful article on the 'Life in Burma'. What a fascinating place it must be in normal days. Course it all just makes us feel sick to think of what you lads are enduring in Singapore and who would ever have thought your job was going to be so tough. Gosh we're not one iota proud of you all oh no only a rumour and just look forward to the great day when this hell is over and finished for all time.

Max our youngest and only brother (since we lost John) has got his wish at last and goes into camp in Queensland on 17th. He tried at the outbreak but was turned down and told to get younger!! Now he's been passed for the Militia being too old for the AIF. Makes me feel more of a granny than ever!! He's joined the 11 Motor Regiment old ALH (Australian Light Horse) and should be in his element. Violet (wife) and two youngsters will hate the separation as they're such a happy lot but the lad feels the time has come when every jack man should be trained. Max, in 1939 when war broke out, would have roped every jack man in and trained them in case the Japs did as we've always feared they would, make themselves a --- nuisance.

I go to the netting in Milson Road now, almost opposite; saves fares and time. It's only been going since June and 500 mark has been passed so we're celebrating with cakes etc. on Thursday week when Mrs Sisle who lent her billiard room can be present.

[Women used to meet in places such as church halls to make camouflage nets on large frames. They used wooden needles made from silky oak by school students in woodwork classes.][396]

Last Thursday Mrs McCoy whose son Bruce is in 2/20 B Coy was on the net next to me, showing me some mag he's sent her last week .

[John Bruce McCoy, NX 31312, was Killed in Action in Malaya on 10 February 1942 just two days after Connie wrote this letter.][397]

Has the old parcel sent out on Dec 29th turned up yet? Hope so as the sweets just might fit into the new picture.

It's bad luck the airmail has pro tem been suspended as letters mean so much to you all, not to mention us at this end so lets hope it will soon be re-instated.

Am getting my new glasses tomorrow. What a joy it will be to see things at their correct prospective [sic].

Well Bill old dear I must drop Max a line and see if he's in need of a house wife or what he needs most. To think the lad hated himself for still being at Shore during the last war

and now has got into uniform after all these years. Hell, that's what war is and what good comes of it all. Enough. Look after yourself and give those little rats hell.
Whacko Bill. All the best and a big cheerio and lots of love
Yours ever,
Connie Cay
PS Am feeling very sad our dear kid Ross Lindeman has been killed in aircraft accident in N. Ireland. Was he at Broughton with you? Course the Malay list in Saturday's paper was just hell C.
To think it was a year ago last Tuesday that you all left. What a hideous day for many.

[Ross Wellesley Lindeman, RAAF, Service Number 403141, was killed on 25 January 1942].[398]

The day that Connie wrote her letter, so full of news at home, was to be one of the worst days possible for the troops in Singapore. These were days of fierce fighting for all the AIF troops on Singapore Island. There is an excellent coverage of the role of the 2/20 Battalion in Don Wall's book *Singapore and Beyond*. It covers most of the action taken from many first hand accounts by the survivors and is recommended to readers who wish for an extensive coverage of events.

The following summary indicates the horrendous nature of the fighting. Bill Gaden was serving as 2IC of 'D' Company but as the fighting progressed all semblance of working in specific platoons or companies was to disappear as casualty numbers rose and men fought for their lives alongside any ally, whatever their company or battalion.

Major Arch Ewart recounted that the 2/20 had three and a half miles of Johore Straights frontage to protect, with nine Japanese regiments likely to land there. The Japanese guns and mortars fired continually for three days, being particularly intense on 8 and 9 February.[399] This huge bombardment was to 'soften up' the defences. There were few casualties but signal communication wires were severed, a devastating loss. Eighty shells fell on one company of 2/18 in just one minute, another platoon had sixty-seven in ten minutes.[400] The noise would have been deafening, artillery, mortars, bombs, shells, and grenades.

The 2/20 men were subjected to this intensive shelling by artillery and mortar. Boat loads of Japanese troops then poured across the Straits of Johore along the length of the coast defended by the 22nd Brigade of AIF. The brunt of the attack fell against the 2/20 Battalion, in particular the land defended by 'C' and 'D' Company (Bill's Company) in the Pala Bulah and Nemazie House area.

Close to midnight troops of the 5th and 8th Japanese Divisions headed across the Straits four thousand at a time. Facing them were just three thousand Australians.[401] The Japanese Commander had chosen his place well, there was a thin line of defence and his plan was to punch a hole in that defence and then infiltrate; our troops were too thinly dispersed and it proved impossible to stop this infiltration.[402]

Early Sunday morning Bill Shelly (NX45908) led a platoon including younger brother George and 'Bluey' Myers (NX45482). They were sent forward to reconnoitre their frontage. They worked towards the Malayu River and found themselves looking down on a huge enemy concentration on the edge of their perimeter. They were able to pick off the enemy virtually at will. A Japanese officer with white gloves started waving his sword, exhorting his men to move forward. George said to Greg Lawrence (NX50739) 'He's mine' and shot him and he fell to the ground still holding his sword. George recalled he thought the Japanese officer to be the 2IC to the commanding officer Yamashito.[403]

He said the Japanese soldiers appeared to be confused and hesitant. They had no air support - the Australians were between two groups of Japanese, so the enemy aircraft could not strafe them or they'd kill their own troops. Arch Ewart arrived by motor bike and told them there was no relief coming, they had to fight their way out. A bayonet charge was the only way.[404] Many members of the platoon were killed in this action including Bill Shelly who threw himself in front of his younger brother as an enemy machine-gunner opened fire.[405] Out of thirty men, just a dozen made it out.

At dawn the remains of 10 Platoon joined up with what was left of 'B' Company and moved forward to support men from HQ Company and 'C' Company who were also under heavy machine gun fire, facing a Battalion strength of Japanese.[406] 10 Platoon had a new replacement commander, their Assistant Adjutant Lieut Alan Maclean. He would lose a leg in the battle but two-thirds of the platoon lost their lives.[407] They were forced into swamps and drains, some managed to work out the enemy pattern of fire and were able to escape.

There was heavy fighting in these areas which initially was done from prepared positions such as trenches so there was some protection from the bombardment.[408] The invaders were repelled by machine guns and hand grenades but were able to get troops ashore elsewhere to press on the flanks of 'D' Company. Capt Richardson asked for artillery backup. It took three hours to arrive. No artillery, no verey flares, no search lights to show up the boats, a major disaster.[409] Much fighting became hand-to-hand; it was done in the open with no protection.

Smoke and vegetation made it difficult to see. Radio communication was impossible. Amid the noise, chaos and confusion would reign. The 2/20 men were pushed back, by daylight they would have over four hundred casualties. [410] Evacuation of the injured troops would have been very difficult. Waves of Japanese troops poured onto the Island through the many gaps in the AIF's defences.

Lack of communication was major problem. Radio facilities were not issued at Platoon, Company or even Battalion level, they relied on land lines which were so very easy to destroy by bombs or sabotage.[411] When lines were destroyed they used 'runners', these men had to brave the territory between their troops and HQ, often when the area was already swarming with Japanese soldiers, a slow and dangerous task.

Even command posts were not communicating with each other. Frank Baker recalled that he passed close to an English regiment who were all 'on parade', they were so used to the noise of the bombardment they didn't even know the Japanese had landed on Singapore Island.[412] George Shelly asked one English gunner why he wasn't in action to be told he was still waiting to hear if the Japs had landed.[413] An English officer refused to issue ammunition to the Australians, demanding a requisition order. George recalled 'Bluey' produced his Bren Gun and advised 'This is my requisition order'.

War Diary of the 2/20 Battalion AIF SINGAPORE ISLAND, KRANJI District 9 Feb '42

'D' Coy under heavy fighting. At 0500 message sent for them to withdraw to the Bn. perimeter. 0545 Heavy enemy fire from our W on a frontage of 2/300 yards. West Flank. 0700 'D' Coy not yet reported in to Bn. Perimeter. Unable to reach Bn. Area owing to enemy pressure. Coy. ambushed, heavy casualties, withdrawn along general line to Aerodrome.

The 0500 message never arrived. 'D' Coy were at the locality of the airstrip at dawn and the company was exposed to the full weight of the assembling enemy.[414]

The Japanese held the high ground and all the Allies were forced into swamps and rubber drains. 'D' Coy was under pressure to the east of Kankar, they needed to cross the river to withdraw. There were some non-swimmers amongst the men ... why had the Australians not been taught to swim during their time at Port Dickson and Mersing? The river was at low tide and at one of the crossings the water was only a foot deep but the enemy opened fire when the Allied troops were half way across. At other crossings the water was deep and canoes and other craft had to be procured. Many Australians died before reaching friendly lines.

Local Chinese Dalforce troops were assisting where they could;

At the first crossing one of the Chinese Dalforce guerrillas was shot. Lt. Harry Woods applied a dressing and Capt. Bill Gaden picked him up on his back and carried him through mud under heavy fire to firmer ground. [415]

All the signal wires between companies and Battalion Head Quarters had been broken by the shells and mortars and there was no efficient back-up system. The Commanding Officer (CO) in the Battalion HQ, Lieutenant-Colonel Assheton, had received no contact from Brigade HQ, nor the 2/18 during the night. Assheton sent Arch Ewart by motor bike to Brigade HQ to ask for orders. On the way there and back he passed some men from the 2/18, men he described as 'a broken Company'.[416] The orders from Brigade HQ were to withdraw towards Tengah Airport, ironically the same area where all the Japanese were told to assemble.[417]

Assheton then went with Arch Ewart on the motor bike to try and find a way out for the troops to withdraw as a fighting force. They ran into a small Japanese force and Arch was shot in the neck, but they managed to retreat. Arch was sent to get all the transport moving out of the area whilst the CO, Charles Assheton, ever aggressive, organized a party of men to try and clear the enemy from this area.

Assheton called for Lieut Roger Cornforth of 2/20 to bring his six Bren guns and Capt. Kenneth Mosher of 2/18 to get his eight Lewis guns and the Australians prepared to attack.[418] At 1130 the CO, Lieutenant-Colonel CF Assheton was killed by machine gun fire whilst leading this party of 2/18 and 2/20 personnel in the vicinity of Tengah Airport. He was to receive a Mention in Dispatches for his Gallant and Distinguished Service.[419]

This day of battle also saw Major Cohen killed with a bullet through his forehead, Major Ewart wounded in the neck, Captains Lowe and Betterridge both killed in action as were Lieutenants Lennon, Porter, Chave and Tipping. It was a horrendous day for the officers of the 2/20 Battalion.

Arch Ewart managed to get the transport moving, the Regimental Aid Post (RAP) truck was the last one to go and it was full of wounded troops. They came under more fire. Cpl David Thompson (NX51413) was one of these men. He was injured in a grenade attack and crawled back to relative 'safety' before losing consciousness. He woke to find Japanese passing over him in large numbers. He was rescued by 'Bluey' Costello and Pte Forrest and put on the truck. John Frederick Kirkland (Bluey) Costello (NX68637) was to survive the war in Naoetsu POW camp. There were two Pte Forrests in the 2/20. Henry Forrest (NX 33291) survived the war but Alan John Forrest (NX 71897) was soon to die, on 15 February. Despite the Red Cross flag clearly on display, the truck was strafed by low flying enemy aircraft and many wounded men were killed. David was lucky to survive and was taken to 2/10 AGH for medical attention. [420]

The Intelligence wagon was blown up by mortars and so was Arch's motor bike, leaving him with shrapnel wounds. At 1000 hrs Arch located a small group of troops and joined them in a move to Tengah airport. His boots were full of blood and he had to be assisted by two men until he was able to obtain opium from a Chinese house. Arch went to hospital for three days before discharging himself and returning to the unit. He found a Military Police motor bike and made his way to 8th Division HQ.[421]

Capt. Richardson's 'D' Company was moving on a south-easterly course, coming out east of the airfield where he ordered Bill Gaden to take the wounded to the Indian RAP. This was done successfully and the troops were safely evacuated. This party of 'D' Company was the last of any size out of Kranji and the Japanese were close behind as they moved across the Tengah Airfield. [422]

Bill Young (NX73630)[423] remembered Bill Gaden had been here, there and everywhere during all the fighting as he tried to encourage and support his men.[424]

Bennett reported that the 2/20 and 2/18 were overrun by the enemy.[425] There were too few men and too many kilometres of unprotected coastline to cover. The gaps in the defence posts could not be plugged.

A line was formed along the road round the aerodrome, it consisted of the remains of the 2/18, 2/19, 2/20, 2/29, 2/4 machine gun battalion and an Indian battalion. They were attacked by two Japanese divisions, the 5th and 18th.[426]

On simple numbers it was inevitable that the Allies had to give ground and the enemy took the aerodrome. General Percival recorded:

During the night of 8-9 February, 13,000 [Japanese] *troops were landed on the island and another 10,000 landed shortly after dawn'.*

The first 13,000, all of them, fell against just two Australian battalions who fought fiercely and inflicted heavy casualties on the Japanese but they suffered grievously themselves. The 2/20 sustained 334 killed, and 214 wounded out of 1,000 men who were in action. One of the battalion's forward companies of 145 men lost 57 killed, 22 wounded and 66 taken prisoner, its complete strength.[427] Thus the forward posts were either overrun or annihilated.

The people of Australia learned of the Japanese attack on 10 February with the headline

ENEMY LANDS ON SINGAPORE ISLAND
SITUATION WELL IN HAND
AUSTRALIAN TROOPS ENGAGE INVADERS

A long communiqué from Singapore gave reports of Japanese landings under a terrific artillery barrage lasting for twelve hours. Oslo Radio and Rome Radio were both quoted saying that Japanese troops had landed and Singapore radio advised some Japanese were wearing Australian hats. The BBC observer told that:

The Australians, after covering the landing, moved back to establish a line covering the whole 10 miles front along which the enemy was landing. The fighting went on throughout the night in a sea of mud caused by torrential rain that afternoon.[428]

Our troops had 'dug-in' during the previous eight days ... no doubt any trenches would have succumbed to the heavy rain!

On 10 February a composite 19/20 Battalion withdrew to the Brigade Assembly area at the racecourse, then, with Major Merrett in command, they set off for the Reformatory Road area. They were surrounded by Japanese troops so they decided to withdraw and fight their way back to Brigade Area, suffering many casualties under heavy enemy fire. They made their way in small groups to the Botanic Gardens.[429]

So many men had been killed or wounded it was not possible to call the men by their own battalion names. A composite had to be put together so 'X' Bn was then formed, under the command of Colonel Boyes, and Capt. Richardson's 'D' Company was part of it. This included Lieut Harry Woods who had been with Bill to evacuate the Dalforce soldier. They had no Intelligence, no communications, no medical services and no support.[430] They did not know the enemy had already occupied the nearby Bukit Timah village.[431] They were walking into an ambush. At 0300 the enemy fired into the adjacent fuel dump. In the ensuing fight for Bukit Timah and Jurong Roads all types of guns were used, even a flame thrower. There was fierce hand-to-hand fighting. Many died and, of the few who got out alive, every one was injured.[432] 'X' Battalion was virtually wiped out. Harry Woods was injured in the shoulder and thigh, and was unable to stand due to loss of blood. A young Chinese man helped him to safety on the West Coast Road where Harry was evacuated to Alexandra Hospital.[433]

'Y' Bn under command Major Robertson was also in process of being formed. Owing to lack of fit personnel not more than one Company could be raised, made up of men cut off from their own units. With this force were Captains WA Carter and EW Gaden and Lieutenants Cowden, O'Keefe and Lee of 2/20 Bn and a number of 2/20 men. This force moved out by truck during the night and debussed in the Holland Road area, moving by route march to Ulu Panden Road. On arrival they received orders from the Brigade to form a perimeter astride the junction of Holland and Ulu Panden Roads. Dispositions were occupied by first light and Robertson was instructed next morning to form a perimeter astride the Holland-Reformatory-Ulu Panden Road and take up a position at 'The Fort',[434] where some Indian troops were already located.

There was some heavy fighting on the north side of Ulu Panden Road during the day with heavy casualties among the Indian and 2/18 troops who had also joined this 'Y' force. The 2/18 were withdrawn during the night and Major Robertson's men took over. The *War Diary* reports that initially there was not much action with just sniping and machine gun fire on the night of 11-12 February. Our artillery caused many casualties but during the late afternoon and early evening the enemy used mortars and attacked the position of the 2/4 MG Bn to the right. The enemy were successful and also attacked the feature held by our right flank, 'The Hill' which was immediately to the north of 'The Fort'. According to Lieut Frank Gaven the enemy attacked 'The Hill' in force and captured it.[435] The previous day the Officer in Charge of 'The Hill', Capt EW Gaden, was evacuated with ptomaine (food) poisoning. That probably saved his life.

Various Companies including those of the 2/18 and 2/20 were ordered to withdraw to the Buona Vista Road then Holland Road, the wounded were safely evacuated.[436]

The Australian public would have woken to extremely worrying news. The *Sydney Morning Herald* headlines of 11 February read:

> *PERIL OF SINGAPORE GROWS HOURLY GRAVER*
> *IMPERIAL FORCES FALL BACK AGAIN*
> *JAPANESE POURING IN REINFORCEMENTS*

There were four full columns of news with details of the battle including hand-to-hand fighting. There was continuous dive bombing by aircraft, strafing using machine guns, and bombing attacks. Combined with the pounding by the artillery, the noise would have been horrific and very frightening. The Island was said to be shrouded in smoke but life was reported to be 'normal'. It was still possible to buy meals without trouble but the civilians were warned against Japanese paratroopers. Several bodies of Australians troops had been found in a location where it was necessary to fight their way out with bayonets after the Japanese had infiltrated their position. In one case a HQ unit had made a gallant bayonet charge driving out several Japanese machine gun crews.[437] How must the families, the mothers and wives, sisters and sweethearts, have felt on reading such horrific news?

There was plenty more worrying news the next day. Trying to be more optimistic, the *Sydney Morning Herald* reported that the defenders were said to be 'counter attacking' and the Australians 'fighting heroically'. Bitter combat was reported on the western and north-western sector, both areas defended by the Australians. Rome Radio reported that British, Australian, Chinese and Indian troops fought with incredible contempt for death.[438] These were hardly words to encourage the families of the Australian soldiers; there would have been major concern and angst in the country.

By 13 February the 2/20 Bn was ordered to occupy 'Hill 90' and the surrounding area in Holland Hill Rd locality. There was a composite force of 2/19, 2/20 and Gordon Highlanders here, under active enemy air attack and artillery and mortar fire.[439] Major Robertson was promoted to Lieutenent-Colonel and appointed to Command the 2/20 Bn.

Capt. Gaden with Lieuts Cornforth and Cowden and a composite force of 100 men were in defensive position as part of the AIF perimeter east of Tyersalls Palace on Clunies Road. There was active patrolling both day and night.[440]

The Japanese could be seen moving to the south to the Alexandra area.

The Japanese claimed to be within the city of Singapore and engaged in fierce hand-to-hand fighting.[441] They had also stormed Bukit Chandu peak, the highest point on the Island only 5.5 miles from the city and scene of fierce defence by the local Malay Regiment.[442]

This first battle between the members of Malay Regiment and the Japanese occurred on 13 February 1942. The Japanese attacked the Pasir Panjang Ridge and the Raja Road and one Company of the Malays made up part of the defence. There was fierce hand-to-hand combat using bayonets. They then withdrew after dark to Raja and Depot Roads, Buona Vista.[443]

On 14 February the Battle for Opium Hill or Bukit Chandu, Map Point 226, occurred. The position was very strategic; if the Japanese gained control of the ridge they had easy access to Alexandra, site of the main British military supplies, ammunition depot and the hospital. The Japanese launched mortar and artillery, there was hand-to-hand combat and many were killed on both sides. The fighting was fierce and bitter between the Japanese 18th Division and the Malay Regiment. Small arms, grenades and bayonets were used and the local troops stood their ground against an all out assault. They ran out of ammunition and the Japanese were brutal in their treatment of the captured wounded.[444]

The Battalion's *War Diary* for 14 February reported an enemy observation balloon was seen in their area and there was intermittent shelling from both sides. The Japanese troops were moving in the direction of Alexandra but it was considered to be a *quiet night* with *normal patrol activity* for the 2/20.

This day Captain William Akins Carter was promoted to Major. He was just above Bill on the Battalion's seniority list. He later spent his time as a POW with 'E' Force in Borneo.[445]

The Japanese were able to make their way to the Alexandra Hospital on the afternoon of February 14. Many of the walking wounded had been told to get out into trucks and were evacuated to other places in Singapore but Lieut Harry Woods, former tent-mate of Bill's, and Sgt Gordon MacDougal, cousin of David MacDougal, remained as patients there. The Japanese troops bayoneted medical staff and roamed through the hospital rounding up patients and staff. Many patients were killed whilst lying in their beds.[446] Sgt MacDougal of 2/20 tried to disarm a Japanese soldier with his good arm; he was killed. Major Beale was one of the 'walking wounded'. He was executed; only moments before he had been talking with Harry Woods.[447] Harry, with a wound to his thigh, was unable to walk and could not move out of the building.[448] It was to save his life.

The 'walking wounded' were crammed into three small rooms in a row of buildings nearby. The doors were barricaded and the men left for the night with no water. Many died during the night. Next day they were taken out and led, two by two, on a 'water march'. Soon those left behind heard screams of anguish 'Oh my God', 'Mother', 'Don't, don't'. The prisoners were being systematically massacred. Suddenly the sound of shelling was heard and one shell ripped off the door and window shutters. Some men tried to escape; most were shot but a few managed to get clear of the buildings and into the scrub in the area.[449]

Harry Woods managed to survive the massacres and was still in the hospital two days later when another Japanese officer arrived and asked that the 'mess' be cleaned up ... the dead had to be buried.[450]

It was the Allied Commander General Arthur Percival who made the decision to surrender to the Japanese. When Major-General Gordon Bennett, commanding officer of the AIF, heard this information, he decided on a final tour of Australian lines (to inspect his troops for a last time and to reconnoitre his escape route) before putting into practice his plan to leave the Island. Disturbingly he recorded in his diary that he found the 2/20 Battalion HQ:

> *... in a beautifully furnished house where I had afternoon tea from unusually high quality dishes.*[451]

Back in Australia on this Saturday, the *Sydney Morning Herald* was reporting:

> *FIERCE BATTLE RAGING FOR SINGAPORE*
> *IMPERIAL GARRISON FIGHTS ON*
> *FIGHTING NEAR RESERVOIR ON ISLAND*

Fighting was reported to be fierce with the artillery being extremely active, with 400 shells an hour falling on Japanese lines. The Japanese broadcasts reported stubborn resistance but they were within three kilometres of the heart of the city. Bombing was being carried out by a large formation of aircraft.

Things were not looking good for the worried friends and relatives back home. February 15 was a Sunday, there was no *Sydney Morning Herald* to read, only the weekend newspapers. The distraught families would probably have relied on the radio broadcasts for up to date information.

On Sunday 15 February 1942, the Allied troops were ordered to stop fighting.

'Orders received to cease fire at 2030 hrs and withdraw patrols' is how the Battalion's *War Diary* notes the surrender of Singapore to the Imperial Japanese Army. These eleven words would plunge the men into the uncertainty of internment.

The message left many soldiers in a state of shock with some weeping openly. The troops were apprehensive about being prisoners of war but they were also angry, feeling they had never even been given a chance to win:

> *We were withdrawing ever since the balloon went up and we seemed to be having strategic withdrawals; it was a great feeling of loss.*[452]

George Shelly remarked that when they were told to surrender, in many ways they were at their strongest.[453]

Capt. Gaven had already complained to General Bennett:

> *The men have been withdrawing all the way from Mersing, there we were well prepared but were ordered to withdraw at a time we were inflicting casualties upon the enemy. We moved to Jemaluang and were again ordered to withdraw. We got to the Island to find ourselves in an unprepared sector, we held out until our positions were overrun and we were told to withdraw. All this with little sleep. The men are very tired. Their rations have been irregular and inadequate, they have been in constant contact with the enemy and they feel they have been badly let down. I feel that too.*[454]

How many lives would have been lost if they had continued to fight? How many were lost as a result of the decision to surrender?

352 *Sydney Morning Herald*, 31 January 1942, p. 13.
353 *ibid.*, 2 February 1942, pp. 4-5.
354 *War Diary 2/20 Bn. A.I.F.*, 31 January 1942.
355 *ibid.*, 1 February 1942.
356 Arneil, *One Man's War*, pp. 8-9.
357 Media Masters *Guide to the Pacific Battlefields (1941-1945)*, The Japanese conquest of Malaya and Singapore.
358 Wall, *Singapore and Beyond*, p. 51.
359 Ziegler, *Men May Smoke*, p. 34.
360 *War Diary 2/20 Bn. A.I.F.*, 31 January 1942.
361 Wall, *op. cit.*, p. 52.
362 Bell and Salter, *Notes on 2/20 Battalion operations in Singapore, Feb 1942.* <http://www.geocities.com/batt2_20/story.htm?200721> and Wall, *op. cit.*, p. 81.
363 Ziegler, *op. cit.*, p. 26.
364 Moremon, *A Bitter Fate*, pp. 98-9.
365 Forbes, *Hellfire*, pp. 156-7.
366 Bennett, *Why Singapore Fell*, p. 166.
367 *ibid.*, p. 167 and Media Masters *Guide to the Pacific Battlefields (1941-1945)*, The Japanese conquest of Malaya and Singapore.
368 *Sydney Morning Herald*, 2 February 1942, p. 5.
369 Wall, *op. cit.*, p. 61.
370 *ibid.*, p. 71.
371 *Sydney Morning Herald*, 3 February 1942, p. 5.
372 Smith, *op. cit.*, p. 435.
373 Ziegler, *op. cit.*, pp. 26-7.
374 Wall, *op. cit.*, p. 62.
375 Media Masters *op. cit.*
376 Bell and Salter, *op. cit.*
377 Baker, personal communication.
378 *Sydney Morning Herald*, 4 February 1942, p. 9.
379 *ibid.*, 3 February 1942, p. 5.
380 Wall, *op. cit.*, p. 52.
381 Media Masters *op. cit.*
382 *Sydney Morning Herald*, 5 February 1942, p. 5.
383 Wall, *op. cit.*, p. 104
384 *Sydney Morning Herald*, 4 February 1942, p. 9.
385 David MacDougal, Personal communication.
386 Savage, *A Guest of the Emperor*, p. 10.
387 *Sydney Morning Herald*, 6 February 1942, p. 5.
388 *ibid.*, 7 February 1942, pp. 1 and 11.
389 Bennett, *op. cit.*, pp. 171-2.
390 *Sydney Morning Herald*, 7 February 1942, p. 13.
391 NSW BDM 30463/1893.
392 NSW BDM 16667/1895 and DVA Nominal Roll.
393 Qld BDM, marriage 1922/C426.
394 NSW BDM 160/1900 and Warden, SCEGS Register and DVA Nominal Roll.
395 *Sydney Morning Herald*, 31 January 1942, p. 12.
396 Personal communication from members of < aus-nsw-sydney@rootsweb.com > 23 November 2007.
397 DVA Nominal Roll.
398 *ibid.*
399 Ewart, interview with Don Wall, AWM S04103.
400 Elliott and Silver, *A History of the 2/18 Battalion*, p. 61.
401 Smith, *op. cit.*, p. 462.
402 Wall, *op. cit.*, p. 65.
403 George Shelly, personal communication.

404 *loc. cit.*
405 *loc. cit.*
405 *War Diary 2/20 Bn. A.I.F.*, 8 February 1942.
407 George Shelly, personal communication.
408 Bell and Salter, *op. cit.*
409 Smith, *op. cit.*, p. 462.
410 Moremon, *op. cit.*, pp. 104-6.
411 Wall, *op. cit.*, pp. 62-64.
412 Frank Baker, personal communication.
413 George Shelly, *op. cit.*
414 Wall, *op. cit.*, p. 77
415 *ibid.*, p. 86.
416 Ewart, Interview with Don Wall, AWM S04103.
417 Smith, *op. cit.*, p. 469.
418 Elliott and Silver, *A History of the 2/18 Battalion*, pp. 70-1.
419 Wall, *op. cit.*, in list of awards for Distinguished and Gallant Service.
420 David Thompson, personal communication, Don Wall, p. 78 and DVA Nominal Roll.
421 Ewart, Interview with Don Wall, AWM S04103.
422 Wall, *op. cit.*, p. 89.
423 DVA nominal roll.
424 Bill Young, personal communication.
425 Bennett, *op. cit.*, p. 175.
426 *ibid.*, p. 176.
427 Legg, *The Gordon Bennett Story*, p. 235.
428 *Sydney Morning Herald*, 10 February 1942, p. 5.
429 *War Diary 2/20 Bn. A.I.F.*, 10 February 1942.
430 Wall, *op. cit.*, p. 92.
431 *ibid.*, p. 94.
432 *ibid.*, p. 97.
433 *ibid.*, pp. 94-96.
434 *ibid.*, p. 103.
435 Frank Gaven, interview with Don Wall, AWM S04104.
436 *War Diary 2/10 Bn A.I.F.*, 11-12 February 1942.
437 *Sydney Morning Herald*, 11 February 1942, p. 9.
438 *ibid.*, 13 February 1942, p. 5.
439 *War Diary 2/20 Bn. A.I.F.* 13 Feb 1942.
440 *ibid.*, 13 Feb 1942.
441 *Sydney Morning Herald*, 12 February 1942, p. 9.
442 Reflections Museum at Bukit Chandu, Singapore, visited February 2007.
443 Hoon, *Battle of Pasir Panjang Ridge*, <http://www.mindef.gov.sg/safti/pointer/back/journals/2002/Vol28_1.1htm >
444 *loc. cit.*
445 Wall, *op. cit.*, p. 371.
446 Smith, *op. cit.*, p. 537.
447 Wall, *op. cit.*, pp. 106-7.
448 Harry Woods, personal communication, May 2008.
449 Partridge, *Alexandra Hospital*, pp. 65-7.
450 Wall, *op. cit.*, p. 108.
451 Bennett, *op. cit.*, p. 194.
452 Wall, *op. cit.*, p. 109.
453 George Shelly, Personal communication.
454 Frank Gaven interview with Don Wall, AWM S04104.

Chapter 9 - Aftermath of Surrender

The families of NSW soldiers learned of the fall of Singapore by radio or the *Sydney Morning Herald*. Surprisingly, the *Herald's* issue of Monday 16 February 1942, did not rate the surrender as the main headline of its war coverage; the invasion of Sumatra with landings from sea and air was deemed more important. There were seven paragraphs on that attack before the Japanese claim of the Allies surrender in Singapore was mentioned. The paper advised that the Domei news agency reported Major Cyril Wild led a delegation of four British officers bearing a white flag. The British and Japanese leaders were due to meet at 5.30 pm local time (8.30 pm Sydney time) the day before to discuss terms of surrender, but this could not be taken as authoritative, and London had no direct information about the situation.[455]

Many families would perhaps have been relieved, thinking that if their son was still alive after the fighting, he would be spared further battle and would be cared for as a prisoner until the war ended. They would expect to hear from their boys soon. How wrong they were.

In the last hectic days of fighting in Singapore, many civilians and wounded had tried to flee the Island by ship. Sadly the British civilians never considered that the Japanese could take the 'Island Fortress' and so they had not evacuated early enough. Now there were wounded troops and nurses who also needed to escape. Inevitably there were far too many people for far too few ships. In addition the Japanese planes were superior in the air, efficiently dropping bombs on all the ships in the vicinity.

News Editor and War Correspondent of the Malaya Broadcasting Corporation, Rohan Rivett, left the Island on the *Siang Wo* on Wednesday 11 February. It was one of the last ships to make an escape. He commented:

> *The fact that our own ship and those around us carried women, the last of whom should have been evacuated at latest at the beginning of January, deepened the general feeling that here there had been bungling on an appalling scale.*[456]

The ships which fled Singapore harbour at this late stage were in for a horrific ride.

The Salvation Army personnel, including George Woodland who had worked so hard for the 2/20 troops, were successfully evacuated, jumping aboard the *Empire Star*, as it was leaving the Island, also on 11 February.

Salvation Army Major Blaskett told how on the last day before fleeing they opened up a storage dump on the lawn of the Anzac Club in Singapore. They had cases of bully beef and biscuits, tins of fruit, boxes of raisins and bottles of soft drinks. The soldiers were in a bad way, hungry and tired. They had all come through a great ordeal and

their uniforms bore testimony to the fighting covered in black oily smoke and, in some instances, blood.

The work of the Salvos in Singapore and Malaya -

> *will be a record of 12 months of untiring labour. The whirl of events has driven them from Malaya and tossed them out of Singapore at scant notice.*[457]

Despite the scant notice *The War Cry* reported that the Salvos had endured a nightmare voyage. Apart from the lack of food and water, the ship was bombed, there were numerous near misses, a direct hit resulted in fires, men were blown into the water. However they eventually made it back to Australia and *War Cry* advised 'They are safe again with their loved ones'.[458]

The nurses that Bill mentioned in his letters were not so lucky; they suffered a different fate. On Thursday 12 February sixty-five nurses were evacuated from Singapore on board the *Vyner Brooke* which was then bombed and sunk by the Japanese. The passengers left the ship in one of two lifeboats, or straight into the sea. They drifted for several days and some came ashore near Muntok. One group included Elaine Balfour-Ogilvy, the nurse with whom Bill had played tennis and golf, gone dancing and enjoyed the social rounds of leave at Fraser's Hill and Singapore. She and twenty-one other nurses, landed on Radji Beach on Banka Island.

The nurses had heard that the Japanese were 'taking no prisoners'. Sister Vivian Bullwinkel (VFX61330) recalled that:

> *When the boys had come into hospital their one cry had been 'They're not taking prisoners'. It didn't matter what members of the forces came in, their cry was the same, 'They're not taking prisoners'.'However when you're young and have a group of over 100 people you can't imagine anything happening to that and we confidently felt we'd be taken prisoner because there was safety in numbers.*[459]

It was not to be. When the Japanese arrived on Radji Beach they proceeded to separate the wounded men from the nurses and took them along the beach out of sight. The Japanese then returned wiping their blood stained bayonets. The girls realised it was true, 'they were not taking any prisoners'.

The nurses, including Elaine, were told to form a line and walk into the sea. They were then machine gunned from behind. All were killed outright except Vivian Bullwinkel who was shot through the hip and knocked headlong into the water where she floated for some time, struggling to the beach only when the Japanese had left.[460]

Vivian Bullwinkel was later recaptured by the Japanese and interned with other nurses and civilian women already captured from other landings. Their story is told in the inspiring book *White Coolies* by Betty Jeffrey and portrayed in the film *Paradise Road* starring Glenn Close and Cate Blanchett.

Another of Bill's tennis playing nurses, Wilhemina 'Ray' Raymont (TFX6012), was part of this group of internees. Sadly Ray did not survive being a prisoner; she succumbed to Japanese brutality. To earn some money in the camp, Ray made and sold small handkerchiefs. One day a guard the nurses had nicknamed 'Rasputin' began shouting at her whilst she was sitting on her bed doing some sewing. A knob of wood was missing from the timber boarding behind her bed; 'Rasputin' accused Ray of damaging Japanese property. Despite being ill she was forced to stand out in the sun. A nurse gave her a hat which 'Rasputin' knocked away. He then punched Ray to the ground and she fell into the sweet potato patch. The guard refused pleas to end the punishment, from Mrs Hinch, the British Camp Commandant, and Dr Goldberg, a female doctor who had also escaped Singapore with the nurses on the *Vyner Brooke*. Eventually Ray collapsed, desperately ill. She was in hospital from many weeks, finally being discharged in November 1944 but unable to do any strenuous activity. She was back in hospital by January 1945 with malaria and subsequently died on 8 February 1945 after thirty-six hours of being critically ill, never having recovered properly from the treatment at the hands of 'Rasputin'. The nurses:

> *gave Ray a military funeral, all wearing their uniform. It made the Japs sit up, they even stood to attention and removed their caps as it went past their quarters, a thing they had never done before.*[461]

As for the soldiers who were left behind on Singapore Island:

> *no Australian could suppress feelings of bitterness and disgust at the thought of the impregnable fortress depicted for, and believed in by the people of Australia and the virtually defenceless island on which our troops with their British and Indian fellow troops were to make their last stand.*[462]

The order to cease fire and surrender left many in a state of shock. Everyone was in a state of apprehension just wondering what was going to happen and they all felt they had been let down by the hierarchy of Malaya Command.[463]

Sgt Alec Hodgson of 2/6 Field Park Company of the Royal Australian Engineers wrote in his diary:

> *Surrender and from my narrow view of affairs a shameful surrender. Feeling of utter disgust and shame, never saw a Jap, never fired a shot and there are thousands like us. Whole damn campaign has appeared to be a dismal tragedy of non-cooperation and blundering.*[464]

The Allied troops were ordered to put up a white flag on their positions but some found it very hard to do. In some instances a white towel between two rifles was all they had. The troops found that, after the terrific din of the fighting, it was the silence that was the most frightening.[465]

The 8th Division of the AIF and their British and Indian comrades-in-arms became Prisoners of War, prisoners of the Imperial Japanese Army whose Government refused to follow the accepted care of prisoners as set out in the Geneva Convention. This lack of care was to lead to thousands more Allied deaths.

Bill Gaden wrote an account of life as a POW. Additional information has been added to give a more comprehensive idea of their days of captivity. It is shown in a different font from Bill's writings.

Bill wrote:

15 Feb. '42 - Capitulation 2000 hours - location Botanical Gardens, Singapore. The following day moved to unit concentration areas TANGLIN. Japanese took all arms and permitted troops to occupy civilian houses but no rations were issued.

By daylight on 16 February 1942, orders were conveyed for arms to be stacked as Japanese started to appear. Capt. Frank Gaven of 2/20 had given Sgt Keith Ainsworth and Cpl Beavan the task of collecting all available food from the homes in the area. He recalled:

We set off and had just turned into Holland Road when a Jap soldier ran over and stopped us. He directed us to drive the vehicle in the opposite direction and place it behind 2/18 Bn. transport, which lined up on the road. It was then obvious that we had no chance of getting the truck and our stores back to the 2/20. Just then a truck with 2/20 men aboard and with Capt. Gaden on the running board came onto the scene. It was stopped by the soldier who tried to drag Gaden's wrist watch from his arm. After some resistance, to avoid an ugly scene, Bill surrendered the watch and the soldier, no doubt to avoid any complaint, signalled the truck to move on. As the truck began to move I called to Ainsworth and Beavan 'Come on' and we jumped onto the truck. We returned safely to 2/20 Bn. minus the truck, the stores and unhappily our personal possessions. We learnt later that the 2/18 Bn. transport had been driven off under Japanese orders and the drivers were not seen again.[466]

The 2/18 drivers were shot by the Japanese on 19 February 1942.[467] The two 2/20 soldiers had a reprieve this time, but sadly neither survived the war; Cpl Geoffrey Beavan, (NX72115) as part of 'D' force, 'U' Battalion, died 22 June 1943 and Sgt Joseph Keith Ainsworth (NX30278) was sent to Naoetsu Camp and died 4 December 1943.[468]

The Japanese appeared very keen to confiscate the Australian soldiers' watches. It may have been because they thought they were compasses similar to the ones they wore strapped to their own wrists, but they also coveted '*Western trinkets such as watches and fountain pens*'.[469]

The men marched from Tanglin, carrying whatever spare food they could find.

18 Feb. '42 - Marched about 16 miles to SELARANG barracks at CHANGI. Troops were tired; battle worn and the effort taxed their strength severely especially those slightly wounded.

Frank Baker recalled the smell of death was horrific on that march. When they arrived at Changi the men were given a tot of rum in hot water.[470]

The accommodation proved inadequate and crowding of all buildings was necessary.

The 2/20 men were allocated Barracks on the south-west corner of Selarang Square, 'A', 'C' and 'D' Companies on the top floor, HQ and 'B' Company on centre floor, ground floor used as a Mess.[471]

I employed myself first on compiling Coy and unit records, later on agricultural work. The object being to relieve the ration situation which was even at so early a stage becoming serious.

At this time the Japanese Command placed the responsibility for the prisoners under the direct control of the Allied Malaya Command complete with Army style hierarchy. It covered camp hygiene and maintenance, medical and cooking, very little different from the usual routine of an Army camp.[472]

Troops were obliged for the first few days to live on the scanty rations they carried from Singapore which were placed in a central dump for equitable distribution. It was already evident that lack of adequate food supplies was going to be an issue.[473]

The Japanese were worried about illness and had devised 'an undignified and unpleasant' dysentery test.[474] They were particularly worried about cholera spreading to their own troops so they regularly tested the prisoners. They looked for signs of mucous in the stools as those of cholera victims rapidly become watery with flecks of mucous. They are known as 'rice water' stools.[475] The specimen was collected from the anus using a bamboo or glass rod or even a piece of wire.[476] The 'glass rod' test certainly was 'undignified and unpleasant' especially when conducted on the parade ground with all troops assembled together.

The AIF troops would have been told of the bombing of Australian soil. On 19 February 1942 the Japanese flew the first of sixty-four bombing raids on Darwin. There were eight vessels sunk in the harbour, extensive damage to the city's infrastructure and two hundered and forty-three lives lost. The severity of the raid was held from the Australian public.

Winston Churchill wanted Australia's 7th Division to go to Rangoon, in Burma. He was of the opinion that Australia itself was temporarily expendable.[477] Australian Prime Minister John Curtin was not. Curtin had his way and the 7th Division did not go to Rangoon.

The names of all the troops who had been captured or killed were collected and recorded by the Battalion's adjutant in the notes for the *War Diary*. The numbers kept changing as a 'missing' was confirmed 'killed' or found to be in hospital, then as wounded 'marched in' from hospital, or stragglers found their way to their own battalion after the fighting. By 4 April the *War Diary* revealed the Battalion's revised casualty list:

Killed and Missing	Officers 15, NCO's 27, ORs 294
Wounded	Officers 10, NCO's 27, ORs 139
Total	512

Lists were passed onto the Japanese who were expected to inform the Australian authorities as per the Geneva Convention. No such list was passed on for many, many months, even years.

Vera wrote to the Red Cross to see if they had any news. Their letter of reply dated 2 March 1942 stated:

We refer to your enquiry for Capt. E.W. Gaden NX12543. The position with regard to personnel in Malaya and Singapore is at the moment obscure and there is no communication, either cabled or postal, with these countries, because as you know they are entirely in the hands of the Japanese.

In a cable from London, dated February 19th, published in the Sydney Morning Herald, of February 20th, it was stated that an announcement had been made that Japan will conform to the Geneva War Prisoners Convention and allow all necessary food and clothing to reach men in Japanese Prison Camps. One of the first obligations upon Japan will be to supply a list of all members of the various fighting forces who have been taken Prisoners of war as well as a list of civilians interned. Naturally it will take some time to collect all the details but as Japan has agreed to do this work it should not be unduly long.

We have every reason to believe that food and clothing will be allowed to reach the Prisoners through the Red Cross in the same way as it is reaching them in Germany and Italy.

The Red Cross believed the Japanese were going to follow the Geneva Convention and care for the prisoners. How wrong they were.

Unaware that letters were definitely not getting through, Connie Cay, former matron from his school days at Broughton in Newcastle, wrote to Bill. The letter was returned to her.

Bill old dear,

I just can't tell you the joy and relief it was to get yours of 29th Jan. and know all was well with you. I could hardly tear it open quickly enough and read all you had to say before ringing your Mum. Words are not in the dictionary explaining her joy and relief. The mail hadn't reached No 10 so I read your letter to your Mum. Later I went across on the boat with her all smiles having got your letter. You poor dears all you have gone through and now unable to further the cause. Your Mum is once more feeling her old self having got 2 letters from you yesterday, latest 2nd Feb. I rang her to say Gladys (sister) had read me a remarkable letter from her 19 1/2 [year old?] *lad Rick Tindal of 2/15 A, and bless your dear soul, your Mum was actually reading your letters. It's been hideous these last few weeks not getting letters, no news of you all. It's quite on the cards that this may not reach you for ages as we understand all communication between Australia and Singapore has been suspended but I just feel I must send you a line as it would be poisonous if mail filtered through and you weren't in the running. Far as I can gather your Mum is waiting till official news about letter writing is received before carrying on with her nightly diary. It is to be hoped you'll now be able to fill in all the blank spaces in your diary. How we all ache to hear exactly just how your days are filled in and conditions generally as to your mode of living.*

Am listening to a most entertaining programme on the air, 'The Big Dipper' instead 'Out of the Bag' is its new title. Few Tuesdays ago I had an invitation to attend 'Take it or Leave it' Quiz at 2CH so took Hazel Clayton of Barry Street to support me. More out of devilment than anything I put up my hand as desirous of taking part. I almost sank through the floor when my name was drawn from the hat and had to take up my position on the platform with 10 others. But I came to grief as only 10 are called upon to take part in the contest. To think I nearly, but not quite, spoke over the air.

You just ought to see me now from the sublime to the ridiculous. You were almost or quite in your birthday suit (what a sight you all must have looked) but how we chortled and would have loved to have stolen a march on you all, if only to see the scatteration [?] *as you wrote in your letter of 29th Jan. and here I am dressed fit for any party but because parties are a thing of the past I take a delight in donning a very long black skirt and evening style blouse complete with ear rings so multi coloured that I'd have a slender chance of retaining it should a darkie get a glimpse of it. Being so gay it helps to make one feel a trifle better.*

Was thrilled to hear Gilbert Spence speaking from Canada a few nights back. Among messages to his pals he mentioned Ian Simpson. We're having some mild Singapore weather last week or so, terribly humid. Today a strong wind has been blowing very cooling but dashed rough on my poor vegetable plot which now boasts of peas, beans, carrots, beetroots, spinach, lettuce that will seed before heartening.

I've had the time of my young life the past few weeks traipsing the city trying to land myself a job, but so far have just about worn out a pair of shoes and possibly temper. Lost a glove and back to where I started. I'll increase the postal revenues answering ads, all so inspiring. However last night I rang a friend of your Mums, put the full facts to her and she's seeing her boss on Monday on my behalf, all of which is really wonderful and most encouraging.

Am having a very trying time getting used to my bifocal glasses. Get lots of neck exercises if nothing else.

My goodness what lots, if weird and various, experiences we'll all have to swap with one another one of these fine days, the sooner the better. In the meantime I have frequent yarns with you behind the glass in the frame. You'll probably say it's the last stages but gosh, one must discuss the situation with someone even though it be photograph.

North Sydney Oval was packed to overflowing last week when the Fire Brigade 'Head' gave a most interesting and instructive talk and his men illustrated how to deal with the various types of bombs. Several of us took sandwiches and thermos and had our repast under the trees then crept through the tiny man trap hole and got a front row position and had a most entertaining time watching everyone file in.

Well Bill old lad all the best to you and your mates now it's our turn to say keep your chin up, keep smiling, we're thinking of you all.

With tons of love. Did the parcel posted Dec 29th turn up?
Yours affectionately
Connie Cay

Connie's nephew Gunner Richard Travers Tindal, NX25015, was destined to die on 10 November 1943 in Thailand.[478]

John Gilbert Spence of Newcastle was a Flight Lieutenant in the RAAF (0210631). He was awarded the DFC. Ian Gordon Simpson also of Newcastle, was a Captain in the Army (NX201581). Both these old school friends of Bill survived the war.[479]

20 Mar. '42 - Moved by MT [motor transport], 60 [men] to 3 ton vehicle into Singapore and camped at The Great World under command of Maj. Schneider R.A.A. [Major George Graydon Schneider QX6178 of the 2nd Anti Tank Regiment survived the war.][480]

I had 320 troops and 5 officers with me. Our work in Singapore was concerned with food and clothing. Daily we loaded trains with rice and foodstuffs for up-country areas. The Japanese were also shipping food out of Singapore and we were required on wharf loading parties.

The food issued to us by Japanese was scanty and poor quality but, by adroit thieving, we managed to keep in reasonable condition.

Singapore city was being systematically raped by the I.J.A. Stores and supplies from shops, now closed, found their way to wharf go-downs. Transport carried furniture from private houses to the wharf for shipment to Japan.

On street corners Japanese guards were forcing the civilian population into submission. Those who failed to bow in the lowly manner required were beaten, thrashed and even murdered. The sanitation facilities were momentarily paralysed and in the gutters bordering the city streets, excreta rotted together with the decomposing bodies of humanity.

Japanese newspapers blared forth propaganda magnifying Allied losses and talking of the invincibility of the I.J.A. One extract quoted from memory appeared consistently in the *Syonan Times* - 'Any person or persons found depositing a body whether dead or nearly dead in any public or private place will be punished. By Order Gunsibu Tie'.

The native civilian population moved about their business quietly, no longer with the gaiety that once was so characteristic.

During the early occupation the Japanese issued a decree that all Chinese males between the ages of 18 and 50 years were to report to one of five named locations. Here they were held for days with no food, water or toilets whilst they were processed. This was part of Operation Clean-Up so all anti-Japanese elements were eliminated. If they wrote their name in English, if they had a tattoo, if they had knowledge of English it was a death warrant. An Indian officer witnessed some of the mass executions ... the Chinese had to dig their own graves and they were then beheaded, one by one. The second row had to bury the first lot and then dig graves for their own bodies. This went on for about 10 days.[481] The Japanese admitted to 6,000 deaths, in reality at least 17,000 Chinese men were massacred.[482]

The Chinese girls and young women from 13 to 25 years old fared little better, 9,000 of them did not return home and were eventually found in forced prostitution, being paid half a dollar a visit by Japanese soldiers.[483]

Looters were busy especially in the areas round Holland, Tanglin and Bukit Timah Roads, the European residential areas. One group of looters made the mistake of breaking into a Japanese Military Store. They were at once beheaded and their heads were placed on stands on street corners in the city.[484] These were to serve as warning to other offenders.

As a young child (born in 1938) Poh Woodland recalled:

One thing I remember distinctly was when a teenager was found stealing from the Japanese storage place. The Japanese believed in severe punishment and they beheaded him. His body was displayed in the park opposite our shop as a warning. That was something I'll never forget.[485]

The POWs reported:

One day the Japs lopped the heads of eight Malays for theft and murder and the heads were displayed in prominent parts of Singapore, and we could see one head outside Singapore Railway Station. We were scared off scrounging for a week.[486]

However another prisoner thought:

Probably more stuff went out than on any other day. I think most fellows worked on the assumption that the Japs wouldn't bother to search, they would reckon we'd be too scared.[487]

The accommodation in The Great World was 'Gilbertian' though adequate. The troops occupied buildings that were once dance hall [2/19] and picture theatres [2/20],[488] whilst officers lived in Shooting Galleries, small shops and 'Hoop-la' Stalls.

Work in Singapore and on the wharves was often hard and the hours dawn till after dark. The troops had the labouring work whilst officers stood as buffer between them and the I.J.A. The officers generally were not required to take off their shirts and labour with the troops.

Sgt Frank Baker (NX59308) was with Bill at this time. He recalled the officers and troops did not really talk to each other prior to the fall of Singapore, there was an aloofness of the officers, but once they all became prisoners of war there was much more open communication.[489]

Some working parties would load rations for the IJA. Bags of rice weighing two hundred pound were easily shifted by country troops who were used to lumping wheat bags. They would complete loading the train then return to camp early. The Japanese objected to this so the men slowed down and delayed the departure of the train. The Japanese eventually realised that they had to compromise.[490]

There was always something to 'scrounge'. Beer was one, so was tobacco; gramophone needles and bicycle chains were valuable on the 'black market', stomachs were filled whenever the chance arose, beer was drunk and replaced with urine and the bottles re-capped and re-boxed. As much food as possible was taken back to camp to build up a stock.

The Great World, a former hub of social activites in the city with its dance hall, amusement arcades and picture theatre, became the principal commercial centre for black market operations. A great assortment of goods was traded with the local Chinese. There was no shortage of money which found its way back to Changi, to mates who were confined to camp on POW rations.

The obligatory radio was scrambled together and kept hidden (under penalty of death) so daily news could be posted in a newspaper-type bulletin for secret circulation.[491] Captain Reg Newton had one hidden in the bottom of his water bottle, another was located in a broomhead.[492]

Prisoners coming back into camp from work parties were adept at smuggling goods through the searches at the work site and camp gates. The penalty was a severe bashing but the Japanese would often then allow the victim to keep his stolen goods. The height of the smugglers' art was reached by those who could conceal bulky goods while dressed only in a 'G' string. They were experts in 'crutching' and one man distinguished himself by crutching a live chook, another by crutching a pineapple ... he was bow legged all the way home, ripped raw and sore but he and five mates had a feed which *was delicious and well worth the effort.*[493]

Scrounging was essential to survival and stories of triumphant looting sustained morale. One Japanese lieutenant got a digger's slouch hat, put a tin of condensed milk on the ground and covered it with the hat. He then mounted a box and he berated the troops for their stealing. He got down and said *You have your hat and under it you are stealing things.* He went to pick up the hat to show the tin of condensed milk but it had gone!

Another incident recalled was when a high ranking Japanese officer and his interpreter arrived to abuse Australian prisoners for stealing petrol and selling it to the Chinese. He said he would behead two prisoners every day until it stopped. Satisfied he had put the fear of death into the prisoners, the officer drove off in his flag bedecked car ... for all of thirty metres until he ran out of petrol.[494]

One Japanese officer berated the Australians. He lined them up and sneered *You Aussies think we know F--- NOTHING. But let me tell you Aussies, we know F--- ALL.*[495]

Back home Vera finally received an official letter from the Australian Military Forces (AMF) dated 30 April 1942, ten harrowing weeks after the fall of Singapore advising:

> *no definite information is at present available in regard to the whereabouts or circumstances of your son Captain Edward William Gaden (Number NX12543) 2/20 Battalion AIF and to convey to you the sincere sympathy of the Minister and the Military Board in your natural anxiety in the absence of news concerning him.*

She was asked that if she received any information from other sources it should be sent on to the AMF to verify or assist with their official investigations.

By 29 June 1942 Vera received another official letter informing her that the Minister for the Army advice was that Bill was posted as 'missing'. Further news was being sought through the AMF and also the International Red Cross. What hell for the families who didn't know if their loved one was alive or dead so long after the cease fire.

> **August '42 -** Moved with 100 men to Delta Rd., a small camp near Havelock Rd, and in the same area as The Great World. Conditions at Delta Rd. were not really bad. Rations were reasonable because we managed to have these supplemented from a nearby store of European foods. The accommodation, although 'attab' huts, were clean and not over-crowded.

The huts had long wooden sleeping platforms down each side.[496]

> The Japs soon introduced us to the Indian National Army and in a hut neighbouring ours they quartered these troops. Their duty was that of guarding British POWs in Havelock Rd. camp.
>
> **Sept. '42 -** During the first days of September the Japanese ordered that POWs sign a non-escape declaration. At Changi the Officers refused to sign and the 'Selarang Square Incident' took place in which all troops were confined in a small area and conditions became nearly unbearable, but morale was high and it was only the threat of having the hospital moved into the Square at Selarang that finally influenced the Officers to order troops to sign 'under duress' the declaration. In Singapore the progress of the 'incident' was watched with interest. If Changi held out then we would hold out also. My camp at Delta Rd. was wired and I was told that rations and water would be cut off and machine guns mounted on the corners of the camp. Eventually when Changi signed I received orders from AIF HQ for all troops under my command to follow likewise.

In the middle of the tension Lieutenant-Colonel 'Black Jack' Galleghan organized a concert ... a platform was built out of bits of wood and there was a captive audience of 15,400. At the end the orchestra struck up 'The King' and over 15,000 men sang 'God Save the King'; it stunned the Japanese. 'The Australians put on a jolly good concert'. When the Allied officers eventually agreed to sign the no-escape agreement, the troops decided on their own form of protest and signed under a variety of names ... there were several who signed as Ned Kelly, Jack Lang or Bob Menzies. One unexpected result of the Selarang Barracks incident was an immediate lift in morale. Officers and other ranks, Australian and British prisoners, all had been united in their gesture of defiance toward the enemy.[497]

> Relationships between the Indians and ourselves were decidedly strained and we were fortunately moved into Havelock Rd. camp before any serious incident occurred.

Ray Ridley of 2/20 reported that the Australians did not like their Indian guards, they considered them sadistic turn-coats who had been recruited by the Japanese to fight the British. *To the Indian's Army's credit however, most Indian troops remained loyal.*[498]

> Havelock Rd. camp, commanded by L/Col. Thomas [of the 5th Bedfordshire and Hertfordshires, part of the British 18th Division][499] proved to be crowded and dirty, but work was easy and living with the Englishmen a welcome change. The 100 AIF established amicable relationships with the British O/Rs.
>
> **Oct. '42** - Red Cross supplies arrived and were distributed. These stores came from Lorenzo Marques [the capital of Mozambique, a Portuguese colony which was a major port on east Africa] and were very much appreciated. They provided valuable food and medical stores.

When Red Cross parcels were being distributed the Japanese supervisors insisted on opening bundles to check them. The prisoner's 'scrounging' skills, coupled with the boredom of the guards, saw many parcels going through unchecked.[500]

> The medical authorities with us were now definitely concerned with diet deficiency diseases such as beri-beri, sore mouths and inflamed scrotums. Even with the addition of Red Cross supplies they were unable to combat these ailments satisfactorily. The Japanese turned a deaf ear to our demands for the necessary medicines and the only relief was obtained by contacting occasional native civilians outside.
>
> Tobacco, cigarettes and other necessities, i.e. soap etc. were retailed through small canteens, but supplies were limited and private trading became established within the camp.
>
> **Nov. '42** - The English moved to Thailand packed into railway trucks at about 30 to each vehicle. They were given no opportunity to carry supplies in bulk so that feverish eating of Red Cross food was necessary before leaving.
>
> When the English moved out of Havelock Rd. and River Valley camps, they wore forced to leave behind much of their unconsumed Red Cross food. This was taken over by AIF and transferred to the hospital at Changi. Australian troops now came from Changi to occupy Havelock Rd. and River Valley camps. Conditions then improved in both camps, the accommodation being less congested.

Dutch troops arrived and also small numbers of English from Changi. Until Xmas conditions were better, much use being made of a football ground where international soccer matches provided good entertainment.

Lt. Schuizoa on one occasion ordered Maj. Schneider to move camp from The Great World to an area near Tanglin. I went forward in advance to clean the new camp site. The huts were 'stale' and in shocking condition. On examination some of the huts were found to contain partly decomposed bodies of Indian troops killed by bombs. Other bodies were located half buried in the area. Fortunately we were able to delay the move, and finally returned to Changi at Xmas without occupying that camp.

Dec. '42 - Transport was provided and movement to Changi commenced. By Xmas Havelock Road, River Valley and Great World were all evacuated.

Generally speaking the year in Singapore was not very serious for the POWs. Rations were very poor and insufficient in vitamin requirements but we were proficient thieves and were given small amounts of food by the native civilians.

Often the men were bashed by Japanese guards and soldiers who exhibited a savage brutality - on occasions these bashings were deserved but on other occasions the brutality was undeserved and inexcusable.

A Japanese Officer, Lt. Schuizoa was directly responsible for POWs and must be held to pay for the rations and the conduct of guards. This Officer was difficult to deal with and incidents can be proved concerning the inhuman conduct he adopted when dealing with POWs.

In all camps the Japanese forbade news of the outside world. POWs were never without news; they always managed to work a wireless even when they knew the punishment for having such a machine meant death.

The wireless sets were carefully hidden in such containers as water bottles, bags of rice etc. They were never discovered but the Japanese constantly searched our quarters.

When we finally arrived back at Selarang, Changi, for Xmas '42 the troops were reasonably well and fit but clothing was showing signs of wear. We were all put through a period of 'smartening-up' in the Square and troops were more like soldiers once again. No persons were allowed outside the wire excepting occasional gardeners, but soon gardening became organized and I worked on a 100 acre plot which soon showed signs of producing vegetables in quantity, certain types of spinach and sweet potatoes being quick maturing crops.

[Byam was a quick growing leaf vegetable, sweetbuck was similar to sweet potato and towgay were small green seeds germinated in water, similar to bean sprouts. Tapioca was one root vegetable planted but troops were horrified to learn it would be nine months before harvest. They hoped the war would be over long before then.][501]

The concert party was well under way and producing light entertainment but good quality. Some artists were professional in peace time. The English gave some musical recitals of extremely high order, some of the musicians being of England's best.

Test matches were played on a good cricket ground.

The accommodation was still crowded but some troops remained in Singapore at Blakan Mati [the Island of the Dead Behind, now known as Sentosa][502] loading and storing bombs for the I.J.A., so things were not quite as bad as previously.

In March 1942 the Japanese War Cabinet decided to prepare for an invasion of India during the dry season of 1943-44. Because American and British submarines were operating in the Bay of Bengal, the Japanese were having trouble getting their supplies through to the IJA.[503] Their administration decided to construct a railway line from Thailand to Burma to connect the railway systems of the two countries and thus ensure the Japanese could supply their troops as they invaded Burma and India.[504] The British Army had surveyed a proposed route as far back as the early 1900s but had decided the terrain was too difficult and tropical diseases would be a serious issue.[505]

The Allied POWs were in fact a huge problem for the Japanese; they were present in such large numbers, there were no facilities to confine and intern them. To remove them to Japan would require vital transport and food, things that were already in short supply. The prisoners were, in effect, a strong, well trained and available labour force. The Japanese Government decided to put the thousands of prisoners of war to work, as slave labour in the mines back in Japan and also to build the Burma-Thailand railway. This would help the Japanese war effort and was therefore in direct contradiction to the Geneva Convention on treatment of POWs. Japanese civilian engineers were to design and supervise the construction of the rail line. The IJA was to be responsible for acquiring material and labour.[506] Much of the labour would be provided by the POWs.

The Japanese selected a work party of prisoners, 'A' Force, to construct airfields in Burma and then commence work on the railway to be built from Thanbyuzayat in Burma southwards. Another work party, 'D' Force, was to go to Nong Pladuk in Thailand and work northwards. The lines were to join at Konkoita on the Thai side of the Three Pagodas Pass border crossing.[507]

'A' Force left Changi early in May '42.

Commanded by Brigadier Varley, it was 3,000 strong. There were some 2/20 troops including Major Ron Merrett and Major Arch Ewart who were in the group under Lieutenant-Colonel GE Ramsay.[508] They sailed to Burma on the *Celebes Maru* to build air strips, and, once the decision to build the railway had been taken, 'A' Force men were sent to Thanbyuzayat to start work on the railway.[509] Both Merrett and Ewart of 2/20 were Mentioned in Dispatches for distinguished service whilst POWs.[510]

'B' & 'C' Forces left Changi at later dates, 'B' Force went to Sandakan, Borneo in July 1942, and 'C' Force was sent to Japan in November 1942, to work in the mines.

The Japanese also did not conform with the Geneva Convention on sending and receiving letters from home. The captured men were desperate for news from Australia but, once they became prisoners, letters from home only filtered through very slowly and were many months, if not years, out of date. The Japanese used withholding letters as a threat and to 'encourage' POW Camp discipline. Men who were lucky enough to receive letters shared them with other prisoners as they knew how much it hurt when you missed out on the Red Cross Mail which came so infrequently.[511]

Likewise the prisoners were not allowed to write letters home; they could only occasionally send a tick-a-box postcard. Often when families eventually received these cards they were saddened to finally find their son had died as a POW many months before.

Bill received his letters in several batches. The first was in February 1943, a year after the surrender, then in January 1944, August 1944, October 1944, November 1944 and finally in February 1945.

It is impossible to know precisely how many letters Bill received, but the undated ones which made it back to Australia with him are placed in the most logical order among the dated ones. From the comments written there were many letters which went missing and only a few postcards made their way from the prisoners back to Australia. It must have been a dreadful time for the families not knowing if their soldier listed as 'missing' had in fact been killed or died as a prisoner. At least they would not have realised the dreadful conditions under which their lads were interned in the railway camps; they would have hoped the Japanese were following the Geneva Convention it its treatment of POWs.

These first letters were addressed to Bill as part of the 2/20 AIF in Malaya. Date of writing unknown, but between June and Dec 1942, received February 1943:

From Mrs V.L. Gaden, 10 Raymond Road, Neutral Bay, Sydney

My darling old Bill

It's time to write my 2nd letter to you now. How I count the days. Again I am glad to tell you we are all well and everything is going along smoothly. I have never seen Sue looking better and she seems so happy and contented with her work. [Sue had joined the RAAF as an aircraftwoman, enlisting on 15 April 1942].[512]

Elizabeth [Bill's sister Ginge] *is with Kitty at Gundagai for a couple of weeks which will be up in a few days.*

[Kitty was one of Bill's aunts, Catherine (Gaden) Walker whose husband was Norman Arthur Walker NX 70675, a Major in AAMC MED. They had three small children, Helen, Richard and Judith].[513]

All Kitty's children were ill and she had no help so Elizabeth went to her rescue. She had left her job with the Trustees and will find another when she comes home.

Your firm [Shipping Company Birt and Co.] *sent me a bonus of £14 dear, the same as last June. Mr Carlyle rang me to say it was coming and hear all the news etc.*

We are getting along well financially and don't owe a penny to anyone. Now that the old house in Scone is sold I feel a weight off my mind. I wish the price could have covered the mortgage but the trustees will adjust all that now.

Mother is still at Bundabarrina [the home in Collarenebri, north-west NSW, of Vera's sister Doris who was married to Hugh Grant] *and will stay there until the hot weather starts. I think she will have had enough of it by then. Marjorie Blomfield is in Armidale. Barbara is at the University there so Marje let her flat in Sydney to be near her. She is looking so young and pretty again. Country life suits her.*

We haven't heard anything of Margaret [Taylor] *for ages. Perhaps you will get a letter from her. Mrs McCully rang me the other day ... came in to see me last Saturday. Dorothy and her children are living in Armidale for a while now.*

Bill and Audrey Tewksbury are proud parents. They own a small daughter. It would have to be small wouldn't it? [Audrey Rose Westgarth was a family friend from Scone. Her father and Bill's were both solicitors.]

Henry Friend is also a father. He might grow up now and be his age.

I went down to the Sautelles one night last week. They were bright as usual. Mr Sautelle has been ill lately but is well again now.

The Griersons [next door neighbours] *are just the same. We see Gordon once a week and the curate is still the centre of attraction.*

Elizabeth is home now and has a good job with York and Kerr [a company of shipping agents][514] *in Bridge Street and is very happy dear. All our love darling.*

Your loving mother
Doukie

Date of writing 26 June 1942, received February 1943

From Miss A.C. Cay, 44 Harriette Street, Neutral Bay.

Bill my dear old lad

It's just too marvellous to be actually having a yarn with you though it be but on paper. All is well with your home folks. I slipped round to see your Mum last Saturday morning, she's 'in the pink' and just about bursting every seam with rude health. Her one big sadness was not being able to write to you, but now she is all smiles again. Sue and Elizabeth are full of pep and looking awfully well. Ginge had a wonderful time whilst on holiday and was able to give me news of many old friends. She grows more like you daily. You'll love the new flat Bill, it's all so cosy. Garden is giving your Mum much pleasure especially the rose plot; my contribution to it being 'General MacArthur' who is growing splendidly and belongs to each one of you. Your Mum and I planted the bush and whilst doing so hoped it would mean a speedy return for everyone of you. Curiously enough I hear you had it in your Scone garden.

Three of your letters have been returned to me, shall keep them for you. How heavenly it will be to hear how all you lads are; be of good cheer. News of you all is what we so long to get.

Have just finished a temporary job at the Egg Marketing Board; never handled an egg but with four others checked millions of cases. Am once again scanning the columns.

We're having a marvellous winter, not too cold as yet and quite enough rain. My vegetable garden is returning good profit as is the flower section.

Have made friends with a Mrs Lewis Kennedy who left Singapore February 5th and have begun to feel I know lots more of your surroundings than previously. She's living with her aunt Mrs Bremmer in Bennett Street. She has had no word from her husband since she left and is very worried. It's just been the greatest help to your Mum, the girls and the rest of us to have had messages from various ones who saw you after the fall.

All the best Bill. Wish you boys had Mike Connors over there, he's just a bundle of cheerfulness. Am in rude health and fit for anything. A big cheerio
Yours lovingly
Connie

Bill would receive no more letters until January 1944, twelve long months later.

And finally, after eleven interminable months of waiting herself, on 6th January 1943, Vera received a telegram from Victoria Barracks, Sydney. Imagine the trembling fingers as she read whether her beloved son was alive or not.

```
6 JANUARY 1943, MRS VERA LYDIA GADEN, FLAT 1, ST DAMIENS
RAYMOND ROAD, NEUTRAL BAY
CAPTAIN GADEN PRISONER OF WAR. I HAVE TO INFORM YOU THAT CAPT
EDWARD WILLIAM GADEN NX12543 PREVIOUSLY REPORTED MISSING
IS NOW REPORTED PRISONER OF WAR INTERNED MALAYAN CAMP
MINISTER FOR THE ARMY
```

Just three weeks later, on 20 January 1943 Bill's sister Elizabeth (Ginge) announced her engagement to Major David Campbell MacDougal, second son of the late Mr and Mrs R.M. MacDougal, Brisbane.[515] He had returned from Mission 204 in China after the soldiers were withdrawn. It was a lucky move from the 2/20 into Mission 204 as David had returned home early, missing the fighting and defeat of Singapore. He renewed his friendship with Bill's sister and proposed to her after a whirlwind six week romance.[516]

It was not until September 1943 that the family finally received Bill's first card home to advise he was still alive. But by then he was miles away from Singapore, up in Thailand working on the construction of the infamous railway line.

455 *Sydney Morning Herald*, 16 February 1942, p. 5.
456 Rivett, *Behind Bamboo*, p. 16.
457 *War Cry* 14 March 1942 reported in Hull, *Salvos with the Forces*, pp. 155-176.
458 *ibid.*
459 ABC TV program, *Vivian Bullwinkel, an Australian heroine.*
460 Jeffrey, *White Coolies*, p. 24.
461 *ibid.*, pp. 82, 98, 123-4, 141, 149-50.
462 Rivett, *op. cit.*, p. 16.
463 Wall, *Singapore and Beyond*, p. 109.
464 Hodgson, Alec, *Diary*, <http://www.s1942.org.sg/s1942/images/pdf/600374.pdf > p. 25.
465 Brown, *Diary of a POW in Singapore*, <http://www.bbc.co.uk/ww2peopleswar/stories/19/a3609119.shtml>
466 Wall, *op. cit.*, p. 110.
467 Ziegler, *Men May Smoke*, p. 32.
468 DVA Nominal Roll and Wall, *op. cit.*, pp. 366 and 369.
469 Braddon, *The Naked Island*, pp. 105, 126.
470 Frank Baker (NX59308), personal communication.
471 Wall, *op. cit.*, p. 110.
472 Arneil, *One Man's War*, p. 19.
473 *ibid.*
474 Poole, *Of Love and War*, p. 178.
475 'Cholera' from *Up to Date Medical Program*, 2006 version, information supplied by Lieutenant Peter Gaden, Medical Officer RAN.
476 Savage, *A Guest of the Emperor*, p. 59.
477 Molony, *The Penguin History of Australia*, p. 285.
478 DVA Nominal Roll.
479 *ibid.*
480 *ibid.*
481 Pillai and Radharkrishnan, *Report on treatment of civilians*, p. 23.
482 Shinozaki, *Syonan*, pp. 20-21, 115.
483 Pillai and Radharkrishnan, *op. cit.*, p. 23.

[484] Shinozake, *op. cit.*, p. 18.
[485] Barrett, *Hidden heritage*, p. 8.
[486] Wall, *op. cit.*, p. 131.
[487] Nelson, *Australians under Nippon*, p. 29.
[488] Wall, *op. cit.*, p. 128.
[489] Frank Baker (NX59308) personal communication.
[490] Wall, *op. cit.*, p. 128.
[491] *ibid.*, pp. 129-30.
[492] Reg Newton, personal communication.
[493] Nelson, *op. cit.*, pp. 32-3.
[494] *ibid.*, pp. 29-30.
[495] Stuart Lloyd, Personal communication.
[496] Wall, *op. cit.*, p. 133.
[497] Nelson, *op. cit.*, pp. 31-2.
[498] Wall, *op. cit.*, p. 133.
[499] Smith, *op. cit.*, p. 266.
[500] Wall, *op. cit.*, p. 133.
[501] Arneil, *op. cit.*, pp. 285-6, 20.
[502] Gaden, *Changi to Hellfire Tour Diary*, p. 15.
[503] Newton, Interview, AWM S01739.
[504] Wall, *op. cit.*, p. 138.
[505] Beattie, *op. cit.*, p.15 and Bradley, *Australian Bicentenary Hellfire Pass Project*, pp. 2-3.
[506] Bradley, *op. cit.*, pp. 2-3.
[507] Beattie, Map of the Thai-Burma Rail Link.
[508] AWM Encyclopaedia <http://www.awm.gov.au/encyclopaedia/pow/general_info.htm>
[509] Wall, *op. cit.*, pp. 140-1.
[510] Wall, *op. cit.*, no page number.
[511] Braddon, *op. cit.*, pp. 242-3.
[512] DVA Nominal Roll.
[513] DVA Nominal Roll and Gaden family history researched by the author.
[514] Personal communication, ANS mailing list, < aus-nsw-sydney@rootsweb.com > 17 May 2007.
[515] *Sydney Morning Herald*, 20 January 1943, Births, Engagements and Deaths.
[516] David MacDougal, personal communication.

Chapter 10 - 'D' Force

The Japanese wanted more working parties of prisoners to build on the Thailand end of the Burma-Thailand railway. One was designated 'D' Force and consisted of four 'battalions' each of around 555 men and a Brigade HQ under command of Lieutenant-Colonel Cranston McEachern (QX6176). The battalions were 'S' Bn. was under Major Graydon Schneider (QX6178), 'T' Bn under Major John Quick (NX70492(N7)), 'U' Bn. under Captain Reg Newton (NX34734)[517] and 'V' Bn under Major Alf Gough.

Reg Newton, the Officer-in-Charge of 'U' Battalion, selected Bill to be his Second in Command, 2IC. Thus Bill Gaden left the relative comfort of Changi and was sent north to work on what became such an infamous railway.

When Reg Newton was advised that he was to be in charge of a battalion of 'D' Force to travel into Thailand, he

> *selected officers who I knew could be rough and tough and could handle the Nips, they had proven this in Singapore work parties. I did not select anybody who had been in Changi throughout because I knew they had not had Japanese experience. But above all they had to be of the rougher and tougher type who could handle themselves and handle troops. I was determined I would only take one officer per hundred: that still left back a number of younger ones who were very good lads. This was unfortunate but I was determined I would not have a superabundance of officers and then be at the beck and call of all the Nips for having too many drones around the place.*[518]

Reg chose Bill as his 2IC because he'd known him from 17 Battalion days and they'd been room-mates and friends when patients in Alexandra Hospital. In particular he took him *for his great administrative ability, particularly the food supplies.*[519]

> **14 Mar '43** 'D' Force left Changi for Thailand. I took troops on this party which was commanded by L/Col. C. McEachern C.R.A.A. [Commander Royal Australian Artillery]. We left Selarang by truck and were taken to the railway station at Singapore. Very little heavy luggage was allowed. The total force of 2,500 men AIF was divided into 5 train parties each of 500.

When Lieutenant-Colonel McEachern subsequently left 'D' Force to command Dunlop Force, allowing Lieutenant-Colonel Edward 'Weary' Dunlop to concentrate on medical duties, the leadership of 'D' Force came to rely on the individual commanders of each battalion. 'U' Battalion were fortunate that Reg Newton was their OIC. Major Douglas Okey (NX35116) of 2/18 recalled

> *He was the sort of man men would sell their soul for, thoroughly healthy in his outlook, with a ready smile and a quick appreciation of a situation.*[520]

Reg was well known for his pat on the shoulder and 'Well done Bonnie Laddie'.[521]

In 'U' Bn Capt. Fred Harris had 6 Coy, all 2/19 men; Lieut Sanderson had 7 Company, also from the 2/19, Warrant Officer 2nd class Ned Turner of

2/19 had a mixed group of men in 8 Company, from 2/18, 2/19, Army Service Corps and some military police troops; Capt. Bill Gaden had 9 Company, all 2/20 men and Lieut Frank Ramsbotham had 10 Company, also from the 2/20.[522] It was important for the prisoners to try and remain with men of their own battalion, their mates who had become their 'surrogate family' once the troops had left home and who had fought alongside each other in the battles, blokes they knew and could trust.[523] Any inter-battalion rivalry had to be superceded by a common goal to survive.

When the prisoners arrived at the railway station they were horrified to see their transport, steel rice trucks. One recalled that orders to board the train

> *brought a chorus of incredulous laughter from the POWs, for it seemed impossible that they could expect thirty-two men and their gear to cram into each truck. Once again we had underestimated our oriental friends who, with kicks and shouts, demonstrated that where there is a will there is a way.*[524]

> The accommodation on the train was appalling, 29 & 30 men to rice trucks enclosed with iron and unmercifully hot. The train crawled slowly up Malaya into Thailand finally to stop on the morning of the fourth day at Nong Pladuk where we detrained.

Chaplain Marsden recalled the gauge was three feet six inches *which did not exactly make for comfortable travelling.*[525]

> The food on the journey was extremely poor, vegetable water being occasionally issued and on one occasion at Prai [near Penang] two small tins of sardines was provided to each truck of 29-30 men, 1/2 pint of boiled rice was also available for each man. The Japs were frightened that the POWs would have strength to escape if provided with sufficient food. On arrival at Nong Pladuk we were given 5 bananas and a pint of tea each. The party was ravenous.

Don McLaren and his five mates recalled how they sold their precious magneto, used to light cigarettes, as it was too heavy to carry. They traded it for a dozen duck eggs, and asked for them to be boiled as they had no facilities to cook the eggs themselves.[526]

> The same afternoon we loaded ourselves on to table top trucks with no sides and commenced a journey to Kanburi by rail. [Kanchanaburi an ancient walled city was about 50km from the designated start of the railway at Nong Pladuk]. The line we now traveled was built by English POWs who had left Changi whilst we were in Singapore. The men were exposed to heat on our departure from Nong Pladuk, the 'table tops' having no covering what-so-ever. Later it rained, became cold and finally hailed heavily, the men suffered from exposure.
>
> At dusk we arrived at Kanburi and marched to an amazing camp consisting of one hut and about one acre of ground - accommodation for our train party of 500.

Kanchanaburi was known as The Desert Camp.[527]

> The I.J.A. interpreter with me said food was ready for us. I followed him to the rear of the hut and was shown a live pit [pit viper snake] in a basket, some eggs and a few skips of a green vegetable we knew well by sight. The men were 'all in' but we managed to provide a meal within an hour or so. The following morning proved to be an important one for us.

> The Thai natives thronged around our crowded acre and soon trading burst into full swing. Our half starving men purchased and ate native food. Bananas and eggs were safe but some ate cooked rice, cakes, omelettes and many other native 'delicacies'. This purchasing was soon controlled but damage was done and soon we had cases of dysentery. 500 men in one acre with dysentery spreading was frightening, and finally the Japanese agreed to find us a new camp which proved to be about 20 acres of scrub, uncleared, with no buildings of any description, into which the whole party of 2,500 was to live. Within a fortnight we were a complete party roughing it in the bush with an increasing dysentery roll. Men were trading trinkets, watches etc. to the natives who in return were supplying local currency and rubbishy food and cigarettes.

'D' Force prisoners were left alone outside the town for a few days. The Thai Command troops of the Imperial Japanese Army had not yet arrived to take over the prisoners from the Malay Command. Thus the men had several days of 'freedom' in which to trade with the Thai locals, unload surplus gear and buy food and other goods in exchange for anything they had - one sold a thick marble desk set with penholders to buy the more necessary food. Some ventured into the town, some ate as much as they could, some were entertained by ladies of pleasure and had to suffer the indignity of a 'short arm parade' to check for venereal disease.[528]

But the most important thing which occurred at this time was the meeting between Capt. Reg Newton, Bill Gaden and Boon Pong, a local trader who had the contract to provide food for the Japanese.[529]

Boon Pong was a provision merchant and grocer, with a sound financial business. He served a couple of terms as mayor in Kanchanaburi. His initial contact with the Japanese was when they wished to purchase land at Chungkai for a cemetery, land which belonged to Boon Pong's mother. Through this contact he won the contract to supply the prison camp canteens for the Japanese prison guards.

Supplies were transported upstream to them by barge. Reg arranged for Boon Pong to also bring food and medicines by barge for the prisoners. Despite the risk, Boon Pong agreed. If this meeting had not occurred, if this trade had not been established, thousands more men would have starved to death.[530]

Ex-patriot civilian internees and other businessmen assisted POWs financially via a couple of aid organisations which were set up, both calling themselves the 'V' Organisation.[531] Much of the money raised by the 'V' organisations was sent to Changi. However only a small amount made it up the railway line to where it was so much more desperately needed to buy food and medicines.[532] The Army hierarchy in Changi did not appreciate the critical plight of the men on the railway line and they did not forward as much money as was required. Reg had little time for the officers in Changi whom he blamed for this neglect.[533]

The people involved in these 'V' organisations risked their lives. They relayed messages in and out of the camps, liaised with the Thai Army and sent the vital food, medicines and radio batteries into the camps. As Rivett says:

The families of the Allied POWs in Siam owe a tremendous debt to all those in this brilliantly organized underground society which helped save the lives of hundreds of British, Dutch and Australian prisoners.[534]

Meanwhile the supply of provisions to 'D' Force was purchased by Reg Newton. He signed cheques which he gave to Boon Pong. There was no payee name, amount or date written to safeguard Boon Pong's identity. The cheque book was for the Bank of NSW, Wahroonga Bank a/c Sgt. John French. All Reg did was alter 'Wahroonga' to 'Head Office', where he had an account. (After the war Reg made sure Boon Pong had been paid all the outstanding money and then tried to claim it back from the Australian Government, who refused to pay. After some publicity in the local newspapers the government threatened Reg with Court Martial. However he was ultimately not prosecuted and was reimbursed, but it was by the Red Cross, not the Government.)[535]

> The order came to move north and after one hell of a trip crowded in the back of trucks over partly-cleared bush roads we arrived at Tarso on 30 March '42.

(Tarso, Tarsao, Tarsau, Tha Sao and Tahsao are all variations on the spelling, depending on which reference is read. For Bill's post-war paintings he used Tarsau but in his diary it was TARSO, so that spelling has been retained. The camp was about 125 km north of Nong Pladuk, the start of the railway in Thailand.)[536]

The 'D' Force troops were lucky, they were one of the few parties to be transported north by motor.[537]

> The camp was even then falling to pieces. The huts were low, evil looking native shelters built of 'attab' and bamboo. To our consternation they were found to be verminous. The latrines were open and breeding flies, kitchens, in fact the whole place was filthy. Some of our troops elected to sleep in the huts but the majority chose the open ground outside.

One member of 'D' Force recalled arriving at the camp where they:

met indescribably gaunt British and Dutch prisoners, some with blood from dysentery running down their legs and mottled with filthy sores. My greatest shock was the sight of beri-beri victims carrying their [fluid swollen] *melon sized testicles before them.*

The Australians wondered how long it would take them *to get like those poor bastards.*[538]

> One good feature of Tarso was the river which was within walking distance and in bounds for bathing and cooking water.

It also had a beautiful view and, according to Weary Dunlop,

the effects of the sunrise and sunset on the rugged jungle clad mountains were indeed gorgeous.[539]

> TARSO at this stage was a base camp containing some 2,000 English. There were camps established further north. We had traveled some 60 km along the line which was later to be cleared and a railway built from Kanburi. The troops already north

were clearing the path - our job was to build the embankment. The cemetery at TARSO contained 33 graves when we arrived.

When the Australians arrived in Tarso it was occupied by British soldiers who had virtually been abandoned by their senior officer. He didn't stand up to the Japs and he spent his days fishing in the river. The camp was in a dreadful state, rations were terrible, hospital supplies non-existent, no hygiene and no canteen. The abysmal state of affairs was very apparent to the newly arrived Australians. Their leader, only identified as the 'Big Australian' made a number of pointed remarks, and eventually gave the Senior British Officer a very public, very wrathful dressing-down. Not long after, things improved, new latrines were dug, firewood and water was collected and clothing and bedding was sterilised.[540]

Tarso became the HQ for 'D' Force. It was a base camp for the Japanese with a large maintenance and repair shop for their vehicles. It had roofed attap [sic] huts sufficient in number for the 'D' Force men, but not enough to accommodate 'F' Force when they later marched through.[541]

Tarso was one of the camps surrounded by a fence on three sides with a formal entrance gateway. The fourth side was the Kwei Noi River. The fence caused a problem with location of the latrine trenches ... the Japanese insisted they were to be built in the narrow strip between the ends of the huts and the fence. They were far too close to the accommodation huts; in monsoonal rain they were totally inadequate and flooded and the contents overflowed. Conditions were very unpleasant.[542]

1 Apr. '43 On this April Fools day we commenced work on the railways which was to cost us so expensively both in health and in lives.
Building the embankment was heavy work with very bad tools. The shovels were made from 44 gallon oil drums and the picks rough cast iron, the handles being hewn from the poor jungle timber.

Officers were once again the buffer between the Japanese and the troops. The job was to obtain from the guards the nature of the work required, and to organise things so that the troops were not imposed too heavily upon. They saw that sick men went home to camp. They argued when the Japs demanded more work. They organised ration parties and in general did their best to alleviate the extreme task of the O/R.

The Australians were prepared to work as a team to overcome the problems as much as possible, their team spirit and behaviour contrasted with that of many of the British.

Capt. Vardy, a British Medical Officer, was very aware of this difference. He observed

Not only could the Australians rough it much better than the British but they were much friendlier. There was a more pleasant spirit about their mess, amongst the officers, amongst the men and between the officers and men. Their CO is friendly - they all chat together, laugh and play the fool - yet he is undoubtedly their CO and if time calls for it they jump to it (I have seen it time and time again) while in our mess there is a bloody barrier almost everywhere you turn. There is hardly any general conversation - just in little groups. We get secret letters sent round the mess telling us how we should behave towards the O/Rs. Ye Gods, such piffle at time like these and when after all, we are all POWs - no we are frightfully British don't you know, while they [the Aussies] *are bloody good fellows.*[543]

The spirit of cooperation in the Australian Camp was important. The men who fared the worst were the ones badly led, with officers who could not stand up to the Japanese. Gordon Gaffney talked about the poor officers he had in 'F' Force. He mentioned two who were frightened, never had any guts and some who wouldn't go to work but hid under a mosquito net all the time.[544]

Capt. Adrian Curlewis, also of 'F' Force wrote on 30 August 1943:

God how weary I am of squalor, mankind and illness. I live in a tattered tent with nine officers who are too ill to work, who talk of nothing but their illnesses (my breakfast in the dark as they lie in bed is accompanied by boasts of the number of their visits to the latrines at night). My day is among foul mouthed animals who have lost self respect and decency, who rob their mates, who cry to me for help on all occasions and then let me down by lying. Razors have been sold for food, brushes and combs gone, soap almost unobtainable, clothes in rags and dirty, tempers on edge and hope gone. Personally I have succeeded by weary hours of sewing, scrubbing and will power to keep a certain amount of appearance. As I lie now in the tent five officers are sitting on their haunches just gazing at nothing or talking in faded voices, men without hope, or if they have hope, they are past fighting for health to get them home. Two are cholera convalescents. Have just supervised 240 men (skeletons) drawing their lunch issue of rice; blasphemy, flies, dirt. God how I hate it all![545]

However Reg Newton commented that keeping score of the number of visits to the 'benjo' was one way for the men to try and keep a sane mind despite the difficulties and stress being encountered.[546]

There were of course poor officers in all camps but the good officer made a huge difference to their men; they were the ones who did what they could to alleviate their suffering. As Kevin Fagan remarked

After a long days march ... a fellow like Newton would be scrounging around trying to buy a few eggs for the sick, trying to organise the men to be together, finding out where everyone was and whether anyone needed a doctor and all this before he even thought of sitting down.[547]

It wasn't just the commissioned officers who acted as a buffer between the troops and guards. Sgt Andrew Keith Wilson (QX10799) of the 2/26 recalled standing up to a guard nicknamed The Black Bomber. Sgt Wilson ordered his men to have a much needed rest. They were hit with rifle butts and he was bashed with the flat edge of a bayonet. This happened day after day.[548]

A sense of humour also played an important part. Jack Boon another member of 'D' Force recalled the prisoners were always talking of places back home and where they would like to be or doing. One man said that he'd like to be before the 'beak' (magistrate) on a charge of being drunk and disorderly; most replies involved food or women.

One Japanese guard had been nicknamed Caesar. A prisoner was given a task by Captain Gaden but a different task by Caesar. The frustrated man said *Things are bad enough without being confused by Gaden and Caesar.* Immediately his learned companion turned round and advised *Render unto Caesar the things that are Caesars.*[549]

> There were two units of Japanese that POWs were concerned with - the railway 'engineers' and the Korean guards from the camp administration staffs. These units were usually at loggerheads but both agreed on the persecution of prisoners.
>
> From the start officers had trouble obtaining permission for sick men to stay in camp. At TARSO there was one Japanese who caused many a sick man to work and indirectly caused many deaths - Oseki the camp interpreter. This individual would on occasions have the sick paraded and send men to work who had been marked 'Bed Down' by our M.O., who we were fortunate enough to have still with us. Oseki also bashed many POWs, sometimes punishment was deserved but brutality was inexcusable.
>
> Our parties of 500 were given alphabetical appellations. My Battalion being commanded by Capt. Newton (Reg) was 'U Bn' others were 'S' & 'T'. Maj. Gough with one of the 500 parties was taken away out of the Tarso area and we did not contact him for nearly a year. When finally we were able to contact him he had received 44% casualties dead.

'S' Bn was sent to Kinsaiyoke and Hintoc and 'T' Bn went to Wampo and later to Kenyu.[550]

> 'U Bn.' troops were from 2/20 Bn, 2/19 and Australian Army Service Corps. Capt. Newton did excellent work and the men were spared many a hardship by his good organization.

'U' Bn were only in Tarso until 1 June when they moved to South Tonchan. This was often called the Waterfall Camp as a stream ran along the edge of the campsite then plunged down the rocks below.[551] This was the Sai Yok Noi waterfall near to Nam Tok. The Japanese officer in charge of the prisoners here was Hiromatsu, known as 'The Tiger' who was considered to be

> *tough and the terror of the whole Japanese army but he kept good control of his own troops and there was less 'touching' of rations. He was known to avenge an unwarranted bashing if it came to his notice, but to iron out a worse one if he dismissed the appeal. The Tiger had great admiration for Capt Newton with his 6 foot height and blockbusting voice and his iron efficiency. Newton became a byword on the Line and fought the Japanese all the way, often getting knocked over as he made his demands for boots, food and protecting his men.*[552]

Captain Reg Newton stood up to The Tiger and even appeared to bully the prisoners in front of him to 'con' the Japanese. The Tiger wanted working parties and generally left the prisoners to sort out for themselves who would go and who would not. He had threatened that an officer would be executed if something went wrong and then left them to run the camp. He was considered to be 'weird but fair'[553] and the prisoners knew that, in general, 'Roaring Reggie' Newton had the measure of him.

The men themselves were subject to around 15 to 20 bashings a day but the officers like Reg who stood up to the Japanese would score twice that amount. Whilst it was not funny for the person on the receiving end, it gave men a talking point that so and so 'copped a good one today'.[554]

Sometimes guards would single out the tall prisoners for particular abuse. Andrew Coventry of 2/10 Field Regiment recalled the time a guard was giving him a severe berating. Coventry was a tall man and drew himself to his full height. The furious guard screamed something in Japanase and another guard raced out, bringing a chair. From his new high vantage point the guard proceeded to slap Coventry around the face. The Australian found it hard not to laugh.[555]

Sgt Frank Baker recalled The Tiger didn't like sick people and therefore he had no time for Frank who was a medical orderly. One day he insisted that Frank plant a tree and water it every morning. The Tiger would get up at 5.00 am to ensure the tree had been watered. For two weeks he inspected the tree, arriving earlier each day, to make his point.[556]

One day the Australians were ordered to carry Japanese rations from the railway to their kitchen. One of the work party, Wally Rooke, was caught hiding a pumpkin in the bush with the intention of returning for it later. He was taken to the Japanese guard room and ordered to stand to attention with the pumpkin held above his head. Each time his arms started to droop he was hit with a rifle butt across the elbows. Capt. Newton went to try and get Rooke off the punishment. The next thing Rooke was released and Newton ordered to take his place. '*Everyone in the Camp came out to see this sight, even The Tiger. Everyone was smirking and smiling.*' Eventually Rooke was called back to the guard room and presented with the pumpkin; Newton was released and was rewarded with a slice of pumpkin pie for his part in the acquisition.[557]

On another occasion Reg intervened when a prisoner sick with malaria, Bill Coombs (NX58188),[558] retaliated after The Tiger pushed him in a physical training session. The Australian was to be sent to Tarso for execution. Reg intervened and eventually The Tiger came out and said Coombs had a temper, he himself had a temper and things had got out of hand, there would be no execution this time, but it was not to happen again.[559] Reg Newton obviously knew how to exploit The Tiger's ego and personality.

Owing to Capt. Newton's strict control on hygiene and the drugs that were smuggled into camp, his group was the healthiest on the Line and The Tiger took the credit for this. However Capt. Newton was astute enough to let Tiger have the credit, he used it as a lever to wrest a thousand privileges from him.

One of these privileges was to arrange with Boon Pong to access the desperately needed drugs of *Magnesium sulphate* and emetine, used to treat dysentery. Reg was allowed, under escort, to collect and then distribute them

*

IT'S THE BIGGEST

LEFT: When Bill Gaden gets down to art, he does it in a big way. President of the North Shore Art Society, and a life member of the Art Gallery Society of NSW, he has been conducting an exhibition at the Mosman Town Hall this week. All the oil paintings and framing are entirely Bill's work, with framing assistance by his wife, and the collection is considered possibly the biggest exhibition of its type ever presented in Australia. Bill's work will be on show until 9 o'clock tonight.

Railway embankment

Supply barge on River Kwai at Tarsau 1943

Hellfire Pass

Kanburi Station

Attap huts at Tarsau 1943

Pack o' Cards Bridge

Nakompathom Pagoda

The Bridge on the River Kwai

Wampo Viaduct

A Prayer

By Janet Muriel Johnston
and Vera Lydia Gaden

Hear us Lord we hum - bly pray make all wars and strife to cease

bring our loved ones safe - ly home bring us near - er Thee and peace

1939-45 Star, Pacific Star, Defence Medal, War Medal, Australian Service Medal

to his own and the British troops.[560] The Tiger received cash to the value of a 10% levy on the transactions.[561]

The Japanese soldiers themselves were frightened of Capt. Newton. One delightful story was told of some Japanese soldiers who, when they spotted Reg entering a hut at one end, all fled out of the back amid cries of 'Aaagh! Number One Australian'.[562]

The Tiger's guns and Capt Newton's voice struck an almost perfect balance of power.[563]

> The Japanese demanded every available man to work. Sick were only excused when they absolutely could not walk and the camp staff allowed was the smallest possible. When opportunity arose we cheated the Japs by keeping men off work and generally endeavouring to do the best possible in the interest of the men. 'U' Bn in this respect was successful; or rather they managed better than others. The Officers, N.C.O's and men cooperated and formed a united spirit. The troops are to be particularly commended for the contribution from their meagre pay to purchase medical supplies at exorbitant cost for sick men. Dysentery was rife and emetine was purchased for men at $100 for course of 10 tablets. 'U' Bn. spent some $3000 on emetine alone. The money being supplied by Officers, N.C.O's and men when the rates of pay were as follows:-
>
> Officers $20 per month.
> N.C.O. $7.50
> Men $6.
>
> The Bn. strength of 500 only included 5 Officers.

This made a general supplement of about 8 cents per man per day.[564] Reg Newton collected this meagre pay issued to the prisoners by the Japanese. He then used it to buy food from the barges. The men referred to him as 'Woolcott Forbes',[565] after John Woolcott Forbes, a well known Sydney builder (whose mansion Burnham Thorpe in the suburb of Gordon was taken over by the Red Cross for injured soldiers in 1940).[566] He had run into financial difficulty and, attempting to avoid charges of fraud, he had absconded to America with the cash.[567]

However despite the troops' 'concerns' Reg Newton reported that the goods received in the Australian Kitchen far exceeded the value of goods which had been purchased from the monies subscribed from the officers' pay and men's contributions. This was due to the *wonderful assistance* of the 'V' organization.[568]

> The small staff remaining in Camp did their best to keep the area clean. Officers often dug latrines for the troops and on occasions worked in cook-houses to enable better food to be prepared. 'U' Bn. weathered the Tarso 'Speedo' period without a death, but the men suffered from overwork and harsh brutal treatment.

Speedo happened when the deadline for the railway was brought forward by the Japanese Command. After March 1943 the tide of the war had turned against Japan. They had been evicted from Guadalcanal, Papua and the Aleutians. At Attu the 10,000 Japanese troops garrisoned there fled before the arrival of the US forces. Thanks to American raids there continued to be a steady diminution in the number of Japanese ships yet they still had a very large area of South East Asia to supply and support. The railway became even more important to the IJA supply lines, it had to be finished earlier than planned.[569]

In addition, the engineer in charge of the railway had made a pagan boast to the Emperor that he would commit hari-kari if the railway was not finished by September 1943.[570] Engineering problems were minimal on the flat country but not the mountainous regions where cuttings and embankments were necessary. More men were needed so more were recruited and men had to work longer hours.

At this stage only 20% of the railway had been constructed yet the date for its completion was brought forward from December to August 1943. The pressure was on to meet the new deadline. When numbers of 'fit' men were insufficient, sick men were forced from their beds to work on the line.[571] The hours of work increased so men worked through the night. The line was lit by bamboo fires and carbide lights. 'Hellfire Pass' earned its poignant name. Work went on despite the monsoon. The guards became even more brutal.

Men were battered. Limbs were broken. Men died.[572]

> The hours of work were from daylight till dark. This meant that breakfast was eaten in the dark. Clothing was scarce and the scanty apparel worn daily at work was washed each night on return. The clothes soon began to show signs of wear and patching was the job of men in camp, sick etc. No new clothes were obtainable but rubber boots were issued. These caused the men's feet to become sweaty and stinking and accentuated the menace of tinea. No hats were issued and straw substitutes were made but provided small protection from the intense tropical sun.
>
> When working, men wore only sufficient clothing to be decent, their torsos and legs bare to the sun became brown and sunburned. Shaving was difficult because of shortage of blades and time. The men's faces grew coarse and hard with exposure and physical strain.

The tools issued were axes, really wedges; the shovels still had the corrugations from the oil drums from which they were cut; the picks were soft and un-tempered. All transport of soil and rocks was by human labour, carrying loads in primitive bamboo baskets or rice bag stretchers with bamboo poles pushed through holes for carrying purposes.[573]

Sgt Keith Wilson recalled his men were expected to cut granite with sledgehammers and load the rocks into skips. If any of them escaped they were told they would be captured and executed and so would one of their colleagues. One day a snap roll call showed that two men were missing as they tried to find a few extra rations. Immediately Keith was forced to his knees, hands tied behind his back and a Japanese officer was taking practice swings with a large two handed sword. Luckily the two men returned from the jungle in time to prevent the execution.[574]

In some areas elephants were used to help with the heavy lifting. Bill told a story of an elephant trained by the POWs to kill Japanese guards. It would happen when a guard was isolated and afterwards the men would shout and scream so all the elephants were quickly brought in. The Japanese could never work out which elephant was the 'rogue'.[575] Frank Baker did not know of this, he thought it could have happened on the Burma end of the line. He did recall seeing a very angry lone elephant; it was pulling up trees and flinging them far and wide, but it ignored the prisoners as they marched past it whilst they were changing camp. Was this the hungry elephant used to haul timber over many long hours? The mahout warned the POWs that it would go berserk for feed and to get out of the way when it did - the elephant went AWOL soon after.[576]

Wood was cut from the local jungle. The prisoners worked out a way of letting any Allied aircraft flying over the area know that the railway was under construction. The unused vegetation from a cleared part of the jungle was piled into the middle of the area, the Japanese were told it was much quicker than pushing it aside. Each evening, as they returned to camp, the prisoners would set fire to the pile in the hope that any passing aircraft would spot a line of fires in the jungle and realize something was happening.[577]

Workers were divided into three groups, the earth moving gangs, who cleared the earth and rubble to expose the rocks; the 'hammer and tap' men who hammered deep holes into the rocks to allow gelignite sticks to be inserted; and finally the 'rock rollers' who cleared the rocks and boulders cracked open by the explosive charge.[578]

The methods of working were as follows:-

The men were given an area to dig close to the embankment and stretchers were provided to carry the earth from the digging party to those on the mound with poor tools and bad stretchers. One hour was permitted for lunch. The men had to send ration parties to camp sometimes two miles away for rations which were steamed rice, vegetable water and rice coffee. The coffee was frightful when unsweetened but wet. On some occasions tea brewed from tea dust was available.

Rest periods during the day were rare. Smokos were sporadic and only occurred when the railway engineers were satisfied with progress. The Japanese never allowed a decent period of rest, usually the men were permitted only 5 minutes. Often men were required to work all day with no rest periods and during the 'Speedo' periods, time off for meals was sometimes stopped.

May and June '43 During May and June work on the railway was consistent and hard. The Japanese would often give us task works i.e. they would mark out a length of embankment to be built up and give us the time necessary. This varied from one day to a week. On nearly every occasion the task was increased before the agreed period was completed. The Japanese could not honour even such a simple contract. The position became acute and finally it was agreed between P.O.W. Officers and I.J.A. engineers that one (1) metric cubic of earth should be moved on to the embankment daily. This arrangement was satisfactory at the commencement because it was within the power of the men. Soon however, the I.J.A. increased the task and before long the troops were moving 1.50 cubic metres of earth. This was really difficult work because the ground was hard and stony. Digging with bad tools was very difficult indeed. As a generalization when the men worked well they were imposed upon and when they worked slowly the Japanese bashed. Conditions were bad for everybody.

Reg Newton recalled how strictly the different Japanese groups stuck to their own orders with no consideration of the others.

> *If a bridge had to be finished at one o'clock, finished it was at one o'clock regardless of anything else. After that time it did not matter to the construction staff for they had handed it over to the maintenance staff and if the bridge fell over at two o'clock then it came under the heading of repairs. Repairing a bridge might mean pulling it down completely and rebuilding.*[579]

> The native slab huts in which the POWs lived were vermin infested both by rats and bugs. Efforts were made to be rid of these pests but even the building of new huts proved unsatisfactory because the new material was bug infested before building commenced. Rats were trapped and even cash prizes given for 'tails' but still the appalling huts remained verminous.

One 'D' Force soldier recalled the attap roof of the huts was invariably rotten with lice, bugs, centipedes, spiders, scorpions and the occasional snake.[580]

> Cooking was difficult because of the painful shortage of containers both for cooking and serving. The jungle was bereft of tins and no local supplies were available. The Japanese issued kualis, a shallow large dish of iron suitable for steaming rice and also good for stews. The kualis were usually issued at the rate of 2 per 100 men and provided insufficient containers. Often the kualis broke under heat and these were not replaced by Japs.

> The meat issue at its best was 1 beast per 500 per day. These animals were very small, diseased, and the quantity of meat was only sufficient for each man to receive a minute portion. For simplicity in distribution the meat was all minced and the bones boiled. The stock thus obtained was boiled with the few green vegetables available and water. The stew thus made was weak and barely nourishing.

Reg Newton reported they pinched two yaks in twelve months and if possible they collected jungle spinach which had been shown to them by the Indonesian troops.[581]

Elliott McMaster (NX639) of 2/20 and 'D' Force recounted how some English prisoners at South Tonchan had the job of droving a mob of cattle up the line for Japanese rations. A few Australian 'bushies' managed to cut out a straggler, caught it and quickly had it slaughtered and butchered so all prisoners had some meat that day. It had to be eaten quickly without discovery and, in any case, the local daily temperatures ensured it would not have stored overnight.[582]

On some occasions the hospital managed to buy rice polishings, the outer husk of the rice grain full of vitamins. Often men refused to eat it so others would collect their share;[583] it saved their lives.

Men would catch what they could for the stew pot; dogs, cats, snakes, lizards, fish, birds and monkeys. On the way back to camp they would collect edible green leaves, roots and mushrooms, they would salvage what they could from the rubbish outside the Japanese cookhouse. Butter was made from peanuts. In some camps ducks, chickens and pigs were raised for the communal pot. If possible, fish were caught from the river using hooks baited with rice grains.

The most important item on the menu, which saved many lives, was the humble duck egg.[584] Glen Skewes (VX61290) recalled how he sold his nickel Eversharp pencil and with the 50c was able to buy some duck eggs. He cooked two for dinner and ate them with his rice. It made him *feel like a new creature.* He thought there was *wonderful life giving food in an egg or two.*[585] According to the Hospital Bulletin, things were so bad, especially for the sick, that eggs and milk were regarded as drugs not eats.[586]

Every man on the line heard of the speech of Colonel Coates, one of the medical officers on the line. He told prisoners the route home was inscribed in the bottom of every man's dixie.

> *Every time it is filled with rice, eat it. If you vomit it up again, eat some more even if it comes up too some good will remain. If you get an egg eat it no matter how bad it may appear. An egg is only bad when the stomach will not hold it.*[587]

The Japanese weighed the prisoners and the less a man weighed the less rice he was allocated.[588] This of course compounded the problems. The Japanese thought that if one of their own soldiers was sick he was of no use to the Emperor so he was given half rations, if he was wounded in battle it was honourable and so he remained on full rations:[589] with that attitude to their own men one can only wonder at their feelings towards men who had surrendered and were prisoners ... they had no time for prisoners.

> Rice usually worked out at about 1 pint per man on the plate and the stew at 1/2 pint. These conditions were the best we experienced on the line. Occasionally dried fish was issued in lieu of meat and even dried vegetables - like seaweed - the quantities as usual were insufficient.
>
> Malnutrition and hard work took its inevitable toll on the men. Hospitals began to swell with patients and these were suffering from:-
>
> Amoebic and Bacillary Dysentery, Nutritional diarrhoea, avitaminosis, ulcers and malaria, cerebral malaria was also in evidence. Cholera also arrived.

Avitaminosis was the general name for a number of diseases caused by vitamin deficiency. As the POWs were given mainly polished rice which had the vitamin-rich husk removed, they suffered several of these diseases. Lack of Vitamin A caused xerophthalmia or blindness. Beri-beri was due to Vitamin B1 or thiamine deficiency; wet beri-beri affected the heart and the body became oedemic and waterlogged, dry beri-beri caused partial paralysis. Lack of B3 or niacin caused pellagra or skin lesions, lack of B12 led to pernicious anaemia.[590]

The POWs had their own names for some of these diseases. 'Changi Balls' or 'Rice Balls' was where the scrotum skin became red and inflamed, split and peeled away. 'Happy feet' caused searing stabs like electric shocks to the soles of the feet but an intolerance to cold; the pain was worse at night so the sufferer walked round at night and, as a result, suffered major sleep deprivation.[591]

The starvation diet affected the prisoner's immune system so small cuts and scratches quickly became infected.[592]

There was an attempt to provide some vitamins in the prisoners' diet; in some camps the troops collected urine for use as a fertiliser on the vegetable garden,[593] in other camps the urine was a basis for yeast production to make a rice-based bread which would be rich in vitamin B.[594] The 2/20 Battalion appointed Capt. Yates as their Yeast Production Officer, Capt Ewart had constructed a rice grinder and it was hoped their efforts would help to alleviate the symptoms of beri-beri.[595]

> The British troops living in bad huts soon became victims of cholera. On the fourth day of the epidemic, 6 AIF, some 700 Tamils and 48 English had died. Work had ceased on the railway because cholera had also entered the Japanese camp claiming 2 men.

Upstream from the polluting native camp, the Australians set up a bamboo pipe irrigation system to collect uncontaminated water for their own camp.

> The efforts of the AIF CO Capt. R. Newton were tremendous. He and his small staff which included MO Capt. D. Hinder and Padre Thorpe worked unceasingly. The troops were ordered to cut all finger nails back to the quick - all eating utensils were kept constantly in boiling water - some disinfectant was obtained and bottles and dishes provided at every tent. Men were required to wash in this fluid every time they passed.

Reg told all ranks that if anyone saw any man attempt to eat from an unsterilised dixie or any receptacle he was to knock it from the offender's hands and prevent him eating any and he would have to go hungry; the risk of infection was so great and all the men would be endangered.[596]

> No raw fruit or vegetables were permitted to be eaten. The AIF obeyed these orders magnificently and the casualties were less than ½ a per cent. The English suffered more heavily and 96 men died during the epidemic. The cholera stopped as quickly as it started and moved on to claim more men in other camps.
>
> **June '43** Men from Singapore arrived and marched through our camp for a destination far north near the Thai-Burma border. These men had already walked from Kanburi some 100 km down the line. They were unfit when they left Singapore, conditions on their tragic march and later in their camps brought about a tragedy, the worst on the railway line.

This was 'F' Force. Their senior medical officer Major Bruce Hunt saw a chance to leave the sickest men here for treatment. He selected 37 of the sickest and, with Major Wild, attempted to persuade the Japanese that the men should be hospitalized. Both Major Hunt and Major Wild were bashed by the Japanese, to the point of fracturing bones. [597]

Roy Mills recorded that when 'F' Force marched into Tarso on 30th March he saw the Senior Medical Officer of 'D' Force Alan Hazelton, as well as Bill Gaden, Reg Newton, Frank Ramsbotham and Dave Hinder, eggs were sent across by Reg Newton and he enjoyed an egg flip and coffee from Lt-Col Knight and a canvas bath which he thought was 'glorious'.[598]

Some of the troops were not so impressed, one 'F' Force soldier caught up with some 'D' Force friends in the camp hospital. He'd last seen them only a few weeks before in Changi. He was alarmed that

> *Some were hardly recognisable. Their faces were hollow and drawn, their eyes sunk back into their heads and their still bodies flat on the bamboo slats were little more than skin and bone. They explained in voices little more than whispers that they had suffered severe attacks of dysentery and malaria.*[599]

Frank Smith who was with 'D' Force changed places with an 'F' Force prisoner so he could be with his two brothers Les and Robert who came through with 'F' Force. From then on Frank was known as Andrew William Pearce (NX54964).[600]

Narromine-born brothers Frank and Les had joined up together, Frank Clem Smith's Army number was NX72734, Leslie Nelson Smith's was NX72733. Both were to survive the war, as did Andrew William Pearce but Robert Edward Smith (NX71853) died in Thailand in December 1943.[601]

For the lads assigned to 'F' Force, their hell was just beginning. An interview with Gordon Gaffney, a survivor of 'F' Force, makes for harrowing reading.

What did you weigh?

> *Well at one stage there I was - I don't know, about four and a half, five stone. When I was up at cholera hill a fellow died along side of me - and he had cerebral malaria which is a dreadful thing - he bucked over on top of me and I couldn't kick him off, I was too poor to kick him off. While I was up there, orderlies came around and wanted to pick up the dead* [to place on the funeral pyre]. *They said* [of Gaffney] *this poor bugger's had it, and they pulled these meal tickets off* [his boots]. *You couldn't talk, your eyes were back in your head and I winked at him, and I think he fainted!*

Tell me, when you actually got back to Changi, what was it like getting off the train? What was the reaction of the people in Changi?

> *They were ... Black Jack, the toughest man in the world, cried when he saw us, he said, where are the rest of my men? Thirtieth Battalion? They said that's it. Well they tipped us off the back of trucks at Changi like a lump - heap of bones and meat - and these fellows in Changi, they couldn't understand it. We were just like skin and bone, there was nothing of us. Filthy dirty ...* [602]

Dunlop reported that barges conveying emaciated men and even corpses, frequently went past on the river. There was no attempt to look after the sick in transit and they frequently went days with no food or medical care.[603]

In June many of the 'U' Bn troops moved out of Tarso to other camps further up the line. They left behind many sick men from both 'U' Bn, 'S' Bn and 'F' Force who had moved through. It was decided to also leave Capt. Bill Gaden behind to look after the Australians. He was thought by Reg Newton to be *the best officer for the job to work with the British, a smooth negotiator with a superb personality.*[604]

However for Bill it would have been traumatic that his own 'family' of friends, his support group, were moving away and he would have no one close with whom to share yarns, experiences or to watch his back.

Reg recalled

> *It was a wise move and choice as it turned out, for the number of desperately ill members of 'D' Force, the Java Battalions and the strays from 'F' and 'H' Force increased as the Line progressed and Bill Gaden carried out a very difficult task*

> *with great success, for we lost very few chaps back behind us, compared with the other nationalities on the line.*[605]

Capt. Newton had

> *long talks with Captain Bill Gaden that night to tidy up the administration at this I.J.A. P.O.W. H.Q. for all the action and decisions would affect us back here at base, from now on we were in his hands; transfer of funds to our hospital chaps; canteen supplementing for our sick and all Australians, for we had not heard from Colonel McEachern and felt somebody had to look after them, for despite being on the same side and Allies and so on, one could not expect the British junior officers and most of the senior to worry about anybody other than their own men. We had the utmost faith in Colonel Alf Knight P.O.W. Camp Commander from the 4 Royals Norfolks and Colonel Bill Harvey, the S.M.O., but as far as we were concerned, charity would begin at home. Another decision was made to leave our first rate and well trained (in cooking with rice and rations supplied and in adding to the issue by judicious scrounging and acquiring and making a little go a long way) staff we had set up under Sgt Norm Healey in the Australian kitchen, with the three section chiefs under him in Don (King) Cole, Athol Nichols and Bob Graham, the 'doover' king.*[606]

Doovers were the nickname for the small 'rissoles' made from camouflaged rice.[607]

Eventually Bill looked after close on 2,000 Australians who had been evacuated down river by other Battalions, usually with no one sent down to look after them. Bill cared for them all and lost very few thanks to the good feeding from Norm Healey's team. (Sgt Norman Henry Healey, NX35150, of 2/19 survived the war).[608]

According to Reg Newton

> *One other important matter tied up with Bill Gaden was the re-direction of canteen supplies from Boon Pong. This was a headache for when you left the river there were carriage problems and if you arranged by rail the costs became much higher and you would be subject to pilfering all the way. We decided to continue to draw from Boon Pong in Tarso, with Captain Bill Gaden taking delivery and that we would get parties back at night to bring goods on up to South Tonchan.*[609]

The distance was around 10 kms.[610]

Reg Newton later recalled

> *... this was one of the best decisions I ever made in my whole army career, leaving Bill back in Tarso because he was a born negotiator, he was a smooth talker, he got on very well with the British and that was a blessing because he had to fight for food, and get more than his share, which he did with the help of the blokes, cooks, I left with him and it proved a blessing all the way. He saved a lot of lives helping the blokes and making sure they got their good food, what little food there was, cooked properly by our own cooks.*[611]

Bill was much the same as Reg in many ways, in the sense that he would not suffer fools gladly if at all. Another reason why Reg left him behind was

... to look after the sick, and the ailing, and the sore and the sorry, because without any bloody playing up, he did not muck about, he exacted his own corporal punishment as we all had to, in command, if you applied it, because you could not let the Nips take over and exact punishment, you had to do it yourself. So you just hit the spot, and devil take the hindmost. Bill did the same down at Tarso, down at Chungkai, if anybody played up he'd just clock them, that's it, finished. Then they'd pick them up and shake them and they loved him for it, because they knew they'd get a belting, but very few of them played up. In my own case, I only had one case of stealing right throughout the whole of the war, that's stealing from one comrade ... from the other, and we caught him with another chap's watch. Now the chap had been killed down at Parit Sulong bridge down in Malaya and his brother was taking his watch home to his mother, and suddenly he lost the watch, and we found it in this particular person's haversack. Now I just had to do something, and I was going to do it, I hit him myself. Then I gave him to five of his chaps in his own platoon, and I told them to take him out, give him the father of a hiding, I don't care what you do with him, I'll bury him tomorrow if I have to. That's the only way you could handle anybody who played up. And he was straight all the way then until we arrived in Japan, and he started to steal from the British in the next camp. So I told the British take him out and do what you like with him. That's the only way you could exact corporal punishment.[612]

August '43 August came and many of 'U' Bn. were moved up the line for work further north. Tarso North became for a short time a camp of some 200 men in the jungle bordering the river bank. This camp started with the men living in tents but after a short period of two weeks the men were moved farther north.

Tonchan South, our next site, was a dirty area. The grounds having been fouled by a native kampong before our occupation. This camp was occupied by both English and AIF troops the two areas being separated by a small running stream of clear water.

Tonchan South was 138.8 km from the start of the railway.[613]

Capt Newton was not happy with their allocated area so the men set up a tent camp at what they called 'Reggie's Retreat' down on the river bank. They were close to the water and enjoyed a daily swim ... until they realized that there were three large crocodiles in the area who grabbed the local monkeys as they came down for a drink.[614]

Shortly after our arrival, Tamil Indians arrived from Malaya. The men were a labour force conscripted by the Japanese to work on the railway. They were of course marching northwards and in even worse condition than POWs. At Tonchan South they developed cholera and within days all men in the area were in danger. The Tamils were living upstream from the POWs and their filth and excreta washed down past our camps. It was necessary to use the water in the stream for cooking being the only water available. Boiling of all water and sterilisation of eating utensils was the order of the day - no fruit or food was purchased from natives with the possible exception of eggs. Still the cholera spread.

Tamils began to die and their death rate reached 200 per day, So fast was the death rate that AIF were called upon to bury the Tamils - a very dangerous business indeed - our fellows were unable to count accurately the number buried.

Later a passable hut was built and the gauze although not fly proof was certainly proof against birds.

Anaesthetics were usually available and so far as I know no major operations were carried out with the patient in a conscious state. The curetting of ulcers was normally done without anaesthetic.

Instruments were boiled and sterilised in buckets and the various surgical instruments included clasp knives, scissors, razors and the occasional scalpels all of which were sharpened on stones. The saws used for amputations were often the ordinary carpenter's type. Gut was scarce and used sparingly, often linen thread was used for surface wounds. My appendix was sewn internally with gut but the surface stitches were linen thread.

It was impossible to have sterile conditions, the medical officers had to resort to surgical conditions which would have been familiar to Wellington and Nelson. Blood transfusions were possible only by defibrination of blood, done by stirring for ten minutes with a bamboo switch, blood typing was done by eye.[615]

Crude lump sulphur [sic] and animal fat was made into an ointment for scabies.

Welfare for hospital patients was attended to by Officers who provided money from their scanty pay for this purpose. Fruit and eggs were purchased whenever obtainable and distributed on medical advice.

Burial parties were called for daily and funerals were attended by all available people in camp. The cemetery records were kept by Padre and individual units. Tarso cemetery buried the 1000 and all graves were tabulated, numbers and records retained.

The Japanese did not allow the use of the Union Jack nor did they permit the singing of the National Anthem at funerals. The Japanese CO Ishi was responsible for this order.

Cholera at Tarso was never very serious but during the sporadic outbreaks the cases were kept under isolation and those that died were buried in a special cemetery. The personal belongings of dead men were given to other men to take home to their families. These could not be held by Officers because the I.J.A. never provided transport. Clothes were always divided amongst those most in need of assistance.

The blanket shortage was extremely bad and men in hospital often developed pneumonia when in weak condition. Having no M & B these men usually died.

M&B 693 was a drug developed by May and Baker in the UK in 1938. It was known as the 'wonder' or 'miracle' drug. It was a sulphonamide called sulphapyridine which seemed to cure pneumonia and meningitis.[616]

The shortage of blankets was of great concern to the medical officers; in November 1943 there were 442 men with no blankets whatsoever and many others had just torn shreds of bedding. Very sick men had just a loin cloth and a rice sack. The Japanese provided 300 bamboo mats for use as mattresses and windbreaks, 250 hemp rice sacks and 200 coarse fibre rice sacks, primitive but welcome articles for use by the prisoners.[617]

Sept '43 'U' Bn had evacuated some 40 men down to Tarso and their welfare was entrusted to me. I moved to Tarso in Sept '43.

The following months were filled in attending the requirements of sick men in the hospital huts. The Japanese had built new huts for the hospital and these were an improvement on previous conditions but still poor. Wards were instituted for malaria, surgical, medical and dysentery patients. The dysentery ward was always stinking but kept passably clean by hospital staff. The surgical ward reeked with the stench of corroding ulcers. The treatment for these ulcers being hot compresses and bathing with aqua-flavin. Small quantities of iodoform were obtained and found invaluable. 'U' Bn. did not have many ulcer cases because M.O. Capt. D. Hinder always managed to produce sulphur-nilamide powder to stop the development of really large ulcers. This drug he had carried with him from Singapore and had used it sparingly and wisely.

Pte Miggins 2/15 Field Rgt. R.A.A. (Artillery) wrote about his visit to the hospital in Tarso on 26 August 1943:

The ulcer ward just stank of rotting flesh, a stink that made the insides crawl. The bandages were filthy and the matter oozing from the gaping wounds. It was not the Doctor's fault as there were no drugs available. In the beri-beri and deficiency wards there were some pitiful sights. It was in these wards that most deaths occurred. Some of the patients were so thin that they were skin and bone. Those with beri-beri were looking fat and it made them look like bloated toads.[618]

The surgical wards at Tarso were also occupied by amputation cases and some operations.

Daily operations were being performed by M/O Capt. McConachy [sic] B.E.F. and Lt/Col Dunlop A.A.M.C. Their work included appendectomy, supra pubic cathetisation, bowel flushing, appendix and amputation of various limbs. Personally I underwent an appendix operation. On occasion patients were insufficiently strong to withstand the operations and these cases were sometimes attended by cardiac massage. Bowel ulcerations caused by dysentery were attended and generally major operations were not uncommon.

The jungle operating theatre in the early stage was a hastily erected bamboo table in the open. The operation being attended by two men whose duty was to wave away the swarms of flies.

Bamboo was used for many things in addition to the jungle operating tables: transfusion needles, water bottles, tableware, water supply and irrigation pipes, beds, huts, fences, animal traps and fires. There were acres and acres of it growing in the jungle; some was as tall as 40 to 90 feet high;[619] some was as thick as a man's thigh.[620] Sadly though the prisoners didn't realise it had medical properties too ... the underground rhizomes when boiled make a poultice for wounds; stomach ailments could be treated with bamboo salt in water; heat rash could be soothed by using the powder left by the powderpost beetles which feed on the sap.[621] Young shoots could be eaten and would have provided 'greens' in the diet.[622] If only the local Thais had been able to pass on their knowledge.

Bamboo brooms were made by sick men if they had sufficient strength.

Coconut oil cans were used to make watertight containers for kitchen and hospital. Surgical instruments were fashioned. The hides from the occasional meat cattle were stretched over bamboo frames to scrape and cure them and the leather was used in the hospital for straps and wooden leg sockets.[623]

The day before Christmas 1943 allied aircraft flew over and bombed an area six miles from the camp. The lines of fires the lads had been lighting in the jungle for the past six months had been seen.[624]

> **December '43** Xmas 43 was not really very bad. Concert parties and entertainments given by an improvised band helped to raise the spirits of the men. The dinner on Xmas day was passable and for once no rice was included in the meal which was made to resemble a normal roast dinner as well as possible. This was achieved by saving the necessary rations for weeks prior to Xmas.
>
> On the day following Xmas I moved with some 80 AIF troops to TARDAN [also known as Tha Dan][625] a small camp 16 km south of TARSO. The work at this camp was dangerous. A bridge had to be built across a river. The men worked the usual hours from dawn till dark.
>
> Fortunately at Tardan there were reasonable supplies of food in a nearby Kampong. The fruit and meat thus purchased helped to provide better meals. The health of the men improved at Tardan. No deaths. This is probably one of the very rare camps without a graveyard.

On a trip down the line from the Kannyu camps to Tarso and Kanburi, Reg Newton managed to obtain half a ton of *Magnesium sulphate*, the appropriate treatment for amoebic dysentery, and 28 capsules of emetine to take back to the Medical officers.[626] On his trip he discovered Chungkai, a big hospital camp with no one looking after the Australians, so he decided to send Captain Bill Gaden from Tarso to Chungkai to take over the Australians and 'U' Battalion patients and finances back there. On the trip back from Kanburi, he called in at Chungkai and primed the way for Bill to become the Australian No. 1 at the hospital and with all authority to look after AIF interests.[627] Chungkai was 60 km from Nong Pladuk, the start of the railway.[628]

Edward 'Weary' Dunlop was Medical Officer in the camp at the one end of the Pack of Cards Bridge. Reg Newton was in the camp at the other end. After discussion it was decided that Dunlop should also move to Chungkai as the M.O. in charge of the hospital medical team.

> During January it was discovered that 700 AIF troops were in the base camp CHUNGKAI. These troops had only 2 Officers with them, both of whom were sick. It was also known that some 7000 Br O/Rs, were in the camp in poor shape.
>
> L/Col. Dunlop and I were sent from Tarso to attend the troops at CHUNGKAI. Col. Dunlop to look after the medical side and myself to attend the administration.

On 17 January 1944 'Weary' Dunlop with 15 other officers including Bill Gaden, as part of a party of 201 troops, moved to Chungkai by train.[629]

[517] DVA Nominal Roll.
[518] Nelson, *Australians Under Nippon*, p. 62.
[519] Newton, Interview, AWM S01739.
[520] Elliott and Silver, *A history of 2/18 Battalion*, p. 145.
[521] Bob Gaden, personal communication.
[522] Newton, *The Grim Glory*, p. 575.
[523] Elliott and Silver, *op. cit.*, p. 25.
[524] Moremon, *Australians on the Burma-Thailand Railway*, p. 22.
[525] Marsden, *Under the Heel of a Brutal Enemy our Catholic Boys Kept the Faith*, <http://.www.military.catholic.org.au/stories/changi-prison1.htm>
[526] McLaren, *Mates in Hell*, <http://www.slsa.sa.gov.au/saatwar/collection/transcripts/ISBN1876070714_i.htm >
[527] Skewes, *Changi Diary*, < http://changidiary.com/changi_april.html >
[528] Wall, *Singapore and Beyond*, p. 152.
[529] Newton, Interview, *op. cit.*
[530] Nelson, *op. cit.*, pp. 39-40.
[531] Summers, *Colonel of Tamarkan*, pp. 200-2.
[532] Newton, Interview *op. cit.*
[533] Newton Reg, Personal communication.
[534] Rivett, *Behind Bamboo*, p. 323.
[535] Newton Reg, Personal communication.
[536] Beattie, *The Death Railway*, p. 56.
[537] Newton, Interview, *op. cit.*
[538] Moremon, *op. cit.*, p. 25.
[539] Dunlop, *AWM 54 Control Symbol 554/5/1*, p. 10.
[540] Peek, *One Fourteenth of an Elephant*, p. 307.
[541] Boyle, *Railroad to Burma*, p. 71.
[542] Peek, *op. cit.*, p. 301.
[543] MacArthur, *Surviving the Sword*, p. 299.
[544] Gaffney, Interview, AWM S01738.
[545] Poole, *Of Love and War*, p. 210.
[546] Newton, *The Grim Glory*, p. 604.
[547] Nelson, *op. cit.*, p. 67.
[548] DVA Nominal Roll and O'Connor, *Digger's yarn worth hearing.*
[549] Boon, *War Experience of Jack Boon*, <http://www.pows-of-japan.net/articles/41.htm>
[550] Newton, *The Grim Glory*, pp. 582-585.
[551] McMaster, *My Experiences as a POW on the Burma-Thailand Railway*, <http:/greatlakeshistorical.museum.com/burmarailway/southtonchan.html>
[552] Nelson, *op. cit.*, p. 62.
[553] Frank Baker (NX59308), personal communication.
[554] Newton, *The Grim Glory*, p. 604.
[555] Francis Andrew Coventry (QX10372) as told to Robyn Crossle.
[556] Frank Baker (NX59308), personal communication.
[557] Newton, *The Grim Glory*, pp. 588-9.
[558] DVA Nominal Roll, William Arthur Francis Coombs survived the war.
[559] Frank Baker (NX59308), personal communication.
[560] Newton, Interview, *op. cit.*
[561] Elliott and Silver, *op. cit.*, p. 146.
[562] Eulogy at funeral of Reg Newton.
[563] Wall, *op. cit.*, pp. 62, 154-5.
[564] Dunlop, *op. cit.*, p. 3.
[565] Frank Baker (NX59308), personal communication.
[566] AWM record < http://cas.awm.gov.au/film/F00505. >
[567] < http://libapp.sl.nsw.gov.au/cgi-bin/spydus/ENQ/PM/FULL1?12707,I > and <http://www.parliament.nsw.gov.au/prod/PARLMENT/hansArt.nsf/V3Key/LA19920319033 >
[568] Newton, *The Grim Glory*, p. 613.
[569] Eade, *Onwards to Victory*, p. 197.
[570] Marsden, *op. cit.*
[571] Beattie, *op. cit.*, p. 46.

572 Moremon, *op. cit.*, pp. 55-6.
573 Newton, *The Grim Glory*, p. 582.
574 O'Connor, *op. cit.*
575 Diana Bradhurst, personal communication.
576 Frank Baker (NX59308), personal communication, and Wall, *op. cit.*, p. 176.
577 McLaren, *op. cit.*
578 Moremon, *op. cit.*, p. 54.
579 Newton, *The Grim Glory*, p. 609.
580 Moremon, *op. cit.*, p. 40.
581 Newton, Interview, *op. cit.*
582 McMaster, *op. cit.*
583 Peek, *op. cit.*, p. 304.
584 MacArthur, *op. cit.*, pp. 195-207.
585 Skewes, *op. cit.*
586 Dunlop, *op. cit.* p. 7.
587 Whitecross, *Slaves of the Son of Heaven*, p. 73.
588 Gherardin, *Lt Col. Albert Coates*, <http://www.pows-of-japan.net/articles/37.htm >
589 Luce, < www.rquirk.com/cdnradar/seacradarfile3a.pdf > p. 151
590 Glynn-White, *Reminiscences*, <http://www.araratcc.vic.edu/fow/JGWhite.html>
591 Braddon, *The Naked Island*, pp. 120, 215.
592 Gherardin, *op. cit.*
593 Braddon, *op. cit.*, p. 247.
594 Summers, *op. cit.*, p. 197.
595 Notes for Battalion's War Diary, 24-25 April 1942.
596 McMaster, *op. cit.*
597 Forbes, *Hellfire*, p. 312.
598 Mills, *Doctor's Diary and Memoir*, p. 53.
599 Moremon, *op. cit.*, p. 27.
600 Frank Smith, personal communication, 30 Nov 2007.
601 DVA Nominal Roll.
602 Gaffney, Interview, AWM, S01738.
603 Dunlop, *op. cit.*, p. 5.
604 Newton, *The Grim Glory*, p. 587.
605 *Loc. cit.*
606 *Loc. cit.*
607 Arneil, *One Man's War*, p. 285.
608 DVA Nominal Roll.
609 Newton, *The Grim Glory*, p. 587.
610 Beattie, *op. cit.*, p. 56.
611 Newton, Interview, *op. cit.*
612 *ibid.*
613 Beattie, *op. cit.*, p. 56.
614 Wall, *op. cit.*, p. 158.
615 Gherardin, *op. cit.* and Dunlop AWM *War Diaries of Weary Dunlop* pp. 369, 406.
616 *Illness, Drugs and Wonder Drugs before Penicillin*, p. 19 < http://fds.oup.com/www.oup.co.uk/pdf/0-19-925406-0.pdf > Accessed 7 March 2009.
617 Dunlop, *op. cit.*, pp. 17-20.
618 Beattie, *op. cit.* p. 50.
619 Skewes, *op. cit.*
620 McLaren, *op. cit.*
621 Hutchinson, *The grass that built Asia*, pp. 63-68.
622 Savage, *A Guest of the Emperor*, p. 25.
623 Peek, *op. cit.*, p. 326.
624 McLaren, *op. cit.*
625 Beattie, Map of Burma-Thailand Railway.
626 Newton, Interview, *op. cit.*
627 Newton, *The Grim Glory*, p. 612.
628 Beattie, *op. cit.*, p. 56.
629 Dunlop, *The war diaries of Weary Dunlop*, p. 368.

Chapter 11 - Chungkai

When Bill arrived, Chungkai was a large hospital camp with no one in charge of Australian troops. It was located downstream from Tarso and Tonchan, and was quite close to Kanburi. On 17 January 1944, Bill was one of the party who were to take over the care for their troops.

> Jan '44 On arrival we found Chungkai an old established camp, dirty and with a hospital full of patients in very poor condition. The troops were living in poor, low, dirty huts and the AIF were spread throughout the camp in groups but with no central control. The first job was to get the troops together and then to get a workable administration going. 400 AIF were in hospital and 300 living in the huts.
>
> Lt/Col. Dunlop made a swoop on the hospital and took over the whole medical side of the camp. Soon the hospital was cleaned up, wards organized, patients classified into their various medical groups. A diet kitchen was put into operation and patients were fed specially cooked foods. This proved an excellent scheme because previously the food given to [the] sick was often wasted.
>
> The Japanese were not helpful with this re-organization but were quick to observe the general improvement in conditions.
>
> Shoes were made from green-hide and old boots repaired. Clogs were also made from wood. All these were provided free to hospital patients but the fit men were charged $1.50 to $3 according to type to defray the expenses of needles, twine, tools etc.
>
> Crutches and wooden limbs were also made, the latter without much success.
>
> The river provided quite good bathing facilities. Col. Dunlop ordered all personnel to bathe daily including hospital patients for whom water was carried.

Bill received a welcome letter this month. Date of writing 17 August 1942, received 14 January 1944:

> *From Miss A C Cay*
>
> *Hullo Bill old dear*
>
> *A big cheerio to you for your birthday; thrills, I'll be off duty on that day so shall collect your Mum and the girls and we'll toast the day. Since last writing end of June I've landed a very congenial billet, replacing a man at one of the City Clubs in the booking office. Duties are many and varied, all most interesting and come in contact with some awfully good sorts. Have been at the game a month. Hours are shift which means quite a lot of spare time during the week. I'll have lots of amusing instances to relate to you one of these fine days.*
>
> *Have had your parcel, sent last December, returned so will take it round to home and get your Mum to include it with hers as I believe there are certain restrictions as regards parcels.*
>
> *I have been at home all today; good part of the day spent in the garden, picked a very nice bunch of stocks and planted a couple of plants one of the members gave me, am taking him some seedlings tomorrow. Soon I'll have to start peddling my lettuces in aid of Prisoners of War Fund. They're growing so quickly these lovely days.*
>
> *Had a photo of brother Max Cay sent me today, a cutting from the Australian Women's Weekly, it's quite good of him but he looks rather stout, his new life must agree with him. His big nose and dimple in chin must appeal to photographers as he's always getting in some paper.*

Am feeling very bucked as my extraordinary land lady has had a gas refrigerator installed, sort of housing it until the flat it belongs to becomes vacant. Will be jolly nice during the hot weather. I'll be sure to have one on ice for you Bill.

Saw your Mum little over a week ago, full of chat as were the girls. Bob Robinson bucked about in my spare bed as he did at Broughton a few years back. He spotted your photo, said 'Gosh, there's good old Bill'. How we yarned about school days, he's just the same only grown up. Lots of love and a big cheerio.

Yours lovingly

Connie

'Weary' Dunlop reported that on 18 February 1944

a number of Group II personnel are to be set aside as a 'Japanese Party'. The health classification of prisoners was M&D (heavy work for the railway), B (light work), C (usually no work for the Nipponese but may work for the camp) and Bed downs (hospital). The personnel for the Japanese party were to come from categories exclusive of C and 'bed down'.[630]

The camp had a small football ground which was used for sport and helped to keep up morale. The Japanese were not very helpful, often issuing orders that sport should not be played during working hours.

However they must have allowed some recreation because 'Weary' Dunlop gives an account of the Spring Meeting of the Chungkai Race Club in which he and Bill raced:

21 March 1944 *There is keen competition and interest at present in the extraordinary human race meeting to be held on 23 March. The idea is to make money for the hospital and provide amusement. The owners enter a horse at approximately one tical each to give prize money and the bookmakers pay 10 ticals for a stand on the course. Various enclosures have entry fees. A tote to pay 10 per cent. I am entered under the name of Manfred by Bill Ongley, an astute racing man. Secret trials are being held. My jockey being 'Punchy' Powell. It is believed that a good time for the 100 yd will be 18 seconds. My trials up to date are about 19 seconds but I have malaria and am not trying very hard. A terrific weight of Australian Bookings has promptly pushed my odds down to evens, starting from 5:2 - most amusing nonsense is going on about trials and times.*

23 March 1944 *Spring Meeting of the Chungkai Race Club. The first race was at 1830, the tote opening at 1800. The course was the dry dusty area of Group II lines, fairly flat going with a few depressions. A very large crowd consisting of most of the camp population. Various enclosures and some important looking race officials. There were six events: The Canberra Maiden Stakes, 75 yd: The Officers' Stakes 100 yd; The Stayers' Stakes 150 yd; The Chungkai Invitation Stakes 100 yd; The newcomers' Stakes 100 yd; The Thailand Stakes 75 yd. The affair was conducted with considerable pageantry. The 'horses' and jockeys first parading around the course, the 'horses' wearing numbers, the jockeys very diminutive and for the most part in suitable costume, peaked cap and colours etc. As 'Punchy' Powell had his tobacco factory on me, he withdrew as a jockey and I was presented with a new boy, a little over 7 stone. Much amusement from the crowd during the parade for* *the Officers' Stakes including Bill Gayden* [sic] *and Captain Hetred, RAMC, with me backed down to evens with a terrific load of AIF money in particular. I got slightly left at the start but won easily in a time of 15.25 seconds. As usual I started to shake with laughter in the middle of the race. McMullen, the camp bugler, won the Chungkai Invitation Stakes with the same jockey in the sensational time of 14.25 seconds for the 100 yd. Otherwise my time stood. Much AIF jubilation and 'Waler' Davidson told me he had won 100 ticals on me. I'm afraid I got a little tiddly on the local brew.*[631]

The work required by the I.J.A. was not hard but men were required to spend long hours in the sun without hats and inadequate headgear. Most of the work was on vegetable gardens, the yields from which was very poor but valuable. The Japanese kept their own kitchen well supplied and only surplus found its way into troops' kitchens.

A Chinese Canteen in the camp provided cooked foods and was a fine installation. A further canteen run by P.O.W. called the P.K sold cooked foods also. The necessary meat, eggs etc. being purchased from outside, the Japs receiving a 'rake off'. This canteen also sold tobacco and sundry necessities, all at a cost nearly prohibitive to the men.

Lt/ Col ...[no name given] took over the AIF because we had no field officer in camp. He was popular with the men and worked well on their behalf.

Lieutenant-Colonel 'Weary' Dunlop reported on his time at Chungkai where he was S.M.O. from January to May 1944. He wrote

At Chungkai which was a hospital camp, there were some 8,000 prisoners of the Allied Nations ... the hospital maintained at over 2,000 accommodation.

This was the period of the most terrible aftermath of railway construction. These areas being 'cities of sickness'.

In the first time it was possible to begin a programme of rehabilitation and in these tumbling hovels the greatest battle was won, and the appalling death rate lowered to reasonable proportions.

The general conditions were of pre-listerian era and hospital gangrene and I will always have memories of the magnificent efforts made by all concerned with these hospitals, and in the presence of tremendous difficulties, the harmonious relationships between the Allied nationals.[632]

On 6 June the I.J.A. advised the prisoners that the railway work was over and the fit men would be sent to Japan. Capt. Reg Newton would lead one group, called Newton Force. Bill Gaden was on the list of those to go, however he was sick at the time and remained behind in Thailand.[633] In the end Capt. Keith Westbrook was left behind as OIC of the remaining 'U' Bn men with Bill Gaden as his 2IC. Lieut Frank Ramsbotham was sick and so also left behind.

On 14 June 1944 Bill Gaden arrived at Tamuang (Tha Muang, 39 km from Nong Pladuk)[634] from Chungkai with Hospital Sick.[635] A few days later another group of sick were evacuated with 'Weary' Dunlop to Nakom Pathom, a new hospital at the start of the line.[636]

It was an emotional parade and farewell when, on behalf of 'U' Battalion, Capt. Reg Newton thanked Lieutenant-Colonel Edward 'Weary' Dunlop for the magnificent effort of him and his medical team. This was now the end of 'D' Force.[637]

The large POW force who constructed the railway were relocated following the completion of the line in late October 1943. Varley and Newton Forces left for Japan. The rest of the 'D' Force men were scattered throughout the region. Some POWs were returned to Changi where they worked on construction of the new airport runway. Many more POWs remained working on the railway, repairing the lines and bridges when they were damaged by bombs, chopping wood for the engines and loading the freight. Increased bombing by the advancing Allies proved to be a problem. The railway itself was often damaged or even totally destroyed in places. The bombs also were a danger for the POWs as their camps were deliberately located close to the line.

Many POWs remained to make tunnels for the Japanese who, by now, were being pushed back by the Allies. Some tunnels may have been defensive but several POWs believed they were probably digging their own graves - none were to be left alive, exactly what happened at Sandakan and detailed in Wall's harrowing chapter on Borneo in *Singapore and Beyond*.

At Chungkai Camp sick Japanese soldiers started to appear, short of food.[638]

Eventually many of the POWs were sent back down the railway line to base camps, none in good shape. Russell Braddon described them as not looking like men, but not quite being animals. He wrote:

> *They had feet worn by bamboo thorns and working long months without boots. Their shins had no spare flesh at all on the calf and looked as if bullets had exploded inside them, bursting the meat outwards and blackening it. These were their ulcers of which they had dozens, from threepenny bit size upwards, on each leg. Their thigh bones and pelvis stood out sharply and on the point of each thigh bone was that red raw patch like a saddle sore or a monkey's behind. All their ribs showed clearly, the chest sloping backwards to the hollows of the throat and collar bone. Arms hung down, stick-like, with huge hands, and the skin wrinkled where muscle had vanished, like old men. Heads were shrunken to skulls with large teeth and faintly glowing eyes set in black wells: hair was matted and lifeless. The whole body was draped with a loose-fitting envelope of purple-brown parchment which wrinkled horizontally over the stomach and chest on sagging fleshless buttocks.*[639]

The men of 'U' Battalion 'D' Force fared better than many thanks to the efforts of their doctors, officers and cooks. They had a death rate of just 8.5%, an excellent survival rate. This was despite the fact the 'U' Bn did some of the heaviest work on the railway and had suffered cholera.[640]

It was during this time that more letters began to arrive for Bill. Did Chungkhai have a more relaxed Japanese commander? Was it because he was stationed closer to the start of the railway? Did the Japanese realise they were no longer winning the war and wanted to appease some of the prisoners? Whatever the reason, Bill received welcome letters with news of home.

Date of writing 23 September 1942, received 5 August 1944

From Miss A. C. Cay

Hullo Bill old boy

You remember how ages ago I told you sister Sue was a beautiful looking lass, well that truism was mild compared with all one could say about how she looked on her wedding day on August 15th. Yes Sue made a magnificent bride, gowned to perfection and oh so happy and not one iota nervous. Her Warwick gasped at her splendour as she approached him. Elizabeth and his sister also looked most attractive. Your Mum, despite the hectic rush, looked most charming and handsome, an aristocrat in every sense of the word. How we all longed for you to have been here to give Sue away but as I told her perhaps on that very day you'd have had a premonition that it was a big day in her life, least that's how I felt about it all and I'm sure everyone else did. Naturally it saddened your Mum you not being present but she hid her feelings and was sweet to everyone. Harvey Barton and I were spectators at the ceremony in the Shore Chapel.

[Warwick Alexander Keeling, like his father Alexander John, was an Old Boy of the Sydney Church of England Grammar School, better known as Shore.[641] The Best man was Bruce Beale and groomsman Henry Friend, both Air Force colleagues.]

Elizabeth Gaden, Warwick and Sue, Pamela Keeling

Your Mum was upset at not being able to invite us all, but we fully understood. Anyway I had a finger in the pie having unpacked some glasses on the previous day.

I was round at the flat a few weeks back and met Warwick who seems a very sound lad, no oil painting but has a very strong expression. Long may their present happiness last. There was quite a gathering; the Badgery's who like myself just popped in then along came Peggy and her husband.

Here we are back to winter after several really hot days all so silly. There's a blustering wind blowing through tonight. My acquaintances at the Club are growing daily, they are many and varied, Rimoeil's owner being one of them. He was tickled pink the other day when I told him I'd won one penny from the switch boy the previous Saturday when his Rimoeil romped home. He's a good sportsman, is giving 20% of all Rimoeil's winning at the Spring Races to Patriotic Funds. His last win produced £150.

Wish you could see the super nasturtiums I picked from my garden this afternoon. Golden Gleaners, yellow beauts but the red (double) have stalks 12 inches long and bloom is 3 inches across. Dashed proud of them I am. Lettuces have been huge, my surplus ones I sell to the flat tenants to help swell the Prisoner of War Funds.

Great will be the excitement at the Capper flat on Oct 16th when Bubbles and Ted Rowe get married. [Joseph Seymour Rowe married Marcia Lydia Capper.][642]

I'll be on duty but may with luck get the lad who relieves me to change duty. There's another fly in the ointment on 24th when I'm on duty and badly want to go to a concert Gwen Selva my old school pal is giving. She's busy training a choir for the purpose, all proceeds to the Prisoner of War Funds.[Gwen Selva was a well known soprano of the time, with articles on her activities in the *Sydney Morning Herald.*]

It's all given us fresh heart seeing the various spring trees in blossom after a comparative dearth of flowers. The bush flowers are a joy to behold just now. How I love a days tramp in their midst, instead I'll have a roam around the city gardens instead. Heard two thrilling plays over the air tonight, one an extract from 'Pickwick's Papers' and the other a ghost story, most spooky but very entertaining. I think a cup of tea and bed will be a good topping up. All my love Bill old dear. What a day it will be when letters come from you lads. I noticed a post card from a lad in Germany the other day when sorting the mail and felt I was bringing joy to some ones house, putting it in its right box. Cheers and all the best of luck Bill.

Yours affectionately
Connie

Sue was discharged from the RAAF on 24 September 1942, just a month after her marriage.[643]

The next letters were addressed to Bill in Malaya via Prisoner of War Post, but soon the country spelling was adjusted to Malai which suggests Red Cross involvement. They were still many months out of date by the time they were delivered. Date of writing 22 December 1942, received 4 August 1944:

From Mrs V.L. Gaden

Bill Darling, we are all thinking of you this week and hope you are well and happy. I am hoping Sue and Warwick will be home on Friday if only for a few hours. Sue will be coming home to stay indefinitely after the New Year.

You are to be an uncle in June! What do you think of that?

We are all so thrilled especially Sue who is looking so well and happy.

Gran is coming down from Bundy [Bundabarrina] *next week. She has been with Doris* [Vera's sister] *almost a year. It will be lovely to see her again.*

I had a nice holiday week at Jervis Bay with the Shellshears. The Professor and I used to fish off the breakwater and catch young Jew fish up to 5 lbs in weight.

I had a game of golf every day. I did enjoy it so much. Such a nice little nine hole course and no green fees to pay.

I have got the garden well under control and have lovely flowers and vegetables. It is so much easier to manage than Valhalla next door. You will love this place dear.

David MacDougal, Joe Moore and Co are home. Elizabeth had lunch with David last Thursday. He has been pretty ill lately and is very thin.

Elizabeth met Margaret Taylor in town last week and what do you think? She is married - I don't know what happened to Elaine. She must have stayed in South Australia and probably married too. [Elaine Warren and Margaret Taylor were both referred to in Bill's letters home from when he first arrived in Malaya.]

I had a letter from Jean Thatcher a few days ago. She says she writes to you every month. Connie has a job in a legal firm now and likes the work so much.

Elizabeth loves being with York and Kerr in Bridge Street. It is so much more interesting than the other place and a much bigger salary.

I wonder if you have received my other letters darling. It will be wonderful to hear from you and to know where you are, and that you know of our doings. Everything is going along well and you haven't a moments worry on our account.

If you see Ron Merrett tell him I saw his mother the other day and she is well, also his wife and children. I hear from his wife very often. The Younger Set [of the Comforts Fund] *had a Xmas party for all the children of 2/20 last Saturday. A good time was had by all. We were glad to hear Brig. Taylor's letter through the air.*
Heaps of love darling from the girls and your loving mother.

Doukie

Date of writing unknown, but soon after 20th January 1943 as that is the date of the engagement mentioned, received 5 August 1944

From Mrs Vera Lydia Gaden

My darling Bill

It was wonderful getting news of you at last. [This probably refers to the publication of Officers listed as POWs in the Sydney newspapers on 14 January 1943.]

I do hope you are getting my letters. I am longing to hear from you dear and know how much you know of our doings.

Sue was married last August [1942] *to Warwick Keeling and now Elizabeth has just become engaged to David MacDougal who returned home a few weeks ago. He is such a nice fellow. You always liked him. He has written to you as head of the family. What a surprise you will get dear.*

[David MacDougal, was originally with Bill in 2/20 but then seconded to Mission 204.][644]

You are going to be an uncle in June. What do you think of that! Sue is home with us again and is busy sewing and knitting for the new arrival. She is well and happy about everything.

Connie brought old Mary Wilson [she was the wife of Bicton Wilson, Bill's former Headmaster at Broughton School] *to see us on Sunday morning. She is so glad to have news of you and talks just as much as ever. Connie has a job with a legal firm and seems settled for life.*

What do you think? Mr and Mrs Sykes from Scone are living almost next door to us and Mrs Sykes' mother, Mrs Thompson lived in that place in Raymond Road called 'Strathbroke' with the stone steps that I always wanted to go up and see what the house looked like. Well I have been up dear, Nell Newton and I went there to afternoon tea last week. It is a lovely place with such a pretty garden and glorious view. Percy Sykes is down and has a job with a wool firm. They leased their property for a couple of years.

Mother is going to stay at 'Tara' near Mrs Waters. I think she will like it there and it is so close to the ferry, no tram fares.

Lee Sautelle, I mean Fallaw, is coming for luncheon tomorrow. She is still hoping to hear something of Charles. She is such a dear. Margaret Burns (nee Taylor) rang me when she saw your name in the paper dear. She married an old love called Burns so all is well.

We went to see Mick and Marge a few nights ago. Bill Badgery from Scone was there too. We had a great yarn and Mick drove us home.

[The Badgery family were close friends, Mick was Ginge's god father and gave both girls away at their weddings. Their son Brian was also a POW.]

The girls send their love darling. Elizabeth is going to write to you and tell you all about David. All my love son and God bless you.
From your loving Mother
Doukie

Date of writing 17 May 1943, received 5 August 1944:

From Mrs V.L. Gaden, 10 Raymond Road, Neutral Bay, Sydney

Darling Bill

I hope you have had letters from us by now. We have heard nothing from you yet but expect we will get a letter or message through the Red Cross.

We are all well dear and everything going along smoothly. Sue's baby is due to arrive in about 5 weeks, she is so happy about it. How will you like being an uncle? Think of me as a grandmother. I do wish Gran Gaden had lived to see it. [Agnes Lilian Gaden, wife of Edward Ainsworth Gaden died in 1942. Her husband had died in 1938.] [645]

Elizabeth is to be married soon, but will be with me for the duration like Sue, she will write her bit at the end of the letter.

Mrs Spain tells me that old 'Stan' is back in civilian life again and not pleased about it either.

[Stanley Spain was born October 1873. He was in the Army, N75405, a lieutenant in the Area Staff section.][646]

The Badgerys have had two radio messages about Brian. He is well but not interned near you. [Sadly Brian died in Borneo.] [647]

I hope you know we are living in St Damien's, next door to Valhalla dear. Old Valhalla got too damp ... you will love this place. We have fixed up a tiny room off Sue's bedroom for a nursery. I painted it cream and it has blue curtains and cream furniture. Elizabeth has the room with the windows along Valhalla fence. It is a lovely room and will be yours when you come home darling.

The Griersons are still next door. Gordon is a long way from home but he sent me a message for Mother's Day. Mrs Davies gave me a bowl of frangipani flowers and some eau-de-cologne from you. She did the same last year. Last year she dreamt she was with you over there and you picked some frangipanni and asked her to give it to me which she has done for each Mother's day.
All my love darling
From Mother

...

Hello Bill

What do you know ... I was practically ready to be married, got the cake and all and then David couldn't make it. How do you think I will go as Mrs MacDougal? Had a letter from him a couple of days ago and he had met Rodger Barry and was very pleased to see him after all this time. Bill my beaut old brother I must go and do some work or I will get the sack.
Lots of love
Ginge

Date of writing 30 June 1943, received 5 August 1944:

From Mrs V.L .Gaden

My Darling Bill

I have such a lot of news to tell you in this letter.

First of all you are now an Uncle dear. Sue has a little baby daughter a week old.

She is to be called 'Diana' Keeling - no middle name. Warwick doesn't know he is a father yet. Sue is so happy and the baby is a pet. She was born at 'Saba' at the top of Wycombe Road. It will be so good to have them both home next week.

Elizabeth and David were married on 22nd May [1943] *and now David has gone away and she is home again and back at the office once more. David is a dear and Elizabeth is very proud of a scarf of the MacDougal tartan he gave her. Mick Badgery gave her away at the wedding, the same as Sue and said in a very nice speech that he was sorry I had run out of daughters.*

Aunt Ida and Biddy came to lunch yesterday and then went to see Sue. They send their love to you dear. Moya lives with Biddy now that Gran has gone.

[Ida Brereton Atherton was sister to Agnes Lilian Atherton. Ida married Thomas Burton Gaden, whilst Agnes married his younger brother Edward Ainsworth Gaden[648] Biddy and Moya were the Goff sisters.]

I hope you had my letter telling you that Gran died suddenly about 7 months ago. She wrote me a lovely letter telling me she was sure you were alright just before she went.

Elaine [Warren] *is back in Neutral Bay after a year in Adelaide. She looks just the same and is still unmarried!!*

Mother is still at 'Tara' and seems happy there. She likes Neutral Bay just as much as we do.

Mr Carlyle rang me today to say the office was sending along a half yearly bonus. They come regularly dear.

We are all well and everything goes along well so don't worry darling.
All our love and blessings from
Mother

Whilst these earlier letters from Bill's family and friends had plenty of news, the later communications were much more like telegrams, with every single word having to count. By September 1943 the Japanese authorities insisted the message contained just twenty-five words. They used the excuse that they had to censor the letters.[649] Many of the Japanese who acted as censors could not understand English; also handwriting can be hard to interpret if you are unfamiliar with the words and sentence construction. News of any Allied progress would have been totally unacceptable. However many letters were received by the Japanese but they did not pass them onto the men even if they were interned in that specific camp. Letters were burnt to reduce the size of piles that should have gone through to Allied troops, or were eaten by white ants or destroyed by damp.[650]

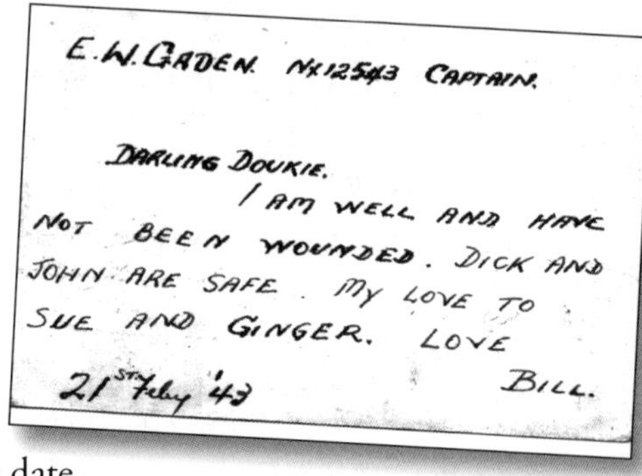
E.W. GADEN NX12543 CAPTAIN.

DARLING DOUKIE.
I AM WELL AND HAVE NOT BEEN WOUNDED. DICK AND JOHN ARE SAFE. MY LOVE TO SUE AND GINGER. LOVE
21st Feby '43 BILL.

Dick and John were Sgt Richard Bodley Gaden NX32954 of 2/15 Bn. and Staff Sgt John Burton Gaden NX26103 of 2/30 Bn, the sons of Ida (Atherton) Gaden who was sister to Bill's grandmother Agnes Lilian. It is not known when the family received this card. Was it the first one? It is the only one of the four received that has a date.

Date of writing 8 September 1943, received 5 August 1944:

From Miss A.C Cay, 44 Harriette Street, Neutral Bay
BILL DEAR
BIRTHDAY GREETINGS. HOME FOLKS WELL.
ELIZABETH MADE CHARMING BRIDE TWENTY-SECOND MAY.
ELIZABETH DAVID VERY HAPPY.
SUE'S DIANA SWEET. SELF SPLENDID
LOVE CONNIE

Date of writing 27 September 1943, received 18 February 1945

From Mrs V.L. Gaden
DARLING BILL
DELIGHTED TO RECEIVE YOUR FIRST CARD.
ELIZABETH, SUE AND BABY KEELING WITH ME,
EVERYTHING IN ORDER, ALL WELL.
FONDEST LOVE
MOTHER

Date of writing 29 September 1943, received 18 February 1945:

From Elaine Warren, 3 Hillside Flats, Shellcove Road, Neutral Bay
DEAR BILL
DELIGHTED THAT YOUR MOTHER HAS HEARD FROM YOU.
I AM LIVING AT HOME AND HAVE A GOOD POSITION AT NEUTRAL BAY.
BEST WISHES ON YOUR 26TH BIRTHDAY.
LOVE FROM ELAINE

Date of writing 5 October 1943, received 18 February 1945:

From Mrs V.L. Gaden
DARLING BILL
OUR THOUGHTS WITH YOU ON YOUR BIRTHDAY TODAY.
BADGERY'S HAD CARD FROM BRIAN, CELEBRATED WITH US.
ALL WELL HERE. FONDEST LOVE MY SON.
DOUKIE

Date of writing 3 November 1943, received 18 February 1945:

From Mrs V.L. Gaden
DARLING BILL
ALL WELL HERE. YOUR AFFAIRS IN ORDER.

SO HAPPY IN THIS FLAT. GARDEN LOVELY AT PRESENT.
MOTHER LIVING 'TARA'. YOUR NIECE BEAUTIFUL.
DOUKIE (MOTHER)

Date of writing unknown, received 18 February 1945:

From Elaine Warren
BILL DEAR
LIFE HAS NOT CHANGED HERE. MY THOUGHTS ARE ALWAYS WITH YOU.
I HOPE YOU ARE WELL, AM STILL HOPING TO HEAR FROM YOU SOON
BEST LOVE FROM
ELAINE

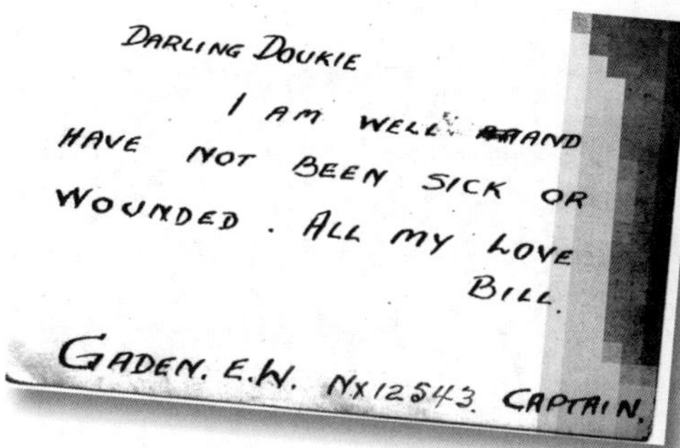
DARLING DOUKIE
I AM WELL AND HAVE NOT BEEN SICK OR WOUNDED. ALL MY LOVE
BILL.
GADEN. E.W. NX12543. CAPTAIN.

Date of writing 3 January 1944, received 7 October 1944:

From Mrs Warwick Keeling
DARLING BILL
MUM, GRAN, GINGER, MY BABY DIANA
AND I WERE TOGETHER FOR XMAS.
WE MISSED YOU, DAVID AND WARWICK.
MAY WE BE TOGETHER NEXT TIME.
LOVE
SUE

Pencilled on the back of this note was the following calculation (no indication of date, but in Bill's handwriting):

AIF in Malaya			
Total			19449
Deaths before war			49
Repatriation (inc boarded and wounded)		981	
2/3 MT evac to Java			377
Nurses and one MO evac			133
Burial Party			47
Official (M Gen B)			78
Killed in Action	378		
Died of wounds	106		
Missing	2309		2793
POW			14991
			19449

Date of writing unknown, received 7 October 1944:

From Mrs J.C. Court, Kingdon Street, Scone [Agnes O'Donohoe cared for Bill and his sisters whilst they were young. She married John C Court in 1929].
DEAR BILL
GLAD WE HAVE HEARD OF YOU. WENT TO ELIZABETH'S WEDDING.
ENJOYED SEEING EVERYONE. WISH I COULD SEE YOU DEAR.
KEEP SMILING. SUE'S BABY IS BEAUTIFUL
AGNES COURT

Date of writing 3 December 1943, received 18 October 44. [Pencil note Chungkai suggesting Bill was located there when he received this card.]

From Miss Betty Wilkinson, 4 Belmont Avenue, Wollstonecraft.
MY DEAR BILL
OVERJOYED HEAR YOU SAFE.
HAVE YOU SEEN CHARLIE?
OUR PEOPLE ALL WELL, HOPE YOU SAME.
AM WORKING AT ARTARMON.
LOVE FROM US ALL, LOTS OF LOVE
BETTY

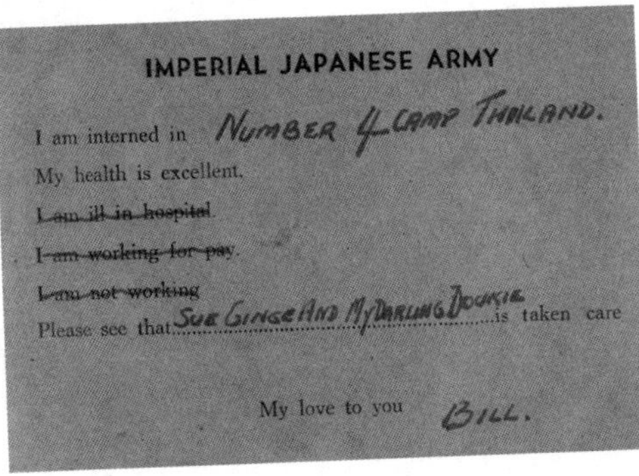

IMPERIAL JAPANESE ARMY

I am interned in NUMBER 4 CAMP THAILAND.

My health is excellent.

~~I am ill in hospital.~~

~~I am working for pay.~~

~~I am not working~~

Please see that SUE GINGE AND MY DARLING DOUKIE is taken care

My love to you BILL.

Date of writing unknown, received 19 October 1944:

From Mrs V.L. Gaden
BILL DARLING
HOME GARDEN IN ORDER. LOVELY FOR SUE'S BABY.
GIRLS EXCITED. WARWICK, DAVID EXPECTED SOON.
HOPE YOU HAVE HAD LETTERS.
PRAYING ALL TOGETHER SOON DARLING
DOUKIE

Date of writing unknown, received 19 October 1944. Pencil note 'Chungkai' on the envelope which suggests that Bill was still posted to Chungkai when he received it.

From Mrs V L Gaden
DARLING BILL TWO CARDS FROM YOU TODAY, ONE FROM THAILAND.
THINKING OF YOU ALWAYS. SUE, WARWICK, DIANA, ELIZABETH, DAVID AND SELF WELL. GIRLS AND BABY WITH ME
LOVE DOUKIE

Date of writing 1 January 1944, received 20 November 1944:

From Mrs V.L. Gaden
DARLING BILL
OUR LOVING GREETINGS. AUNT IDA HEARD FROM THE BOYS.
BIRTS REMEMBERED YOU CHRISTMAS. DELIGHTED AT ANY NEWS.
IF POSSIBLE WRITE SIGNATURE ON NEXT CARD.
LOVE DARLING DOUKIE

[Aunt Ida's sons were the Dick and John referred to by Bill in his first (?) post card home. They were Sgt Richard Bodley Gaden NX32954 of 2/15 Bn and Staff Sgt John Burton Gaden NX26103 of 2/30.]

Date of writing 16 April 1944, received unknown:

From Mrs V.L. Gaden
BILL DARLING,
DAVID, ELIZABETH MACDOUGAL AWAY SECOND HONEYMOON. WARWICK HOME SOON. HIS BABY DAUGHTER SO LIKE SUE.
IF POSSIBLE SEND BROADCAST MESSAGE.
ALL WELL HERE DARLING
LOVE MOTHER

Date of writing 18 June 1944, received 18 February 1945:

From Mrs V.L. Gaden
DARLING BILL
DIANA'S FIRST BIRTHDAY TODAY. WARWICK HOME FOR IT.
I HAVE BEEN GOULBURN FOR HOLIDAY. AGNES COMING TO STAY. ELIZABETH GOING LEURA SOON. WE ALL SEND LOVE
MOTHER

David MacDougal recalled that in late 1944, Vera gave him a card which had arrived from Bill. It had many 'squiggles' and at the bottom was 'Contact Pitman, Metropole Hotel, and give him my regards'. At the time Army Intelligence was located there and Bill's letter, when the 'squiggles' were translated by a Shorthand expert read 'Railway completed, suggest bombing soonest'. (The family no longer has this card.)

Date of writing unknown, received 18 February 1945:

From Elaine Warren
BILL DEAR
FOR THE PAST YEAR I HAVE BEEN HAIRDRESSING AT NEUTRAL BAY AND AM STILL DOING SO. HOPE YOU ARE WELL AND CHEERFUL ALL MY LOVE
FROM ELAINE

Date of writing 2 January 1945, received unknown:

From Miss C Cay, 44 Harriette Street, Neutral Bay
DEAR BILL
ALL LONG KNOW HOW YOU ARE, ALSO IF RECEIVING LETTERS.
SAW MUM, GRAN, SUE, DAUGHTER DIANA SUNDAY, ALL SPLENDID.
GINGE AND DAVID HAVE SON. CHEERIO, CONNIE

[James Campbell MacDougal was born in November 1944.]

Date of writing 5 January 1945, received unknown, possibly re-directed to Vera on 26 February 1945:

From Mrs V.L. Gaden
DARLING BILL
HOPE YOU RECEIVE CABLE. REPLY IF POSSIBLE. FAMILY WELL INCLUDING YOUR NIECE AND NEPHEW. HOPING TO SEE YOU BEFORE LONG. LOVE AND PRAYERS FROM ALL DEAR.
MOTHER

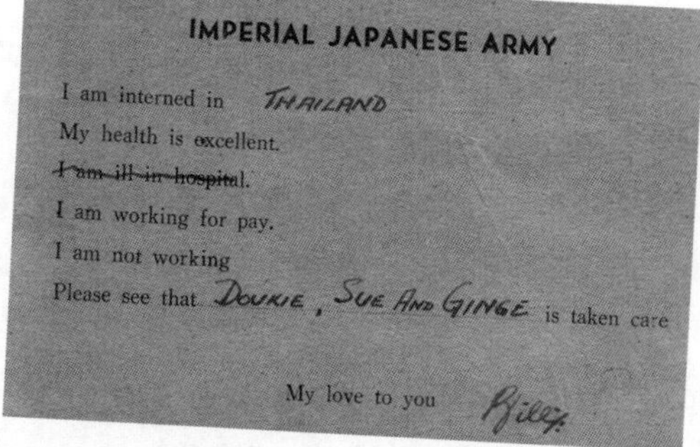
IMPERIAL JAPANESE ARMY

I am interned in THAILAND
My health is excellent.
~~I am ill in hospital.~~
I am working for pay.
I am not working
Please see that DOUKIE, SUE AND GINGE is taken care

My love to you Billy.

Date of writing 19 January 1945, received unknown:

From Mrs B Wilkinson, 4 Belmont Avenue, Wollstonecraft, Sydney.
MY DEAR BILL
MOTHER AND GIRLS WELL, DELIGHTED GET YOUR CARD. HOW ARE YOU AND CHARLIE?
PEGGY MARRIED TO SOUTH AUSTRALIAN. I AM WORKING BOOKSTALL.
YOUR LOVING SISTER
BETTY

In fact Miss Betty had written before, in December 1943, and she was trying to ensure the message went through by referring to herself as Bill's sister. Again she refers to Charlie, her brother. A search in the Nominal Roll and Australian War Memorial records for a 'Charles Wilkinson' revealed a Charles Reid Wilkinson, Service number 2191641 (NX54635) He was born in Glenfield on 5 Nov 1919. His Next of Kin was Ethel Wilkinson. He was Lance Sergeant in the 2/20 Bn, the same Bn as Bill, and was listed as a POW. Later letters from Betty reveal Charlie was a POW in the same Thailand camp as Bill. She had another brother David born 1925 whose next of kin was also Ethel and she mentioned the family was no longer living at Glenfield. Charlie survived, he was discharged 19th December 1945.

Date of writing 8th June 1945, was not received by Bill, it was redirected back to Vera.

```
From Mrs. V.L. Gaden
DARLING BILL
ALL LOOKING FORWARD TO SEEING YOU SOON.
SUE, DIANA, CRONULLA,
JOINING THEM THIS WEEKEND,
ELIZABETH, DAVID, BABY WELL, ALSO GRAN
ALL SEND LOVE DARLING
DOUKIE
```

Date of writing unknown, it was not received by Bill, it was redirected back to Vera.

```
From Mrs V.L. Gaden
BILL DARLING
HOPING TO GET RADIO MESSAGE FROM YOU SOON.
ALONE HERE AT PRESENT
GIRLS WITH THEIR HUSBANDS
GETTING READY FOR YOUR RETURN
ALL WELL, LOVE
DOUKIE
```

In July 1945 Vera and her friend Janet Muriel Johnston of 26 Aubin Street, Neutral Bay wrote a musical prayer for which they applied for copyright to the Copyright Office. It was number 41657 and dated 18 July 1945.[651]

The music was composed by Janet, the words written by Vera and they reflect her concern for her son.

Hear us Lord we humbly pray, make all wars and strife to cease,
Bring our loved ones safely home, bring us nearer Thee and peace.

The following month saw the war take a dramatic turn for the better for the Allied prisoners. The dropping of the two atomic bombs, one on Hiroshima on 6 August 1945 and the second on Nagasaki on 9 August 1945, led to unprecedented destruction and death. Around 140,000 were thought to have perished in the first attack. The Nagasaki bomb landed just 1700 metres from

Prison Camp 14 which housed 24 Australians in its complement of 169 men. They survived but 75,000 Japanese civilians did not.[652] Capt. Reg Newton was one of the survivors in Nagasaki.[653]

At noon on 15 August Japanese Emperor Hirohito ordered the acceptance of the Potsdam Declaration which had been issued by the Allies on 26 July in an attempt to encourage the Japanese to surrender. Hirohito did not say the word 'surrender' nor issue an apology for all the death and destruction that had been caused.[654] After Hirohito's 'settlement' the official end of the Second World War came on 2 September 1945.

The news rippled through all the POW camps. At Kanburi Boon Pong cycled past waving V signs and shouting 'War Finish'.[655] On the road to Pitsanlok a Chinese man wore a coat over his sweatshirt; when the Japanese guards were distracted he opened the coat and pointed to a sheet of paper pinned to his shirt THE WAR IS OVER. THE JAPS ARE DEFEATED AND HAVE SURRENDERED.[656]

At Ratburi a Thai man sang to the tune of 'God Save the King':

Please listen to me now, I have to let you know,
The war is done
England victorious, American victorious,
Japan has surrendered
The war is done.[657]

Louis Baume wrote in his diary:

> *Yes it is all over and we have reached the bitter end. We are free. O God can it really be true? 3 1/2 years of eternity and at last we have reached the end. All those weeks, all those months, that suffering and now it is all finished. All that agony, bombing, disease, hunger, death and we have lived to see the end! We have vainly hoped, prayed, planned for this day for how long - and now it has come suddenly, unexpectedly, quietly. Just like this. I suppose we ought to sing, to dance, to go mad and scream with joy but we cannot. The going has been too hard and anyway the magnitude of the event is so great that it is quite beyond us to fully appreciate it. It is a particularly beautiful night: the stars are glimmering bright and ghostly wisps of white cloud are lazily drifting round the dark hill tops.*[658]

The Burma Thailand Railway was constructed at the cost of large numbers of allied prisoners and Asians. Seventy percent of the terrain was malarial jungle, much of it was in difficult country. The railway was completed in just ten months ... four million cubic metres of earthworks were built, three million cubic metres of rock were shifted, fourteen kilometres of bridgework were constructed.[659]

The labourers included 30,131 British prisoners of war, 17,999 Dutch, 13,004 Australians, 686 Americans and an unknown number of Burmese, Malay and Javanese - a total workforce of 240,000.[660] They were all malnourished, racked with disease, bashed and beaten as well as being denied Red Cross food and medical treatment by the Japanese.

The Prisoners of War held by the Germans and Italians had a death rate of 4%;[661] the total workforce of the Japanese had an average death rate of 41%, the Australians lost 22% of their men.[662] None of these men had died in battle, they had not been

> *given the chance to fight for his life. They had been ordered to surrender and all died in captivity - prisoners dying of starvation, brutality, slavery, dreadful tropical diseases, malaria, diphtheria, dysentery, cholera, beri-beri and terrible leg ulcers.*[663]

No wonder it can be claimed that a man died for every sleeper laid and the reason was simple; they starved. The Japanese did not feed them, they did not issue the Red Cross parcels that were available and that they had stored. Men were given 4,220 calories daily in their 1941 Australian Army ration. A ration of 3,000 calories would allow survival and some work. In Changi the daily issue was around 2,000 calories. On the railway things were much, much worse. The prisoners received a small amount of rice, some watery vegetable stew and tiny amounts, if any, of fish or meat. These men were expected to work at maximum effort, they were expected to overcome dreadful diseases, but they were starved, in many cases, starved to death.[664]

Legendary medical officer Lieutenant-Colonel Edward 'Weary' Dunlop wrote:

> *Perhaps the main battle for the lives of prisoners of war was fought in these crude jungle hospitals of Burma and Thailand. It is an enduring commentary on the civilisation of the detaining power, that having broken these men by inhuman conditions of labour, they denied them adequate rations for recovery, and allowed the burden of equipping the hospitals and the provision of special foodstuffs and essential drugs to be borne largely by the prisoners themselves.*[665]

At the Hellfire Pass Museum is a quote from Medical Officer Major Bruce Hunt:

> *I would say that ... (the Burma-Thailand Railway) was the most searching test of fundamental character and guts that I have ever known. That so many men ... came through this test with their heads high and their records unblemished was something of which we ... may not be unreasonably proud.*[666]

A survivor summed up the prisoners of war:

> *Beneath the rags and grime of those who limped back to Singapore stood some of the finest men to have worn an Australian uniform. Theirs had not been the role of the fighting soldier, but one of combat against an enemy whose methods would not have been found in army training manuals of any civilised nation.*[667]

[630] Dunlop, *The War Diaries of Weary Dunlop*, p. 378.
[631] *ibid.*, pp. 387-8.
[632] Dunlop, *Report on Base POW hospitals, Thailand*, AWM 54, Control symbol 554/5/1. p. 5.
[633] Dunlop, *The War Diaries of Weary Dunlop*, p. 409.
[634] Beattie, *The Death Railway*, p. 56.
[635] Newton, *The Grim Glory*, p. 637.
[636] Beattie, *op. cit.*, p. 56.
[637] Newton, *op. cit.*, pp. 634-5.
[638] Bart Richardson, as told to James Keady, and Wall, *Singapore and Beyond*, pp. 196-7.
[639] Moremon, *Australians on the Burma-Thailand Railway*, p. 87.
[640] Elliott and Silver, *A History of the 2/18 Battalion*, pp. 145-6.
[641] Warden, SCEGS Register.
[642] NSW BDM register 27150/1942.
[643] DVA Nominal Roll.
[644] *ibid.*
[645] NSW BDM Register.
[646] DVA Nominal Roll.
[647] *ibid.*
[648] Gaden family history researched by the author.
[649] Rivett, *Behind Bamboo,* p. 318.
[650] Summers, *The Colonel of Tamarkan*, p. 241.
[651] Johnston and Gaden, *A Prayer*, National Archives of Australia, Series A1336, Control Symbol 41657.
[652] Forbes, *Hellfire*, p. 455.
[653] Newton interview, AWM S01739.
[654] Forbes, *op. cit.*, p. 464.
[655] Summers, *op. cit.*, p. 286.
[656] Peek, *One Fourteenth of an Elephant*, p. 481.
[657] Forbes, *op. cit.*, p. 467.
[658] Baume, *Diary*, IWM 66/310/1-2 quoted in Summers, *op. cit.*, p. 289.
[659] Forbes, *op. cit.*, p. 263.
[660] Beattie, *op. cit.*, p. 52.
[661] Gordon, *Miracle on the River Kwai*, p. 46.
[662] Beattie, *op. cit.*, p. 52.
[663] Cooper, Carol, My father's Diary, in *Legacies of our fathers*, p. 22.
[664] Nelson, *Australians under Nippon*, p. 51.
[665] Dunlop, *Report on Base POW Hospitals*, p. 26.
[666] Hellfire Pass Museum display.
[667] Moremon, *op. cit.*, p. 91.

Chapter 12 - Freedom

Once the Allies were able to officially declare victory over the Japanese, on 2 September 1945, the massive job of repatriation of survivors could begin. The prisoners had to be sought out from their many locations scattered across the countries of the region. They had to be transported to centres ready for their return journey home. They had to be clothed, they had to be treated for their many diseases and they all needed good nutritious food. It would be a massive task.

Many families in Australia rejoiced that the war was over but they had no idea if their loved one was still alive or had been killed or injured; the joy at war's end was muted until they actually had good news from their son, husband or brother, or the girls who had also gone to war. In September 1944 six Japanese transport ships had been sunk by Allied torpedoes. The cargo consisted of American, Australian, British, Dutch and Filipino prisoners of war and Javanese slave labourers; about 10,600 prisoners lost their lives in these sinkings. American submarines picked up 114 survivors, all they could carry.[668] These few men were the first to pass on the horrific stories of the treatment of the POWs at the hands of the Japanese. The families were devastated to hear such dreadful news. Now the war was over they could hope for information again and pray it was good news.

It was not until ten days after the official end of the war, on 12 September 1945, that Bill finally managed to get a cable through to his mother to tell her he was well and it was only on 14 September that Vera received confirmation from the Army that he was alive. What an eternally long wait those days would have been.

For many families the news was not so good. The family of Tom Scollen (the 2/20 lad who was a member of Bill's relay team which won the Athletics Championship in 1941) received three cards from him from Sandakan, then on 15 August 1945 the family were overjoyed to learn of the unofficial end of the war. Just one hour later the postman delivered a letter to say Tom had died in the POW camp. Tom's sister Patricia recalled that less than twelve months later her father, who had never had a day of illness, suffered a heart attack and died within a few hours.[669] In the doctor's opinion his death was the result of delayed shock after learning of the loss of his son. Tom's mother soon became ill with early onset memory loss and Patricia nursed her for years until she died. She was still asking for 'her boy'.[670]

After the Japanese surrendered, the surviving allies were eventually transported from the many POW camps to larger Reception Centres where they awaited repatriation. During this time they were given medical treatment, good food and clean clothes. Many quickly recovered their weight and good spirits. Bill was involved in the administration of the repatriation process and would not be sent home as quickly as some of the others.

Letters to and from the released prisoners flowed more freely once the war was over. But there were still frustrating delays as can be seen by the letters received by Bill from his family. Prisoners had to be re-located, letters were sent to incorrect places, men had to be found and their mail delivered. It would have been a time of hope but inner turmoil until a letter written by a loved one was safely delivered into their hands, tangible evidence that they really were alive. Bill's family heard from him by cable on 12th September but it was a few more weeks before they received a letter penned in his familiar handwriting. Only then were their hopes realised and their joy unbounded.

Mrs. V.L. Gaden
St Damien's
10 Raymond Road, Neutral Bay

Bill darling *17th August 1945*

This is a letter I pray you will receive and very quickly too. There is so much to say dear. First of all we are all well and you will see by the address we have moved next door. We did this in January 1942 but my letters telling you were returned and we don't know if you received any mail from us afterwards.

It is lovely here. Old Valhalla got too out of repairs so we jumped at the opportunity of getting this flat. Mother is living at 'Tara' in Kurraba Road and is very well too.

Sue and Elizabeth are both married and you will be getting letters from them too. It will be a surprise to know that David MacDougal is a brother in law but not such a surprise about Warwick Keeling as one. They are so happy and have a gorgeous child each. Elizabeth and David have a little son 8 months old and a miniature David. Sue has a little daughter 2 years old. They will give you all their news themselves. Sue and Diana have been with us all the time until a few weeks ago when they moved into a tiny flat at Balmoral in readiness for Warwick's return.

Darling Gran Gaden died over two years ago. She wrote me a sweet little letter just before she died. It was very sudden. Vermont [the family home in Bowral] is sold, everything was left to Kitty [Walker, sister of Bill's father] *except the big picture of the Blue Mountains which is yours and which I have waiting for you. Kit sent us down some furniture and a big carpet too.*

Birt and Co have been looking after your interests dear and our other affairs are much as they were.

I am alone just waiting for you darling; although the war is over, it is not really for us until we hear you are safe and on your way home.

We have kept the Comforts Fund going all the time and now there is an 8th Division Association to look after you all on your return.

Bob Grant is home from Canada where he got his 'wings'; after returning from the Middle East he transferred to the Air Force. [Hugh Balcombe (Bob) Grant was the son of Vera's sister Doris.[671] He enlisted in the Army in June 1940, to the 2/101 General Transport Company NX28293 and was discharged on 22 July 1943. The next day he enlisted in the RAAF and was a Flight Sergeant at 5 Service Flying Training School.] [672]

Poor old Gordon (Bill's son) was lost over Berlin last year. [Gordon Robertson Balcombe was a Flying Officer in the RAAF, Service Number 420825. He was the son of Vera's younger brother William Gould Balcombe and his wife Annie Laurie Robertson who lived in Binnaway. Gordon, a Shore Old Boy, died on 15 Feb 1944.][673]

Oh dear there is so much to tell dear, it is hard to know when to stop. I have received six cards from you altogether dear, the last one written in June 1944 which arrived just after Christmas. I was a lot luckier than some. The lads in Japan have been able to write such long letters and far more often than you others in Malaya and Thailand.

Tony Walter is home and looking so well I believe. I haven't seen him myself.

The Griersons are still at Valhalla but it is sold and they will have to go before long. Gordon has been in the AIF for years and has grown up. He has been in the Solomons and is very thin but has been so good to us whenever he is on leave. Betty is engaged and is just as much a dill as ever. [Dorothy Betty Grierson married John Eddis Linton in 1946.][674] *They can't use the front balcony because it's not safe to walk on, which will give you an idea of how the old place has been left to rot. I have such a pretty garden here dear; I know you will love it all.*

Margaret [Taylor] *married about 2 years ago and I haven't seen or heard of her since. Elaine* [Warren] *came back from South Australia, still unmarried and continued hair dressing in Neutral Bay. Then she joined the W.A.A.F.'s so goodness knows where she is now. She is just the same if you know what I mean.*

The Fowlers have returned from the Bank at Goulburn and are building a house at Palm Beach. Robin is in the Army and Frank the Navy. Doesn't that make you feel old? [Francis Bursill Fowler S/10260 was an Able Seaman. He was on HMAS *Moreton* on discharge.][675]

David did great things in China as you will hear when you return dear.

Barbara Grant [another of Bill's cousins on the Balcombe side of the family][676] *married Dick* [Richard Gowland] *Young in 1942* [677] *and they have an infant 2 years old. Think of all your new relations!*

Poor Jack Kitchen [one of Bill's cousins on the Gaden side of the family] *lost his life in a crash when he was instructing in the RAAF and left Margaret with a dear little son and no money!!* [John Edward Kitchen married Eleanor Margaret Ball Fleming in 1940.[678] He enlisted in the RAAF on 7 November 1942, service number 419852.][679]

I have had some nice holidays at Armidale with the Johnstone's, friends we have made since you went away dear, but otherwise have just gone on as usual, trying to keep young and beautiful for your return. God bless you darling. Hope to have you home very soon.

Your loving
Doukie

The Armidale friends were Brigadier John Lorimer Gibson (known as JLG) Johnstone, a solicitor and his wife Noemi Marie formerly de Lepervanche. They had five children, the oldest being Joan, born 1921. She studied physiotherapy at Sydney University. Her family sometimes stayed in Sydney in the Hotel Australia. Was this where they met Sue when she was running her manicure business, or did the Johnstones and Gadens know each other through the Law fraternity? Joan was mentioned in one letter as helping Vera and the girls to move from their flat in Valhalla to the new one next door in Raymond Road.

Bill's sisters would have liked Joan to become Mrs E.W. Gaden. However Joan married Richard Pollock in 1944 and son Timothy arrived in August 1945. Her sister Jennifer recalled that Joan's wedding dress was a borrowed one[680] and a study of the photographs reveal it was more than likely the same dress of ivory cream satin as Sue Gaden wore when she and Warwick Keeling were married in August 1942.

The families did visit and stay with each other. Joan's youngest sister Jennifer can recall staying with the Gadens in Raymond Road; she remembered walking down the side of the house to the entry. One visit her mother became sick and the doctor had to be called. Jen chuckled as she told of her mother ill in bed but still fussing to put on her pearls and look smart before the doctor arrived.[681]

Sue Gaden

Mrs. D.C. MacDougal
Willumbong
22 Redan Street, Mosman

Darling Bill *Saturday 18th August 1945*

Well sweetie so much has happened and there is so much to say that I hardly know where to begin. I suppose Sue and Mother will tell you the same things too. Mother is very well and has been all along. Warwick came back from England and he and Sue were married on August 22nd 1942 and Diana was born the following 18th June or was it July? She is a bonzer kid.

Joan Johnstone

David came back from Burma, China via India in December 1942 and we were engaged almost immediately and married on his next leave May 22nd 1943 and James arrived on November 28th 1944. David was discharged in July of same year. Still gets miserable about it at times. We have not been able to find a house yet and are living with his two aunts; the third died a couple of months ago.

Agnes and kids are very well.

Margaret, can't remember her other name, however she married an army bloke ages ago, saw her once and she's very happy.

Tony Walter came back a few weeks ago after being a POW in Germany; he has improved but Mick and Marg say he's slipping into his old ways already. [Anthony Rutherford Walter, NX12271 was a Lieut. in the 2/1 Infantry Bn.][682]

Rolfe [Barker, NX28141] *died of typhus in Burma. John Richards is married can you believe it and has a daughter; he has a property in Queensland I think it is.*

Norman is discharged and has bought a practice at Roseville and he and Kate and kids are all very well. [Dr Norman Arthur Walker, NX70675, was married to Catherine (Kitty) Gaden one of Bill's aunts.]

Sue has a dear little flat down at Balmoral. She was living at Raymond Road until recently; since leaving Mother looks younger. Diana is, as Warwick say, a demolition

David and Elizabeth's wedding

squad concentrated into one small child, not far wrong. Gran is the same and loves listening to the races. No more space and anyway could not run the risk of missing the mail. Next letter will have a few more details. Tons and tons of love Bill old boy and a kiss from Jamie.
From Ginge

...

David C. MacDougal
22 Redan Street, Mosman

Dear Old Bill, *18th August 1945*

I sincerely hope that this finds you as well as may be in the circumstances and strong enough to stand a pretty severe shock. I wish to ask you if you are quite agreeable to accepting me as your brother in law because truly when I arrived home from China at Christmas '42, I was completely bowled over by Ginge and in fact everything was over so quickly that I feel that the forces of good were really on my side.

We were married in May '43 and have more or less been in bliss ever since apart from 12 months in the North and NG, some malaria and dysentery which carried on from China. When Singapore fell we were in Kweiyang, Southern China and on our way north to help our 'comrades-in-arms' and I can tell you that we went on with a good deal of trepidation and soon after, Burma was lost. We spent 9 months in the blue, with Mr. Forde (Army Minister) and the general staff denying our existence when suddenly Smith's Weekly found us and got a story plus photographs (we were then between Changsha and Nanchang in some of the filthiest country I've been in). With us of course were all the local diseases, malaria, blackwater, cholera etc. which you know all about. After everyone becoming too crook to do anything we were withdrawn and brought home. Of course we were split up and went all over the shop, I went to 2/33, 7 Div and was with them in N.G.

I'm afraid at that time people were a bit upset that we hadn't held S and been in Tokyo and the most ridiculous stories were circulating and which we couldn't stomach. No doubt some Staff Corps Wallah will only be too pleased to condemn the General and indeed poor chap has received a filthy deal and has made us all thoroughly fed up. However we still stick and mustered about 140 for the Victory Parade through the City which was very good really.

Now for some news of the lads.

Rolfe Barker contracted typhus in Burma and went, also Cecil Martin.

From Don Company Bob Ward (the Tommy) was killed in Northern Burma also.

Charles Moses [NX12404] *is back in Civvy Street as is the General* [Bennett],

Stuart Burt is in the West and Pat Reynolds is almost discharged.

Fenton Braund [NX12551] *who was with me and also in the 17th is also out.*

Keith Magno [NX12306] *and Tim McCulloch were killed at El Alamein, at the time Keith was commanding the 2/17th.*

Tony Walter was taken prisoner and arrived home last week looking very fit and feeling v. good.

Wallace Betts [RAAF 402563] *is in England with Gerry O'Donnell* [NX23058].

Col O'Donnell [NX19326], *Harold McLachlan* [NX20771], *Bevan Ellison* [NX20775],[683] *Swede Weldon, Vord Burgess are all discharged.*

Brian Badgery was lost in Borneo last November.

[Brian Lloyd Badgery was a Shore Old Boy, attending the school from 1928 to 1933, the son of Keith Pitt (Mick) and Marjorie Evelyn Badgery of 4 Alexander

Avenue, Mossman. His Service number was NX65880. He was a Sergeant in 8th Div HQ. He became a POW in Borneo, died 30 March 1945, aged 30. His memorial is on Panel 8 at the Labuan Memorial.][684]

Pat Paton is up in N.G. with Movement Control and Harks is with Water Transport.

George King has been boarded 'B' Class and is instructing down at Wagga. Poor old George is still a Lieut. and the most junior in the Army, he still gets in a lot of strife.

I saw Ern Smith in Cairns last year and he is with 2/4th Pioneers. I think that that is the lot of them I can remember for the moment, oh! Your cousin Jack Kitchen was killed in an aircraft last year, very bad luck as he was instructing at the time.

I'm sorry to say that we have been unable to get a house yet and cannot build although we hope that restrictions will be lifted very shortly without much delay and then I will be able to give your young sister a home.

We have a son James Campbell who is supposed to be like me but I get a glimpse of you now and then. Susie's daughter Diana is a cracker with eyes as big as oranges and very brown.

Gran is well and bearing up wonderfully and still as keen as ever on the horses.

Your Mother has been wonderful Bill and if it hadn't been for her marvellous work with the 2/20 Comforts Fund would have gone to bits long ago. She has kept her spirits up very well and is preparing everything for your arrival. What a party it's going to be!!

I hope you are pastured in alright and that the Red Cross are as good as they have been. We have an 8th Div. Association going here and we are trying to get extra comforts for you all, the women have been splendid, Jeanie Ewart [wife of Arch], *Madge Linscott* [wife of John] *and Nell Merrett* [wife of Ron] *who we see most of are all so full of excitement that they don't know which way to turn.*

Give my very warmest wishes to Ron, Arch, Johnny Brooks, Rod Richardson and all the mob. We heard that Jimmy Lowe, Dick Cohen, Ken Hutton and young Howard P got it on the Island; I hope our reports were wrong and that they are okay.

[Capt. James Lowe NX35117, Major Richard Cohen NX499 and Lieut. Howard Porter NX12556 all died 9 Feb 1942, Lieut. Kenneth Hutton NX35003 died on 11 Feb 1942. They were all from the 2/20.][685]

Well Cheerio Bill old boy and I can't really tell you how terribly glad we will all be to see you
Cheerio
Mac.

...

Mrs. W. Keeling
243 Raglan Street, Mosman

Billy dear *19th August 1945*
At last we are allowed to write proper letters to you and there's so much to tell you that it's hard to know where to begin.

We can't wait to have you home and be prepared for a terrific ear bashing and lots of happy surprises, for we only need you home to make everything perfect.

Mummy has been wonderful during all these years. She has worked like a galley slave at the Comforts Fund, running it of course and running it well. And in between times taking care of Ginge and I and later our babies. Can you imagine us mothers or your self an uncle? We're very good mothers too and be prepared to be very much an uncle.

It will be three years on Wednesday since Warwick and I were married. We became officially engaged a year before that when Warwick left for England with the Air Force. I gave up the Rowe Street rat hole soon afterwards and joined the W.A.A.F. [Women's Auxiliary Air Force], *on 15 April 1942 and became an odd thing called an Office Orderly. But it carried a beaut blue uniform and cap, worn only on leave. During 'active service' we were extraordinary looking females in navy blue shapeless overalls. Mine shrank and there was a gap of 3 inches between pants and shoes. Luckily I was able to do a bit of string pulling and was able to stay near to home, at Bradfield Station just out of Lindfield, for I didn't want to go far away from Mum.* [Date of discharge was 24 September 1942].[686]

Warwick came home from England after only being away a year. The Japs were getting very close to us so they sent a Spitfire Wing out. We were married three days after he arrived and it's the best thing I've ever done. We're incredibly happy and we have an adorable devil's whelp Diana, she is just two. Warwick has spent two of the last three years away, he didn't see Diana till she was a year old and he's in Darwin now, but it won't be long before he's home for good.

You must have been happy to hear that you've got old David Mac for a brother in law. He and Ginge came to see me tonight. By the way I've been living with Mum until about a month ago when I managed to find a flat of my own, they are scarcer than gold. I'll try and fill up the rest of the space about non family, for no doubt you'll get all that from Mum and Ginge.

Old Connie Cay is still talking, maybe a little bit fatter but really unchanged.

The Waites at 55 are unchanged too, but they've given up boarders. Funny old Mr. Waite, Diana adores him and insists on kissing him no matter where we meet, will be returning soon and they are off up the mountains to live.

Tony Walter has just come home after being a POW in Germany for four years. Ginge and David saw him today and say he's improved out of sight. Both his sisters are married, the one that married that Burbury bloke who used to come to the old 17th turnouts has three kids already ... he couldn't talk much but ...!! [James Halley Burbury married Betty Eleanor Rutherford Walter in 1940.][687]

Henry Friend gave up at last and married Ruth Docker, poor Ruth has been busy having a baby every year ever since, the third is en route, and Henry rushing round in the Air Force, flying Liberators now.

[Henry Bell Friend, N74658 joined the Army from June to October when he re-enlisted in the RAAF and became a Flight Lieut with a new Service number of 34555.[688] He was a groomsman at Sue and Warwick's wedding.]

'Poop Face' Elaine Warren still about, in W.A.A.F. uniform now.

Mum is terrified she'll appear and grab you. Please steel yourself, we couldn't bear it.

David Bjelke was evacuated home from the Middle East early in the piece, badly shell shocked. He promptly married a little Floozy with lots of cash and has lived happily ever after.

[Captain David George Bjelke-Petersen, NX12211, was discharged from HQ 20 Australian Infantry Brigade on 24 September 1941 and married Joan Margery Lewis in 1942.][689]

Poor old Valhalla is almost in bits. I don't know what keeps it standing. Thank goodness we moved, you'll love this place, remember the odd room with all the glass windows we could see over the Valhalla fence, that is your room.

Roy Masters is a civilian, unwillingly, and Mrs. M says she wishes he really would realize that she isn't his batman and his daughters aren't troops.

So you see Bill you will find us all a little different and you will have so much to catch up, but you will be coming back to a much happier home than the one you left. For if we have changed then it's an improvement. Lots of the old faces will be around, none have forgotten you. So take care of yourself and don't worry about us. Being a grandmother

has given Mum a new joy in life, so just get yourself ready to come home to a lot of settled sane happy family and be loved.
Sue

Ruth Friend and Sue Keeling

When Bill left to go overseas the family was still reeling from the breakdown of Noel and Vera's marriage and his subsequent death with the resulting debts. In the ensuing years the debts had been settled, the girls had both found happiness in marriage and motherhood, Vera had grandchildren to enjoy and her beloved son had survived the war. Bill certainly would be returning to a much happier family.

Miss Betty Wilkinson
4 Belmont Avenue, Wollstonecraft NSW

My Dear Bill
20 August 1945

Well Bill I just can't tell you how pleased I am to think you will soon be home again. I am so looking forward to seeing you, we all are. Congratulations Bill.

We have been in touch with your Mother all the time; in fact Mum was speaking to her on the phone only this morning. All the family are very well and of course are very excited. Both of the girls seem very happy, married and have their wee babies. We haven't seen the babes yet but believe they are beautiful.

Peg is married too and has a baby son, he is such a sweet dear little chap. David has been up in Bougainville for over 18 months. Mum had a letter from him this morning and he says he is very well.

We often wondered if you saw anything of Charlie when you were both in No. 4 POW Camp, Thailand. We are hoping to get word from him soon. It is going to be wonderful when you are all home again. As you will see by the above address we are not living at Glenfield now. This is all I can write so will close for this time. Your Mother sends her love, so do all my family. Do hope you are well. Lots of love. Always yours,
Sincerely
Betty

...

Miss Elaine Warren
No. 3 Hillside Flats, Shellcove Road, Neutral Bay

Bill Dear *21 August 1945*

Even yet I cannot register the fact that the war is over, it has been so long. As I try to write this letter I am at a loss for words to express my feelings to you, knowing that at last you are freed from that ghastly Japanese tyranny. Although I have written you often, I am very doubtful if any of my notes reached you and am hoping that this one will.

Whether you feel the same towards me as you did I of course do not know. I naturally am hoping that you do, but realize that I must understand that it is possible that you don't, you are older now and in a position to know definitely one way or the other. I feel the same as ever towards you and have lived through these years with the knowledge that one day you would return.

I am now serving in the Women's Auxiliary Australian Air Force. I have not been in for many months and will not be for much longer now that the war is over. I am stationed at Point Piper, Sydney and come home often. [Elaine Hampton Warren, Service Number 178063, enlisted as an Aircraftwoman on 17 May 1945.][690]

I always thought that when peace was declared I would be overwhelmed with joy but instead it did not affect me, for on 2nd August my Father, who was on one of his trips away in the country, died unexpectedly, after just having examined the interior of a mine, from a heart attack. Daddy had always been in the best of health and we had no idea anything was wrong, the shock was frightful. I adored my Father and he was a wonderful Father to me and it will be sometime before I get over the fact that he is no longer here. [Percy Hampton Warren died at Queanbeyan on 2 August 1945.][691]

I have always had the feeling you would return and when you do I am hoping that you will wish to see me. As yet we have not had much news about you all over there but hope to soon. Hoping that you are as well and as happy as your present surroundings permit and that before long I will either see or hear from you.
With all my love
From Elaine

...

Gwen Clarke
17 Shell Cove Road, Neutral Bay

My Dear Bill *21 August 1945*

Well Bill I just had to drop you a short note to let you know we were all thinking of you when the excellent news came through last week. I do hope you are quite well and that it will not be long before we see you over our side of the water once more.

I'm sorry this note is so brief but have just noticed in the paper we could send letters now, so am writing before knock off time.

Mother and Dad are quite fit but Mother is feeling a little tired sometimes as she is still working at the Transport Office, they have kept going all this time and hope to continue for a while longer. Dad is very perky these days and gets around like a two year old, it's the good life he leads so the family tell him. [Gwen's father worked with Bill at Birt and Co prior to the war.]

I have no complaints but now and then moan a bit but think to myself there are lots worse off than I am, so pull myself together again.

Well Bill I shall have to go now but will write a longer note soon only I really had to let you know you were or should I say have not been forgotten in the Clarke household after all this time and we often speak about you.

Cheerio for the present and with all my good wishes for your speedy return to sunny Sydney; and a good boat trip to work each day.

Lots of love
Gwen Clarke

...

Connie Cay *21st August 1945*
44 Harriette Street, Neutral Bay

Well Bill old dear, it's just too marvellous to be able to write in an unrestrained manner. There's so much to tell you but just now our main thoughts are for your welfare and the longing to see you again. Gosh Whacko!!

Uncle Bill you, with your niece Diana Keeling, Sue's 2 year old daughter, a sweet soul, and nephew James Campbell MacDougal. Sue and Ginge are most happy whilst you will be equally so having David for a brother in law.

Your Mum is in the pink, was round to see her last Sunday morning week three days before the 'Big Day' when peace was announced. I've just been speaking to her as how to address this letter. Not until the poor dear has word from you can your Mum really let up as it's a very anxious time waiting to hear how you lads are.

You'll find many gaps after all these hideous years. One that will sadden you is our well beloved Broughton Head, Bicton [Bicton Clemence Wilson][692] *who said 'farewell' on 29th January 1945. Dear old Missie is just too sad, yet being wonderful. Various bouts of pneumonia, kidney trouble and gassing from World War I were responsible for ending Bicton's life at 64; it was less than a week thank goodness. What a character and so lovable.* [Bicton Clemence Wilson from Parramatta was a Church of England Chaplain (4th class) who embarked on 2 October 1915 on RMS *Moldavia*. He became head master of Broughton School until 1933 then he moved to St Luke's in Scone from 1935 until his death. He was the only incumbent to die in office.][693]

Bet you all, in your hearts if not outward, made 'Whoopee' last Wednesday as did the world. No wonder! Sydney went mad, why not, so did I, yet feeling sad for my sister Gladys Tindal whose lad Rick has seemingly gone. I'll enclose particulars just in case you could make some enquiries. Last letter card was received from Malaya about 2 years ago but last April Gladys was advised he had presumably died from illness in Thailand. No date or cause given and information was gathered from rescued lads from Hell-ship torpedoed Sep 12th 1944. Man who told authorities here said he had been told by another that Rick had died, all rather vague. Four days before various people had rung her after picking up a radio message saying he was well getting lots of [word unknown].

[Richard Travers Tindal NX 25015 of 2/15 Field Regt. died on 10 Nov 1943.][694]

Have still got the sherry waiting to be cracked, been in store since fall of Singapore. Ferry and ships tooted loudly after we heard the British PM broadcast. I joined in with my Norwegian bell on the lawn outside my verandah and drank to 'World Peace and speedy return of our lads'. With the Grants (front flat) toured the City in afternoon and again with the Grants and several others at night. Marvellous sights, radio stations at various points amusing the crowd, everyone sang, danced and yelled but hard on ones feet!! Our party of 8 consisted of 3 English, 3 NZ, and 2 Australians, good mixture. Delightful NZ Lieut. Colonel (Engineers) on his way back to India took charge of another lass and me and was a tower of protection and did so enter into the spirit of everything. Now it is all like a dream and all one prays is that this will be the end of all wars.

Oh your dear old Granny is still as game as ever.

Am longing to repost your parcel sent 29.12.41 as yet unopened and received back soon after fall of Singapore. Should so love you to get it before your return but if not you can collect it yourself.

Far as I know Gilbert Spence R.A.A.F. is the only lad from Broughton to collect a decoration.

[John Gilbert Spence of Newcastle, born 11 Nov 1919, next of kin Frederick Augustus Spence, enlisted 3 March 1941. He was a Fl. Lieut in the RAAF and in January 1944 was awarded a DFC, for 'large number of sorties at night as W/Op and A/Gunner' with RAAF 482.][696]

Several lads have given their lives unfortunately but many have come through unscathed thank goodness and been in from the jump. Paddy Cramer [RAAF 405676][695] *should be back from England soon, he'll have much to tell.*

Life for my own part has flowed on up hill and down dale and at present I'm enjoying some freedom after 2 1/2 years registration clerk in solicitor's office which cooked my cheap feet but I got to know city. Possibly I've been a fool as jobs of that nature don't hang on branches.

We're already missing the British Fleet not to mention weird and wonderful American ships that came and went. It's all been too exciting for words and how thankful I am not to be living up the [North shore railway] *line or somewhere. Possibly the most (or one of) perfect harbour view you get yourselves from that glorious drawing room window.*

Am so glad your Mum was able to move next door. No. 10 you know it from the Jones being there or isn't that their name. I mean the ones who'd lived in Formosa or nearly returned to S. Africa. You'll love your room Bill and everything about the flat as does your Mum.

Wonder how many of my letters have reached you. All your cards having been addressed to your previous flat rather looks as if all letters have been held from you, a ghastly thought and one that worried your folks and us all, as that alone would help you lads to hold on getting news from home. We've only just been told today that ordinary letters can be written. It was poisonous having to print them like a kid; bet you were all amused. Never mind it's over now.

I've still got my decorations up. Bunting was everywhere. Weather now is perfect, spring very much in the air. Conditions really have been wonderful, very few shortages really. We queue up for lots of things but its fairer and more orderly.

On V.P. Day at night we saw strings of people in a new queue at drinking fountains, poor throats were hoarse from shouting and singing.

Bet all the ferries will just about be hoarse when you lads return. Oh what a day that will be. Your Mum tells me Brian Badgery has died in Borneo; poor dears only heard last week.

Must scoot and catch the mail Bill. Oh it's too wonderful but what a nightmare these last 6 years have been and what for!

The wireless has been one long joy, so marvellous hearing what's happening everywhere. Peace celebrations in London were stupendous and no wonder.

Well my lad all the best. Your Mum is ringing me first news that comes from you direct.

All my love, a big cheerio and happy home-coming any day.

Yours affectionately
Connie Cay

So Bill was catching up with all the news from home. But what of his family? Were they getting any news from Bill?

668 Allies sink six prisoner laden ships < http://www.navalorder.org/09-Sep-99%20MistHist.PDF >
669 NSW BDM Index, 21667/1946.
670 *ibid.*, 5068/1966 and Williams, Patricia, Personal communication.
671 Gaden family history researched by the author.
672 DVA Nominal Roll.
673 Gaden family history researched by the author, DVA Nominal Roll and Warden, SCEGS Register, pp. II-263.
674 NSW BDM Index 30874/1946.
675 DVA Nominal Roll.
676 Gaden family history researched by the author.
677 NSW BDM Index 26480/1942.
678 *ibid.*, 18432/1940.
679 DVA Nominal Roll.
680 Johnstone, Jennifer, personal communication and Johnstone, *Reverend Thomas Johnstone*, p. 172. Photograph of Joan published with permission of Jennifer Johnstone.
681 Johnstone, Jennifer, personal communication.
682 DVA Nominal Roll.
683 *ibid.*
684 DVA Nominal Roll, CWGC and Warden, *op. cit.*, pp. II-184.
685 DVA Nominal Roll and Wall, *Singapore and Beyond.*
686 DVA Nominal Roll.
687 NSW BDM Index, 19728/1940.
688 DVA Nominal Roll.
689 DVA Nominal Roll and NSW BDM 9819/1942.
690 DVA Nominal Roll.
691 NSW BDM Index, 20192/1945.
692 *ibid.*, 5665/1945.
693 AWM, *First World War Nominal Roll*, <www.awm.gov.au/cms_images/awm8/6_6-3/pdf/0085.pdf>, and McLellan *History of the Parish of St Luke's Scone*, p. 107.
694 DVA Nominal Roll.
695 *ibid.*
696 DVA Nominal Roll and AWM <http://www.awm.gov.au/cms_images/awm192/00203/002030643.pdf>

Chapter 13 - Letters at last!

The family must have been beside themselves with worry that there was no tangible news from their beloved son and brother. Was he really still alive, had he been injured, was he 'whole'? The anticipation of finally receiving something in Bill's own handwriting would have been colossal.

DOUKIE DARLING BANGKOK 26TH AUGUST 1945

I SHALL SOON BE HOME. 'AND NOW SITS EXPECTATION ON THE AIR'. WE ARE FREE. LIFE IS REAL AND VITAL. WE FEEL YOUNG AND HAPPY GRIPPED BY THE SURGE OF RELIEF.

STORIES MUST WAIT FOR THE PRESENT. I AM WELL, WEIGHT 12 1/2 STONE.

ACHING TO SEE YOU, THE GIRLS AND MY NIECE AND NEPHEW.

LETTERS FROM YOURSELF (7), SUE (1), CONNIE (4) AGNES (1), ELAINE, THATCHER, WILKINSON.

ARCH AND RON M OK BANGKOK.

LOVE TO ALL
BILL

One can only imagine the shaking hands which opened the envelope, the trembling fingers which held the letter, the tearful eyes that devoured the words, the joy and relief that followed.

Mrs. V.L. Gaden
St Damien's
10 Raymond Road, Neutral Bay

Bill darling *28th August 1945*

We are counting the minutes until we hear how you are.

I have written one long letter to you letting you know all the news but feel it may miss you so will write a few more lines. You will have so much to hear and see when we meet again.

The main thing is we are all so well and your niece and nephew are such sweet wee things. Diana kisses Uncle Bill's picture every day, she is two, but Jamie MacDougal is only 8 months and thrills us all by clapping hands and waving goodbye. David and Elizabeth have written to you. Warwick is still in Darwin. It's grand the girls married such fine men, no more responsibility for you dear.

Birt and Co will be glad to see you, they have been terrifically busy all the war years and the Boss is the big man in this part of the world now.

This house has just been bought by George Davies and he is going to do it up through and through and not turn us out. You will love it. Poor old Valhalla is a wreck but has been bought recently and is going to be done over too. It was a grand move on the one part to leave when we did, we would be house hunting now with no houses to find. The Griersons are still there but it won't be for long I'm afraid.

Heaps of love and happy meeting very soon darling.
Doukie

...

DARLING DOUKIE BANGKOK 27TH AUGUST 1945

MY SECOND NOTE SINCE OUR RELEASE. STILL IN A WAREHOUSE AT (CENSORED). THE DAYS ARE PASSING SLOWLY BUT EACH HOUR BRINGS THE SHORE OF BLESSED AUSTRALIA CLOSER.

DECENT FOOD IS AVAILABLE; WE GORGE OURSELVES ON FRUIT, EGGS AND MEAT AND ARE HAPPY BUT IMPATIENT TO LEAVE THIS LAND OF UNPLEASANT MEMORIES AND DARK SKINS.

DARLING I THINK OF YOU AND THE GIRLS AND THEIR CHILDREN ALWAYS.
MY LOVE
BILL

Darling Doukie Bangkok 30 Aug '45

At the moment of writing I am in the most colossus warehouse you could possibly imagine. It is nearly 10pm but the noise and babble of excited voices is appalling. Somebody is pushing an accordion and hundreds yell with song. The excitement is terrific, we are waiting evacuation by aeroplane from Bangkok.

Today is Ginge's birthday. Heavens I wish I was home!

We are going to India before returning to Australia. Many people have already gone.

For the first time for years we have some new clothes, new boots, in fact we are only now making use of the American Red Cross supplies that have been kept away from us by the Japanese since November '42. Everything is a novelty. We are Rip Van Winkles from the jungle.

Civilians from Bangkok have now been released from their internment camps. They come to see us. Today a woman brought in a child aged about 4. The troops' reaction was amazing they patted and cuddled the kid for hours fighting for a chance to hold it. Many of them have children at home they have not seen. I thought of the two kids that I have not seen, bless them. They will soon know their mysterious uncle.

This is my third letter dear. The other two were written here and went by aeroplane to Rangoon. This will probably follow by the same route.

I came through the fight without a wound and all I have to show now is a scar or two from ulcers received in the jungle. Oh! I nearly forgot my appendix; that was removed in Thailand in Aug '43.

Sue's marriage in the Shore Chapel must have been wonderful - in Connie's letter she said you looked 'the perfect aristocrat'.

I was very pleased about Ginge and David - a wonderful match dear. The boys here who know David were all pleased with the news. It flashed up and down the camps of Thailand. People from all over the place told me but I heard it first from Ginge's own letter.

I sent you a cable today. The local agent of the P and O sent it for me.

We are itching to get out of this place. There are 34,000 of us; it will take a few more days.

The little snap you sent me of yourself and Diana is a treasure. Every now and again I take it out and look at it - it takes me right home.

Some of our officers are quartered in the city. They say Bangkok is a magnificent place. Somehow I can't become sufficiently interested to even walk up to town. I think always of home and remain completely divorced from the East. Perhaps it is only shyness. I run at the sight of a woman now whilst others flock around those that come to see us, so far I have avoided speaking to any of them. They are for the most part French, Eurasian anyway.

Darling you must have had a lot of worrying work squaring up the estate of father, Gran Gaden etc. I have been worried concerning your financial position because mine now seems satisfactory, but I just can't find a way of sending you money at all. From India it should be easy. I have no idea how much I have but it should be a fair lump.

A small leather wallet that Aunt Doris gave me is all I have left of the vast amount of luggage I departed from Australia with. The Japanese took the rest. We have lived in rags for years. My proficiency with a needle and thread like fishing line saved my few clothes from passing out altogether. Now I wear a new American uniform but just yearn for grey flannel bags and sports coat with a clean white shirt.

St Damien's [10 Raymond Road, Neutral Bay] sounds good. The move was a good one. Old Valhalla [8 Raymond Road, Neutral Bay].

Here the letter suddenly ends a quarter of the way down the page. We don't find out what he thought of 'Old Valhalla' or the reason why he did not return to finish the letter.

Darling Doukie — Bangkok 2 Sept '45

I have written several letters since we were released but this one is the first I know will travel to you through official channels.

Today I am in a warehouse in Bangkok .We have been here for two weeks, thousands of men, English, Australian, American, Dutch and heaven only knows what the others are composed of. Evacuation by air goes on every hour but our turn seems far off. Australians will leave by boat so the story has it at present. Our feet itch to be moving our hearts ache to be home once again with you. For the first time for 3½ years we have reasonable clothes and decent food.

The enormous concrete building echoes with the excited singing, yelling, cheering of men who cannot really believe they are free.

Japanese move about with bleak faces, tired unlifelike eyes, we know only too well how they feel. They know the price they will soon be called upon to pay. The judgment of the Lord must be just.

Bangkok is a really modern city. Definitely well laid out, spacious and clean. In times of peace this must be one of the most beautiful cities of the East. I have seen little of it but the occasional visits have been a rare pleasure.

Last night I talked for the first time with officers from the world outside. We are Rip Van Winkles from the jungle knowing very little of what the world has been doing during our period of captivity. They talk of new weapons, new songs, new dances, new clothes. We are being born again into a 'new world' and we feel the luckiest beings in it.

My health is OK, no wounds only a few scars from when in the jungle and Oh yes, one across my tummy where my appendix came out in August '43.

Both the girls' marriages are excellent news, that they have children I find hard to believe!

We hear very little Australian news. The wireless blares forth one hour of tripe for POWs each night. They say in a soppy sweet voice 'be patient, calm and wait just a little longer etc'. It makes us sick, we want to know how much your allotment is, the price of beer, tobacco and food, who will win the Melbourne Cup.

We have done our waiting, years of it, and are free now in a real world and are only interested in realities.

Please spread my love and regards to my old friends, Connie, you know them all.
My love and best wishes dearest
Bill

Mrs. Agnes Court, Kingdon Street, Scone
My Darling Bill *September 4th 1945*

I do hope we will be seeing you soon, it will be lovely to have you home again. You will find all sorts of changes since you went away with your two brothers in law and a niece and nephew. I am coming down to meet you when you arrive.

We are having some heavy frosts here. Scone looks beautiful. We have had a wonderful season, grass for miles. Joe is a working man now he is fifteen, works at the Advocate office learning to be a linotype operator. He is doing real well. Jim is still at School.

I have not seen Elizabeth's baby yet. I saw Susie's little girl, she is lovely.

Do you remember Noah Tanner? He got married to a girl in Perth, his wife and baby are over here with the Tanners. Ponty Spicer is married to Bob Mackay. She is living at Dungog. [In 1944 Robert Theodore Mackay married Jessie Elizabeth Hume Spicer.][697]

Well my dear boy I am overjoyed to think you will be home soon.
All our love
Agnes Court

...

Darling Doukie Bangkok 10 Sept 1945

This time I can write much more cheerfully. We live in really decent quarters, sleep in beds, smoke decent cigarettes and even have a drop of good old Scotch. Luxury beyond our expectations has at last fallen into our hands and we are fairly lapping it up. Still in Bangkok but now we occupy buildings that were used by the Thai university. The quarters are clean and comfortable.

Red Cross supplies are coming our way slowly but surely and all those normal amenities to civilization are arriving. There are hundreds of our troops quartered here with us and we nine officers have established a small but super mess. Chinese boys attend our needs and at last we feel clean normal beings, perhaps a little coarse in speech and feature but those attributes are fast departing. When I return you will not see much difference in my appearance.

We are to stay here in Bangkok for about 8 weeks and then fly to Singapore and catch a boat home. I find it hard to be patient.

The wireless is grand but heavens what a lot of rot they talk, especially about released prisoners and internees. The civilian internees in this city are a good crowd. They have provided us with many a party. Conditions in their 'camp' were not really bad and they have weathered the storm quite well. The Thais have seen to their welfare. The couple of hundred internees include people of all ages from babies to the limit. Kids that were 'run in' when Singapore fell are now grown young men and women. Some even married in the camp which is a poor name for a collection of rather excellent buildings.

I always thought that when released we would be returned home and most certainly not do any more work. Things have turned out differently; we are working hard administrating ourselves and troops coming in. We have all gone back to our old jobs so to speak. The boys drive trucks and stand guard with weapons as if nothing had happened.

When possible I shall send you cash. That may not be for some weeks, we have not been able to establish pay offices as yet.

Every hour I think of you all. Please spread my regards to Connie, Sue, Ginge and their kids. No mail has turned up from you but I know it is coming as fast as planes can carry it.
For the present darling cheerio.
My love
Bill

Sue Keeling

243 Raglan Street, Mosman

Date unknown, but the contents suggest before 12th September

Willy darling

We're still waiting to hear news of you, but it must come soon.

Diana and I went round to see Mum today. Ginge and David and young James have packed up and gone to stay with her for a while. Poor Kids they are both fed up with living in other people's houses but the housing shortage is incredible, people living in boatsheds just anywhere there is a roof. Can't you see everyone rousing on to the ruddy government, not that it's much help. Still we haven't had a bad war; plenty of food; meat, butter, sugar and tea have been rationed and clothes of course, but we've had no meatless days nor have we gone cold.

Gran was there too today, she's just the same Bill, spent the afternoon with an ear to the wireless, races at Randwick today and an eye on her great-grandchildren. On V.P. Day, when we stayed soberly at home, Gran tore into town where seething masses celebrated and danced in the streets, and stayed there all day without a bite to eat and had a wonderful time - and she's eighty if she's a day!

I saw Connie today. Poor old Con had most of her money invested in rubber or tin shares, she has had to get back to work. She had a job in a solicitor's office, glorified office boy for quite a while but had to give it up for she got so tired running messages. Now she comes to Mrs. Johnston who lives in the back flat and does her housework and cooks her breakfast and lunch and so earns a few bob. She sends her love to you, her white haired boy.

Thank goodness we left Valhalla when we did. It has been gradually falling apart ever since. Mrs. Grierson's balcony has been unsafe for over a year, no longer can she go out and peer at the neighbours and ships. Nor will her front window work, she went to push one up one day and the woodwork on the wall crumbled and she was left holding the bottom pane!

At last the old landlord MacPhee died. Remember how Mum dosed him with her precious whisky when he fell up the steps! And the place was sold.

Now the Griersons have been asked to leave, the new owner wants the place himself. Poor old Dolly is in a dither. Gordon is off to Singapore with the occupational forces and happy about it. He has done a wonderful job; he's been in an AIF wireless unit and has been on most of the island campaigns and working part time with the Yankees. You won't know him Bill, he's full of life, has stories and as happy as a lark and never stops talking! And it's all worth listening to! [Charles Gordon Grierson NX190190 of 5 W/LESS SEC.][698]

Little Ray Walker comes to see us whenever he's on leave. He went to the Middle East with the ack-acks and was transferred to water transport when they came home. He's in some special branch of that, they snoop around in small sea going launches and map and take photos, not a pleasant job at all. Colin had been in the Navy in England and has seen plenty of fun too. [Ray Osbourne Walker (NX80836) enlisted in Neutral Bay and Colin Osbourne Walker (RAN S/6627) both had Keith as next of kin.][699]

Mum had David at work this afternoon digging out a hydrangea bush. It has grown peacefully for thirty years or more and had roots about as big as the stump we all took out at Valhalla. Poor old David, but alone he did it.

We had photographs taken for you last week, so you'll be getting some soon. There's been a film shortage and so we haven't taken any snaps for ages. But these will be ready very soon and will send them straight on.

We see a lot of Madge Linscott, Jack Linscott's wife and we're all fond of her. As yet she's had no word of him either. [Capt. John Robertson Linscott, NX70193 was eventually discharged from the 2/20 Bn. on 19 Sept 1949.][700]

Well Billy dear, no more tonight, so ta-ta for now love!

That Betty Payne is married to a Hardon, of course and has a son, in fact she's had two but the first died when it was born. Saw Peggy Walter and her brat yesterday, she spent her nine months with her nose in an illustrated medical book, just finding out where it was up to and produced a two pound tadpole! There must have been some pages missing!

Tons of love
Sue

The general population suffered restrictions which were quite severe. They had to have an identity card and there was rationing of food including meat and clothes, tobacco and alcohol and petrol. Many people grew vegetables in their gardens. The arrival of 120,000 American troops meant the arrival of cigarettes, chocolates and silk stockings to impress the local girls. The Americans were 'over paid, over sexed and over here' much to the chagrin of the Australian troops and civilian men still in Australia.[701]

According to the NSW Birth, Death and Marriage Indexes, there were no Hardon marriages in the 10 years from 1935-1945 and only 15 Harden, 36 Haydon and 40 Hayden marriages. None married a Payne. As Betty Payne was a former Scone friend, it is very likely that Payne would be the correct surname for the bride. There were 306 Payne marriages with one in 1939 when Mary Elizabeth Payne married George Haynes in Forbes (16100/1939); in 1944 Mary Elizabeth Payne married Thomas Mitchell Hale in Muswellbrook (11061/44) and another Mary Elizabeth Payne married Thomas Mitchell Hale in Sydney also in 1944 (14061/1944). Which, if any, is the couple Sue refers to? The other former friend mentioned in the letter, Peggy Walter, was Margaret Rutherford Walter who had married John Gavin Rutherford Drummond in 1942 (19580/1942).[702]

I CABLE 693 RANGOON
12 SEPT 1945
GADEN ST DAMIENS 10 RAYMOND ROAD NEUTRAL BAY
ARRIVED SAFELY AT INDIA HOPE TO BE HOME
SOON WRITING ADDRESS LETTERS AND TELEGRAMS
TO AUSTRALIAN RECEPTION UNIT BANGALORE INDIA COMMAND
BILL

Mrs. V.L. Gaden
St Damien's, 10 Raymond Road, Neutral Bay
Bill darling *12th September 1945*

Your cable sent Elizabeth and me wild with excitement when it arrived this morning and also glad to see you knew the new address at last. We know now that you have received mail and are longing to get your first long letter and learn what you know.

We have all written c/- Army base P.O. since the surrender so those letters should chase you to earth soon.

David is wondering what you will think of him as a brother in law and feels rather worried at living here for the present. Well I know how glad you will be to know the girls are so happily married to the men being all we could wish for. Their little children are lovely and you will soon see. Diana Keeling is two and a bit and has brown eyes and hair and is like both Sue and Warwick, and Jamie MacDougal is a tiny edition of David, very blonde with blue eyes. He is 9 months old and trying so hard to walk alone.

A miracle happened and Sue got a tiny flat at Balmoral, so the others came to live here to keep me company. They were living with the Cormack aunts at Mosman since Xmas 1944. It is impossible to get a cottage or flat, the demand is a million times greater than the supply and just as hard to buy land to build on if one could build at present.

When you write to David tell him it will be nice to have him here; you will both have so much to tell. His exploits in China are most interesting and he was acting Lieut Colonel at 23!!! [David's date of birth was 18 June 1918], *but came down to Major on his return here. He's out of the army now and back at the Permanent Trustee and has settled down well.*

I rang Birt and Co and everyone was so pleased and said how glad they will be to see you on your return.

Mrs. Wilkinson is all thrills and waiting to hear about Charlie. He was moved to Fukuoka in Japan and she has had letters and cable from him recently but not since V.J. Day.

[Lieut] *Tony White* (NX35100), [Capt.] *Frank Gaven* [NX34885], [Major] *Bill Carter* [NX34852], [Major] *John Fairley* [NX34719 were all in the 2/20 Bn][703] *are some that are in Kuching, Borneo and well but poor old Brian Badgery died last November somewhere in Borneo. It is so awful for Mick and Marg as you can imagine.*

The men have started to arrive home by plane. I hope you will come in a comfortable ship dear. The sea trip will do you good.

Old Tony Walter is home just the same as ever. No doubt Elizabeth has told you of his welcome home party she and David went to.

How are you yourself? I expect I will soon have a letter. The telephone has gone ceaselessly since your news has got abroad. John Brookes is well and in Singapore. [John Henry Brookes NX38735 was with the 2/11 General Hospital.][704]

Gordon Grierson is going to Singapore with an entertainment unit. He is a radio expert now.

We are getting your room ready dear. It is the one with the round end nearest Valhalla and perfectly charming. You can lie in bed and look all over the harbour, you will love it Pet. And can enter by the verandah door when you come in with the milk!! and disturb no one.

Elizabeth is off to town now and will post this at the GPO. Your friend Mr. Hart is still there. Mother is well and all thrills. Sue told Mr. Waite the news yesterday and he was so excited he was incoherent for minutes. Mother is still at 'Tara'.

Lee Sautelle's husband is presumed dead. Poor old Lee she has been wonderful and is now a Red Cross official. [Lee (Ellen Bentley) Sautelle had married Charlton Fallaw in 1940. He was a Captain with the 2/19, NX34869, and had died on 22 January 1942, when the 2/19 were trying to take the bridge at Parit Sulong.][705]

Dick Gaden has turned up but no news of John yet [two of Bill's cousins, sons of Ida and Thomas Burton Gaden].

I will write again tomorrow dear and send some snaps if possible; films have been almost non existent. Heaps and heaps of love dear
From
Doukie

Elizabeth MacDougal
10 Raymond Road, Neutral Bay

Darling Bill *Wednesday 12th* [Sept 1945]

Today at 11.25 a.m. your cable arrived and boy it was good. Ma literally snatched it from the postboy. No good trying to describe the excitement, telephone has been going all day. We sent a telegram to Agnes and by the amount of telegrams received tonight she has spread the news all over the district in no time at all.

Warwick arrived yesterday from Darwin on a months leave and Diana follows him like a dog. At 5.30 a.m. today they were wide awake and playing together. You can imagine how Sue would appreciate that.

Tonight Gran has been up. As you can see David, James and I are around here now. Did you get an awful shock when you heard? Think we get a bit of one ourselves!!

David is in town tonight at an 8th Div. meeting, has had a couple of interviews lately with Minister for Army, Forde, and as a result of it some of the nurses who escaped were included to go over on reception unit, also some of 8th Div. blokes. Think they mostly went to Singapore. In original draft only one was included although dozens had applied. Fat-belly Blamey does not like Bennett and Bennett stands for 8th Div. therefore you are all included. Gee he is disliked (Blamey I mean). However enough of that.

How are you feeling, gosh it will be grand to have you home again. David and I are still looking for a house but it is impossible. Sue was terribly lucky, interfering mother-in-law got it for her. [Sue's mother-in-law was Mrs Alexander John Keeling, formerly Jessie M. Stigings. They lived at Zweena, Spit Road, Mosman.][706]

Mick and Marg were awfully thrilled when I told them but Marg's voice was beginning to crack by the time she said 'good bye'. Poor old Brian was in Borneo.

Was speaking to young Jean Ewart today, she is a grand kid, her mother (Mrs. Ross) came to my rescue and made my wedding dress one weekend when we thought David was arriving from Queensland but then his leave was cancelled. Gosh it was funny. Even had the cake here. Luckily leave came 3 weeks later so although the icing was dulled and a bit soft it was pretty good.

Sue was a WAAF when Keelo arrived from England one Tuesday and they were married on the Saturday. I bought her frock, a cracker; Bruce Beale (since killed) and Henry Friend were best man and groomsman. [Flying Officer Francis Bruce Beale, Service No. 402842, son of Francis Joseph and Myrtle Gwendoline Beale was killed 28 May 1943, aged 26, Panel 6 Northern Territory Memorial.][707]

Henry married Ruth Docker and their third is on the way! Just as well Sue didn't!

Think I will have to make this do for tonight Bill and will scratch again tomorrow, but it is 11 p.m. now and Jamie will be wide awake by 6 a.m. and he is a handful, so goodnight old boy and sleep and sleep.
Tons of love from all 3,
Ginge

...

Connie Cay
44 Harriette Street, Neutral Bay

Well Bill old dear *September 12th 1945*

This has indeed been a red letter day for your dear Home folk and all of us who have anxiously waited for actual word from you. Now it's come and, as on surrender day, one feels weak with joy. As you can imagine it's just been hell for your dear brave Mum, Sue and Ginge these many long years, but none of us ever gave up hope.

It was wonderful to see your Mum today, full of pep, smiles. I trot round to Mrs. Johnstone's every morning to cook her dinner etc and so got the joyful news direct from your Mum. Directly I heard her calling 'You there Mrs. Johnstone?' out I dashed, feeling all was well. 'Oh Con I've had a cable from dear old Bill. He's safe and at Rangoon etc. etc.' A huge embrace I feel spoke volumes from me. After a bit I went along and saw Ginge who was bubbling over with joy as was her Jamie. Next excitement was when Sue and either her or Ginge's in laws dashed in to make merry with your Mum. It was good to hear the shrieks of joy and laughter. I've not seen Granny Balcombe yet but Mrs. Barton travelled back from town with her and told me how overjoyed the old dear is. Now your Mum can hop into bed knowing you are safe and soon she'll be seeing you. Would to God [my] *sister Gladys Tindal could hear news of her Rick.*

What's so lovely is knowing at last you boys have received letters, if even years old, about some home news that has been gathered.

Tonight I heard the Melbourne journalist Rivett speak from Melbourne, all terribly interesting and comforting to so many thousands. What a help the wireless has been to everyone, even to you lads whilst guarded by those evil devils.

Wonder if you have received my letter sent airmail through Red Cross on August 16th or 17th. What I have here is your parcel returned after the fall of Singapore. Today I listened to the surrender terms read by Admiral Lord Louis Mountbatten and signed by the yellow slit eye. Heard the 'Missouri' broadcast also, all most interesting. [The broadcast of the official signing of the surrender by the Japanese onboard the USS *Missouri* on 2 September 1945.]

Were you very surprised to hear David MacDougal is now your brother in law, as is Warwick Keeling. Diana Keeling is a perfect reproduction of Sue yet at first she was so like Warwick but on Saturday when Sue walked through the gate with her I couldn't help remarking to Sue 'Now I've seen you in your youth'.

Snowy haired James Campbell is David's double and a most quaint little soul. David has put on weight of late. They are a happy pair as are Sue and Warwick.

Beth will be thrilled to hear you'll soon be home as will Wes. They are both in Melbourne at present, he being in charge of Army food lab.

Fear you'll find lots of old faces missing one way and another, war casualties and otherwise, among them being our beloved Bicton Wilson who left us on January 29th after less than a week's illness. Kidney trouble, heart and gas recurrences from World War I. The awful gassing he got in France and several bouts of pneumonia last few years in Scone really were the cause of his premature death only 64. I just can't believe he's gone. Missie is being very brave. Oh how relieved she'll be to hear you're safe.

I'm off to bed now Bill but just want to send you a big heap of love and cheerio before going shut eye. Whacko!! What a day it will be when you set foot on Neutral Bay terra firma again. Not long now, glorious thought. At last the day is dawning when my four year old (least that's how long it's been in my linen cupboard) bottle of sherry can be cracked. It will be your honour to draw the cork!!

Gosh I'm going to throw a Gaden party, am going to Lapstone on October 23rd for 10 days, first holiday for 6 years. Do hope you get home long before that date.

Until the big day all the best Bill, don't worry about your Mum, she's in the pink and oh so happy now she's heard from you and will I feel sure have your bed made up tomorrow. You'll love your room in fact every inch of the flat. And you're all returning to gorgeous weather and a big welcome.
See you soon, in the meantime take care of yourself Bill old lad.
Yours affectionately
Connie Cay.

Gwen, Nell and Stuart Clarke
17 Shell Cove Road, Neutral Bay

My Dear Bill — *12 September 1945*

Well Bill I really don't know quite what to say but when Dad rang me this morning and told me he had just heard about your release I just could not settle down to work again until well after lunch.

It's the best news we have had for a long time and believe me we have been hoping to hear that you were safe. I'm very pleased.

Dad rang your Mother this evening and had a chat to her and then I spoke and after hearing the cable and the address I thought I would drop you a note straight away, but I believe it is going to be a community affair as both the folk are going to put a fast note.

I do hope you are going to enjoy a bit of comfort until your trip home and I suppose it won't be so very long before you come to sunny Sydney again.

I do hope you are reasonably well after your hardships, however our sunshine and good food will soon pick you up again.

You will in all probability be able to do some sailing this season and of course, surfing. I'm rather looking forward for the summer to come this year myself as I have hope of doing a fair bit of swimming, our pool down the front is not very shark proof at the moment but later I will go down at low tide and do a bit of hammering up.

We are having very warm days at present and by the looks of things a very early spring this year, as the flowers and gardens up the North Shore line are just perfect.

I had a very enjoyable trip last Sunday afternoon to Kuringai. The padre (or rather in the Navy they call them Chaplain) took seventeen British Navy lads for a trip and of course called on Mother for transport, so five loads set off. We had afternoon tea at the Sphinx and the boys boiled the billy and it was great. The lads enjoyed every minute of their outing and hoped it would not be the last as they all like the Australian bush. I have had one or two days outings in the bush lately. We have not been able to go very far but far enough to boil the billy and grill chops.

Mother has been for a very nice drive today and she called in on our friends at Wallacia, in fact we are going there this coming weekend. Pop's coming too so I'll put in his music for him as he has done quite a lot of playing over the last couple of years.

Well Bill I will have to go now and I'm really very, very pleased to hear the good news and it will be better still when you come back to the Bay again, we will be looking forward to seeing you.
Love
From Gwen.

...

Dear Bill

Great news and seeing that Gwen has told you all the gossip I will give you a bit of sport.

Football - the Grand Final next Saturday 15th is between University and Parramatta at North Sydney No. 1 with the odds on Parramatta. I saw Randwick play both of these sides and my tip is Parramatta. Randwick's display against both of these sides was disappointing although from all accounts the Wicks had a lot of casualties and cracks against Unis last week.

League football is booming, large crowds and big dividends for the players. Eastern Suburbs carried off the major Premiership with Balmain, Newtown and Wests finishing in that order.

Sailing - All the sailing races were conducted up the harbour in and around the Lane Cove and Parramatta Rivers. The Yachts did not sail at all.

Cricket - Last year the Clubs reverted to 2 day games but prior to that one day was the vogue, daylight saving was in force then but the clock was not put back, the Association was obliged to come back to the old style.

Office - with the exception of Lance Crowther, lost in Jap waters after coming through all the European business, [Lance Crowther RAAF 403560 died 6 April 1945.][708] *and Watson lost in Europe also, the rest of the mob are OK to date. We have not heard from Ron Eaton* [Lieut Ron Eaton of 2/30 Bn., NX70758, also a prisoner of the Japanese].[709]

Fred Harrison and Win Harper [John Winston Harper, NX120250] *are over in India somewhere with the Ministry of War Transport, Alan Fraser, Geoff Johnson also were posted and served about 2 years but are back again. Nell wants a bit of room for her little greeting so until we see or hear from you, all the best.*

Stuart.

PS I called in and told the King's (next door), needless to say, delighted.

...

Dear Bill

They can't leave me out so just a few lines to say how pleased we are to get the good news that you are safe and I hope you will soon be on your way home. Your mother was almost too excited to speak on the phone tonight and I'm not a bit surprised. The waiting to hear news of you boys has been a terrible strain to all the mothers but we all know the waiting has been much worse for you lads, and now it is all over we now wait your arrival. Until then good luck, good health and good sailing.

Kindest regards

Nell Clarke

...

Sue Keeling
243 Raglan Street, Mosman

Billy dear *13 September 1945*

It's an incredibly happy time for us all for yesterday came your cable and today your letters and we were among the first to hear, more than we had dared to hope.

Yesterday morning I was pottering round the flat in a bit of a daze when I heard Mrs. Gifford calling that I was wanted on the phone. I haven't a phone on yet and had given the Gifford's number to both Mum and the Keeling's should they want me urgently. This was the first ring and of course I thought of you and never have the stairs seemed so long, and it was the news we've waited so long to hear. Mummy was too overcome with sheer joy and relief to talk so it was Ginge who read me your cable and we laughed and wept together.

I was excited already for Warwick had arrived home from six months in Darwin the day before and when I'd rung off I didn't know what to do, such happiness was almost too much to bear. Warwick was out, he had to go up to Bradfield and didn't know when he'd be back. I had to tell someone and the other people from the flats were in the front garden and they were almost as excited as I was. We were all nattering and jumping about when a car drew up with a scream of brakes and out rushed David's two aunts. He'd rung them so they dropped their brooms and tore down to collect Diana and I to take us round to see Mum. The two old dears, they were as happy as though you'd been their own. Diana was having her morning sleep so we pulled her out of bed and shoved her on the pot and then into the car and off to St. Damien's, collecting some flowers on the way. Mummy looked radiant. Both she and Ginge had been trying to collect their scattered wits to send wires but they couldn't stand still for long enough to even write names down. Oh Bill it was a day.

Warwick and Diana and I hopped round for a while this afternoon too, the phone rang all the time, either telegrams or people to say how happy they were for your name was in the Herald this morning. Not just the people we expected either, while we were there a long distance call came from Gosford. It was a chap called Darling (I think); he was in your Company. He's working in the goods shed there and could hardly wait to knock off time to ring! Wasn't it good of him?

The Waites were very excited. We saw Mr Waite pottering down the road when the aunts drove us down yesterday and I yelled for them to stop and tumbled out and grabbed him. Oh Billy he was happy. We held hands!

Old Bill Delory (I never can spell that name) rang this afternoon too. He has just come home and taken unto himself a wife after three years in England with the RAAF.

The wires from Scone came thick and fast. We sent one to Agnes and asked her to ring the Badgery's and Throsby's. She must have stood on Campbell's corner - yelled - for everyone knew and wires came from half the district last night, from the Cowdreys, old Mary and Pen, the Firths and so many more.

Birt and Co's were very happy. Mum rang of course and they rang back to say Sir Thomas had cabled you and that should we want to send anything they'd fix it up.

So you see Billy dear, it's rather a wonderful world really and you'll find many happy welcomes when you come home. And how wonderful it will be to have you back. Warwick sends you his love though he's sure you won't remember him, I'm sure you will, I'll be hurt if you don't. No more darling, a big kiss to Billy from Diana.
Cheers, Much love
Sue

Campbell's Corner in Scone was named after Malcolm Campbell who began trading in the town in 1880. He moved from his original store to one which was destroyed by fire in 1909. It was rebuilt and the store remained there until 1928[710] when the fourth store was opened on Kelly Street, the Old Northern Road through Scone. This was the one which became known as Campbell's Corner. It was the largest store in the town and even today, with the family long gone, the corner is known as Campbell's Corner.[711]

Bangkok [Date unknown, but the ink suggests close to the middle of September]
Darling Doukie

Tonight I dined, wined and had a very excellent dinner at a superb hotel in Bangkok. This is the first occasion that I have used fish knives, soup spoons etc. and was agreeably surprised to find that handling such unaccustomed tools was not difficult.

News has just come over the air that a party of fellows I sent from this building some days ago has arrived home, the first men from the area to reach Australia. It makes me feel impatient to be moving but this cannot be helped, my turn will come.

The men are now dressed in jungle green uniforms; they look fine and have lost their POW look. In fact it really is extraordinary how quickly the fellows have returned to 'normal'. Good food and clean clothes has worked a miracle.

Daily I walk and drive through Bangkok. I told you in a previous screed that the city was good and now have more details. There are some streets with large buildings far more modern than those of Sydney. The shops in those areas are magnificent to look at but there is always something lacking, such as beautiful taps through which no water will run, bottles of glorious foreign perfume decorate windows but inside you can't buy anything but cheap 'scents'. I have literally searched the place for a pair of shoes and cannot find a pair large enough when in shops as palatial as DJs.

Behind these beautiful shops there exists abject squalor. Beautiful clean looking girls are terrifically dangerous so our troops are finding out.

I shall not be sorry to leave Bangkok and return home to you all. The aeroplane can't come quick enough for me.

Cheerio darling
Love Bill

...

Doukie dear, Bangkok Sept, after 13th

Today I received a personal cable from Sir Thomas Gordon. Decent of him wasn't it!

I have no news but a few minutes to spare so here goes for a few lines meaning nothing.

Two English V.A.D.'s [Voluntary Aid Detachment, a branch of the Red Cross] turned up in our camp this afternoon. They got lost and were directed to us. We were only too pleased to produce cups of tea and gather round the girls like a pack of buzzards. Eventually we had to take them back to their hospital reluctantly.

Our Chinese boys turned on an act after their departure. They considered it their job to hand around the tea cups but they had been told to get to hell and we had waited on the girls, literally fighting each other for the privilege, such is life.

The dammed wireless alarmed us last night by broadcasting horror stories of fighting and shooting in Bangkok. We are in no danger whatever; the shooting was only a minor show between Chinese bandits and the Siamese police.

Our evacuation seems to be speeding up. More planes are on the job. We are told that all of us will be out by October 3. I was hoping to be home for your birthday and it looks as if that may still be possible.

Mail is coming in at last. I have two letters of yours and many others from various people at home including Ginge, Sue, Connie Cay, Betty Wilkinson, David and one or two others. Gran must have had a wonderful time on V Day. Sue writes an excellent letter full of news and very bright like yours.

Poor old Brian has gone. I did not even know he was in Borneo. Mick and Marg must be very cut up about it.

So you have Ginge and David with you. Sue says you have been making David work in the garden. That is good oh! All the best for a while. My regards to all dear,

Cheerio Love
Bill

Thomas Gordon, the man who sent Bill the cable, joined Birt and Co in 1902 and became Chairman and Managing Director in 1929. He was a member of the Shipping Control Board and, from December 1939, the representative in Australia of the British Ministry of Shipping (War Transport). He was Director of Shipping in the Department of Supply and Shipping from 1942, controlling all shipping in Australian waters. He resigned in 1945.[712] He was a keen golfer and no doubt it was at the Golf Club that he met another keen golfer in Bill's grandfather Edward Ainsworth Gaden, a solicitor who dealt in shipping matters, and they arranged the job for Bill at Birt and Co. in 1934.

14 SEPT 1945
POSTAL ACKNOWLEDGEMENT DELIVERY PERSONAL
MRS VERA LYDIA GADEN
ST DAMIENS FLATS, 10 RAYMOND ROAD, NEUTRAL BAY

IT IS WITH PLEASURE I HAVE TO INFORM YOU THAT NX12543 CAPT EDWARD WILLIAM GADEN PREVIOUSLY REPORTED PRISONER OF WAR IS REPORTED ALIVE IN SIAM.
26 AUG 1945 ADDRESS LETTERS LIBERATED AUST PW CARE 2 AUST PW RECEPTION GP AUSTRALIA
ANY FURTHER INFORMATION RECEIVED WILL BE COMMUNICATED UPON RECEIPT
MINISTER FOR THE ARMY
IO IOB

Sue Keeling
243 Raglan Street, Mosman

Billy darling *18 September 1945*

We've had three letters from you now, everyone has been read over and over again, for it's still hard to believe they are real.

We're longing for you to come home, there's so much to show you and tell you. I knew you'd be happy about our weddings and you'll love our children. They are both devil's whelps but adorable. Diana and I spent the whole day with Mum. We arrived at nine this morning to read your newest letters, one came yesterday and the others today and to hear about the two 8th Div. men David brought back to stay last night. They had been among the first to arrive home. They came by air reaching here on Sunday. They were both South Australian and weren't continuing their journey till today. Mummy loved having them; they had been working on the Burma railway and then sent down to Changi. Both were very fit and so completely happy to be in a home, to put their noses in the kitchen, have a hot bath, play with Jamie and sit by the fire and then to sleep in a bedroom. One slept in the sitting room, the verandah didn't appeal so they brought the bed in!

David is doing a wonderful job, he is a grand person. He's been meeting trains and planes. Today he and General Bennett met a train bringing men down from Cairns. They were thrilled to see the General and cheered wildly. You'll think that only natural but it's all a very long story. Poor old Bennett was given a rotten spin by the shiny arses here, forcing him to resign. For a while public opinion ran hot against him but not now. He's always been our hero, Mum's especially, for he told her he remembered you soon after he came home.

The letters and telegrams from people hearing of your release have made an alarming pile, alarming because poor Mum has to answer them all! But it's been good getting them; one came from Penny Fussell today, now a sister in the Gunnedah Hospital; and a funny little girl, a W.A.A.F. from Bradfield days who has been in Melbourne for the last two years, rang today, she saw your name and remembered.

Oh Bill, you'll love being home. No more worries or fussation - both Ginge and I happy and sensible and so efficient!! And Mummy happy - no jumps any more. Our babies have done more to help her through these years than anything. 'MumNanny' Diana calls her - they love her and she loves them. We took lots of snaps in the garden today and will send them to you as soon as they are developed. Mum took the film into town so they shouldn't be long.

No more - there's so much to tell you I can't get round it all. Judy Sayers sends you her love, she came to see me this afternoon.

With tons of love from
Warwick, Diana and Sue

...

Betty Wilkinson
4 Belmont Avenue, Wollstonecraft
My dear Bill *18 September 1945*

Well I hope that by the time you receive this letter you have already received a couple of others from me. Above all I hope you are on your way home, it is almost too wonderful to believe that you and Charlie will soon be home. We had a Red Cross message from Charlie last month and it was sent on the 13th of August from Fukuoka POW camp and he said he was well and hoped for an early reunion, that is the last word we have had, but of course we are hoping every day to get word of him.

I am writing at work, hence the awful paper and the scribble but is fairly quiet here and I have quite a bit of time to myself although during that time I am up and down attending to people.

In my last letter I told you we were going to an American Tea at the 2/20 Comfort Fund Rooms, well we went in and of course your Mother was there and I don't think she has missed any of the meetings, she has been wonderful. At the meeting your Mother showed us some photos of your little niece and nephew and really they are such dear little children. I feel sure you will love them when you see them. Also Peg's baby, he is 5 months old and is just full of life, he is named Ian Robert. I told you in my last letter all about him so I won't tell you again. Peg's surname is now Arrowsmith, Bruce her husband comes from South Australia; he is in the Bank of N.S.W. in Civvy life in South Australia, so Peg will be going over there to live, but at present he is a Captain in the AIF up on Bougainville but he expects to be home the first week in November, it is going to be a race between he and Charlie to see who gets home first. [Robert Bruce Arrowsmith SX26063, Captain with 16 Australian Army Ordnance Depot on his discharge in May 1946.][713]

We went into Martin Place on Sunday and saw the lot of POWs arrive home; it was wonderful to see them back again even though we didn't know any of them.

We have been having some beautiful weather but today is quite cool again, in fact I am sitting here shivering.

Mum and I are going into town this afternoon, we want to get some new curtains for our balcony. We are well and truly settled in to our home here; we moved here 4 years ago in November; it is a nice big house with plenty of ground around it and we have our cat and dog and some fowls. Well Bill I must close now. We will be looking forward to seeing you soon.

Tons of love. Yours sincerely

Betty

Mrs. V.L. Gaden
10 Raymond Road, Neutral Bay
Bill Darling *19th September 1945*

All 4 letters have arrived from Bangkok. It is wonderful to know you are well and 'whole'.

Now I will tell you all you want to know.

I have been getting £7-14-0 allotment per fortnight and last week the military have raised the dep. allowance to 2/6 per day instead of 2/- on account of the MacDougal family being with me. They are paying £3 per week so we manage beautifully. I have kept your insurance policies up to the mark twice yearly and have the furniture and personal belongings insured against fire, burglary etc. also had a war list policy during the dangerous years. I have banked £50 for you in your pass book you left behind and the military allotment is in a separate thing at the bank. I also have £20 in War Bonds for you dear.

We have fared very well really during the war. Meat, butter, sugar and tea and of course clothing have been rationed. We have the coupon books and can manage alright. The allowances are quite adequate.

The family were lucky to have had no shortages of food during the war because rural Australia had been in the grip of a drought. It was so bad that the *Sydney Morning Herald* commissioned artist Russell Drysdale to accompany a reporter looking at the 1944 drought in outback NSW. Many men who found themselves without work had signed up to join the AIF ... there was even some suggestion that by joining the AIF their families would at least get an income from their allotment. Prime Minister John Curtin recognised the importance of the rural struggle. In 1943 he said that the war would be won in the factories and farms as much as on the battlefields and American President Roosevelt agreed that 'Food is a weapon of war'. But people were needed to produce that food. Before the Second World War rural workers numbered 416,000, by 1943 the number had declined by 32% to 284,000. The women and children left behind had to run the farms. On top of their new responsibilities the fearful families also worried and wondered each day about their loved ones fighting overseas.[714]

Doukie's letter continued:

Beer, wine and spirits are very hard to get, there is no such thing as walking into a hotel and buying it. W. Keeling gave Sue and me a bottle of Scotch to celebrate 'peace' with, and the Shellshears have given us some wine for your homecoming. I often crave for a gin and lime!!! and will be glad when we can have it again.

We had a dress circle view of our one big thrill of the war when a Jap submarine tried to torpedo the American Capital Ship Chicago off Garden Island [on the night of Sunday 31st May 1942].[715] *The torpedo hit the island and the explosion at midnight made us all leap and think the bombers were overhead. It missed the ship and was destroyed in quick time. No one was as scared as we thought we would be, but it made us realize there was a war on!!! One could have got a house or flat on the waterside for about two pence a week in those days and now £1000 won't go anywhere near.*

I don't think you will like the fashions out here dear. Most of the girls look very tarty with their hair done over big pads in front and dangling to their shoulders at the back and hats that dolls used to wear perched on top. Our girls don't do it of course, but the rank and file do.

Peggy Wilkinson is married and has a lovely little baby boy. Both she and Betty are getting so black looking, like Mama who is worse than ever, but oh so kind and enthusiastic. They live at Wollstonecraft now.

Bob Stanistreet [NX59135] *and Roger Cornforth* [NX59134] *are on their way home, also Tony White* [NX35100] *and Bill Coates.*

I have been secretary for the 2/20 Comforts fund all these years. We are in the Exchange at the corner of Bridge and Pitt Street. We have met on Wednesdays and Fridays every week and when you see our balance sheet you will be proud of our War effort. We have £300 odd in hand to help any needy 2/20 [men].

Phil Murray's mother comes in regularly. Poor dear has never heard of Phil since the fall. And the other son is in Borneo and the news from there is so awful it looks very bad for both. [Phillip Charles Murray NX 34248 was a Sergeant in the 2/20 who was killed on 10 February 1942.][716]

Mrs. Russell French asked me to ask you for any news of her two sons. Peter was one and I don't know the other's name. I hope you will be home soon to tell them yourself. [Peter Russell French NX32834 was a Sgt in 2/20 and was discharged 9 Jan 1946.][717]

David was so thrilled and relieved when your letter came saying you approved of him as a brother in law. He is such a dear and you won't know Elizabeth, she is so happy and efficient. Sue too is wonderfully happy and a model wife and mother. Warwick is a dear and no one could ask for better.

As you say your responsibilities are lifted and now only Mum to worry about.

All legal affairs are as they were when you left dear. A few payments have been made from Grandfather's estate but they have gone to liquidate Dad's debts, not really enough though. We will survive though dear and can talk over our affairs later.

Great jubilation at Birt and Co's for you and Sir Thomas sent you a cable which I hope you received and sent word to me to say if I wanted to send you anything to just let then know and they would do it.

We got some furniture and your big picture (Crossing the Blue Mountains) from Bowral after dear old Gran died. All property up there has been sold. Biddy is still in her little cottage. Moya is off to England soon. [Biddy Moriarty and Moya Goff were sisters and friends of the family from Bowral.]

The Fowlers have left the Bank at Goulburn and are building at Palm Beach. Dan has returned. [Daniel Arthur Fowler, N75306, enlisted in Goulburn.][718]

Oh darling there is so much to tell you so come home soon.
All our love dear
Doukie

...

Mrs. D. L Wilkinson
4 Belmont Avenue, Wollstonecraft
My dear Bill *20 September 1945*

It is great news to know you are well and safe. Your Mother has been so very brave and an example to all, you must be very, very proud of her. I was at the 8th Div. Association meeting last night and saw her there. She said she had received 4 letters from you and was so thrilled about it.

Amidst all our rejoicing there is a sadness for those who won't return. I have not had any word of Charlie's liberation yet but had a Red Cross message from him in August to say he was well and hoping for an early reunion. He is now in Fukuoka Camp, Japan and I hope I will soon hear he is in Manilla and on his way home. David my younger son has been up in N.G. and Bougainville for 20 months and hopes to be home the first week in November - just can't realise I am to have them both home again. David has been in all the heavy fighting in Northern Bougainville and says he has yet to see a small Jap.

[Charles Reid Wilkinson NX54635 was discharged 19 December 1945. His brother was David Curtis Wilkinson NX17247 who was eventually discharged in September 1946.][719]

You have a niece and nephew to greet. Charlie has a new nephew. Peg married Bruce Arrowsmith from South Australia. He is a Capt. and the adjutant of his unit - 16 Aust. A.O.D. and is on Bougainville - he and David met the other day for the first time in 2 years.

I have had over 900 men of the forces through the home since war started and they have been a wonderful lot and all of them so grateful for the home. Some of my Naval lads were in the Tokyo Bay for the signing of the Surrender.

Of course all the Mothers and wives are preparing now for our boys to return - it will be wonderful to see you again. Your photo sits on our piano. Your Mother was at Peg's wedding - Peg was married in St. Andrew's Cathedral and we had the reception here - it was a very jolly wedding - she has a dear little son - not so little now, he is 17 pounds 10 ounces - Ian Robert is his name and he is a real pickle just over 5 months old. I don't know what I will do without them when they go to live in South Australia.

Joan of course you wouldn't recognize, she is quite grown up - 18 now and very modern. We all tease her although I say it who shouldn't, everyone says she is very attractive, she is fair. Betty has put on a lot of weight and looks very well. She works for the NSW Bookstalls and is on the stall at Wollstonecraft so it is nice and handy to home.

I wonder will you come home by plane or boat. The 8th Div. boys are getting a great reception and so you should - nothing is too good for you lads.

We have quite a bit of land with this place, two blocks, so we don't feel a bit closed in- we are looking forward to showing it to you soon; we must have some more parties when you get back.

Mrs. de Meyrick used to often ask after you during the long dreary years of waiting.

The Eddison's haven't heard anything of Jack for over 2 1/2 years and he has lost both his brothers. We are very anxious about him. I do hope he is alright.

Well Bill this is all for this time. Your Mother looked so pretty last night in a black dress and hat. With love from us all and hope you have a good trip home and that we will see you soon.
Yours affectionately
Ethel Wilkinson

The Eddison family were to have much sadness. Jack Osbaldeston Eddison, NX60320, was in 2/20 and died as a POW on 7 June 1943 in Yokohama. His brother Edward Dalkeith Eddison was a Flight Lieutenant in the RAAF and died 27 May 1943 in Lae. The name and death of a third son of W or Walter (next of kin) could not be confirmed but the Commonwealth War Graves Commission lists the above two and also Frank Newman Eddison, VX5419, next of kin Reginald, who was in the 2/31 Bn AIF and died 11 June 1941. He is buried in Damascus.[720]

No 2 Aust. PW Reception Centre, Singapore 21 September 1945
[This is a postal address, Bill is still writing from Bangkok.]

Darling Doukie

This evacuation is going on much slower than we expected but our conditions here in Bangkok are reasonable so the matter is not really serious.

Really the boys are having a good time in this city. Dance clubs are opening all over the place - picture theatres with shows from Rangoon are fair entertainment. The local Siamese shower invitations upon us and have given us some fine parties.

There are in Bangkok some very fine sights such as the palace and many temples - one of the temples sports an enormous green Buddha supposedly world famous.

The local museum is well worth a visit and so are the strip-tease shows provided in an iniquitous setting in Chinatown. The city is gay and carefree; doing its best to make our stay as pleasant as possible.

Every night now some of us have dinner in a first class pub. The meals are passable but the atmosphere is what we like best. It makes us feel free and important - a lovely feeling.

The local whisky and wines are playing havoc with many of the lads. They have been off hard drink for so long that this crude spirit bowls them over quickly. The fellows rarely come back for a second dose.

A reporter turned up today from the Sydney Morning Herald; the boys grilled him with questions. Fortunately he is staying close handy.

We now know all about the shortage of tobacco, cigarettes, beer and who won the football competitions, races and all the rest of such information - just the stuff for us.

The wireless is still blaring forth about Japanese atrocities and does not tell us what we really want to know.

Still no mail - it is terribly slow coming in but we are assured every day that the stuff is on the way.

We have been issued hideous jungle green uniforms. They are a good battle dress but their social efficiency is limited. The lads are all hoping that they will have old khaki to arrive home in. My old uniforms were lost years ago so I shall probably arrive looking like one of Smith's Weekly unofficial diggers.

How did the estates eventually wind up? There cannot be much money for us, I know, because of the heavy taxation [death duties etc.]. My army pay should amount to a decent figure between £1,500 and £2,000 I think.

Plan a good holiday dear. We will let our heads go and really enjoy ourselves.

The city is full of cheap silver broaches [sic] and trinkets. They are attractive but not cheap in reality. I am not going to waste money on such rubbish.
Cheerio for the present dear. Love to all.
Love
Bill

...

No 2 Aust. PW Reception Centre, Singapore 24 September 1945
Darling Doukie

This letter should arrive in Sydney within a couple of days. It is going home with a reporter from the *SM Herald*.

Today your telegram arrived and at last dear I know you are well - by gosh I am relieved - soon now we will all be together.

Our days are busy. We are looking after ourselves still. I mean the army people from outside have not arrived to take over the troops and arrange the evacuation for us. We are doing the work - probably a good thing because the business of waiting in an Eastern city now that we are free makes us impatient.

Conditions here are not bad. The local food supplies are good and the local civilians in Bangkok are attending our requirements very well. Many of the boys have been to dinner parties and have generally accepted the local hospitality. The Siamese does not appeal to me very much although I admit that many have charming manners, speak English and their girls often look snappy.

In the city there is not much for us to buy. The place is full of cheap Eastern junk and the few good things are very expensive. There is some very attractive silver ware but I am not buying any because the quality is awful when compared with Hardy Bros.

Every day people come in from Australia; these fellows are war photographers, correspondents, newspaper reporters, air force officers and the occasional army officer who has been sent in to report upon 'our condition'. The chaps give us all the news. The boys here are following the races and football fixtures on the wireless already.

Surprises happen here every hour; some RAF parachute officers turned up yesterday with a small crocodile in a basket.

All leave in Bangkok was stopped for a couple of days because some local bandits ran amok and started to shoot up the Siamese police. The most modern bombers and fighters roar so low over our heads that they are positively frightening.

Civilian women turn up at odd moments and tell us they were in Australia, England and some other blissful place a week ago.

Self satisfied masculine looking girls in military uniforms stand with their feet apart, hands on hips and discuss the necessary steps to be taken in connection with Japanese atrocities. The wireless talks about us every time we turn on the news.

Cheerio darling, See you soon.
Dick Gaden is okay and John I believe is in Singapore.
Love to yourself the girls etc
Yours truly,
Love Bill

...

Mrs. V.L. Gaden
10 Raymond Road, Neutral Bay *24th September 1945*
Put this on something dark and it is easy to read.
Bill darling. [Vera had written on both sides of the thin paper and the ink showing through from the back made it difficult to decipher. By placing it on a dark background it was easier to read the writing].

Just received your 5th letter from Bangkok and am worried now because I have addressed all your mail to Bangalore, India Command as you said in the cable. However this one will be addressed differently as apparently you are not to be in India at all.

It is wonderful getting long normal letters from you dear. Don't worry about sending money darling everything is under control and I have told you in a previous letter which I hope you will have received by now.

The POWs are arriving almost daily now and you will find an 8th Division Association all functioning and waiting to receive you. David is Treasurer and meets planes and boats etc. We have opened a Club room in Macquarie Place (St. John's House) where you can meet and have a cuppa and sandwich and talk with your mates.

I am sending a photograph of the children and me. It will give you some idea of what we all look like.

Diana opened her eyes and mouth at the wrong second but Jamie enjoyed the photographer's antics and looks like a little frog. Sue and Ginge look exactly the same dear, just as young as ever.

You are going to be so happy in the house. The glorious landscape window in the lounge is the envy of everyone and from your room you can see all over the harbour as you lie in bed. It is a fascinating room altogether. I bought you a lovely big loughboy [sic] *with*

Vera with grandchildren Diana Keeling and James MacDougal

some of your bonus money from the office and have given you a bed I had as I have Mother's big four poster with the canopy top.

In case you haven't received the other letters dear, I have been getting £7.14.0 a fortnight allotment and Sue paid her board while here. Now she is in her own home David and Elizabeth pay £3 per week so you can see we can manage beautifully. The rent of this place is only £2 per week, 2/6 more than old Valhalla.

The old place is going to be reconstructed as soon as the purchaser can get Mrs. Grierson and a Mrs. Grinstead, who has one flat, out. Gordon Grierson is off to Singapore with a broadcasting unit. He has become a radio expert during his service which has been mostly in New Guinea and Bougainville. Betty is engaged to a man called Eddis Linton, a Neutral Bay lad and a nephew of Prof Shellshear's. [Professor Joseph Shellshear was an army officer and professor of anatomy who provided classes for young surgeons-lieutenant to help them gain their formal surgical qualifications. His mother's name was Eddis].[722]

Practically all your friends are returning except poor old Brian Badgery who was in the Borneo tragedy. You won't know David, he has put on so much weight, almost portly!! We will celebrate our best days when you return darling so get fit to eat all before you.
All our love
Doukie

...

Mrs. D MacDougal
10 Raymond Road, Neutral Bay

Darling Bill *24th September 1945*

Another letter from you this a.m., your 5th and gosh was it good. Am only scratching a few lines because I have a heap of sewing to do. Summer has come and David has no cool clothes and on Saturday we are going up to Baan Baa for a week to stay with Margaret, David's sister. [Margaret Stewart MacDougal had married Kenneth Bertram Latham in 1941.][722]

Can't stay longer because he wants to be back to meet the ships from Singapore coming in. Yesterday he arose at 4.00a.m. to go out to Mascot to meet some POWs arriving by plane. They had been there about 20 minutes and found they would not be arriving until today, luckily for him a little later so he did not have to get up till 5.00 a.m. They were all from Japan included 'Bluey' Parkhill and the M.O. from the 2/20. The 8th Div. Assoc. now have a room in 21 Macquarie Place which is open all day and they serve tea and cake. As funds permit they hope to include lunches. Rang Jeannie Ewart and she was terribly pleased you had mentioned Arch as she still has had no word. Tell him (if he is around) that Little Nell (Jean's Mother) made my wedding dress for me, all in a weekend too because we thought David was coming down, even had the cake at home then all that arrived was a telegram 'Leave Cancelled'; three weeks later he got it. However had it not been for Jeannie and Little Nell heaven knows what I would have done. They are wonderful.

Tony Walter is home again. He was a POW in Germany. We had to go to a party there. Gee it was awful. Luckily no play reading though.

What a pity you paid for your accountancy course, the Army gives you one for nix. David is doing it; goes to Tech at North Sydney on Tuesday and Thursday from 6.30 p.m. to 9.30 p.m. every week.

Mother is very well but we want to get her away for a few days before you come back because it would do her lots of good, but our chances are pretty low I think. Jamie is very well and is beginning to stand by himself now. You would have died if you had seen him when he first arrived, there was very little of him, only a bit over 5 pounds, and a mop of hair which he still has, very fair. Diana was a hulk, nearly 9 pounds.

Well will have to go and do some work, we are longing for you to come home. Did you know David was an acting Lieut Col in China? Major on arriving home.
Tons of love Bill from all of us.
Ginge

...

No 2 Aust. PW Reception Centre, Singapore

Darling Doukie 24 September 1945

Your telegram arrived today advising that you are all well at home - heavens I am thankful - we shall all be together soon.

There is really no proper news so I shall tell you again about the camp here and our doings.

We live in an enormous building which was once a university. Men are everywhere sleeping all over the place. They are a cosmopolitan bunch of AIF, English, Chinese and sundry others. We are all waiting for repatriation.

Local Siamese are running canteens all over the place. The men crowd around, bash pianos, sing and booze. A lunatic asylum would be far easier to administer than this dump. Parties leave continuously in trucks bound for the aerodrome, to Singapore thence by ship home. Drafting boozed men on to the trucks is like handling sheep and preventing others stowing away on the trucks is a man sized job. We are muddling along and should be home soon.

They are using us ex POW fellows for disarming Japanese, a job we like!!

Bangkok is full of thieves. We cannot leave any of our rooms without a guard and hanging clothes on a line is fatal, they are always pinched by the natives.

The Siamese shopkeepers who run the canteens are funny. They set up stalls and drink bars everywhere. The day before yesterday one crowd set up shop in our orderly room whilst the staff were at lunch. Last night a whole bunch of natives were found sleeping in our quarters, they were a laundry organization come to stay. All received the order of the boot.

The men are looking well and deliriously happy. Some mail is trickling in and fellows are hearing real news from their families. Dick Gaden is OK but not with me. John is probably in Singapore.
Love
Bill

...

44 Harriette Street
Neutral Bay

Bill old dear *26 September 1945*

I just can't tell you all it meant to get your letter on Monday 23rd, do think it's so splendid of you to have singled me out to write to when you must have so many letters to write. Your dear Mum shared her first long and real letter from you with us all. Gosh it was good to see your handwriting again and hear you say you are fit and well for which I thank goodness. I feel inches taller being the only one mentioned by name when it came to the messages. Now I've had your letter which, like your charming English woman, was a veritable breath of fresh air.

It is good to hear you are all being so well looked after; only wish I were there to see the reaction. Loved the story about the fellows sniffing the feminine perfume. I took your letter along to the family. Your Mum got one the same day in which you said you'd got 8 of her letters, 4 of mine. So glad; hope you've had lots more of your Mum's since then. We all wrote post haste Air Mail to Bangalore as advised in your card but evidently you didn't go to India. David seems to think it might have been a purely official cable, perhaps you did go to Rangoon and just as quickly been returned to Bangkok.

Saw the aircraft carrier 'Glory' speeding on her errand of mercy this afternoon, she did look a picture. [HMS *Glory* was a light fleet aircraft carrier of 13400 tons built during the war. After the Japanese surrender she was part of the Australian and British equivalent of 'Operation Magic Carpet', the repatriation of troops to their homeland.][723]

I'm doubly interested in her as Kath Davis (a lass I know and great friend of Bubbles Capper (now Rowe) ground floor of the front flats here) is one of the 10 V.O.W.'s on board whilst her Commander is a delightful person, Hicks by name and an Englishman who came out on the same ship as Charlie Tindal's Mother and sister Jan and has become a bosom friend of the family, so should you be returning by her, make your self known to him through Charlie Tindal. He was on loan to RAN and attached to HMAS Stuart prior to the war when we all had a very cheerful late afternoon gathering in his cabin one Sunday, poor old Rick [Tindal] *was with us.*

Dear old Missie Wilson is so happy to know you're well and will be home soon. Gosh that's going to be the day Bill. Was so hoping you'd have been with your own folks for your birthday on October 5th as this year it can be a happy one but, as in all those years now to be forgotten, we'll raise our glasses as has always been done.

At the moment am listening to messages from lads now as free as the four winds; each night from various stations messages are broadcast. Have heard several whom I know or know of and may yet hear you.

Jove it must be an amazing sight seeing all those planes. What a magnificent job they're doing. We had the skies more or less blacked when masses of planes flew over the city to boost the new war loan opened yesterday and their Fourth Victory Loan. Can't exactly be a shortage of petrol as is supposed to be.

Hope the snap reached you, perfectly charming one of your Mum and her grandchildren, in fact good of them all. Goes to show England can produce the goods; my camera which I got in London in 1923 did the trick.

It's good to see the look of relief on your Mum's face and general expression since hearing from you. She's been wonderful all through but also anxious. Dear old Gran yet can't grasp the glad news of you being safe and well. She's so happy and has a very devilish glint in those eyes of hers, she's a pet. And is, I wouldn't mind betting, daily turning over in her mind which horses she'll back in the Epsom, Metropolitan and other races. I must have an earnest conversation with her on the subject. Anyway you'll be home well before the Melbourne Cup. 'Russia' and 'Peter' have been mentioned to me. 'Peter' if I remember rightly was 2nd last year.

[Connie was right, 'Peter' was second to 'Sirius' in 1944, she was also a year early with 'Russia', he won in 1946. The 1945 winner was 'Rainbird'.][724]

Hope you'll be home before I start for Lapstone on October 24th, am going to the Hotel for 10 days with a cousin, first holiday away from Sydney for 6 years. Days fly so quickly, you'll all be sailing through the Heads before any of you or us realize it or flying over our heads, planes are arriving all and every day, it's all so marvellous.

Must to shut eye. What about a good old cup of tea with me first? Will you ever forget how we discovered one another after many years on the ferry and you came home with me and had supper?

Very Happy Birthday Bill dear and each one to follow as you would have it.
Cheerio and all the best. Yours truly,
Connie with love.

...

Doukie Darling — Bangkok, Date unknown

Yesterday I sent you a message over the air on an ABC recording unit. You will probably hear it in a couple of days.

Things in Bangkok are much the same as my last letters described. The town is now literally full of booze houses, night clubs and other types of houses. The fellows are behaving themselves and really their conduct has generally been good.

We have seen some very artistic Siamese dancing, really first class stuff that would cost a fortune to see at all under other circumstances. The magnificent costly costumes made of white satin with interwoven silver threads combined with the slow sensual oriental movements of the actors are at first absorbingly interesting. As the show goes on the repetition becomes monotonous but well worth seeing for all that.

There is also a popular show in which girls perform in the nude. The standard is not classical but once again well worth seeing a couple of dozen times!!

Letters are coming in very slowly. I still only have received two of yours written recently.

A very decent fellow from the ABC has been to see me and together we have roamed Bangkok in search of fun. His name is Fred Simpson. The blighter has been pestering me to give atrocity talks on the air but so far yours truly has not been enthusiastic, a cheery quick talk or nothing say I. Just at the moment Simpson is banging a story out on a typewriter which may possibly come over the air by myself.

In letters that the men have received you receive a prominent mention for the work done with 2/20 and 8th Div. Comforts Organisations. Darling you must have worked hard.

Your birthday is coming fast and this evacuation so slowly that I only have a faint hope of being home on October 19th. It can't be helped; you will have plenty more birthdays.

What clothes have I left at home? I can't remember how many suits but anyway have them ready dear because I am anxious to cast uniforms to the wind after this.
Yours, Love
Bill

No doubt Vera, who was informed of the upcoming radio broadcast, would have been surrounded by friends and family as they listened to the wireless, all desperate to hear the voice of their beloved Bill.

[697] NSW BDM Index, 6984/1944.
[698] DVA Nominal Roll.
[699] *ibid.*
[700] *ibid*
[701] Molony, *The Penguin History of Australia*, p. 287.
[702] NSW BDM Index, marriages.
[703] DVA Nominal Roll.
[704] *ibid.*
[705] NSW BDM Marriage Index, 22876/1940; DVA Nominal Roll; Newton, *The Grim Glory*, pp. 221-228.
[706] NSW BDM Index and Warden, SCEGS Register, pp. II-188.
[707] Commonwealth War Graves Commission CWGC web site.
[708] DVA Nominal Roll.
[709] *ibid*
[710] Scone Town Walk, http://www.upperhuntertourism.com.au/index.cfm?page_id=1073&page=Town+Walk.
[711] McLellan, *History of the Parish of St Luke's Scone*, pp. 73, 77.
[712] *Australian Dictionary of Biography*, <http://www.adb.online.anu.edu.au/biogs/A090056b.htm>
[713] DVA Nominal Roll.
[714] McKernan, *Drought the Red Marauder*, pp. 169-193, 205.
[715] *AWM Encyclopaedia*, < http://www.awm.gov.au/encyclopaedia.midgetsub.doc.htm >
[716] DVA Nominal Roll.
[717] *ibid.*
[718] *ibid.*
[719] *ibid.*
[720] *ibid.* and Commonwealth War Graves Commission.
[721] *Australian Dictionary of Biography*, on line edition http://abdonline.anu.edu.au/biogs/A160268b.htm
[722] NSW BDM Index, 2451/1941.
[723] HMS *Glory* < http://www.fleetairarmarchive.net/ships/GLORY.html >
[724] Melbourne Cup Winners, < http://au.geocities.com/melbournecups/1940-49.html >

Chapter 14 - Over the airwaves

The story 'banged out' by Fred Simpson was recorded on 30 September 1945. The former prisoners were reluctant to talk about the atrocities they had seen but were also given a carefully scripted conversation which was designed to not upset the families back home. Was this ABC policy at the time, or Simpson being very aware of the sadness of many grieving families back in Australia?

Broadcast from SIMPSON for A.B.C
Anecdotes of the infamous Thailand-Burma Death Railway
Recorded September 30th at Bangkok, University Camp, AIF
Speed 33

Opening announcement recorded on disc is as follows:-

Capt. Bill Gaden of Neutral Bay, Sydney, Padre Harry Thorpe of Saratoga, NSW, Lieut. A.A. [Alick] Davis of Launceston, Tasmania and Capt. Claude [Doc] Anderson talk to me a little of some of their experiences while they were on the recently completed Thai-Burma Railway. It is a very brief story in which so little of their experience can be told in a very little time. I thought you would like to listen, so here they are:-

BROADCAST FROM SIMPSON FOR A.B.C.
Anecdotes of the infamous Thailand-Burma Death Railway Speed 33 Sep 29
Please notify the following addresses:-
Mrs. V.L. Gaden, St Damien's, 10 Raymond Road, Neutral Bay, Sydney.
Mrs. A.A. Davis, 5 Line Avenue, Launceston, Tasmania.
Mrs. C. Thorpe, C/o Post Office, Saratoga, via Woy Woy, NSW.
Mrs. H.G. Greiner, Wahronga Estate, Tongala, Victoria.
Mrs. E.A. Anderson, 14 Wooldridge Avenue, Millswood, Adelaide, S.A.
Mrs. W.G. Harris, 30 Bates Street, Homebush West, NSW.

Harry Well Fred, let's get a picture of the set up first. Bill here was with me on the Thailand side of the border.
Doc Alick and I were on the Burma portion of the line.
Fred And the length of the line would be what ... ?
Bill 400 kilometres over some of the roughest country in South East Asia.
Harry Better make that miles, Bill, we are back in Australian terms now and the mileage would be about ... Oh ... about 250 miles.
Bill It was actually a link between Bangkok and Moulmein. Bangkok was of course base of operations. Moulmein was already connected by rail to Rangoon which was the base of operations for Burma and India.
Doc Our party named 'A' Force left Changi, Singapore in May 1942, 3000 strong AIF troops. We began work on the job at the Burma end in September 1942.

Bill Harry and I knocked about Singapore for about a year and did not start work on the Thailand side until 'April's Fools Day' 1943.

Fred Let me get this straight. There were two forces working towards each other from both sides ...

Harry No, no Fred, that's not quite right. There were several forces, we arrived at different times.

Doc British, American, Dutch ...

Alick And not to mention the thousand upon thousand of native coolies.

Doc As far as we know there must have been about 10,000 Australians.

Bill And anything up to 53,000 other Allied POWs.

Fred Well now what is the story with mechanical equipment.

ALL Mechanical equipment!

Harry Ye Gods.

Alick All we had were a few lousy shovels, picks and baskets made of cane to remove the dirt.

Fred I've heard a story about 'G' strings.

Harry Yes a few battered hats, no boots and you should have seen me walking round in an old loin cloth.

Bill And there wasn't any change of clothing for dinner at night

Harry And will you ever forget those meals. Rice every day for 3.5 years. What we'd have given for a good pork chop.

Fred But wasn't there any variation at all?

Doc Our cooks did a very good job but the only vegetables to be had were such things as lily roots, bamboo shoots, pie melons, Chinese radishes ...

Alick But Doc we didn't have all of those at the one time. It depended on where we were. Christmas Day 1943 I had 3 meals of plain rice with approximately half a pint of water in which some ginger root had been boiled in it.

Doc In any case the vitamin content of these vegetables was far below our requirements.

Bill Particularly when you have in mind the men worked from dawn till dark and sometimes in the 'Speedo' period for 36 hours at a stretch.

Fred What do you mean by the 'Speedo' period Bill?

Bill The final rush to link up the line on the Nip schedule.

Harry And the rails were actually joined on 17 October 1943 at approximately 153 kilo peg from Moulmein.

Fred A bit more about the work now.

Harry And didn't we put it over the Nips.

Alick One neat little trick we had was for someone to engage the Nip guard in talking. Then the boys would roll logs, bamboo and any old rubbish into the embankment.

Bill That meant a lot less dirt to be carried.

Harry Another fine little method of delayed action was the introduction of borer grubs into the wooden bridge piles.

Alick The first wet season saw the end of the bridges

Harry The one that tickled me most was on the night shift. When the Nip was careless, if you looked closely, you would see the boys in a steady stream moving up the embankment with empty baskets and bringing dirt back when they should have been taking it up.

Doc But it was bad if you were caught.

Harry You're telling me!

Fred The usual bashings eh?

Bill A little more than that too Fred. How would you like to hold a 50 pound boulder at arms length over your head for two hours, no hat and in the sun?

Fred What can I say ... I didn't have to do it. I don't think anybody could realize what such treatment would mean.

Harry It is impossible to tell you here of the unspeakable things that the boys had to suffer. The filthy living conditions are a story in themselves. The huts were dark and dirty, the roofs leaked time and again and the ground was riddled with bugs, lice and rats.

Bill Often enough they had been abandoned by the natives and on occasions bodies had to be removed of natives who had died of cholera.

Doc And the overcrowding was extreme. Sometimes as many as 18 men were placed in an area the size of a very small bedroom. On these occasions they built 3 decker beds of bamboo.

Harry There were no woollen blankets like at home ... many of the lads ... all they had for bedding equipment was only a rice sack when they could scrounge it from the Nips.

Fred What about the mosquito nets?

Doc Some were issued but we were always very short of them and also many of these had to be cut up for use as ulcer dressings.

Harry I even cut up my church robes for dressings and the odd 'G' string.

Bill The Doc here can tell a story on the medical side ...

Doc Yes things were really grim, particularly throughout the whole period of 1943 and that seems to have been general throughout all the railway camps ...

Harry You see Fred there was a very serious shortage of medical supplies.

Doc Quinine was received in moderate quantities but was always insufficient ... other supplies were extremely scarce ... perhaps about 1% of what we really required.

Bill Dysentery Doc ...

Doc Emetine would have saved the lives of hundreds of men suffering from amoebic dysentery ... but that was quite unobtainable.

Harry Malaria figures were pretty high on the Burma side as early as March 1943 ... Doc ...

Doc In one camp of eighteen hundred ... our first month in the heart of the jungle ... we had nine hundred cases.

Fred Tropical ulcers Doc ...

Doc Terrible things ... in many cases the men who had amputations were lucky to get away with their lives. Amputation in their case was their only possible hope of surviving.

Fred And the surgical treatment of course would be ... Doc ...

Doc Very difficult and primitive owing to the lack of instruments and anaesthetics.

Bill You ask the boys what they think of the Doctors.

Fred Yes I've heard the story so many times.

Doc Well the job was difficult and heartbreaking at times for us all, but the lads knew of our difficulties and helped us through.

Bill Do you remember at Tonchan South how we graded the cholera patients according to their severity into different tents.

Harry That reminds me of one lad who was placed in the suspect tent ... then when he was declared positive promised me that even if he had to go through every tent in the row he would eventually walk out.

Fred And he did?

Harry He did and he was typical of the way that so many thousands of men battled for their lives.

Bill What strikes you chaps as the finest qualities about our blokes ... for me I'll name one ... The spirit of super cooperation when things were tough ...

Doc If a man was very sick for instance, his mates would spend their last cent in endeavouring to buy extra food for him.

Harry The religious faith of these lads was a lesson to me, often a man would timidly come to me and ask for a prayer to be said for his mate who was perhaps dying.

Bill Remember Harry at Tha Muang when you reckoned you could get a thousand men to attend a church service ...

Fred And did you Harry?

Harry We certainly did and other places when the Nip allowed us to hold services.

Alick And what jungle cathedrals we had ...

Harry You know better than that old boy ...

Alick Yeh, I do ...

Harry We were never allowed to have a church building of any kind in our group. We made shift with small bamboo tables for communion purposes and even these at times were ruthlessly smashed by the Nips.

Fred Harry I think I heard you speaking of a Mother's Day.

Harry Each year we observed Mother's Day in our jungle area. It was moving to see a thousand men going to work with white paper flowers in their mixed kinds of headgear.

Alick Where the heck did you get the paper. We used all our paper for cigarettes.

Bill You ... heathen Alick.

Doc But there was always a lighter side. The boys had a wonderful sense of humour.

Bill Some of the female impersonators at our concert parties ... well they even fooled the Nips.

Alick You'd be surprised at what turned up during the search for props, even silk stockings and suspenders that had been carted round the jungle and been kept as souvenirs.

Fred Anyway here you all are and on your way home.

Harry What do you think chaps, how about erecting a monument to the old Thailand duck?

Bill Yes, often the old egg that we were able to scrounge pulled us through.

Fred Well I know you haven't told me a fraction of the story and I know that you kept off the atrocities side of the story.

Doc I think it's best left alone.

All I agree, so do I.

...

Sue Keeling
243 Raglan Street, Mosman

Willy dear *3rd October 1945*

Diana and I returned from a couple of hours on the beach this morning to find a letter from you waiting. It is good to know that at last you've had mail from us- it must have taken quite a while to get to you.

Every day brings men home - both by air and sea. David went out to Rose Bay a few days ago to meet some planes and the first person he saw was Arch Ewart. Their yells of 'Mac' and 'Arch' drowned the official speech of welcome. We're all impatient for your turn to come - it must be soon now.

Yes nothing will stop Agnes' trip down [from Scone] *when you come home. She has a pair of ducks up there getting very special care and attention - little do they know what for! My God, I hope she doesn't get too fond of them - remember the ones we had once, they ended up being pensioned off on the river at Camperdown instead of being eaten!*

Ponty is married and in production. She's Mrs. Bob Mackay now and far too snooty to include us in her list of friends.

I'm glad you've gone off Poop-Face [Elaine Warren] *though the poor kid has my sympathy now. Her father died a little while ago and she has had to leave the W.A.A.F. to look after her mother.*

You ask me to line up a few co-dallyers - that's hard. Mum had the future Mrs. E.W.G. picked out a few years ago - Joan Johnstone from Armidale. We did our best to shoo off the pursuers but it was no good. She's the mother of a fine boy now, and married, nearly forgot that!

[Joan Lorimer Johnstone married Richard Allan Pollock in 1944, with son Timothy born in August 1945].[725]

But we'll find something for you, my young sister in law just loves to dally and she's very attractive, has her own car too!

David and Gingie and their young horror leave today for a weeks holiday with David's sister and her husband at Baan Baa. It will do them both good. Gingie is as thin as a rake these days, David the opposite. Young James would keep anyone thin; he spends his days crawling round looking for dreadful things to do.

Diana isn't much better. It is good being so close to the beach here though and it will be fun when you come back for you'll have a month's leave and its getting warmer every day so you'll have to come down often and 'frin' (Diana's version of swim).

Yes the picture from Vermont was the one from the dining room. Never will I forget the day it arrived not very long ago. We knew it was far from small but had forgotten just how large. This whacking great thing about 6 feet by 4 feet was carted in, filthy dirty and almost falling apart. Mum and I just stood and gaped. There didn't seem to be a wall in the place to fit it but a wall had to be found for there was nowhere to hide it. And as well as a wall a steel cable had to be found to hold the darned thing up. Madge Linscott came in and saved the day. Mum and I were helpless laughing, the darned thing was face down on the floor and Diana thought it was a skating rink and was cavorting around on it! Madge, unlike us at times, has a respect for heirlooms and marshalled us round to find dusters and hammers and nails and before long it was on the wall.

But poor rude 'Nicholas' from Gran Balcombe's was removed from his place to make room. Once again Nicky is behind the door, just as he was in the dining room at 'The Briars'. But never mind Bill, when you build yourself a house you'll only need three walls in one room, they can stick the heirloom in for the fourth and save lots of bucks.

No more now Willy, time to cook lunch for the brat.
Tons of love Sue
Many happy returns for the 5th, sorry this won't arrive in time.

The painting was about the only thing the family received following the death of Agnes Lilian (Atherton) Gaden, Bill's grandmother who had died on 17 March 1942 at 'Tellara', Bowral. Her Will, written on 20 October 1939, just one month after the death of her son Noel, listed daughter Catherine (Kitty) Walker, wife of Dr Norman Walker, as executor. Everything was left to Kitty, or her children if she predeceased them, nothing was left to her other children or grandchildren. According to probate it was valued at £1904, a far cry from the £50,000 left by her husband in 1938. Most of that money was tied up to look after daughter Nancy for life; she had epilepsy and needed care.[726]

Mrs. V.L. Gaden
10 Raymond Road, Neutral Bay

Bill darling *3rd October 1945*

Another long letter from you today making the 6th. I am so disappointed to think you hadn't any of ours when you wrote on 21st September.

Your first cable said safe at India and address all mail c/- Aust. Reception Centre Unit, Bangalore, India Command. Well we sent the return cable to that address, also letters from us all and Birt and Co sent letters and Sir Thomas Gordon sent you a cable so I do hope you have some of them by now.

I sent the last cable and letter to Singapore so they must be there for you when you get down.

Arch Ewart arrived yesterday afternoon by flying boat. David saw him for a few minutes and got the latest news of you darling. He took 6 days to do the trip!!!

I am sure I will be getting a call from you on the phone any day to say you have arrived. Jean didn't expect Arch until today so she had to come down helter-skelter in her car. When you arrive dear you will be taken to Ingleburn for a medical inspection where next of kin will be waiting. I am going in a launch to meet the ship, if it is a ship? And see you all the way up the harbour. The 8th Div. Association has a launch for that purpose.

It is a great movement darling and an Auxiliary has been formed of relatives and friends and we have got a nice big room in Macquarie Place as a rest room and meeting place for you all, light refreshments etc free!! It's grand to see all the men come in and greet one another and get all the news.

General Bennett is President of the Association, Bill Duncan secretary and David Treasurer and Mrs. Assheton is President of the Auxiliary and Mrs. Davidson secretary and Alex Stanistreet (Bob's father) treasurer. I am Vice President among others.

We will close the Comforts Fund down at the end of the year after the Xmas tree for the children. Sergeant Major Chapman came in today to see us and was in your company and was glad to hear news of you dear. He has just returned from Japan. Roger Cornforth is back. He has had a bad time with beri-beri etc but is improving daily. He has already put on five stone since his release.

All the estate affairs are just as they were when you left dear and likely to be for ever as far as I know. I think it would be a good idea to get two congenial men as boarders when the MacDougal's depart. This flat has three nice bedrooms and a small dressing room which has been the babies nursery and then we can manage beautifully darling and you are not to be burdened with keeping me. Your own bedroom is lovely. The nicest room in Neutral Bay and mine the next nicest. We are very lucky to have such a gorgeous flat and nice landlord. You are going to be very happy here. No more for present dear. It is after midnight.

See you soon darling,
Doukie

...

Marguerite Purcell
Birt and Co
4 Bridge Street, Sydney

Dear Mr. Gaden *4th October 1945*

This is just a little note to say a big Welcome Home to you! There was great excitement at the office when your Mother kindly phoned Mr. Ward to say she had received a cable from you and that you were safe. You have so often been in our thoughts and always when collecting Comforts Money for the parcels folk always enquired if anything had been heard of you and Ron Eaton. We heard of Eaton the day after your news and how thankful we all were! We do hope it will not be long ere you are home again and look forward to seeing you again.

I am sorry to tell you that Lance Crowther is posted 'Missing' - he was a Flight Lt. and went down at the beginning of this year. [Flight Lieutenant Lance Dixon Crowther, 403560, of 24 Squadron died 6 April 1945.][727]

The girls are all well - Miss Gourlay retired a couple of years ago and Miss Robinson took her place - my sister Ivy is next in charge.

Geoffrey Johnson was married last Friday to Helen Gordon - Sir Thomas' youngest daughter. She worked in the Office for a while during the war- is a very sweet little lady. They seem so happy together.

Joan Pennings was engaged to a Len Pollard at the beginning of the war but unfortunately he was taken prisoner by the Japs and about 3 months ago she had word that he had died about 2 years ago. Poor Joan, we do all feel so much for her.

[Leonard Pollard, NX55420, of 2/30 Bn died on 6 September 1943 and is buried in Burma.][728]

Mr. Lee has been in America for about a year or more now. Representing the Australian Shipping in America and Canada.

Ian Hunter is now a Major, so also is John Russell-King, the latter is in S.E. Asia Command at present, although we have not heard from him for a long while.

Should you happen to go through Balikpapan look out for Marcel Wattel. He is a Flying Officer, Group No. 292, was asking after you in a letter I received yesterday.

Chapman is married - is in the Army - been right through the business and is somewhere North now, I think in Borneo. Gilbert is in New Guinea - in the Army.

Tony Hughes got his discharge from the Army at the end of last year and is back at the office now. He does not look nearly so well. He was married recently.

Jim Ramsay transferred from the Army to RAAF and is at Darwin I believe.

Jack Bradley also transferred from Army to RAAF. He married Alison Aikins and they now have a little daughter.

Fred Harrison is in Calcutta, representing the British Ministry of War Transport - he was in the RAAF.

Scottie is in the Army and in New Guinea at present. Will West is ditto Scottie.

Ted Willing is a Flying Officer and in India.

We are terribly busy in the Office - at least I always seem to be so, so will have to let this suffice for now. We do hope you are well Bill and are so looking forward to seeing you - we hope that will not be long now.
With kindest regards from all and from yours sincerely
Marguerite W Purcell

Bill also received this invitation, written in Thai with an English translation, to a party in a Bangkok home. It reads:-

It's a fine day. With warmest greetings
We all welcome you, brave men of the Australian Army.
War is ended. People all over the world rejoice.
The Allies bring happiness and peace everywhere they go.
With friendly cheer we cordially invite you
To this party. Be merry and gay and enjoy with us
When you reach home may you find unending joy and prosperity

Sam Saligupta Kua Saligupta (Sally)
Khanha Saligupta Chait Pashoujotin
Chanahaha Saligupta Varan Seributra
5.10.1945

...

Doukie darling — Bangkok, Date unknown

Last night I spent one of the most pleasant evenings in years. 10 officers from our camp at the University building in Bangkok visited a Siamese family who literally killed all the fatted calves in the district in our honour.

The family atmosphere was charming, all relations being present including the aunt who had been to school in America and the clever grandson who is a music teacher to the Prince of Siam.

We sat on the floor and ate an enormous meal of delicious curries, pickled fruits and heaven knows what else. Following the dinner we played all the ridiculous children's games we could think of including 'Here we go gathering nuts in May'. The dainty shy Siamese girls soon fell in with the spirit of the thing and the party became a riot of fun.

The women all were barefooted but otherwise were in quite snappy evening frocks.

Our host's house was a three roomed affair suspended on posts above a swirling dirty river. When you required to wee etc you used the hole in the floor.

No doubt you will hear of this party over the air because Fred Simpson, A.B.C., was with us and says it was one of the best examples of Eastern entertainment he has seen or heard of.

We have only a couple more days in Bangkok, then for the next step. Home.

Yesterday I sent you a cable hoping it will arrive for your birthday.

Have endeavoured to buy silks and dress material but the stuff here is poor quality, rationed and difficult to obtain. Cheerio dear
Love
Bill

Nuts-in-May is a children's rhyme and game, with children dancing round in a circle then facing the centre, with a different person going into the centre for each verse:

Here we go gathering nuts in May, nuts in May, nuts in May,
Here we go gathering nuts in May, on a cold and frosty morning.
Who will you have for nuts in May, nuts in May, nuts in May?
Who will you have for nuts in May, on a cold and frosty morning?
We will have (name) for nuts in May, nuts in May, nuts in May,
We will have (name) for nuts in May, on a cold and frosty morning.
Who will you have to fetch him/her away, fetch him/her away, fetch him/her away?
Who will you have to fetch him/her away on a cold and frosty morning?
We will have (name) to fetch him/her away, fetch him/her away, fetch him/her away,
We will have (name) to fetch him/her away on a cold and frosty morning.[729]

Bill received a cable from his mother for his twenty-eighth birthday on 5 October 1945.

NX12543 CAPTAIN E.W GADEN, AIF SINGAPORE
MANY HAPPY RETURNS
LOVE
DOUKIE

...

No 2 Aust. PW Reception Centre, Singapore
Darling Doukie 6 October 1945

Yesterday I saw the most magnificent sight in all the East, the Royal Temple of the Emerald Buddha, Bangkok. A small party of us were actually taken right into the temple which was about the size of a picture theatre. The walls some 50 feet high inside, were covered with paintings and the ceiling gilt with real gold wash. The Buddha itself, a masterpiece of sculpture in pure emerald stands some 3 feet high on an enormous structure of gold. The idol has real diamonds for eyes and wears a robe of gold woven lace draped across its left shoulder. There are numerous other idols about the place each worth many fortunes. I am enclosing a rough sketch of the inside of the temple. We were amused to find amongst the treasure of the temple an old grandfather clock no doubt of historical value. Western civilization was represented by some excellent Italian marble sculpture obtained by the late king during his wanders around the world.

In my last letter I told you of a party, now in this letter more about another party in the same Siamese house on the waterfront and the fun we had broadcasting the show on a field recording set for the ABC. Fred Simpson did the recording job and had to work like a Trojan in order to get the work finished. The Siamese were all out to help but the fascination of hearing their own voices was too much and the excitement became terrific … screeching kids, giggling girls etc. At times it was nearly pandemonium. We would never have managed had it not been for a charming person one Kua Saligupta who in the capacity of interpreter saved the situation and brought about law and order.

You will not hear the broadcast for about a month owing to the fact that so many records were ruined by people missing their parts and kids making a noise when absolute quiet was required for a 'mike' to record satisfactorily. However it will eventually be OK and then you will hear on the air the type of entertainment given us.

Today we had the whole crowd to lunch with us in the University buildings. They normally live on rice, curry and coconut. We fed them on cold tomato soup, sheep's tongues, frankfurts and vegetables, all cold out of a tin. Kua Saligupta who had been to America announced that we were lazy and extravagant and should have heated everything but we went to great trouble to explain that for years we had been cooking and now that tins of food are available we have closed down the kitchen and refuse to cook anything more until we arrive home. Generally speaking they did not like the food but when we produced tins of peaches with cream they gobbled seven tins.

All our men have gone out on planes, we are going tomorrow and with any luck we should travel all the way by air. In that case I shall be home before this letter.

Japanese working parties are busy cleaning up the place for us. The tables have turned entirely. The Japs are reduced to the social level that suits them best. They work very well and perform wonders with washing and cooking, but for us they only clean up and wash clothes. The Siamese who were our servants have all been discharged.

I am bringing Smithy home with me, the little fellow is thin but quite well. He has been with me most of the time and now just won't leave me. He could have left by plane ages ago but no he wanted to wait. In Sydney he has his sister to look after and will live with her and some uncle and aunt.

[Smithy was Bill's former batman, Pte Robert Smith NX20508 who reverted to his real name of Oswald Burne after the war. He died on 22 September 1946.][730]

Cheerio dear, this will be my last letter before arriving home. Love to all

Love

Bill

Undated and no address, but written from Singapore:

Darling Doukie
About an hour ago I finished a letter to you but here goes for another.

The camp we occupy in Singapore is beside the old buildings at Changi where we were originally interned. Things have changed for now we have nearly everything we want, even beer and chocolate. Australian Red Cross supplies are ours for the first time and are they good!

I believe we are to leave here on 18th Oct by ship for home. My chances of a trip by air are slender because my health is blooming. Anyway there are many 8th Div. men here and I feel that I should stay and leave with them.

A rough and ready sketch of the Emerald Buddha sitting in state in the Royal Temple. The background is gold gilt and excellent mural, paintings not shown. The wealth of this stand alone is beyond computation being built of gold and precious stones and teak timber.

This morning Paddy Turner, no longer a miserable looking runt, came up and introduced himself, you would not know him! He tells me that Charlie his father is a Cpl in the army stationed in a Q store at Scone. He was full of news about people we knew. Paddy is a Pte. and one of the units attending to our welfare. [Arnold Patrick Turner N267768 was with the 114 General Hospital.][731]

It was cold in the plane coming down from Bangkok, but the trip was full of novelty and interest, at times the old Douglas bumped about and we had to cling to straps, not dangerous of course, but an experience.

They have given us khaki uniforms to wear and they are fairly good. The jungle green things given us in Bangkok we now gladly discard, perhaps I shall bring home the jungle stuff it may be handy when working in garden!

Jamie's hair is fair like David's, it could not be any other colour having two tawny parents. Love all
Love Bill

...

Jean Ewart
Woodstock
Emu Plains, Via Bathurst

Dear Bill *14 October 1945*

Your last letter saying you hadn't had any letters made me feel rather badly but there are two from me which you should have by now. It is lovely to be able to write to you again but this will have to be brief as I have to go to the train. I have a new nephew who is being christened this afternoon and, as I hate christenings, I'm looking after the other children while the doings are on; Jim aged nearly three and Mary who is toddling and their cousin aged four. We are going to the park and I don't expect to have any trouble, they do as they are told so that makes it easy and I'm afraid I'm a very doting aunt.

I had a night out last night; it was great after the quiet life I have been leading; the Lieut. Col. and Army put on a show for us out at camp to entertain all the Bathurst women who have worked at canteen etc. Wasn't it good of them, an army entertainment unit put on the 'Laird of the Mountains' and it was extra good. I have seen it twice but had forgotten how lovely it was. You will probably see it somewhere. After the show we had a sit-down supper and I arrived home at 2.00 a.m.

Am rather amused by the papers, Women's Weekly etc. who are writing articles telling us how to treat returned POWS as if they were a strange species, they should be honoured of course but they are still men and I'm sure won't want to be treated as invalids or children, but of course that is just my idea. I do hope Australia will always remember what you have all done.

Had a very nice letter from your Mother yesterday. She says she has heard from other returned men what a good job you have done and I'm sure it's quite true.

Do hope you will come up for a while - the country at shearing time should make you forget prison camps if anything could. Bathurst is looking very lovely just now. Our phone number is Bathurst 1334 and I can meet you any time. We usually get the mail on Wednesdays and Fridays.
Yours sincerely, Jean.

...

16 OCTOBER 945
MRS VERA LYDIA GADEN
ST DAMIENS FLAT 1, 10 RAYMOND ROAD, NEUTRAL BAY, NSW
DARLING DOUKIE SAILING TO YOU TOMORROW
BILL

...

18 OCT 1945
POSTAL ACKNOWLEDGEMENT DELIVERY
MRS VERA LYDIA GADEN
ST DAMIENS FLAT 1, 10 RAYMOND ROAD, NEUTRAL BAY, NSW

IT IS WITH PLEASURE I HAVE TO INFORM YOU THAT NX12543 CAPT EDWARD WILLIAM GADEN PREVIOUSLY REPORTED ALIVE IN SIAM IS NOW REPORTED RECOVERED AND EMBARKED FOR SINGAPORE 15 OCTOBER 1945 FOR AUSTRALIA. ANY FURTHER INFORMATION RECEIVED WILL BE IMMEDIATELY COMMUNICATED
MINISTER FOR THE ARMY
CPD 9P FK

...

Mrs. V.L. Gaden
10 Raymond Road, Neutral Bay
Bill darling *20th October 1945*

You are nearly home at last!

Well dear yesterday Sue arrived with the loveliest flowers I have ever seen with your card attached. Oh dear they were a thrill. Thank you darling. [On 19th October 1945 Vera celebrated her fifty-eighth birthday.]

Everyone is bubbling over with excitement these days and houses are swept and dusted as never before. Roger Cornforth is home and getting bigger than ever and Bob Stanistreet and Tony White are back looking well and happy and there is so much to say and talk about it is impossible to begin in a letter.

The list with your name on it for the 'Moreton Bay' only came out this morning so I am hoping this will reach you in time. I am sending it to the Agents and they will forward it to Adelaide if too late for Fremantle.

David and Elizabeth bought some land away out of Wahroonga and this week Tim Halstead is building at Wahroonga and hopes to be in by Xmas.

All well and the little tiddlers bubbling with joy about Uncle Bill.
Tons of love
Doukie

20 OCTOBER 1945
CAPTAIN E W GADEN
SS MORETON BAY FREMANTLE
HELLO BILL SEE YOU SOON LOVE FROM ALL THANKS FOR FLOWERS DEAR DOUKIE

...

Doukie Darling 21 October 1945

Scribble from the high seas. The old 'Moreton Bay' is giving us a pleasant enjoyable ride - no rough stuff and consequently no Mal-de-mer.

There are girls on board! Only a few. They feed us with Red Cross chocolate, cigarettes, provide pyjamas and encourage light social conversation. They are charming company and we lap up such attention with the mild enjoyment that kittens exhibit when drinking milk. English nurses too, healthy lasses who wear drab grey uniforms and manage to keep their noses shining cheerfully - a nondescript variety of multi coloured civilians frequent the boat deck - bound for Lithgow. Now for the boys, over 1000 of us - all are placidly happy to be returning but most are bored with the slow plodding movement of the lady SS Moreton Bay.

I thought of you two days ago and quietly soaked a gin, toasting happiness in the future and many more birthdays.

Nobody seems to know if we will plod around the coast to Sydney in this old cart (water cart) or travel from Melbourne by train, or fly from Perth or ______ however dear we are coming and will let you know how, when 'the veil of secrecy' lifts.

On board is a shrewd pleasant and slightly crusty gentleman, one Mr. Johnstone from the Orient Line, in fact he is a general manager of that organisation and in that capacity he has given me lots of dope about ships. He knew Grandfather Gaden well, we chat gaily about scandal of mutual interest. I have made a useful friend!!

Moya's sister, the Morry-Arty, simply loved those black hideous brass birds that stood fierce and stork like, on the mantelpiece at Vermont. Where are they dear? Dig 'em up please - I hope to see M-A dressed as she will be in trousers holding affectionately to her breast (manly) one of those beady eyed hungry idols. Just to get in first.

Yours truly is about to make a fool of himself. Together with other stooges, tomorrow night, a ballet darling, can you imagine it? No! Not Russian, my hair is still short; the tune Hoky Poky, other members of the ballet seem to ooze with rhythm whilst I follow with difficulty, 'perspiring profusely the while.' This is all done for a good cause - non nobis nascimur - tell you what that means later. ['We are not born for ourselves' …. he is going to make a fool of himself to help others.]

Once already today virtue has prevailed and our padre saw me at church - will go again later - in a holy mood.

By the way I hear that Holy Charles Moses is a civilian. I wonder if you have had his support in your 8th Div. welfare organization.

Darling it is time to stop. Love to S, G, D, and W and products. With luck we will be able to clear up that dammed estate business soon after my arrival. Sailing to you dear.

Love
Bill

P.S. Oleography, look it up in dictionary, a new hobby of mine

An oleograph is a coloured lithograph impressed with a canvas grain and varnished to make it look like an oil painting or a lithograph which is printed in oil colours to imitate an oil painting.[732]

'Moya's sister, the Morry Arty', was Barbara Ierne (Biddy) Goff who, with Moya, had been friends of the Gaden family in Bowral. She had married Orpen Boyd Moriarty in 1932. He sailed with the 6th Division to the Middle East. Biddy followed him as a representative of the Australian Comforts Fund and then the Australian Red Cross. He was killed in Crete in May 1941. She returned to Australia in 1942, working with the Red Cross. Biddy returned to the Middle East in 1943 to deal with recovered prisoners of war. In 1944 she was promoted to Commandant and prepared for the reception of released Australian prisoners after the German surrender.

She was next sent to Singapore to assist with the 2nd POW Reception Centre and returned to Australia with the last of the released troops in November 1945.

She was awarded the Florence Nightingale medal in July 1947. After the war she worked on the staff of David Jones Ltd.[733]

24 OCTOBER 1945
MRS VERA LYDIA GADEN
ST DAMIENS FLAT 1, 10 RAYMOND ROAD, NEUTRAL BAY, NSW
FREMANTLE DEAR TEN DAYS HOME RECEIVED LETTER LOVE TO ALL
BILL

...

Mrs. V.L.Gaden
10 Raymond Road, Neutral Bay

Bill darling *25th October 1945*

Your telegram has just arrived. So glad you got my letter and I hope the wire also.

A Bangkok letter also came today asking which clothes you have, one good suit (the navy double breasted one with pencil stripe), one pair grey slacks, one dress suit and lots of shirts, pyjamas, new socks, sweaters etc. I disposed of the old suits and sports coat a long time ago, they were in bad order. The navy and dress suits I had cleaned to be sure of no moths and tied them up in calico bags so they are in perfect order waiting for you.

David told Smithy!! to keep some time and material to make you a suit as soon as you arrived and he said he certainly would. He made a lovely DB grey suit for David. Clothes for kids are very hard to get to say nothing of the Coupon value too. Anyway you will get a coupon issue and then go shopping. Hang onto any issue towels dear, they are hard to get and cost 3 coupons each out of our dress allowance. No special issue for house linen, so I haven't bought any since the war.

I thought how lucky you were not to have young brothers to rat your shirts, pyjamas etc. Most of the men have come back to empty cupboards. David had plenty but had outgrown everything. He is a big fellow now. You will get a surprise.

We are going out on a launch to meet the ship if you arrive that way so hang onto the side Pet.

Charlie Wilkinson flew down from Japan. He looks so well now. He is a nice kid isn't he? He got into civilization so quickly he was almost stunned and very shy.

The 8th Div rest room is becoming very popular. Lots of men come in and find a mate they haven't seen for years. The enquiry on Lieut. Gen. Gordon Bennett takes place tomorrow. The place is seething with rage. He has had an awful spin. All spite in high places. I am keeping the papers for you to read Pet. You will get a lot of shocks at the doings of some people since you have been away.

Ron Merrett arrived yesterday. His wife was nearly beside herself. She is such a dear. We have all become such friends through our war work.

We are closing the 2/20 Comforts Fund early in December after the final Xmas tree for the kiddies. I won't be sorry; two days a week for 5 years was beginning to tell but oh it has been worth it all. We will just concentrate on the 8th Div from now onwards.

Agnes is coming down to welcome you home plus the pair of ducks for dinner!! So you had better be hungry.

I hope that this will meet you in Adelaide like the other letter. I got the agent address from Birt and Co.

Moya leaves for England tomorrow. She is so sorry to miss you but thrilled you saw her sister Biddy Moriarty in Singapore.
Ton of love darling
Doukie

...

Connie Cay
Lapstone Hotel, Glenbrook

Bill old dear *25th October 1945*

A cheerio and word of welcome to you and all your ship mates on once more touching your first Aust. port - that great longed look for coast which means 'Home' in a very short time and union with your very own family circle. Guessed you must be on the 'Moreton Bay' directly your Mum told me she'd received your cable and have since seen your name in the list. 'The Largs' I saw streaming up the harbour not so long ago, my old warrior on which I returned from my almost world cruise in 1924 a few years ago.

My idea is to go to the wharf where you disembark for a peep of you (that too providing you don't return before my cousin and I leave here on 2nd Nov.) and shall look forward to a yarn and visit to or from you when the family can spare you. It makes me so glad you and your Mum and girls care and can be together again. Gosh the years that have to be bridged.

Don't have forty fits on beholding the above address. But I'm being half shouted this holiday which is quite easy to take and entertained as each guest seems to spend the entire day appearing in fresh garments a la board ship life in normal times.

We've struck a patch of really hot weather after coming prepared to semi-freeze; said Fairy Barton 'you'll live in your costumes'. [This is a reference to being forced to wear the clothes they'd brought, however unsuitable.]

The grounds here are very lovely, very expansive and quite continental in appearance with a green paved swimming pool set in the midst of lawns and gardens. At night it's particularly attractive with the glittering lights of Penrith and Glenbrook in the distance. Apart from the pool, golf and tennis are the other forms of sport for which one has to dip into the pocket. As yet normal service and conditions have not returned, yet the Hotel is crowded always. The normal night routine seems to be three games of Housie from which the Red Cross benefits, followed by dancing for those who so wish, whilst others play cards etc. or yarn. We only came on Tuesday so are still finding out things, Tomorrow if it is cooler we're taking the bus to Penrith to look see. Last night we raised a 'four' and played 'auction' till almost midnight ending up 6 pence richer than when started.

Was delighted to get your air mail card Bill and hear you'd at last been receiving letters from us all written since the surrender.

Since writing you about Rick Tindal his mother has been officially advised the poor old lad died from dysentery (or however it is spelt) on 10th Nov 1943 and Bruce Abbott of Glen Innes who is back and was with Rick's lot has been able to tell them odd bits. Still any information you may have gathered I'd like to hear sometime and many thanks for doing all you have.

I'd so wish you'd been home last Saturday for the opening of the Sailing season, 1st for donkey's years. It really was a sight though my glimpse was only from the flat window's lawn. Expect you lads will take up the old life again and either dig out your old craft or acquire another. Sadness as I think some of the old crew may be missing, perhaps not.

Cay Armstrong, our sister Lorrie's eldest lad, who is in Fleet Air Arm attached to 'Indefatigable' has several exciting years ahead of him. They leave before long for a 'social' visit to N.Z., from there goodness knows where but with London always on the foreground, and a very depleted banking account but what an education and experience.

You'd laugh at me here cos I'm on holiday 1st time for 6 years. I, like you, am lapping it all up and going right through the menu and just pray too many pounds won't be the outcome of it all. It's so new to have my tea made, meals prepared and served and be able to lead an idle life. Only snag is I'd adore to be about your age. Can't say the guests here are over exciting and possibly they think the same of us. What I do miss is not being able to slip out and make a cup of tea etc before going to bed, only tea served here is at breakfast, none at luncheon, so my supper has been a homely glass of water and cake or biscuits I brought up as advised.

Did so adore your remark about the girls with their new husbands. Sue and Warwick loved it, he teasingly said to Sue is there something you haven't told me about. You'll like Warwick Bill, quite different to David but most friendly.

Now until we next meet, not long now, all too wonderful for you lads and us all the best and expect your Mum etc. will go down to Ingleburn, don't know really, I anyway hope for a fleeting wave if nothing more from you.

Much love Bill old dear,
From Connie Cay,
Excuse pencil, pen silly C

Bill was one of more than fourteen thousand prisoners of the Japanese who were recovered or repatriated after the war. Over fifteen thousand had been wounded on injured in the battles; over nineteen thousand of those young men and women who had enlisted so long ago were not coming home, they were dead.[734]

Bill arrived home on the Steamship *Moreton Bay* in early November 1945. The joy of his family was immense and as soon as Connie returned to Sydney she organized a party at which Bill was a guest of honour.

Reg Newton proposed that Bill Gaden should receive an O.B.E.for his war time work. He received nothing.[735]

Reg himself was recognised for his particular efforts in keeping so many prisoners alive. He received the Special Immediate Award. P.W. M.B.E. The citation reads:

NX 34734 Captain Reginald William James Newton, 2/19 Battalion AIF

He was a Camp Commander of various Prisoner of War camps in Malaya, on the Thai-Burma Railway, and in Japan. He was frequently brutally ill treated by Japanese guards while endeavouring to ameliorate the bad conditions of those under his command and he was outstanding in his complete disregard for the Japanese in the interests of his own troops. His consistent inspiring leadership, courage and personal example over a long period and under very adverse circumstances, inspired and raised the morale of those under his command and his fellow prisoners. His efforts on many occasions were directly responsible for saving many lives and casualties.[736]

The men of the 2/20 had fond memories of Bill. He was known as a 'bloody good bloke' and 'a good soldier'.[737] Arch Ewart agreed that he was a good officer.[738] Frank Baker said he was always a bit aloof but was a good officer, a correct sort of man. He was well educated and an old-school-tie sort of chap.[739]

In 1990 Major Reg Newton gave a book to Bill's son Bob Gaden, *Prisoners of War: Australians under Nippon* by Hank Nelson. Reg wrote on the flyleaf:-

This book gives some indication of difficulties encountered as P's O.W. of the Japanese 1942-45. Your Father, as O.C. Australian troops in Tarso and Chungkai Hospitals on the Thai Burma Railway, managed to surmount the many problems and achieve a very proud record in losing less men in his 'U' Battalion than any other Battalion of all Nationalities who worked on the Line 1943-45: 45 men out of 1000 whereas some Battalions lost up to 700 men, through harsh working conditions, lack of food and medical supplies. But Bill Gaden managed to acquire extras and stand up to the Japanese and minimize many bashings and general ill-treatment. Thank God he covered our back and we all felt much safer with his controls and outstanding administrative ability.

Reg Newton. 'U' Bn.

725 NSW BDM Index 14281/1944 and Johnstone, *Reverend Thomas Johnstone*, p. 173.

726 Gaden family history researched by the author.

727 DVA Nominal Roll.

728 DVA Nominal Roll and Commonwealth War Graves Commission.

729 Wikipedia, < http://en.wikipedia.org/wiki/Nuts_in_May_(rhyme) >

730 DVA Nominal Roll and NSW BDM 16402/1946.

731 DVA Nominal Roll.

732 *Oxford Dictionary of Art*, <http://arts.enotes.com/oxford-art-encyclopaedia/oleograph>

733 *Australian Dictionary of Biography*, <http://www.adb.online.anu.edu.au?biogs/A150577b.htm>

734 Australian Bureau of Statistics, 1301.0 *Year Book Australia 1946-1947*, Summary of Australian Services during World War II, 1939-45 (Enlistments, Casualties, Decorations etc.) <http://www.abs.gov.au/ausstats >

735 Newton, Interview, AWM S01739.

736 Newton, *The Grim Glory*, p. 803.

737 James Keady, Secretary of the 2/20 Bn Association, personal communication.

738 Arch Ewart interview with Don Wall, CD from AWM, S04103.

739 Frank Baker (NX59308), personal communication.

Chapter 15 - After the Homecoming

Bill left Singapore on 16 October 1945 on the ship *Moreton Bay* along with a thousand other former prisoners.[740] Before leaving, Bill was vaccinated but there is no indication which of the diseases this was to protect against. He was issued with a 'Record of Service' book which detailed the clothing he received on 10 October 1945. The Australian uniform included hats, badges, jackets, shirts, towels, boots and the Pacific ribbon.

But 'F' Force survivor Gordon Gaffney remembered arriving back in Darwin on 9 October:

> *We had no clothes to come home in! The stinking wharfies in Sydney had refused to load our ship because they knocked the danger money back. The war was over, and they struck for danger money. So we had no clothes to come home in.*
>
> *I landed in Darwin with a pair of Japanese boots, a pair of Japanese shorts, a slouch hat and a dirty old khaki shirt. A bloody disgrace to Australia! They said 'what did you look like, Gaff?' I said 'like an emu standing in two oil drums!' What happened on the way over, they issued us on the boat with Indian army labour corps uniform, which was a khaki drill thing, like a giggle suit, a pair of old khaki trousers and tan sand shoes and a Scotch tam-o-shanter cap. Now you imagine, fellows who had been away out of the country and fought for their country, for over four years, and that's what happened. So it was all put out, and we lined up on the deck of the ... 'Duntroon', and as we drew in, we just threw it all overboard. I can still see in the wake of the ship these bloody tam-o-shanter hats, bouncing, waving goodbye, and tan sand shoes.*[741]

By the time Bill left Singapore a few weeks later one can only hope the repatriation authorities were better organized.

No doubt the troops on *Moreton Bay*, like all the men returning to Australia from a war in far off lands, would have been able to smell the unique fragrance of the Eucalyptus trees that are part of the Australian bush long before they saw their much loved homeland, land so many of their friends and colleagues would never see again.[742]

The ship arrived in Sydney on Thursday 1 November.[743] One can only imagine the joy of the families and the returning men, and the apprehension about how they would all cope. Hope Herridge's brother (Arthur John Cronin NX71795 of 2/19 and 8 Corp of Signals)[744] was one who worried how they would be received because they had been ordered to surrender and they had not continued to fight for Singapore.[745]

They need not have been concerned.

The prisoners were met by small boats escorting the troop ships into the harbour, and they received a cheering reception in the city. No doubt Vera was, as promised, on one of the small boats.

The returning men were expected to go to the Army Barracks at Ingleburn for medical examination and discharge. Bill went along to finalise all the paperwork but some like Gordon Gaffney refused to do so[746] so he missed receiving the clothing coupons, leave and pay entitlements.

The discharge procedure was quite extensive. Each soldier had to go through a series of dental and medical examinations, they had to attend a rehabilitation interview and a Vocational Guidance interview; they were issued 160 clothing coupons. There was the Australian Military Forces Discharge depot procedure and the Inter-Service and Civil procedures making sure each man was entered on the Nominal Roll. In all there were eight different departments who had to sign off on each of the soldiers. It was a lengthy process.

When Bill enlisted his weight was shown as 190 pounds (86 kg). His lowest weight as a prisoner was 163 pounds (74 kg) or 11 stone 9 pounds. When he first had arrived in Malaya in 1941 his weight came down to 12 stone (168 pounds, 76 kg) and he said he had never felt fitter. The fact that he did not lose a huge amount of weight as a prisoner is a reflection that, as an officer, he was not doing the hard physical labour on the railway. Also he was located in POW camps close to the food supply barges. The men in 'F' Force, well away from the supply lines, suffered a much worse weight loss. Robert Peacock dropped to a mere 77 pounds (35 kg)[747] Gordon Gaffney who spent nine days on 'Cholera Hill' deteriorated to a similar low weight.[748]

Following chest X-rays on 1 November, Bill was given twenty-eight days leave with pay from 2 November to 30 November with a further seven days sick leave from 6 to 12 December. He was entitled to thirty-four days of recreational leave, sixty-eight days due to war service and a further thirty days for re-establishment; leave to be paid in lieu.

However like all the returned prisoners, Bill was let down by the Army who refused to pay the extra 3/- per day subsistence they were entitled to for the years they had provided their own food.[749] They had all contributed to the purchase of food during their time as prisoners and the army didn't acknowledge it. For many men this was a bitter financial disappointment as it would have been worth close to £200 each on top of their discharge and leave pay.

However they fared better than the Australian civilian prisoners of the Japanese who lost everything, were interned for the duration of the war and were then pursued by the Australian Federal Government to repay the cost of their own repatriation.[750] This decision was only reversed after public protest from the civilians, led by Gallipoli veteran Frank Merritt and his wife Mary who were interned in the Phillipines, who pointed out that they had received no pay from the Japanese but at least the soldier-POWs had received a sum equivalent to what their own soldiers received.[751]

Bill was entitled to five Service Chevrons - overseas service stripes worn on the lower right sleeve [752] one for each complete year of service with the AIF from the date of embarkation from Australia. He was approved to wear the Ribbon of the 1939-1945 Star and the Pacific Star as well as the Defence Medal, the War Medal and the Australian Service Medal.

He was given a Certificate of Services as an Officer. It showed he had served on continuous full time war service for one thousand nine hundred and ninety-one days which included Active Service in Australia for 53 days and outside Australia for one thousand seven hundred and thirty four days.

His War Badge was numbered RAS A201269 and his Service ceased on 24 December 1945, the best Christmas present a soldier from the Second World War could have received!

His Final Statement of Account on discharge was £630.4.0 which included his earnings and accrued pay, less other payments already paid. He kept an allotment of £2.2.0 but as from 6 May 1946 the allotments ceased as the accrued leave payment was finalised.

The Demobilization Procedure book shows Bill's education record and noted that as a POW he had studied water colour painting. He listed Oleography (printing a lithograph in oil colours to imitate an oil painting)[753] as the training he desired under the CRTS (Commonwealth Repatriation Training Scheme). CRTS assisted returning troops with university or trade training, land settlement, establishing a business or purchasing tools of trade.

```
AMF PW MEDICAL HISTORY CARD
NX 12543 GADEN, E.W. Capt 2/20 BN.         Age 28 years
Date and Place of Capture 15 February 1942 Singapore
History: Pre-enlistment   Right Fibula fracture 1934
                          Left Clavicle fractured twice 1933
Before Capture            Pneumonia February 1941
After Capture             Malaria (18)
                          Dysentery March 1943- December 1944
                          (Intermittent diarrhoea)
                          Appendectomy August 1943
                          Small leg ulcers
                          Lowest weight 11 stone 9 lbs
                          (September 1943)
Physical examination      Well nourished
Weight                    184 lbs        (13 stone 2 lbs)
Cardiovascular            NAD
Respiratory               No comment made on card
Nervous inc mental state  No comment made on card
Alimentary                No comment made on card
Cutaneous                 No comment made on card.
```

He moved from the Active to the Reserve of Officers list for the Second Military District. Reserves had to report annually to the Military HQ of their State to advise their address. (Bill was a Reservist for a couple of years, he was still on the list in 1949, but he then let it lapse.)

Prior to the war Bill had enrolled to study accountancy, a course which his brother-in-law David MacDougal was currently pursuing at evening class. Bill had changed his mind about accounting and painting was his preferred

COMMONWEALTH  OF AUSTRALIA

COMMAND PAY OFFICE
Victoria Barracks
Paddington N.S.W.

EX-PRISONERS OF WAR OF THE JAPANESE — FUNDS DISTRIBUTION

Dear Sir or Madam,

In 1952 the Commonwealth Government set aside certain moneys available from the liquidation of Japanese assets in Australia to enable a distribution of £32 to be made to, or in respect of, each Australian serviceman who was a prisoner of war of the Japanese. Later, in 1956, a further distribution of £54 per head was made from moneys which included portion of Australia's share of moneys derived from the realisation of Japanese assets by the International Committee of the Red Cross.

Additional moneys have now become available, including the remainder of the share of Red Cross moneys, which will permit a final distribution of £16.10.0 to, or in respect of each former prisoner.

In the case of a prisoner of war who died whilst captive or since release, payment, as was the case with the earlier distributions, may be made to such person or persons who are entitled thereto by virtue of the fact that such person or persons —

(a) Stood to the deceased in the relationship of wife, child, parent, step-parent or foster-parent, etc., or

(b) were actually dependent on the deceased at the time of his death.

If you claim to be eligible to share in the distribution of the moneys now available it will be necessary for you to complete and forward the enclosed application form to the above address.

Yours faithfully,

R.W. [signature]

Acting Command Paymaster
Eastern Command

vocation for the future, be it using water colour, oil painting or oleography. However an artistic career in the austere post-war climate was unlikely to be financially viable. Bill needed to earn money to bring into the family home and so he returned to his job as a shipping clerk with Birt and Co. in Bridge Street, Sydney. One can only wonder why did he not join David is pursuing the extra qualifications.

The adjustment to ordinary civilian life was hard for the returning men, both mentally and physically; harder than they expected or cared to admit.[754] Former soldiers arrived home emotionally frail and badly affected by their experiences. In those days there was no such thing as counseling and debriefing. We now recognise that such life-threatening trauma, such loss for so many years would be counted as significant stressors. The personality and coping style of the individuals would affect their ability to recover.[755]

Bill would have learned to cope with trauma following his parents' separation and the subsequent death of his father, so his coping mechanism should have been already tested when he became a prisoner. However the years of malnutrition and ill treatment by the Japanese would have a profound and everlasting effect on every returning POW.

For many men the reality of returning home was not the joy they had imagined. Lieutenant George Blackford (NX51473) returned to his former job with the Post Master General. Whilst he had been away his wife Mavis had joined the PMG to be a little 'closer in spirit' to her husband. She climbed telegraph poles in all weathers and worked very hard as a linesman. But she was abused and bullied by workmates who could not understand why her husband, in a reserved occupation, had bothered to enlist and leave her to go out and work. When George himself returned to his old job he too was subject to even more bullying because he had been 'stupid enough' to enlist and then become a POW.[756] No wonder some men were distraught at such appalling treatment.

Many of them returned to broken homes, some found their clothes and possessions had been passed on.[757] Excessive alcohol, abusive violence and mood swings became the norm for others. Several preferred isolation to social contacts. Some would need to go bush for a while. Some would hoard tins of food,[758] some could not bear to see anything go to waste. Some former prisoners, who were often tolerant of weakness and differences in their fellows, would churn with rage at inconsequential things in civilian life. Depression was a common indication of their mental stress; as many as sixty committed suicide.[759] We now know that war is far more likely to break, rather than make, the man.[760]

Nightmares were very common[761] and Bill suffered from them particularly in his first year home. However unlike many of his fellows, he did not seem to have them continue throughout his life.

For families the reality of their husband and father's return was often stressful. Communication was difficult, each side being hesitant to talk about what had happened. In fact families were told not to talk about the war and to steer the conversation away. Soldiers found they didn't fit in and they felt lost, only able to talk to each other.[762] It was of course painful to wean themselves from their war time 'families' - the men with whom they had served and struggled together to overcome the depravities of incarceration. It is only natural they wanted to stay in contact with each other, it was difficult to sever those ties and often more difficult to re-weave new bonds with their pre-war and post-war family.

These silent men, practising what we now call avoidance, used whatever tactics they could to try and keep control of the frightening images that came to them as daytime shows (flashback) and night-time screenings (nightmares). By not speaking they indefinitely deferred the possibility of being overwhelmed once again.[763] Neville Mansfield, the lad who lost his arm in the truck accident back in July 1941, worked for years with Bob Gaden and never once mentioned being in the 2/20 with his father.[764] Diane Elliott recalls that in the 1960s she knew Bill as her boss, 'Mister Gaden', and had no idea he had been a soldier and POW along with her own father who had served with the 2/19 Battalion.[765]

For men of the 8th Division their fighting days had ended in surrender - they had seen all the blood, all the gore but had seen none of the glory. They could not discuss the horrors of the POW years so their silence hid the double-edged emotional devastation of the shame of surrender and the humiliation of incarceration. The men were silent, but at what cost to their families? At what cost to themselves? After the First World War the youngsters had been shielded from the truth of what damage those years had wrought, the war was considered to be a forbidden topic. Now those youngsters had, in turn, borne the brunt of another war and again the returning men were silent.[766] The same mistakes were made once more and the human expense of war, the wiping out of a generation, was not discussed. At what price to the men who survived, their partners and their own children?

These wives and children found it hard to understand and cope with the mood swings, the silences, the rages, the depression. Carolyn Newman's book *Legacies Of Our Fathers* documents the stories of more than twenty families. There was incredible unhappiness on so many sides.

For the wives of surviving prisoners it would have been so traumatic to realise that the man you loved and married was not the same person who returned after the war was over.

Those who met and married the men once they arrived back in Australia did not have the comparison of a returning partner who had changed. Jack Pidcock of 2/18 was thankful that he was young and unattached when he left. He thought:

> *I was lucky ... It would be bloody awful, fellows who were married and had a couple of little kids, they used to suffer a bit.*[767]

Major John Turrill of the 85 Anti Tank Regiment, an English POW, wrote to Bill in January 1946 advising:

> *I'm terribly lucky coming back to find I have got a good home, a fairly good motor car and most of all I've still got a wife. Literally dozens of my friends' marriages have gone awry. It must be unbearable to come home, as so many have after 3½years in the jungle, and find that your wife has a couple of kids that don't belong to you and that anyway she doesn't think much of you.*[768]

Bill's sister Elizabeth (Ginge) said he too was a different person from the one who sailed overseas. He had changed. However Bill was lucky to come home to a welcoming family. His two sisters were happily married to men Bill liked, and they each had their first child. His mother was much more content, she had rebuilt her life after the trauma of her separation and husband's subsequent death. She had been very busy with the Comforts Fund for the Battalion and now looked forward to post-war life with her son safely back home.

For Bill's family and friends there was much joy. Connie Cay threw the promised Gaden party and invited many of Bill's old friends. She also invited some new ones including twins Judith and Gertrude Gillespie and their younger sister Marie. The girls were working in Sydney but were originally from

Queensland, having lived in Warwick and then gone to school in Toowoomba. Connie's brother knew the Gillespie family. Bill went off to find some more beer and Judy Gillespie went with him as she thought he was 'rather nice' and thus started a new romance.

At some stage before Christmas that year Bill went to Palm Beach for a few days. He wrote to Jean and Arch Ewart from there in November. On his return to Neutral Bay he also received a letter from Elaine Warren who must have had her hopes shattered ... she wrote to ask why he had walked out on her without explanation. By then Bill was going out with Judy and no doubt Elaine also did not realise the immense opposition to her from Bill's mother Vera and sister Sue in particular. Her dreams were dashed and it was not for another nine years, in 1954, that Elaine finally found happiness when she married Carl Bernard Gregory in Petersham.[769]

Meanwhile Bill and Judy's relationship went from strength to strength. The excitement of a blossoming romance and the thoughts of a future ahead would have been a positive goal for a returning POW. They became engaged in July 1946.

Bill and Judy were married at St Augustine's Church, Neutral Bay on 15 February 1947, exactly 5 years after the fall of Singapore.

In post-war Sydney it was almost impossible to find places to live, so Bill and Judy continued to live at St Damien's at 10 Raymond Road with his mother Vera. Their first child Bob was born less than a year later and Helen followed in April 1950, putting increased pressure on space in the small flat.

During the war Vera had shared the flat with her daughters and their babies Diana and James. Now she had to do it again with Bill, her daughter-in-law and their two children. A generation earlier Vera had not had much time for her own children; it would have been a difficult time for everyone, especially as the spectre of war was no longer hanging over their heads.

As early as September 1948 Bill and Judy had bought some land, (Lot 9) in Coolaroo Park Estate, 24 Coolaroo Road, Lane Cove and a two bedroom double brick house was commissioned to be built. The house, to be called *Gay Shadows*, was designed by architect Gordon King of Joseland & Gilling and Gordon King Architects of Castlereagh Street, Sydney. Shortages of building materials meant long delays and it was more than eighteen months before the family was able to move into their new home in late May 1950, soon after the arrival of daughter Helen.

Painting was completed prior to the move and Venetian blinds were ordered for the windows. Bill constructed much of the initial furniture himself, using skills he had learned as a POW. The beds rattled and squeaked and the lounge chairs were very low, but at least the dining room table did the job.

By 5 February 1951 an application was made to Willoughby Council to make a two bedroom addition to the house. This was due to the imminent arrival of twins Susan and Barbara who were just 15 months younger than Helen. The eventual building took some years to complete. Cash was always in short supply, so to save money, Bill undertook to do much of the work himself, with some assistance from a carpenter for the roof. Bob can recall sharing the second bedroom with his three younger sisters until his early primary school years.

The standard of building was not particularly high. Bill didn't add lime to the mortar so the bricks were difficult to lay. This was basic building knowledge he needed but, as a former officer, he was reluctant to ask anyone for advice, preferring to get on with the job in his own way. He made everything himself, the doors, the windows and frames, but he was not noted for his attention to detail so the windows would not lock and the doors sagged on their hinges.

The children recalled the bedrooms were cold and draughty and the occasional funnel web spider was spotted inside, which caused terror and great disruption!

In October 1965 a roof was placed over the U shaped courtyard to enclose it. For years afterwards there were always problems during heavy rain; the box gutter would overflow down the inside walls.

A family of six all trying to rush for work or school inevitably caused much competition for the single bathroom but it was not until 1966, when all the children were in their teens, that a building application went to Council for small bathroom with shower and toilet to be added to the end of the verandah to ease the congestion. It was built by Bill and Bob.

Like many returning soldiers Bill drifted back into his old job after the war. Former prisoners often found it hard to take up study or to work in a job with a monotonous routine; many had difficulties working under the authority of a woman; some had unrealistic expectations and found it hard to cope with the pressures of post war life.[770]

Bill did not return to his pre-war study of accountancy. Despite the many schemes available to returned servicemen, he did not seek further vocational training. However he rose through the ranks at Birt and Co. to become Passenger Manager where he organised overseas trips for many clients. This often involved meeting ships at various times of the evening and at weekends.

Like many ex-POWs, Bill was rather unsettled, and didn't really enjoy his work. He would have been happier if he'd been able to farm, or earn a living from his painting.

Looking back it may seem strange that Bill did not try to increase his qualifications or gain new ones. In those early years, the 1950s, money was always tight and it was hard work for Judy with four children under four, three in nappies, a copper boiler and hand wringer and no decent clothes line in the back yard. Some extra income from an improved position would have been very welcome to ease the financial strain as the children all progressed through primary then high school.

There was certainly not much compensation from the Funds Distribution for former prisoners of the Japanese. However Bill was no different from many

Bill and Judy with the children outside the house in Coolaroo Road, Lane Cove

other former prisoners in that he knuckled down and worked hard to provide a home for his wife and family.

As was normal for men at that time Bill took very little part in helping in the home. He would hold one of the twins when he arrived home from work but he basically expected the house to be neat and tidy and a meal ready for him on the table. A typical officer, he was good at giving orders!

He also expected the family to all bow to his wishes and discussion or debate was not really encouraged, especially by the womenfolk. He was very much a man of his era.[771]

> *He was king of the castle and everyone accepted that's the way it was. Changing a nappy? You've got to be kidding. If he wanted to read the paper in peace, that's exactly what he did. If he was away all day playing golf, we all accepted he was entitled to that.*[772]

Holidays always seemed to involve camping so Bill could indulge in his passion for fishing. Unfortunately the fishing places were inevitably remote beaches, the camping holidays always seemed to be dogged by rain and the children's memories of these trips were not all that happy - words like wet, cold, primitive, unpopulated, uncomfortable and smelly all sprang to mind - the success of catching any fish was lost on them.

Bill's four children all have different accounts of their childhood. Like all siblings with the same parents and the same upbringing, some come out with less happy memories than others.[773]

September school holidays were usually spent with Gaden relatives on their livestock and cropping farm at Wheogo, Dunedoo. Here the children loved the relaxed, caring atmosphere and home grown food provided by Aunty Dot and the freedom of running round the farm. Here Bill could unwind from his constant stress and enjoy the lifestyle of being a farmer just for a short while.

Bill had attended an Anglican School but was not a churchgoer before the war. On his return he became a regular worshipper. He was involved with the St Augustine's Men's Committee in the early post-war years. Later the whole family attended St John's in Lane Cove each week before moving to Mowbray Chapel in the 1960s. He insisted they had to squeeze into one pew despite there being plenty of room elsewhere. Bill was one of the volunteers who had been involved with the move and rebuilding of the Mowbray Chapel stone by stone. Each stone block was numbered and successfully replaced in the correct position.

He was interested for a while in politics, assisting at the polling booths for the Liberal Party in the 1949 Federal election and the 1950 State election.

When the children were pupils at the nearby Mowbray Public School, Bill became involved with the Parents and Citizens Association, becoming President and running the Chocolate Wheel at the school fete for many years.

Bill eventually joined Sydney Legacy in 1968 and, being interested in youth, he joined the Intermediate Committee. Later he transferred to the Chatswood Group.[774] He had several Legatees that he cared for and he was involved with the adolescents living at Archbold House.

As with so many POWs, ANZAC day became an important date in the calendar. The men had depended on each other for survival in the camps where their surrogate 'family' had supported them through the horrors which they endured but they couldn't discuss those years with their current families. ANZAC day was one time when they could reminisce and re-discover that period of intense mateship.[775]

Bill also joined the Masons rising to the position of Grand Master of Blue Lodge. He used to rehearse his lines in front of a mirror or when marching up and down the timber floor of the verandah, much to the angst of younger family members trying to read and study inside the adjacent rooms.

Things were changing at work for the employees of Birt and Co. By July 1961 the company was part of Birt, Potter and Hughes and then became part of the Federal Steam Navigation Company[776] a subsidiary of the Peninsular and Oriental Steam Navigation Company, better known as P&O.[777] Some time after this take-over, Birt's office at 4 Bridge Street was closed and the staff moved to the nearby P&O building.

Bill was not happy with the new arrangements; from being Passenger Manager at Birt's, he found himself swallowed up by a much larger organisation. In 1967 due to the 'development and rationalisation of P&O', Birt and Co. was officially dissolved and ceased to exist. On 30 June 1967 Bill and other Birt and Co. employees were given notice that their services had been 'terminated due to the merger with P&O Lines of Australia'.[778]

Bill must have seen the writing on the wall, or he had started to actively search for another job as early as the previous September when he had sought a reference from his old commanding officer, Brigadier FG Galleghan who wrote:

29 September 1966

> *This is to certify that I have known Edward William Gaden for the past thirty years. He joined the Australian Army in the regiment I commanded in 1937, and was commissioned, on my recommendation, in 1939. He was in the 8th Division of the AIF in Malaya in which I also served. In war he reached the rank of Captain and I have no doubt that had the Division not become Prisoners of War he would have attained a much higher rank. His military service was always beyond reproach and he was an officer in whom I had the utmost confidence.*
>
> *In his civil avocation Captain Gaden has become Passenger Manager for Birt and Co. Pty Ltd. I have also had a fairly close contact with him in this capacity. He has contributed a great deal to the tourist industry of New South Wales for which I consider he should receive some recognition.*
>
> *In his general character he has always proved himself as a man of the greatest integrity and high moral character. I have no hesitation in recommending Captain E.W. Gaden as possessing enthusiastic capacity in any avenue he chooses and particularly that of the tourist industry.*[779]

By this time the children were all teenagers. Bob had left school to study at Sydney University. He was awarded a traineeship with NSW Agriculture, so he was almost financially independent. Helen remembers her uncertainty about whether or not to go to university. Bill was very supportive of her decision to leave school and attend North Sydney Technical College where she had a great year and came top of the Secretarial Course. She was one of 12 out of 150 who were chosen to start at Qantas and it proved to be an excellent career for her.

Now only Susan and Barbara were 'dependents' in their final years of schooling. Judy did some part time work driving autistic children to school. After his redundancy Bill did not return to the workforce, he took up painting full time. By now he had finally been awarded a small repatriation pension.

Fellow POW officer in 'U' Battalion, Reg Newton, was a great believer in his men, the 'U Beauties', chasing up war pensions and encouraged them all to apply on the basis of any illnesses they may have in the post-war time.

Ready for an ANZAC Day march

He was noted for his dogged fighting on their behalf against 'bureaucratic ineptitude'.[780]

Intermittent periods of illness were normal for many POWs.[781] As far back as 1950 Bill had applied to the Repatriation Department for a War Pension based on his illness. The Department accepted that his intestinal problem was a result of his war service but there was no pension for the particular condition available at this time. His claim for a heart condition was not accepted.

Bill later applied for a Repatriation pension for a duodenal ulcer due to his war service. It was accepted. Early in February 1961 he was duly awarded a Repatriation Pension of £2/16/2 per fortnight to date from 4 May 1960 and an extra 17/9 per fortnight was added for his wife and 6/11 each for the children.[782]

Dr Edward 'Weary' Dunlop was one of the first to recognize that the Repatriation Commission, (later Department of Veterans Affairs, DVA) had made medical and psychological assessments of POWs too soon after liberation. He and others campaigned to receive official recognition of the relationship between being a prisoner and having ongoing health issues.[783]

In 1967 the Department added recurrent functional diarrhoea and recurrent renal calculi to the accepted illnesses due to Bill's war service and increased his pension. He obtained $8.56, Judy was awarded $2.84 and the two children still at home $1.92 per fortnight.

Bill suffered from angina and fought for many years to have his cardiac condition recognised as war related. In 1973 he wrote:

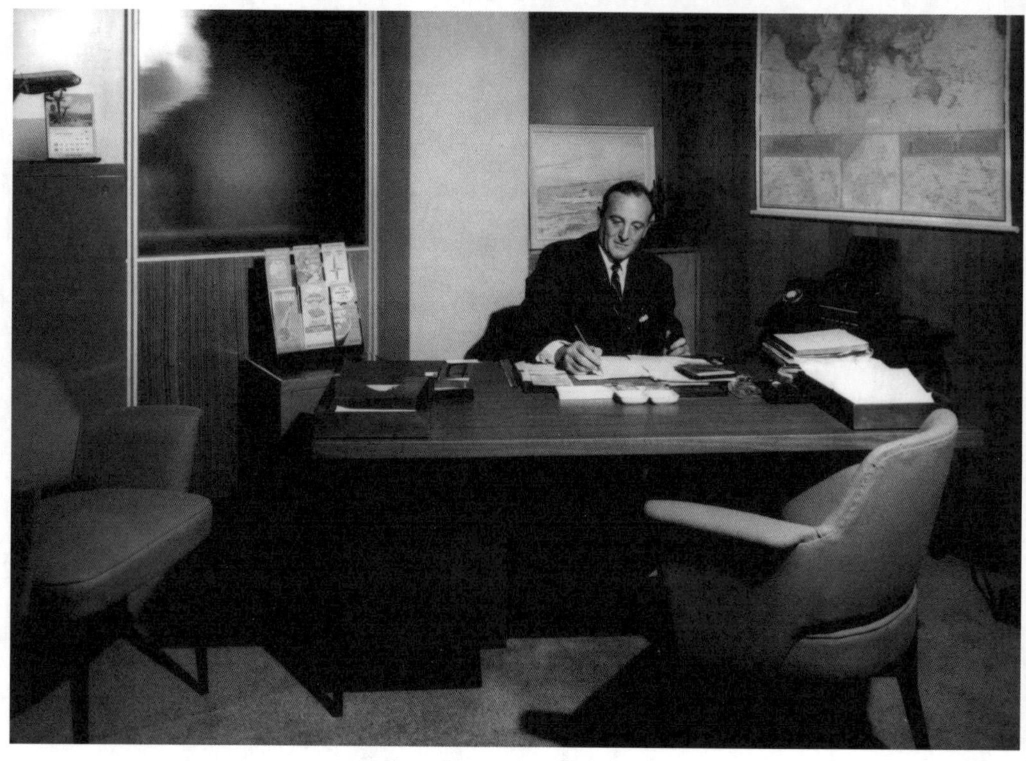

Bill working in his office at P&O

> *My ischemic heart disease was caused in part by an anxiety neurosis induced during 3.5 years as a P.O.W. of the Japanese which included 3 years on the Burma/ Thailand Railway.*
>
> *The effort to survive the work pressure and slave conditions imposed by the Japanese, aggravated by inadequate and vitamin deficient food and consequent diseases, is the basic cause of my anxiety neurosis. The effort to keep this neurosis within due bounds is constant and becoming more difficult year by year.*

He added

> *Starvation caused Beri-Beri, Pellagra, Dysentery, Malaria with swollen spleen ... Each of these ailments caused an extra load on the heart to pump blood through the systems. Heart condition was reported to Repatriation in:-*
>
> *1950 when POWs were called up for examination - nothing found*
> *1967 EEC and extensive examination by Dr Barrett, Chatswood - nothing found*
> *1973 (20 Mar) Examination by Dr Bestic - nothing found*
>
> *1973 (18 April) Dr Stewart Mitchell - admitted to Sydney hospital.*

In 1973 Bill applied again to the Repatriation Department for medical treatment costs and a war pension. In August he had been in hospital with chronic cholecystitis (gall stones) and had a cholecystectomy and his claim also included recurrent synovitis of the left knee. However the application was mainly on the grounds of his ischemic heart disease as diagnosed by Dr L.V. Armati.

The application was again rejected but this time Bill sought Legal Aid, went to the War Pensions Entitlement Tribunal and successfully appealed the decision. However the Board would only accept the Ischemic Heart Disease for pension allocation, not the other conditions.[784] An additional pension was made available from 2 April 1974.

By the early 1970s the children had all completed their schooling. Susan and Barbara had worked hard striving for their father's approval. Both attended Sydney University to study medicine, a concern to their parents because it was such a long course. Susan subsequently specialised in radiology and Barbara became an anaesthetist. Helen had become a Personal Secretary with Qantas.

Bob was working as a Beef Cattle Advisor with NSW Department of Agriculture. He spent close to a year as a jackaroo at Clonagh Station near Cloncurry. Whilst he was there Bill and Judy with friends David and Jo Wrathall travelled through outback Queensland and the Northern Territory. It was on these trips that Bill gleaned copious inspiration for his wonderful paintings.

He painted in oils. Some of his early works were scenes from his POW days, Hellfire Pass, Wampo viaduct, Tarso Camp. Like many POWs who undertook such therapeutic activities, the painting helped Bill come to terms with his time as a prisoner in Thailand. Subsequent paintings were scenes from the countryside and many were of the harsh landscape of the Australian outback.

He was a life member of the Art Gallery Society of NSW and joined the North Shore Art Society which had been founded in 1946. His mother Vera had been a longtime member. He was elected their President in 1956, a position he held until his death.[785]

By the 1970s the family was expanding as all four children were married. Bill was able to give away each of his daughters at their weddings; Barbara married Tony Luey in August 1972, Susan married Wally Kos in November 1973 and Helen married Ron Griffin in May 1974. However Bill was too sick to travel to Yorkshire, England for the wedding of son Bob when he married Caroline Ford in December 1973.

Bill kept up his painting and bought a machine to assist with the framing. He and Judy constructed the frames for all of his works. By late 1974 Bill had accumulated sufficient paintings to hold an exhibition which was duly held over a week in November at Mosman Town Hall.[786] Over 200 people signed the visitors' book.

He held his second exhibition in December 1975. It was to be his last as by then he was too sick to do much painting.

Bill died on 26 July 1976 due to myocardial infarction and coronary atherosclerosis. He was just 58 years old. As ischemic heart disease was classed as an accepted disability by the Repatriation Department, they accepted his death was 'service related' and his widow Judy was eligible for a War Widows pension.[787] Judy continued to live in the house in Coolaroo Road until 2004 when she moved into Lourdes Village, Lindfield where she died in July 2008.

Most of the POW paintings are now located at the Army Museum of NSW in the Victoria Barracks in Paddington, Sydney. It is a most appropriate place. Bill Gaden completed his final medical examination, received his pay book and started his life as a professional full-time soldier at these same Barracks in Sydney on 13 July 1940.

The 2/20 Battalion Association gave the painting of Wampo Viaduct to Don Wall in appreciation of his writing the history of the battalion in *Singapore and Beyond*. On his death the painting went to Gordon Gaffney who had been interviewed by Bill's daughter-in-law in 1995. When Gordon died some years later it found its way to the walls of the office of the Tamworth Returned Services League.

In February 2007, just over thirty years after Bill's death, his son Bob and daughter-in-law Caroline visited many of the places in Singapore, Malaya and Thailand that Bill never talked about but which had such huge impact on his life. They visited battlegrounds and barracks, gun batteries and command centres, cemeteries and massacre sites. They stood on the water's edge where the Japanese landed on the north-west corner of Singapore Island, land defended by the men of the 2/20 Battalion.

On the sixty-fifth anniversary of the fall of Singapore they were in the beautifully-maintained Kranji War Cemetery on the Island. At 12.15 pm air raid sirens suddenly started to howl their mournful warning. It was a routine test to ensure they were all working properly and could be heard all over the island. But it was an eerie, gut-wrenching feeling to be standing in this huge war cemetery, this place so poignant, so heart breaking, on the sixty-fifth anniversary of the fall of Singapore when that terrifying sound reverberated through the air. They shivered with goose bumps as thousands upon thousands of ghosts stirred in silent but tangible response, ghosts of men and women who had been Bill's friends and colleagues.

The couple moved on to Malaysia. They saw the bridge at Parit Sulong, the roadway where the wounded men of the 2/19 were left, the hut where they were herded, the site where they died. They took the train north and stayed in the E&O Hotel where Bill had 'found perfect bliss' so many years before. They moved on to Thailand where they travelled by the local train over the 'Bridge on the River Kwai' and Wampo Viaduct. They descended into the abyss that is Hellfire Pass. They walked through the grounds of the former POW camps at Kanchanaburi, Tarso, South Tonchan and Chungkai, places where Bill spent many months of his life, places were so many of his friends and compatriots died.

It was a journey of discovery, of pain, of intense emotion, of amazement that men could build such a railway with so little equipment, and admiration for those who endured their incarceration by so brutal an oppressor. It is of little wonder that the survivors who finally returned home to Australia were all physically affected and emotionally scarred by their experiences.

But it was also a journey of hope; a hope that nations learn from their past mistakes, from the sacrifices made by these men and women so future generations can be free to grow and develop in peace.

Bill Gaden has thirteen grandchildren; twelve were born after his death. Three of them, Philip and Peter Gaden and David Luey have served their country in the Australian Defence Forces, Philip and Peter as officers in the Royal Australian Navy, David in the Army. They are part of another generation of young men who carry their grandfather's legacy forward.

At the 2005 ANZAC Day Address at his old school, the Guest of Honour, Bill's grandson Lieutenant Philip Gaden, remarked that he'd concluded from his extensive travels that all people, whatever their culture, religion or beliefs, want the same thing: to be safe, to have a full belly, to live with family and friends and to grow old together.[788] It is something for all nations to aim for.

But

If we do not remember our heroes, we will produce no heroes.

If we do not record their sacrifices, their sacrifices will have been in vain.

The greatest strength we have as a people is our common memories of the past and our common hopes for the future,

For without these memories the next generation will not have the fighting spirit to carry on.[789]

740 *Sydney Morning Herald*, 15 Oct 1945, p. 4.
741 Gaffney interview, AWM SO1738.
742 Black, A home never revisited, *Sydney Morning Herald Weekend*, 10-11 November 2007, p. 28.
743 *Sydney Morning Herald*, 2 Nov 1945, p. 3.
744 DVA Nominal Roll.
745 Hope Herridge, Personal communication.
746 Gaffney *op. cit.*
747 Peacock, 'F' - Death Force, <http://www.far-eastern-heroes.org.uk/html/f-death_force.htm >
748 Gaffney *op. cit.*
749 Nelson, *Prisoners of war, Australians under Nippon*, p. 211.
750 The 7.30 Report, Book reveals suffering of civilian war prisoners, Broadcast 18 August 2007.
751 Twomey, *Australian Journal of Politics and History* < http://goliath.ecnext.com/coms2/gi_0199-6968584/In-the-front-line-Internment.html >
752 Badges < http://www.diggerhistory.info/pages-badges/qualifications.htm >
753 *Dictionary* < http://www.allwords.com/word-oleography.html >
754 Savage, *A Guest of the Emperor*, p. 133
755 Cochrane Review of Post Traumatic Stress Disorder.
756 Waring, Joy, daughter of Lt GHS Blackford, personal communication.
757 Nelson, *op. cit.* p. 211.
758 Crisp, Louise, personal recollection.
759 Savage, *op. cit.*, p. 131.
760 Horin, Traumatised diggers - the never ending legacy of war, *Sydney Morning Herald Weekend*, 10-11 Nov 2007, p. 33.

[761] Peters, *The life experiences of partners of ex-POWs of the Japanese*, <http:www.awm.gov.au/journal/j28/j28-petr.htm >

[762] Nelson, *op. cit.*, p. 211.

[763] Bell, *Shot - a personal response to guns and trauma*, p. 79.

[764] Gaden, Bob, personal recollection.

[765] Elliott in *Legacies of our fathers*, p. 33 and personal communication.

[766] Winn, *Scrapbook of Victory*, p. 119.

[767] Elliott and Silver, *A history of 2/18 Battalion*, p. 206.

[768] Turrill, John P, letter to Bill Gaden dated 6 January 1946, in the possession of the author.

[769] NSW BDM, 10538/1954

[770] Savage, *op. cit.*, pp. 130-3.

[771] Mackay, *Advance Australia - where?*, pp. 42-49.

[772] *ibid.*, p. 50.

[773] Patrick Gale in an interview with Richard Fidler, The Conversation Hour, ABC Radio, aired 14th September 2007.

[774] *Sydney Legacy Bulletin*, 26 August 1976, p. 7.

[775] Peters, *op. cit.*, p. 5.

[776] Rabson, Personal communication 26 September 2007.

[777] P&O history, < http://www.pocruises.com.au/html/history.cfm >

[778] Birt and Co., Letter of termination, in the possession of ER Gaden.

[779] Galleghan, Reference letter, in the possession of ER Gaden.

[780] Nelson, *op. cit.*, p. 63.

[781] Peters, *op. cit.*, p. 5.

[782] Repatriation Pension papers, in the possession of ER Gaden.

[783] Hearder, *Memory, methodology and myth: some of the challenges of writing Australian Prisoner of War history* <http://www.awm.gov.au/journal/j40/hearder.htm.

[784] No. 3 War Pensions Entitlement Appeal Tribunal (MX224051), copy in the possession of ER Gaden.

[785] North Shore Art Society < http://www.northshoreartsociety.org.au/ >

[786] *The Daily*, 30 November 1974, p. 8.

[787] Repatriation letter, 8 October 1976.

[788] Gaden, ANZAC Day address, The Armidale School, 2005.

[789] B G (NS) George Yeo, Minister for Information and the Arts, 21 June 1997, at the launch of *The Price of Peace* booklet, Bukit Chandu, Singapore.

ACKNOWLEDGMENTS

This book has been an emotional six years in the making. It has been possible with the help and encouragement of all these people - all the errors are mine.

Family members:-

The late Judy Gaden, Susan Gaden, Barbara Gaden, Helen Griffin for their support of this project and their memories. Philip and Peter Gaden for their Naval and Medical knowledge.

The late David MacDougal and family for the recollections, assistance and photographs.

John Keeling and Diana Bradhurst for their help and photographs.

The late 'Roaring' Reggie Newton, of 2/19 Bn, for his interview and a wonderful friendship for many years.

Penny (Fussell) Hargreaves and Jennifer Johnstone for their memories of the Gad en family and Jennifer for the photograph of that wedding dress.

'2/20 Originals' George Shelly, the late David Thompson and Bill Young for reading the manuscript and correcting my errors and sharing some of their stories. Thank you so much.

'2/20 Originals' Frank Baker, Noel Harrison, Bart Richardson, Frank Smith, Harry Woods for their interesting, sometimes funny, sometimes painful, POW recollections. Thank you.

James Keady and Peter Salter of 2/20 Bn Association for their support and putting me in touch with the 'Originals'.

The late Gordon Gaffney, of 2/30 Bn for his interview and harrowing honesty.

Graham Mansfield for the report on the accident involving his father Neville.

Louise Crisp, former daughter-in-law of Roland Oakes for her reminiscences.

Joy Waring, daughter of Lieutenant G.H.S. Blackford for her recollections.

Patricia Williams, sister of Tom Scollen, for her sad memories.

Australian War Memorial Canberra for the 2/20 Battalion War Diaries, Routine orders and photographs of nurse Elaine Balfour-Ogilvie, Pte Tom Scollen.

Bill Brassell, Sound Preservation Officer, AWM.

Mary Pollard, Research Centre, AWM.

John Hamilton, AWM Volunteer for finding answers to my questions.

Sonia Gaden for her patient proof-reading.

Wendy Taylor, DVA Nominal Roll team.

Denise Bell and Betty Pinkerton of Scone Historical Society.

Sonia Gidley-King for her help.

Stephen Rabson, P&O Archivist and Historian.

Lawrence Czarnik of 2/18 Bn Association.

Di Elliott, a 22nd Brigade researcher who coincidentally worked with Bill at P&O.

Richard Wall for permission to copy one of his father's maps.

John & Libby Fuller, current owners of 'The Briars'.

Tamworth RSL for access to one of Bill's paintings (Wampo Viaduct).

Capt. Linda Graham and the Victoria Barracks Museum, Sydney for access to the other paintings.

Colonel John Flynn a current Army surgeon for his continual encouragement and his concern for the veterans.

The publishing team, Lily, Elizabeth and John McRobert.

Sally Lloyd for her cover design.

James Laurie for turning black dots into sheet music.

Janet Johnston and Vera Gaden for the words and music of 'A Prayer'.

Terry Hunt, son of Alfred George Hunt who died in Thailand, for his surprise and delight on finding a 2/20 connection when he eventually realised his wife was godmother to one of Bill Gaden's grandsons.

Members of the Sydney NSW 'Rootsweb' online Genealogical Mailing list for answering so many questions on wartime Sydney.

To others I should have named but have failed to do so, please accept my thanks.

The members of the 'Changi to Hellfire Pass Tour', February 2007, our own 'A' Force, for their friendship and being there to share the many tears and, in typical Australian fashion, all the laughter.

Stu Lloyd, Tour Leader for his inspiration on the tour and Kevin Bell, Peter Bertram (whose father was a medical orderly when a POW), Pam England, Judith Fisher, Margaret and John Hamilton (AWM volunteer), Pat and Allan Harding, Sue and Grahame Hellyer (Sue's father was Lieut IR MacDonald of the 2/18 Bn and 'A' force when a POW), Hope Herridge (whose brother AJ Cronin was in 2/19 Bn), John Hill, Trevor Hill, Sandra and Martin Kelly (who wrote a lovely tour diary of the trip), and David Mitchell.

My late father, Air Transport Auxilliary (ATA) pilot Ron Ford, for passing on his interest in the Second World War, and my mother, Joan, for her continued support and encouragement.

My sons Philip, Paul and Peter Gaden, their wives and their children for all the reasons to keep looking to the future.

Bob Gaden, my rock. Thanks mate, I couldn't have done it without your love, support, encouragement and your shoulder to cry on.

TIMELINE

September 3, 1939	*Australia declares war on Germany*
February 18, 1941	*22nd Brigade of the 8th Division arrives in Singapore*
August 1941	*27th Brigade of the 8th Division AIF arrives in Singapore*
December 7-8, 1941	*Japanese attack Singapore, Malaya, Pearl Harbour, and the Phillipines*
January 14, 1942	*27th Brigade and 2/19 Bn in battle for Gemas and Muar*
January 21-24, 1942	*Japanese engaged on east coast of Malaya by 2/18 and 2/20 Battalions*
January 31, 1942	*Causeway between Singapore Island and Johore blown up*
February 14, 1942	Vyner Brooke *sunk in Banka Straight*
February 15, 1942	*Allied forces on Singapore Island surrender to the Japanese*
February 19, 1942	*Japanese bomb Darwin*
May 1942	*'A' Force of the POWs sail from Singapore to Burma*
July 1942	*'B' Force of the POWs sail from Singapore to North Borneo*
August 1942	*POW senior officers sail from Singapore to Taiwan then Korea and Manchuria*
January 1943	*Dunlop Force sails from Java to Singapore and Thailand*
March 1943	*'D' Force of the POWs travel by train from Singapore to Thailand;* *'E' Force sails to North Borneo;* *'F' and 'H' Forces follow 'D' Force north by train.*
October 16, 1943	*The railway from Burma to Thailand is completed when the lines are joined at Konkoita*
December 1943	*Survivors of 'F' Force are returned to Singapore*
July 1944	Byoki Maru *sails from Singapore taking ten weeks to get to Japan with its cargo of POWs*
May 7, 1945	*Germany surrenders*
August 6, 1945	*Atomic bomb dropped on Hiroshima*
August 9, 1945	*Atomic bomb dropped on Nagasaki*
August 15, 1945	*Cease fire against Japan*
September 2, 1945	*Japanese surrender*

BIBLIOGRAPHY

Books

Air Transport Auxiliary, *Ferry Pilot Notes*, 26 June 1941.

Arneil, Stan *One Man's War*, Sydney, Alternative Publishing Co., 1980.

Australian War Memorial, Australian Army War Diaries, Second World War, Infantry Battalions, 2/20 Battalion, AWM52, Item 8/3/20 - 2/20 Infantry Battalion, available for download from < http://www.awm.gov.au/diaries/ww2/folder.asp?folder=474 >

Beattie, Rod, *The Death Railway, a brief history*, Bangkok, Image Makers, 2005.

Beattie, Rod, *Map of the Thai-Burma Railway Link*, Kanchanaburi, Thailand, T.B.R.C. Company, no date.

Bell, Gail, *Shot, a personal response to guns and trauma*, Sydney, Picador, 2003.

Bennett, Lieut-Gen. HG, *Why Singapore Fell*, Sydney, Angus and Robertson, 1944.

Bennett, JM, *A History of Solicitors in New South Wales*, Sydney, Legal Books, 1984.

Boyle, James, *Railroad to Burma*, Sydney, Allen and Unwin, 1990.

Braddon, Russell, *The Naked Island*, 1952, First published by T Werner Laurie Ltd, this edition by Pan Books London (7th printing 1960).

Commonwealth Electoral Roll of NSW, State Electorate Liverpool Plains, Sub Division Scone, 1930, available Scone and Upper Hunter Historical Society.

Dodkin, Marilyn, *Goodnight Bobbie*, Sydney, UNSW Press, 2006.

Dunlop, Edward E, *The war Diaries of Weary Dunlop, Java and the Burma Thailand Railway 1942-1945*, Ringwood, Vic., Penguin Books, 1986.

Eade, Charles, *Onwards to Victory, War speeches by the Right Hon. Winston S. Churchill 1943*, London, Cassell and Co., 1944.

Elliott, Di and Silver, Lynette, *A History of 2/18 Infantry Battalion AIF*, Pennant Hills, NSW, 2/18 Battalion Association, 2006.

Falk, Stanley L, *Seventy Days to Singapore*, New York, G Putman, 1975.

Forbes, Cameron, *Hellfire, the story of Australia, Japan and the Prisoners of War*, Sydney, Pan Macmillan, 2005.

Gordon, Ernest, *Miracle on the River Kwai*, 7th imp., London, William Collins-Fontana, 1963.

Hull, Walter, *Salvos with the Forces*, Red Shield Services during World War 2, Hawthorn, Vic., Citadel Press, 1995.

Jeffrey, Betty, *White Coolies, Australian Nurses behind enemy lines*, Sydney, Angus and Robertson, 1954.

Johns, Fred, *Who's Who in the Commonwealth of Australia-1922*, Sydney, Angus and Robertson, 1922.

Johnstone, Ian M, *Reverend Thomas Johnstone D.D. The Evangelical Boundary Rider*, Armidale, Ian Johnstone, 2007.

Kinvig, Clifford, *Death Railway*, London, Pan Ballantine, 1973.

Legg, Frank, *The Gordon Bennett Story, from Gallipoli to Singapore*, Sydney, Angus and Robertson, 1965.

Lloyd, Stuart, *The Missing Years, a POWs Story from Changi to Hellfire Pass*, Dural, Rosenberg, 2009.

MacArthur, Brian, *Surviving the Sword, Prisoners of the Japanese 1942-45*, London, Time Warner Books, 2005.

Mackay, Hugh, *Turning Point - Australians choosing their future*, Sydney, MacMillan, 1999.

Mackay, Hugh, *Advance Australia - Where?* Sydney, Hachette Australia, 2007.

McKernan, Michael, *Drought the Red Marauder*, Crow's Nest, NSW, Allen and Unwin, 2005.

McLellan, AA, *History of the Parish of St. Luke's, Scone, 1839-1989*, Quirindi Press, 1989.

Mills, Roy, *Doctor's Diary and Memoirs, Pond's Party, F Force. Thai-Burma Railway*, New Lambton, NSW, R Mills, 1994.

Molony, John, *The Penguin History of Australia*, Ringwood, Victoria, Penguin, 1988.

Moremon, John and Reid, Richard, *A Bitter fate, Australians in Malaya and Singapore December 1941 - February 1942*, Canberra, Department of Veterans' Affairs, 2002.

Moremon, John, *Australians on the Burma-Thailand Railway 1942-43*, 2003, Department of Veterans' Affairs, Canberra.

Nelson, Hank, *Prisoners of War, Australians under Nippon*, Sydney, ABC Radio, 1985.

Newman, Carolyn, (Editor), *Legacies of our fathers*, Sydney, Lothian Books, 2006.

Newton, Reginald WJ, (editor), *The Grim Glory of the 2/19 Battalion AIF*, Sydney, 2/19 Battalion AIF Association, 1975.

Noonan, William, *The Surprising Battalion, Australian Commandos in China*, Sydney, NSW Bookstall Co., 1945.
Norton Smith and Co., *Norton Smith & Co. 1818 -1988,* Norton, Smith and Co, Sydney, 1988.
Ong, Chit Chung, *Operation Matador World War II, Britain's attempt to foil the Japanese invasion of Malaya and Singapore,* Singapore, Eastern Universities Press, 2003.
Onn, Chin Kee, *Silent Army*, London, Ballantine, 1953.
Parkinson, Roger, *Blood, toil, tears and sweat*, London, Hart-Davis MacGibbon, 1973.
Partridge, Jeff, *Alexandra Hospital, from British Military to Civilian Institution 1938-1998*, Singapore, Alexandra Hospital and Singapore Polytechnic, 1998.
Pease, Allan and Pease, Barbara, *Why men don't listen and women can't read maps,* Sydney, Pease International, 2006.
Peek, Ian Denys, *One Fourteenth of an Elephant*, Sydney, Random House, 2004.
Pitkin Pictorials, *The Right Honourable Sir Winston Churchill, a pictorial memorial,* London, Pitkin Pictorials, no date.
Poole, Philippa, *Of Love and War, the letters and diaries of Captain Adrian Curlewis and his family 1939-1945*, Sydney, Lansdowne Press, 1982.
Richards, Rowley, *A Doctor's War*, Sydney, Harper Collins, 2005.
Rivett, Rohan D, *Behind Bamboo, an inside story of the Japanese Prison Camps*, Sydney, Angus and Robertson, 1946.
Savage, J Russell, *A Guest of the Emperor,* Boolarong Press, Brisbane, 1995.
Shinozaki, Mamoru, *Syonan - my story, the Japanese occupation of Singapore*, Singapore, Asia Pacific Press, 1975.
Silver, Lynette Ramsey, *The Bridge at Parit Sulong, An investigation of a Mass Murder Malaya 1942,* Sydney, Watermark Press, 2004.
Smith, Colin, *Singapore Burning, heroism and surrender in World War II* London, Penguin Books, 2005.
Summers, Julie, *The Colonel of Tamarkan*, Philip Toosey and the Bridge on the River Kwai, London, 2005 Simon and Schuster, 2005.
Wall, Don, *Singapore and Beyond, the story of the 2/20 Battalion*, Dee Why, NSW, 2/20 Bn Association, 1985.
Warden, Andrew and Watson, Brian, joint editors, *Sydney Church of England Grammar School Register 1889-1994,* Sydney, Shore Old Boys Union, 1994.
Whitecross, Roy H, *Slaves of the Son of Heaven*, Sydney, Dymocks Books, 1952.
Willcocks, Wendy Lavinia, *Without glamour, the social history of the 2/18 Battalion*, UNE thesis for M.A. (Hons), TH000/W697/2006, located UNE Library, Armidale.
Williams, John and Williams, Jeanette, *Pop's War Service, 28123 Corporal Fritz Leslie (Lofty) Williams*, J Williams, Townsville, 2002.
Winn, Godfrey, *Scrapbook of Victory*, London, Hutchison, 1945.
Zeigler, Oswald (Editor), *Men May Smoke*, Sydney, 2/18 AIF Association, 1948.

INTERVIEWS

Baker, Frank, 2/20 Bn, with Caroline Gaden, January 2008.
Ewart, Archibald Clyde Menzies, NX498, as a Major, 2/20 Battalion and Prisoner of War 1941-45, interviewed by Donald Wall, no date, available as a CD ROM from AWM, S04103.
Gaden, Caroline, discussions with George Shelly, David Thompson and Bill Young.
Gaffney, Leslie Gordon, NX71862, Interviewed by Caroline Gaden on 04 May 1995, about his service with 8th Division Headquarters in Malaya and Singapore and his experiences as a POW, available as a CD ROM from AWM, S01738.
Gale, Patrick, Interview with Richard Fidler, Conversation Hour, Friday 14th September 2007, ABC Radio 11.00am.
Gaven, Frank, NX34885, as a Lieutenant, 2/20 Battalion and Prisoner of the Japanese, 1941-45, interviewed by Donald Wall, no date, available as 2 part CD ROM from AWM, S04104.
Newton, Reginald William James, NX34734, Officer Commanding 2/19 Battalion relates his experiences and those of Edward William Gaden, 2/20 Bn as prisoners of war of the Japanese on the Burma-Thailand Railway, 1942-1945 to the Gaden family, 25 April 1991, available as a CD ROM from AWM, S01739.
Richardson, Bart, Address at 2/20 Dedication Ceremony, AWM, Canberra, 30 Nov 2007.

NEWSPAPERS, MAGAZINES AND OTHER

Australian Women's Weekly, Microfilm available National Library, Canberra.

Barrett, Peter, 'Hidden Heritage, Yearning for Learning brought Poh to Armidale', *My Life, New England's original Lifestyle Magazine*, September 2007, pp. 8-9.

Black, Ray, 'A home never to be revisited', *Sydney Morning Herald Weekend*, November 10-11, 2007, p. 28.

Bradley, Ken, (Chairman) *Australian Bicentenary '88 Hellfire Pass Project, Burma-Thailand Railway Memorial proposal* Australian-Thai Chamber of Commerce, 1986.

Dimmock, Edna, 'House in Johore, The Road that leads to Singapore', *Sydney Morning Herald*, 24 January 1942, p. 11.

Horin, Adele, 'Traumatised diggers - the never ending legacy of war', *Sydney Morning Herald Weekend*, November 10-11, 2007, p. 33.

Hulsman, David, 'An Ordinary Bloke', *The Northern Beaches Weekender*, 1st February 2001, p. 1. (Torch Publications).

Hutchinson, Jim, 'The Grass that built Asia', *Readers Digest*, April 2002, pp. 62-68.

Malay Mail, July 28, 1941, in the possession of the author.

Media Masters' World War II, Series 1, *Battlefield Guide, The Japanese Conquest of Malaya and Singapore*, December 1941-February 1942.

O'Connor, Mike, 'Digger's Yarn Worth Hearing', *The Courier-Mail*, Brisbane, 23 April 2008.

Rose S, Bisson J, Churchill R, Wessely S, 'Psychological debriefing for preventing post traumatic stress disorder (PTSD)'. *CochraneDatabase of Systematic Reviews 2002*, Issue 2. Art. No.: CD000560. DOI: 10.1002/14651858.CD000560.

Scone Advocate, microfilm available at National Library of Australia.

Scone and Upper Hunter Historical Society Journal, Volume 2, 1961.

Scone and Upper Hunter Historical Society Newsletter 144, June 2007.

Scone and Upper Hunter Historical Society Newsletter 145, September 2007.

Second Two Nought, the newspaper of the 2/20 Battalion, Issues 1-11, June to August 1941, in the possession of the author.

Smith, Adele Shelton, *Australian Women's Weekly* articles, 29 March to 3 May 1941. Viewed at NLA, Canberra.

Sydney Morning Herald, 1941-1945, Microfilm available from UNE Library.

PERSONAL COMMUNICATION

Family members: Bob Gaden, Judy Gaden, Helen Griffin, Barbara Gaden, Susan Gaden, David MacDougal, John Keeling, Diana Bradhurst.

2/20 Battalion 'Originals': Frank Baker, Noel Harrison, Frank Smith, Bart Richardson, George Shelly, David Thompson, Harry Woods, Bill Young.

Penny Fussell and Jennifer Johnstone who knew the family in war time Sydney.

Louise Crisp daughter-in-law of Capt. Roland Oakes and Joy Waring, daughter of Lieutenant George HS Blackford.

Di Elliott, historian and AWM volunteer.

Lt-Cmdr Philip Gaden, RANR, ANZAC Day address at The Armidale School, 2005.

Lt Peter Gaden, Naval Medical Officer

Members of the NSW-Sydney Genealogical Mailing list. AUS-NSW-SYDNEY@rootsweb.com.

Stephen Rabson, P&O Archivist and Historian, re History of Birt and Co. which was taken over by P&O.

Scone Historical Society members Denise Bell and Betty Pinkerton.

Wendy Taylor, DVA Nominal Rolls Team, re Pte Robert Smith/Oswald Charles Burne (NX20508), June/July 2007 and re McLaren, Melvin Donald, (SX8918) August/September 2007.

VIDEO/MICROFILM/CD/DVDs

Coroners Inquests 1834-1942, State Records of NSW, Microfilm SR Reel 2768, Inclusive Numbers 34/1-40/967, Reference Number 3.959-960.

Dunlop, EE *Prisoners of War Camps, Thailand. Report on Kinsayok Camp and Hospital, Report on Tarsau Base Hospital, 1943-1944.* Australian War Memorial Research Centre, Series Number AWM 54, Control symbol 554/5/1, DPI 200.

ABC TV, *Vivian Bullwinkel, An Australian Heroine*, Firebyrd Filmz, Shown ABC TV 2007.

Wall, Don and Lewis, Wallace Chauvel, *Malayan Moments*, Australian War Memorial Research Centre, F03436, Black and white movie made 1941. [790]

INTERNET SITES

Army Battle Honours <http://www.army.gov.au/AHU/HISTORY/Battle%20Honours/Battle_honours_WWII_infantry_Unitspsl.htm>. Accessed 20 September 2007.

Australian Bureau of Statistics, 1301.0 *Year Book Australia 1946-1947.* Australians at War by Matthew Higgins <http://www.abs.gov.au/ausstats>. Accessed 8 October 2007.

Australian Bureau of Statistics, 1301.0 *Year Book Australia 1946-1947,* Summary of Australian Services during World War II, 1939-45 (Enlistments, Casualties, Decorations etc.) <http://www.abs.gov.au/ausstats>. Accessed 7 October 2007.

Australian Dictionary of Biography, online edition Gordon, Sir Thomas Stewart (1882-1949), at < http://www.adb.online.anu.edu.au/biogs/A090056b.htm>. Accessed 21 May 2007.

Australian Dictionary of Biography, online edition Moriarty, Barbara Ierne (Biddy) (1902-1979) at < http://www.adb.online.anu.edu.au/biogs/A150477b.htm>. Accessed 15 June 2007.

Australian War Memorial < http://www.awm.gov.au/>. Accessed many times.

Bathurst Army Camp Memorial Wall. < http://www.skp.com.au/memorials2/pages/20505.htm>. Accessed 20 September 2007.

Bell and Salter, *Notes on 2/20 Battalion operations in Singapore, Feb 1942.* http://www.geocities.com/batt2_20/story.htm?200721. and Wall, *op. cit.*, p. 81.

Birch, Jean, *The 2nd AIF in Malaya 1941-42*, <http://www.htansw.asn.au/teach/war/JBirch%20Malaya%20Article.pdf>. Accessed 3 May 2007.

Bjelke-Petersen School of Physical Culture, < http://www.australiadancing.org/subjects/4021.html>. Accessed 18 November 2008.

Bobs Table <http://www.qualitycaretraining.com.au/active%20games.htm#Table%20Bobs>. Accessed 20 December 2007.

Boon, Jack, *War Experience of Jack Boon, 2/20 Bn. Prisoners of War of the Japanese 1942-1945* <http://www.pows-of-japan.net/articles/41.htm>. Accessed 18 June 2007.

Britain at War <http://www.britain-at-war.co.uk>. Accessed many times.

Brown, George, *Diary of a POW in Singapore* <http://www.bbc.co.uk/ww2peopleswar/stories/19/a3609119.shtml>. Accessed 30 April 2007.

Bulletin, *The Bulletin* publishes for the last time <http://news.ninemsn.com.au/article.aspx?id=108987> 24 June 2008. Accessed 16 Nov 2008.

Commonwealth War Graves Commission <http://www.cwgc.org/>. Accessed many times.

Department of Veteran's Affairs Second World War Nominal Roll <http://www.ww2roll.gov.au/>. Accessed many times.

Digger History <http://www.diggerhistory.info>. Accessed many times.

Frei, Henry P, *Malaya in World War II, The Revolving Door of Colonialism: Malaya 1940-46* <http://www.kasei.ac.jp/library/kiyou/2001/3.FREI.pdf>. Accessed 23 March 2007.

Fuller's Earth <www.netdoctor.co.uk/ate/childrenshealth/1203209.html>. Accessed 25 November 2007.

Gherardin, Tony, *Lt Col Albert Coates* <http://pows-of-japan.net/articles/37.htm>. Accessed 30 April 2007.

Glynn-White, JG, *Reminiscences, Royal Womens' Hospital Melbourne 9th November 1982* <http://www.araratcc.vic.edu.au/fow/JGWhite.html>. Accessed 13 April 2007.

Google Maps, <http://www.google.com.au/help/maps/tour/>. Accessed many times.

Hearder, Rosalind, *Memory, methodology and myth: some of the challenges of writing Australian Prisoner of War history* <http://www.awm.gov.au/journal/j40/hearder.htm>. Accessed 2 June 2007.

Hell Ships sinking <http://www.navalorder.org/09-Sep-99%20MistHist.PDF>. Accessed 7 June 2008.

HMS *Durban* <http://uboat.net/allies/warships/ship/1207.html>. Accessed 24 November 2007.

HMS *Glory* <http://www.fleetairarmarchive.net/ships/GLORY.html>. Accessed 7 June 2008.

Hodgson, Alec, *Diary of Sgt Alec Hodgson, 2/6 Field Park Company, Royal Australian Engineers* <http://www.s1942.org.sg/s1942/images/pdf/600374.pdf>. Accessed 30 July 2007.

Hoon, Lim Choo, *The Battle of Pasir Panjang Revisited* <http://www.mindef.gov.sg/safti/pointer/back/journals/2002/Vol28_1/1.htm>. Accessed 23 March 2007.

Luce, Oswald (Oss), *The War in South East Asia and the contribution of the Canadians*, Part 3, We were there <www.rquirk.com> specifically <www.rquirk.com/cdnradar/seacradarfile3a.pdf>. Accessed 7 June 2010.

Malaya-English Dictionary <http://kamus.lamanmini.com/index.php>. Accessed 16 May 2008.

Magazines: Powerhouse Museum, Sydney <http://www.powerhousemuseum.com/collection/database/search_tags.php>. Accessed 15 May 2008.

Man magazine, the Australian publishing icon <http:collectingbooksandmagazines.com/man.html>. Accessed 18 May 2008.

Quiz magazine <http://www.tnet.com.au/~wirrigalozpulp.html>. Accessed 29 May 2008.

Magnusson, Sigurdur Gylfi, *What is microhistory?* <http://hnn.us/articles/23720.html>. Accessed 26 June 2007.

Malik, Knene, Race Pluralism and the meaning of human difference <http://www.kenanmalik.com/papers/new_formations2.html>. Accessed 26 June 2007.

Marsden, L, Under the Heel of a Brutal Enemy our Catholic Boys kept their Faith <http://www.military.catholic.org.au/stories/changi-prison1.htm>. Accessed 21 June 2007.

Mary Poppins Birthplace <http://www.mary-poppins-birthplace.net/mary_poppins_spit_spot_short_version.htm>. Accessed 15 June 2007.

McLaren, Melvin Donald, (SX8918) *McLaren, Mates in Hell* < http://www.slsa.sa.gov.au/saatwar/collection/transcripts/ISBN1876070714_i.htm>. Accessed 30 April 2007.

McMaster, Elliott, *My experiences as a Prisoner of War on the Burma-Thailand Railway* <http://greatlakeshistorical.museum.com/burmarailway/index.html>. Accessed 18 June 2007.

Melbourne Cup Winners <http://au.geocities.com/melbournecups/1940-49.html>. Accessed 5 June 2007.

Moonstone <http://www.exoticindiaart.com/jewelry/moonstone/>. Accessed 20 December 2007.

National Archives of Australia <http://www.naa.gov.au/>. Accessed many times.

National Archives of Australia <http://www.naa.gov.au/> record for Elaine Balfour-Ogilvy, Barcode 6397185, Series B883, Accession number 2002/05081482; record for Bill Gaden, Item Barcode 4841125, Series number B883, Control Symbol NX12543; and record for Janet Muriel Johnston and Vera Lydia Gaden 'A Prayer', Series number A1336, Control symbol 41657, Item barcode 4008069.

National Library of Australia <http://www.nla.gov.au/>. Accessed many times.

New South Wales Registry of Births, Deaths and Marriage <http://www.bdm.nsw.gov.au/familyHistory/search.htm>. Accessed many times.

New South Wales State Record Office, Kingswood, Coroners Inquests.

North Shore Art Society, *History* <http://www.northshoreartsociety.org.au/>. Accessed 26 March 2008.

Oxford Dictionary of Art. Ed. Ian Chilvers. Oxford University Press, 2004. eNotes.com. 2006. 4 June 2007 <http://arts.enotes.com/oxford-art-encyclopedia/lithography>. Accessed 5 June 2007.

P&O <http://www.pocruises.com.au/html/history.cfm>. Accessed 18 November 2008.

Peacock, Robert, *'F' - Death Force* <http://www.far-eastern-heroes.org.uk/html/f-death_force.htm>. Accessed 21 June 2007.

Peters, Betty, The life experiences of partners of ex-POWs of the Japanese, Journal of the Australian War Memorial, Issue 28, April 1996 <http://www.awm.gov.au/journal/j28/j28-petr.htm>. Accessed 11 May 2007.

Photograph collection of British Association of Malaysia and Singapore <http://www.janus.lib.cam.ac.uk/db/node.xsp?id=EAD%2FGBR%2F0155%2FBAM%202%2F46>. Accessed 19 Oct 2007.

Pillai MM, and Radharkrishnan, V., Treatment of Civilians <http://www.s1942.org.sg/s1942/images/pdf/N600014.pdf>. Accessed 30 July 2007.

Port Dickson river <http://www.britannica.com/eb/topic-470857/article-9060916>. Accessed 29 May 2008.

Pownall, Singapore Defences Memorandum by Lieut.-General Sir Henry Pownall <htttp://www.britain-at-war.org.uk/WW2/ Malaya_and_Singapore/html/body_singapore_defences.htm>. Accessed 20 September 2007.

Puttees from <http://en.wikipedia.org/wiki/Puttee>. Accessed 20 September 2007.

Rainforest animals: Common Palm Civet <http://www.animalport.com/rainforest-animals/list/Common-Palm-Civet.html>. Accessed 20 December 2007.

Rolls Razor: High-tech shaving - circa 1950 <http://www.geocities.com/RodeoDrive/3696/Intros02.html?200825>. Accessed 25 Jan 2008.

Ryerson Index <http://ryerson.arkangles.com/notices.php>. Accessed 21 Jan 2008.

Scone Town Walk <http://www.upperhuntertourism.com.au/index.cfm?page_id=1073&page=Town+Walk>. Accessed 5 September 2007.

Taylor, *British Preparations* <http://www.britain-at-war.org.uk/WW2/Malaya_and_Singapore/html/body_british_prepare.htm>. Accessed 23 July 2007.

Thulaja, Naidu Ratnaia, Communicable Diseases Centre <http'//www.infopedia.nlb.gov.sg/articles/SIP_336_2005-01-03.html>. Accessed 19 Oct 2007.

Twomey, Christina, 'In the front line - Internment', *The Australian Journal of Politics and History*, 1 June 2007, published online at <http://goliath.ecnext.com/coms2/gi_0199-6968584/In-the-front-line-Internment.html>. Accessed 29 May 2008.

Travers, Pamela Lyndon, *Biographical note* <http://www.sl.nsw.gov.au/mssguide/ptravers.pdf>. Accessed 15 June 2007.

Troop ships <http://www.ocean-liners.com/ships/asp> and <http://en.wikipedia.org/wiki/RMS_>. Accessed 30 January 2008.

Up to Date Medical Program, version 2006, accessed by Dr Peter Gaden, Medical Officer RAN 10 October 2007.

Woolcott Forbes AWM Film collection F00505 <http://cas.awm.gov.au/film/F00505> <http://libapp.sl.nsw.gov.au/cgi-bin/spydus/ENQ/PM/FULL1?12707,I> and<http://www.parliament.nsw.gov.au/prod/PARLMENT/hansArt.nsf/V3Key/LA19920319033>. Accessed 10 January 2008.

Yam Tuan's Palace <http://www.malaysia.sawadee.com/negri_sembilan/places.htm> and <http://www.malaysiahotels.cc/nsembilan.html>. Accessed 6 September 2007.

Index Erratum

Grant, Barbara see also Gowland should be see also Young, page 316
Brooks, Lt would be John Seymour Brooks NX 34659, page 104
Brooks, John would also be John Seymour Brooks NX 34659, page 237,250, not John Henry Brooks of the 2/11 General Hospital

INDEX

F

G

H

I

J

K

N

O

P

Q

R

S

T